# Applications in Litigation Valuation

## A Pragmatist's Guide

by Jeffrey A. Johnson, MAI, and Stephen J. Matonis, MAI, MRICS

Appraisal Institute • 200 W. Madison • Suite 1500 • Chicago, Illinois 60606 • www.appraisalinstitute.org

The Appraisal Institute advances global standards, methodologies, and practices through the professional development of property economics worldwide.

*Chief Executive Officer:* Frederick H. Grubbe
*Director, Communications and Marketing:* Ken Chitester
*Senior Manager, Publications:* Stephanie Shea-Joyce
*Senior Technical Writer:* Michael McKinley
*Technical Book Editor:* Emily Ruzich
*Manager, Book Design/Production:* Michael Landis

**For Educational Purposes Only**
The materials presented in this text represent the opinions and views of the authors. Although these materials may have been reviewed by members of the Appraisal Institute, the views and opinions expressed herein are not endorsed or approved by the Appraisal Institute as policy unless adopted by the Board of Directors pursuant to the Bylaws of the Appraisal Institute. While substantial care has been taken to provide accurate and current data and information, the Appraisal Institute does not warrant the accuracy or timeliness of the data and information contained herein. Further, any principles and conclusions presented in this publication are subject to court decisions and to local, state and federal laws and regulations and any revisions of such laws and regulations.

This book is sold for educational and informational purposes only with the understanding that the Appraisal Institute is not engaged in rendering legal, accounting or other professional advice or services. Nothing in these materials is to be construed as the offering of such advice or services. If expert advice or services are required, readers are responsible for obtaining such advice or services from appropriate professionals.

**Nondiscrimination Policy**
The Appraisal Institute advocates equal opportunity and nondiscrimination in the appraisal profession and conducts its activities in accordance with applicable federal, state, and local laws.

© 2012 by the Appraisal Institute, an Illinois not for profit corporation. All rights reserved. No part of this publication may be reproduced, modified, rewritten, or distributed, either electronically or by any other means, without the express written permission of the Appraisal Institute.

**Library of Congress Cataloging-in-Publication Data**
Applications in litigation valuation : a pragmatist's guide / by Jeffrey A. Johnson, and Stephen J. Matonis.
   p. cm.
  Includes index.
  ISBN 978-1-935328-27-8
  1. Real property--Valuation--United States. 2. Evidence, Expert--United States. 3. Real estate appraisers--Legal status, laws, etc.--United States. I. Johnson, Jeffrey A. II. Matonis., Stephen J., 1943-
   KF8968.65.A96 2012
   346.7304'37--dc23                          2012005867

# Table of Contents

| | | |
|---|---|---|
| About the Authors | | vii |
| Acknowledgments | | ix |
| Foreword | | xi |
| Preface | Jeffrey A. Johnson, MAI, and Stephen J. Matonis, MAI, MRICS | 1 |

## Practical Considerations in Litigation Appraisal

| | | |
|---|---|---|
| Chapter 1 | **The Engagement**<br>Stephen J. Matonis, MAI, MRICS, with<br>Jeffrey A. Johnson, MAI | 3 |
| Chapter 2 | **Executing the Commitment**<br>Jeffrey A. Johnson, MAI, with<br>Stephen J. Matonis, MAI, MRICS | 13 |
| Chapter 3 | **The Appraiser as an Expert Witness**<br>Jeffrey A. Johnson, MAI, with<br>Stephen J. Matonis, MAI, MRICS | 19 |

## Litigation Case Studies

### Section I. Eminent Domain and Condemnation Cases

| | | |
|---|---|---|
| Case Study 1.1 | **Partial Taking–Corner Clip Road Project**<br>Stephen J. Matonis, MAI, MRICS | 35 |
| Case Study 1.2 | **Partial Taking– Electric Transmission Line**<br>Jeffrey A. Johnson, MAI | 53 |
| Case Study 1.3 | **Partial Taking–Petroleum Pipeline**<br>Jeffrey A. Johnson, MAI | 81 |
| Case Study 1.4 | **Partial Taking–Loss of Parking**<br>Douglas W. Nitzkorski, MAI, SR/WA | 103 |
| Case Study 1.5 | **Permanent Easement–Access**<br>L. Burl Wilson Jr., MAI | 117 |
| Case Study 1.6 | **Special Benefits**<br>Lori E. Safer, MAI, MRICS | 151 |

**Section II. Title Issue Cases**

Case Study 2.1 **Missing Waterline Easement–Water Rights**    161
Randy A. Williams, MAI, SR/WA, FRICS

Case Study 2.2 **Missing Waterline Easement–
Property Boundary**    171
Shawn Wilson, MAI

Case Study 2.3 **Missing Utility Corridor Easement–
Valuing Grandmother's Oak**    183
Shawn Wilson, MAI

**Section III. Environmental Contamination Cases**

Case Study 3.1. **Leaking Underground Storage Tank–
Former Gasoline Service Station**    189
Thomas O. Jackson, PhD, MAI, AICP,
CRE, FRICS, and Stephanie Norwood

Case Study 3.2 **Environmental Contamination and
Proximity**    205
Michael V. Sanders, MAI, SRA

Case Study 3.3 **Radioactive Contamination of
Nuclear Weapons Test Site**    221
Randall Bell, MAI

**Section IV. Nuisance Case**

Case Study 4.1 **Transmission Line Construction–
Wooden Poles to Metal Pylons**    233
Shawn Wilson, MAI

**Section V. Taxation Case**

Case Study 5.1 **Tax Assessment–Gas Wells**    243
S. Warren Klutz, MAI, SRA, CCIM

**Section VI. Matrimonial Case**

Case Study 6.1 **Matrimonial Dissolution**    259
Anthony S. Graziano, MAI, CRE, FRICS

**Section VII. Bankruptcy Case**

Case Study 7.1 **Bankruptcy–Fractional Interest in a
Leased Fee Estate**    279
Michael Y. Cannon, MAI, SRA, ASA, CRE, FRICS

**Section VIII. Lease Renewal and Arbitration Case**

Case Study 8.1 **Lease Renewal–The Periodic Setting of
Market Rent in a Long-Term Lease**    299
John G. Ellis, MAI, CRE, FRICS

Glossary    319

Index    325

# About the Authors

Jeffrey A. Johnson, MAI, is a partner in the Minneapolis office of Integra Realty Resources. Mr. Johnson is a frequent speaker at valuation seminars and has taught many appraisal classes. He codeveloped the seminar *Appraisal Practices for Litigation* for the Appraisal Institute in 1992. He is a co-recipient of the Appraisal Institute's 2001 George L. Schmutz Award. He holds a master's degree in mathematics and is coauthor of two books: *Practical Applications in Appraisal Valuation Modeling: Statistical Methods for Real Estate Practitioners* and *Shopping Center Appraisal and Analysis*, second edition. His real estate appraisal practice focuses on litigation matters.

Stephen J. Matonis, MAI, MRICS, is a principal of Integra Realty Resources-Orlando and has been appraising real property for 35 years. For the past 25 years, Mr. Matonis has limited his personal practice to the specialty of litigation valuation. He has been active in the Appraisal Institute, serving on the national level in the areas of admissions and education resources. Mr. Matonis chaired the General Demo Report Subcommittee, coauthored the grading manual, and served on the development team for the litigation valuation courses. *The Appraisal Journal* has published his work twice.

# Acknowledgments

A book such as this, with multiple case studies from many contributors, requires the efforts of many people to complete. The authors would like to acknowledge and thank these generous people for their valuable contributions.

First, we would like to thank all of the contributors listed in the table of contents for submitting their case studies. These experts have freely shared their time and expertise to further the educational efforts of the Appraisal Institute and our profession. We sincerely appreciate the contributions of Randall Bell, MAI, Michael Cannon, MAI, SRA, ASA, CRE, FRICS, John G. Ellis, MAI, CRE, FRICS, Anthony S. Graziano, MAI, CRE, FRICS, Thomas O. Jackson, PhD, MAI, AICP, CRE, FRICS, S.Warren Klutz, MAI, SRA, CCIM, Douglas W. Nitzkorski, MAI, SR/WA, Stephanie Norwood, Lori Safer, MAI, MRICS, Michael V. Sanders, MAI, SRA, Randy A. Williams, MAI, SR/WA, FRICS, L. Burl Wilson Jr., MAI, and Shawn Wilson, MAI.

The individual case studies were reviewed by members of a team of content reviewers that included Sandra K. Adomatis, SRA, Gail Cooper, MAI, Don M. Emerson, MAI, SRA, Mark R. Freitag, SRA, Frank E. Harrison, MAI, SRA, Harry B. Holzhauer, MAI, SRA, Dale J. Kleszynski, MAI, SRA, S. Warren Klutz III, MAI, SRA, Karen J. Mann, SRA, George R. Mann, MAI, SRA, Richard Marchitelli, MAI, Michael S. MaRous, MAI, Leonard J. Patcella Jr., MAI, Richard A. Stephens, MAI, SRA, and Nick A. Tillema, MAI, SRA., many of whom reviewed multiple case studies. We particularly appreciate the work of Peter D. Bowes, MAI, Stephen T. Crosson, MAI, SRA, W. West Foster, MAI, Stephen D. Roach, MAI, and John A. Schwartz, MAI, who all reviewed many of the case studies, and of David C. Lennhoff, MAI, SRA, the chair of the Publications Review Panel, who served as a manuscript reviewer and also contributed material to Chapter 3 from a working paper, "Litigation Lessons" (unpublished manuscript, April 2, 2012). The input from all of these reviewers on the individual cases was greatly appreciated.

We wish to offer our special thanks to Mark Lamb, CPA, MAI, who brought forth the idea of such a book. His innovative nature conceived of the idea of a case study-based book in which seasoned practitioners could share their work with the entire real estate appraisal profession.

We also offer our very special thanks to Appraisal Institute staff members Stephanie Shea-Joyce and Michael McKinley for their generous support and enthusiasm in the development of this text.

The authors also wish to thank their business partners for their understanding and support during this time-consuming book development process.

# Foreword

Most people dread the possibility of being called to appear in court, but many appraisers seek out assignments that will put them on the front lines of disputes between condemning authorities and property owners, spouses in divorce proceedings, or other parties involved in contentious legal situations. These appraisers have found a fulfilling niche appearing as expert witnesses or providing litigation support in matters involving real property. The Appraisal Institute's newest text, *Applications in Litigation Valuation: A Pragmatist's Guide*, presents a diverse collection of case studies from appraisal professionals highlighting what they've learned in the courtroom.

The first three chapters of the book provide an overview of the fundamentals of litigation appraisal, filling a need in the literature for practical advice on this complex appraisal specialty. Rooted in the direct experience of the authors, this discussion focuses on the appraiser's engagement, the execution of the assignment, and the eventual expert testimony.

These early chapters are followed by a series of case studies based on actual appraisal litigation assignments involving eminent domain and condemnation, title issues, environmental contamination, taxation, and other topics. The case studies illustrate a broad range of litigation appraisal issues and provide tangible examples of appraisers in action. They are based on real-life situations and include material pulled directly from appraisal reports.

The case study format of this book makes it a pioneering publication for the Appraisal Institute. We hope that this work is just the start, paving the way for fruitful discussion of practical strategies for litigation appraisal assignments and perhaps a second edition of this text in the future.

Litigation valuation is undeniably an interesting and rewarding discipline of real property appraisal. Few appraisers currently venture into this type of work, but more could take advantage of the opportunities offered. Whether you are new to litigation valuation and want to learn more, or you already have some litigation experience and want to refine your skills and expand the types of assignments you take on, *Applications in Litigation Valuation: A Pragmatist's Guide* is a worthy addition to your library.

**Sara W. Stephens, MAI**
2012 President
Appraisal Institute

# Preface

Since the beginning of the modern appraisal profession–which includes the establishment and evolution of the American Institute of Real Estate Appraisers (AIREA), the Society of Real Estate Appraisers, and the Appraisal Institute–many articles have been published in *The Appraisal Journal* and other technical periodicals relating to real estate law and litigation valuation. Several books have also been written on these topics, including volumes 1 and 2 of *Condemnation Appraisal Practice* (published in 1961 and 1973). Both volumes contained selected articles published by AIREA and were specific, for the most part, to eminent domain.

J. D. Eaton wrote the first edition of *Real Estate Valuation in Litigation* for the Appraisal Institute in 1982, and a second edition followed in 1995. The Appraisal Institute has also developed three courses on litigation valuation:

- *The Appraiser as an Expert Witness: Preparation and Testimony* (which includes a mock trial)
- *Condemnation Appraising: Principles and Applications*
- *Litigation Appraising: Specialized Topics and Applications*

In our opinion, Eaton's book is a must-read and the three courses are essential educational opportunities for anyone who is practicing in the field of litigation valuation.

During the summer of 2010, we discussed the need for a new book on litigation valuation that was more practical than earlier texts. We thought that a compilation of case studies would allow someone facing a litigation assignment (such as a lawyer, an experienced appraiser, or possibly a person new to the field of litigation valuation) to develop a basic understanding of the real estate valuation principles and techniques for various litigation assignments by seeing how other appraisers have handled these situations. As the saying goes, "An ounce of example is worth a ton of abstraction."

We developed a working table of contents that was then sent to leaders in the field of real estate law and litigation valuation, and we asked them to contribute case studies describing court cases they had participated in. The response was extraordinary, as virtually all participants felt the need for a practical text that would outline, in case study format, the nuances of this type of work and the issues encountered in particular assignments.

This resulting text includes accounts of actual cases from well-known practitioners in our profession. The case study authors have distilled workfiles and appraisal reports that are inches thick into readable narratives that describe the data and analyses that they found most useful in supporting their conclusions. The case studies do not dwell on the application of quantitative analysis techniques in the sales comparison approach, the derivation of capitalization rates in the income capitalization approach, or other fundamental skills in the appraisal of real property. These topics are well covered in other publications and educational programs. Instead, this book focuses on the unique issues encountered by appraisers in specific litigation situations.

All the contributors to this book have their individual styles, developed through extensive experience in the litigation arena. Neither we nor the Appraisal Institute suggest that these case studies demonstrate the only way to handle such work. In all litigation cases, different assumptions may be made and case law may differ. After all, without differences in opinion, there would be little or no need to litigate. Still, we do believe that worthwhile lessons can be learned from any of the case studies presented in the book, and we hope that the information presented here provides some basic guidelines about the careful, thorough analysis and the objectivity and integrity needed to be successful in litigation valuation assignments.

Because laws differ between jurisdictions, we ask you not to focus on the legal basis for the evaluation presented in each case study. Also, keep in mind that different real estate markets react differently to the detrimental conditions and property changes presented in these cases. Finally, try not to focus on the damage conclusions reached by each individual appraiser. Instead, we hope you learn from these cases by seeing how seasoned practitioners have used familiar appraisal procedures and techniques to measure the effects on value and solve the unique valuation problems they encountered. We consider the diversity of approaches to the different appraisal problems shown in this book to be one of its greatest strengths.

The purpose of this book is to give appraisal practitioners a jump-start on a very interesting and rewarding discipline of real property appraisal that only a few venture into. Keep in mind that each litigation assignment is an opportunity to learn and *no one* has all the answers.

Enjoy.

Jeffrey A. Johnson, MAI,
and Stephen J. Matonis, MAI, MRICS

## Chapter 1

# The Engagement

*By Stephen J. Matonis, MAI, MRICS, with Jeffrey A. Johnson, MAI*

*. . . The phone rings . . .*

You receive a call regarding a litigation case for which the value of real property is an issue. Where do you begin?

## Case Management

We first suggest a basic screening process to establish the *who, what, where,* and *when* of the case. Let's call this "case management." You will want to know who is calling and the caller's role in the process. For example, is the caller an attorney, property owner, CPA, or lender? Are you familiar with the caller's expertise or reputation? The Uniform Standards of Professional Appraisal Practice (USPAP) require client identification. Good business practices also require this identification for the very important engagement letter.

What qualifications are needed to handle the assignment? The answer to this question is obviously important under the Competency Rule of USPAP. What is the appraisal problem, type of litigation, and effective date of value? Is the effective date of value retrospective, such as 10 years ago? The answers to these questions will have a major impact on whether you accept the assignment and your professional fee. What type of value opinion is being sought–market, investment, insurable, or liquidation value? What property interest is being evaluated–the fee simple, leased fee, or leasehold estate, or an easement, air rights, or life estate? The client may need to be educated on dates of value, types of value, and interests.

### Conflicts of Interest

At this point it is necessary to explore potential conflicts of interest with the subject property as well as the parties involved in the case. Problems could result from previous appraisals made for others by you or others in your company. If you are part of a national appraisal firm, your conflict check should include everyone in the firm, not just the local office. You should also discuss conflicts in regard to issues as well as the property and the various parties involved.

## Scope of Work

The *scope of work* is very important in a litigation assignment and needs to be specifically outlined in the engagement letter. For example, are all three approaches to value required? Is there some innovative or creative theory involved in the case you are being asked to assist with? If the legal instructions provided fall outside of generally accepted appraisal standards and are contrary to USPAP, can you accept the assignment? Maybe or maybe not.

As in any other appraisal assignment subject to USPAP, the scope of work of a litigation appraisal assignment must identify the following assignment elements:

- the client (often an attorney) and any other intended users
- the intended use of the appraiser's opinions and conclusions (e.g., as an estimate of just condemnation in a taking, as an estimate of damages or a cost to cure some defect)
- the type and definition of value (often market value but also either retrospective value or prospective value)
- the effective date of the appraiser's opinions and conclusions (again, often a retrospective or prospective date, depending on the particulars of the situation)
- the subject of the assignment and its relevant characteristics
- any relevant assignment conditions such as hypothetical conditions and extraordinary assumptions but also including legal instructions and jurisdictional exceptions

## Litigation Timeline

The next step of case management is to find out where the case is on the *litigation timeline*. This is very important if the trial is scheduled to begin within 30 days or less. Can you complete the assignment in that short time period? On the other hand, you may be told not to worry because the trial is set for six months in the future. That is fine, but what if the *discovery cutoff* is only 30 days away? This means that all evidence, including your appraisal, must be completed in 30 days. This is obviously very important to know and again leads to the question of being able to get the work done on time and credibly. The exhibit below provides an outline of the litigation timeline.

If the trial has been set, is it for a two- or three-week trial docket, or is there a *time certain*? Before accepting the assignment, it is important to check if your calendar is clear during that two- or three-week trial docket so that you can be ready to testify if and when needed. If you are told that there is a time certain–meaning that the case is expected to start on a specific date–you will want to know how long the trial is scheduled to run so you can set that time

## Litigation Timeline

Phone Rings → Client ID → Conflict Check → Scope of Work → Discovery Process → Trial

| Client ID | Conflict Check | Scope of Work | Discovery Process |
|---|---|---|---|
| Lawyer<br>  Experience<br>  Reputation<br>Property Owner<br>CPA, etc.<br>Other Intended Users<br>Time<br>  Trial docket<br>  Time certain<br>Property Type<br>Competency | All Persons Involved in Case:<br>  Lawyers<br>  Appraisers<br>  Clients<br>Past Reports:<br>  You (current and historical)<br>  Corporate-wide (current and historical) | Value Type and Definition<br>  Market value<br>  Retrospective value<br>  Prospective value<br>Effective Date of the Appraiser's Opinions and Conclusions<br>Interests Appraised<br>  Fee simple<br>  Leased fee, etc.<br>Subject of the Assignment and its Relevant Characteristics<br>Assignment Conditions<br>  Legal instructions<br>  Hypothetical conditions<br>  Extraordinary assumptions<br>Other Experts | Subpoena Duces Tecum<br>Deposition<br>Case Review |

aside on your calendar. Unlike bank-related work, for which you can usually get extensions, courts and lawyers do not look too kindly upon failure to meet deadlines. There have been cases, for example, in which the appraiser missed a discovery cutoff date and the courts would not allow the appraisal to be entered as evidence for the trial. This will ruin your reputation in the community very quickly. Once your reputation has been questioned, it will be difficult at best to recover.

> **docket.** A schedule of pending cases. Also termed *court calendar; cause list; trial calendar.*
>
> **time certain.** A definite, specific date and time.
>
> (*Black's Law Dictionary*, 9th ed.)

## Other Experts

Another important question to ask your client is about other experts—such as land planning, engineering, and business valuation experts—who may be involved in the case. Are they "on board," and where do they fit in the timeline? What is the status of their reports?

> **expert.** A person who is presumed to have special knowledge of, or skill in, a particular field due to education, experience, or study. (*The Dictionary of Real Estate Appraisal*, 5th ed.)
>
> **predicate fact.** 1. A fact from which a presumption or inference arises. 2. A fact necessary to the operation of an evidentiary rule.
> · For example, there must actually be a conspiracy for the co-conspirator exception to the hearsay rule to apply.
>
> (*Black's Law Dictionary*, 9th ed.)
>
> **case in chief.** 1. The evidence presented at trial by a party between the time the party calls the first witness and the time the party rests. 2. The part of a trial in which a party presents evidence to support the claim or defense. (*Black's Law Dictionary*, 9th ed.)

The answers to these questions are especially important if their testimony is a *predicate* to your conclusions. Again, if your report can't be completed prior to your receiving information from the other experts involved, you need to take this into consideration before accepting a time-sensitive assignment.

## Engagement Letter

Now you are ready to move on to the very important engagement letter. Who should the engagement letter be addressed to and what are the fee arrangements going to be? The Appraisal Institute currently offers three courses involving litigation valuation.[1] These courses recommend "phased assignments" when participating in litigation work. The scope of work needs to be very specific so that there is no misunderstanding regarding what is expected of you.

Generally, the scope of work in "Phase 1" involves the due diligence needed to reach a reasonable value, value range, or some answer to the appraisal problem you have been retained to solve. If your client feels that your conclusions offered in Phase 1 help the case in chief, then the client can ask you to move forward into "Phase 2," which will involve the more formal and detailed appraisal document or preparation for trial. In Phase 1, you are often considered a consultant, and as a consultant the information you provide the lawyer is protected under attorney-client privilege and may not be subject to discovery.

Most of the work you will do will fall under Phase 1, so you should account for this in the fee negotiation portion of your engagement letter. A client once asked an old-school appraiser to do whatever was necessary to reach a value conclusion but added that he didn't need "the book." When it was time to talk about the fee, the appraiser simply said that the cost for the due diligence is $5,000 and "the book" is free. It should be no surprise that your actual

---

1. See also Guide Note 9, Use and Applicability of Engagement Letters, of the Appraisal Institute's Guide Notes to the Standards of Professional Appraisal Practice at www.appraisalinstitute.org/ppc/ethics_standards.aspx/.

report needs to follow USPAP. To protect yourself and your client, your engagement contract itself should generally be with the lawyer handling the specific case. As indicated previously, only then can the lawyer regulate which information is discoverable to the opponent's case and which is not.

## The Discovery Process

Let's move on to the *discovery process.* Discovery is the vehicle used by lawyers on either side of the case to ascertain the strengths and weaknesses of the opposing argument. This is accomplished though the exchange of each side's evidence, which includes appraisals for lawsuits involving real estate. In most states, this involves subpoenas and the taking of depositions.

A *subpoena duces tecum* is a request for "production" that includes all information used by the appraiser in forming an opinion. An attached exhibit usually lists all the specifically required information that is to be brought to the deposition. Today, that information may include all draft reports, notes made in the field, e-mails, and all other correspondence (letters) between parties to the lawsuit. The appraiser can "organize" the file prior to receipt of the subpoena. However, once the subpoena is received, nothing should be removed from the file or altered.

USPAP requires that the appraisal be completed prior to testifying under oath, as in a deposition. This doesn't mean that the workfile or appraisal report needs to be a 150-page Magna Carta. However, the documentation needs to be complete. Most of us subscribe to the KISS ("Keep it simple, stupid.") format in litigation assignments. While a "less is more" approach to documentation is often considered the most readable and useful, your report must include all the relevant data and analysis that a reader would need to understand and follow your logic and value reconciliations. Another important consideration is that many experienced

**discovery.** A legal procedure in which lawyers prepare for trial by obtaining factual information from an expert or fact witness(es) through written or oral questions. In discovery, an attorney may also have court authority to examine the files of all appraisals and related information for the purpose of preparing a case. (*The Dictionary of Real Estate Appraisal*, 5th ed.)

**subpoena duces tecum.** A subpoena ordering the witness to appear in court and to bring specified documents, records, or things. (*Black's Law Dictionary*, 9th ed.)

**produce.** 1. To bring into existence; to create. 2. To provide (a document, witness, etc.) in response to subpoena or discovery request. (*Black's Law Dictionary*, 9th ed.)

**exhibit.** 1. A document, record, or other tangible object formally introduced as evidence in court. 2. A document attached to and made part of a pleading, motion, contract, or other instrument. (*Black's Law Dictionary*, 9th ed.)

> From the start an attorney admonishes the appraiser to keep file contents to a minimum in order to limit inviting avenues of discovery for opposing counsel. In recent years [before 2003] such admonitions have run afoul of the *Uniform Standards of Professional Appraisal Practice* (USPAP), which requires that specific data and analysis be included either in appraisal reports or, if formal reports are not prepared, as file memoranda.
>
> Attorneys and even appraisers in recent articles and educational forums have pointed out the glaring weakness of appraisal files that are missing information mandated by USPAP; many see such gaps as an opportunity for the attorney to attack the appraiser in cross-examination. Appraisers subject to cross [examination] must be prepared to defend against the accusation of USPAP noncompliance.
>
> —Paul Talmage, "Cross-Examination at a Jury Trial," *The Appraisal Journal* (April 2003): 150.

> **material witness.** A witness who can testify about matters having some logical connection with the consequential facts, esp. if few others, if any, know about those matters.
>
> **protective order.** 1. A court order prohibiting or restricting a party from engaging in conduct (esp. a legal procedure such as discovery) that unduly annoys or burdens the opposing party or a third-party witness. 2. RESTRAINING ORDER (1).
>
> (*Black's Law Dictionary*, 9th ed.)

appraisers believe unnecessary information in the report gives the opposition additional fodder in cross examination. By keeping it simple, you can help the judge or jury understand the appraisal problem and keep the opposing counsel from clouding the important issues.

When attending the deposition, it is important to understand that the lawyers in the room represent their clients. The lawyer who has hired you will do his or her best to make sure you do not muddy the waters in the case, but keep in mind that you are not represented by counsel in that deposition. When being questioned in a deposition, you are on your own. Most experienced appraisers who do a lot of litigation work have a lawyer they can call upon if they need legal consultation.

It is important to make sure that it is clear whether you are being asked to act as a fact or expert witness before a deposition is taken. You may be subpoenaed as a fact witness only to find yourself being asked expert opinion questions at the deposition. As a fact witness, you need to comply with the subpoena but are only supposed to provide facts, such as your stated value conclusion, date of report, client, intended use, intended user, and so forth. Anything more would probably enter into the realm of real estate expertise, and you should be paid for that type of testimony and information. If a question arises as to whether you will be treated as a fact or expert witness and the lawyer who has subpoenaed you is being uncooperative, call your lawyer to intervene. If your lawyer finds that you may be questioned as to your expertise and there is no engagement regarding fees, your lawyer can obtain a motion for protective order, which essentially silences the subpoena. If you receive two subpoenas for the same trial date, the first one received prevails.

Finally, in a deposition you are to simply answer the questions asked truthfully and to the best of your ability. This is not the time to impress everyone in the room with your intelligence or to anticipate a question that has not been asked. A good point to remember is that you can't ever win a lawyer's case in a deposition, but you sure can lose one. Simply answer the questions asked. You are not there to help the lawyer taking the deposition. Additional information on depositions can be found in Chapter 3.

## The Trial

The last step in the litigation timeline is the actual trial. Expert testimony at the trial will be discussed in more detail in Chapter 3.

## Hypothetical Conditions, Extraordinary Assumptions, and Jurisdictional Exceptions

Just as most appraisal assignments for nonlitigation purposes are subject to certain assumptions and limiting conditions, litigation appraisal work often involves extraordinary assumptions and hypothetical conditions that might affect the credibility of the appraiser's testimony. For example, a typical *extraordinary assumption* in an eminent domain case could be the assumption that information provided by another "predicate" witness is accurate and correct. Suppose that the appraisal of wetland areas is outside your area of expertise. In an eminent domain case, you could rely on the "other" witness and, with validation, assume that the wetland expert's opinions or calculations are correct.[2]

As a specific example, in a recent Florida case an appraiser assumed that the entire site he was appraising was high, dry, and 100% "buildable." However, 50% of the site was actually jurisdictional wetlands, which in Florida cannot be used in any building calculations. As such, the appraiser's assumption that the site was 100% buildable was questionable at best. In this case, a second appraiser was hired. The first appraiser assumed the site was 100% buildable, and the second appraiser indicated by use of a predicate witness that the site was 50% buildable. Because of the substantial differences in "assumed"

---

2. According to Standards Rule 2-3, "When a signing appraiser(s) has relied on work done by appraisers and others who do not sign the certification, the signing appraiser is responsible for the decision to rely on their work. The signing appraiser(s) is required to have a reasonable basis for believing that those individuals performing the work are competent. The signing appraiser(s) also must have no reason to doubt that the work of those individuals is credible." (USPAP, 2012-2013 ed.) See also Guide Note 4, Reliance on Reports Prepared by Others, of the Appraisal Institute's Guide Notes to the Standards of Professional Appraisal Practice.

wetlands, the court—by virtue of a *motion in limine*—instructed both appraisers to use a wetland computation of 40%, implying a 60% buildable site.

A motion in limine is appropriate when the two (competent) appraisers involved in a case rely on substantially different assumptions prior to the motion. This can be confusing to the *trier of fact*, or the party responsible for determining the facts in a trial. The appraiser's job as an expert is to assist the trier of fact, whether it is simply the judge (in a bench trial) or jury (in a jury trial), in reaching a reasonable conclusion to the case at hand. A motion in limine limits the testimony of the two appraisers to a reasonably close conclusion regarding the issue at hand (such as wetlands), and as a result their testimony will be clearer to the judge or jury.

Another example of an extraordinary assumption is the concept of "reasonable probability." In most jurisdictions, if you find it is reasonable and probable that the property you are appraising can be rezoned to a higher, more intense use, you can conclude that this extraordinary assumption is correct in your appraisal. Since this zoning is not a fait accompli, adjustments must be made for the risk and time to obtain the assumed use.

A *hypothetical condition* deals with factors that are known to be false but are assumed to be true. In an eminent domain case, you are always dealing with a hypothetical condition regarding a proposed

> **motion in limine.** A pretrial request that certain inadmissible evidence not be referred to or offered at trial.
> - Typically, a party makes this motion when it believes that mere mention of the evidence during trial would be highly prejudicial and could not be remedied by an instruction to disregard. If, after the motion is granted, the opposing party mentions or attempts to offer the evidence in the jury's presence, a mistrial may be ordered. A ruling on a motion in limine does not always preserve evidentiary error for appellate purposes. To raise such an error on appeal, a party may be required to formally object when the evidence is actually admitted or excluded during trial.
>
> **fact-finder.** One or more persons—such as jurors in a trial or administrative-law judges in a hearing—who hear testimony and review evidence to rule on a factual issue. Also termed *finder of fact; fact-trier* or *trier of fact* (in a judicial proceeding); factfinding board (for a group or committee).
>
> (*Black's Law Dictionary*, 9th ed.)

> **hypothetical condition.** A condition, directly related to a specific assignment, which is contrary to what is known by the appraiser to exist on the effective date of the assignment results, but is used for the purpose of analysis.
> - Comment: Hypothetical conditions are contrary to known facts about physical, legal, or economic characteristics of the subject property; or about conditions external to the property, such as market conditions or trends; or about the integrity of data used in an analysis.
>
> (*Uniform Standards of Professional Appraisal Practice*, 2012-2013 ed.)

"project." To consider damages or benefits to a remainder property for a project in a partial taking of a property, you need to presume the project is complete when, in fact, it is not.

A *jurisdictional exception* is an assignment condition established by applicable law or regulation that precludes an appraiser from complying with USPAP. Certain governmental agencies have additional requirements that are often beyond professional appraisal standards. Jurisdictional exceptions are rare but can affect an appraisal assignment when an actual law or public policy contradicts specific appraisal standards.

> **extraordinary assumption.** An assumption, directly related to a specific assignment, as of the effective date of the assignment results, which, if found to be false, could alter the appraiser's opinions or conclusions.
>
> Comment: Extraordinary assumptions presume as fact otherwise uncertain information about physical, legal, or economic characteristics of the subject property; or about conditions external to the property, such as market conditions or trends; or about the integrity of data used in an analysis.
>
> **jurisdictional exception.** An assignment condition established by applicable law or regulation, which precludes an appraiser from complying with a part of USPAP.
>
> (*Uniform Standards of Professional Appraisal Practice*, 2012-2013 ed.)

## Legal Instructions

The employing attorney may provide you with *legal instruction* concerning how he or she would like the appraisal analysis to be considered. If the *legal instruction* is "reasonable" and explicitly discussed in your appraisal without being confusing or misleading, it is allowed in most jurisdictions.

A recent eminent domain case in Seminole County, Florida, provides an example of reasonable legal instruction. In this case, the lawyer for the property owner was looking to create some new "case law" in Florida. The lawyer had copies of case law in other states that he shared with his appraiser but that were contrary to the consistent use theory of appraisal. This case involved a high-volume commercial corner with a highest and best use as if vacant for a national-brand drugstore. The appraisers for both the owner and the county agreed. The property was improved with a like-new warehouse that the property owner used to operate his construction company. The acquisition was a total taking, including land and buildings. It would normally be inappropriate to add the contributory value of the building to this very valuable parcel of land under the typical standards of the market. Both appraisers again agreed that the existing building did not contribute to value over and above land value. However, some states do allow compensation for "the total property as it exists on the date of acquisition."

In this case, a legal instruction was given to the property owner's appraiser to disregard the "consistent use" theory, value the land based on its highest and best use, and include the value of the warehouse. The appraiser was very explicit in his report that the work was in violation of the "consistent use" theory and stated so in the letter of transmittal, scope of work, highest and best use, and reconciliation sections of the report. The case eventually settled, and the court did not rule on this issue. The point here is that in litigation valuation, appraisal theory may not always be "black and white." In this case the judge could have ruled either way and, in fact, his interpretation of the law seemed to be leaning in favor of the property owner prior to settlement.

## USPAP

We end this chapter with a brief discussion of the Uniform Standards of Professional Appraisal Practice. USPAP is the appraiser's friend. It outlines what we can or cannot do in the completion of our appraisal assignments. USPAP outlines the standard for whichever "hat" we are wearing. It is imperative that anyone who works in litigation valuation has a strong grasp of USPAP. If you don't remember anything else in Chapter 1, remember that lawyers spend a great deal of time studying USPAP. Unfortunately, in many cases they know USPAP better than practicing appraisers and use it to try to trip up appraisers in their expert testimony. If you practice in real estate appraisal litigation, you need to be very familiar with what's in USPAP.

CHAPTER 2

# Executing the Commitment

*By Jeffrey A. Johnson, MAI, with Stephen J. Matonis, MAI, MRICS*

In the first chapter we discussed the engagement: contracting for valuation services, defining the valuation problem, and determining the scope of services. In this chapter we will address the execution of that commitment made to your client. The scope of services specified in your engagement letter defines the minimum amount of work to be accomplished to do a credible job and earn your fee. In the litigation setting, the scope of services often changes in the course of the engagement. What was originally planned for the appraisal opinion and report will frequently change, and the additional litigation support services are always changing as one side reacts to each move made by the opposing side.

## The Appraisal Opinion and Report

In all appraisal assignments we appraisers like to have people accept our value conclusions. But in litigation assignments, it is a primary goal. At trial, the attorney you are working with is trying to produce and demonstrate ways to separate your work from that of an appraiser on the opposing side, so anything you can add to your scope of services that will differentiate your work from that of the other appraiser is important. As a simple example, it is better and more credible if you have measured the building yourself rather than relying on measurements from the county assessment records. Also, you may want to include data and analysis for all three approaches to value in your report, even when one of the approaches is commonly considered to have little applicability because the opposing attorney may tell the jury that you purposely ignored one or more of the approaches to value and the other appraiser did not.

In Case Study 8.1, "Lease Renewal–The Periodic Setting of Market Rent in a Long-Term Lease," author John G. Ellis, MAI, CRE, FRICS, explains that he actually used four independent sales comparison approaches to estimate the market rent for a very unique property. In the closing arguments in this case, the attorney would be able to tell the jury about these extra efforts to measure market rent. The scope of work of the appraisal was to develop an opinion of market rent for a former theater building to be used as a church. Ellis concluded that the unit of comparison should be "monthly rent per seat." Rather than stopping there, Ellis states that his research led him to find two brokers who specialize in church properties. Through his investigations, he determined that this unit of comparison was used by those brokers and other market participants. He also cited the 13th edition of *The Appraisal of Real Estate* as support for his choice of that unit of comparison. We always want to have a sound basis for our opinions in litigation appraisals and to be able to demonstrate that basis. Having more legs to stand on is always a good idea. Being a better litigation appraiser is not only about being a better witness, it is also about being a better appraiser. Any work you can do to "go the extra mile" may well prove to make a difference that the jury will appreciate.

In Chapter 1, we encouraged you to contract your appraisal assignments for litigation on a Phase 1/Phase 2 basis. In Case Study 6.1, "Matrimonial Dissolution," author Anthony S. Graziano, MAI, CRE, FRICS, illustrates this phasing concept in detail. The Phase 1 service is usually a more limited service to identify the approximate magnitude of the valuation case and determine if the case can be settled through negotiations. The Phase 1 service may result in a verbal report, but more often this opinion is transmitted in a restricted use appraisal report. Be careful not to limit your Phase 1 evaluation service so much that the value opinion is later found to not be fully supported by the Phase 2 service. This can be misleading to the litigants. For the Phase 2 service, the report can take any form but is usually either a summary or self-contained appraisal report. There seem to be two main schools of thought on writing reports for litigation. The minimalists hide the pearl and only release it at trial; other appraisers show everything they have in their reports. I personally believe that the latter approach fosters settlements because both sides understand more fully the issues on both sides of the case before the trial begins.

File and record keeping responsibilities apply to both electronic media and the hard copy written file. Some courts may conclude that e-mail correspondence regarding an appraisal is part of that file. Therefore, it is good practice to think of any e-mail you send as being copied to the opposing side, since they will see it once the case moves to the discovery stage.

The big question here is what needs to be kept in the file. The Uniform Standards of Professional Appraisal Practice (USPAP) gives us a partial answer by instructing us to include within the file all data, information, and documentation necessary to support the appraiser's opinions and conclusions. Some appraisers also like to keep information about sales and rent data that was considered but not used in the valuation analysis, along with a note explaining why these data were not used. Always be aware of any state rule that may address record keeping. While there is no standard way to organize a workfile, it is good practice to have some categorized sections in it since you might have to refer to it many years later. Once you have received a subpoena for deposition, you must not destroy or alter anything that is in your entire file.

An appraiser may not have originally coined the phrase "a picture is worth a thousand words," but to an appaiser it does sound like a statement made about a valuation opinion. In litigation work we might even say that "a thousand words" underestimates the true contribution of pictures. In preparing a litigation appraisal report, consider using exhibits, maps, photos, graphs, and charts that may be helpful in explaining your position. Remember that the jury will have little or no real estate experience. These illustrations can be included in the report, used as trial exhibits, or both. You will notice that most of the case studies in this book include exhibits. An image that demonstrates a relative condition can also be used as an exhibit, as is the case with the accompanying graphic that appears in Case Study 2.1, "Missing Waterline Easement–Water Rights," by Randy A. Williams, MAI, SR/WA, FRICS. An illustration such as this is not going to win a case

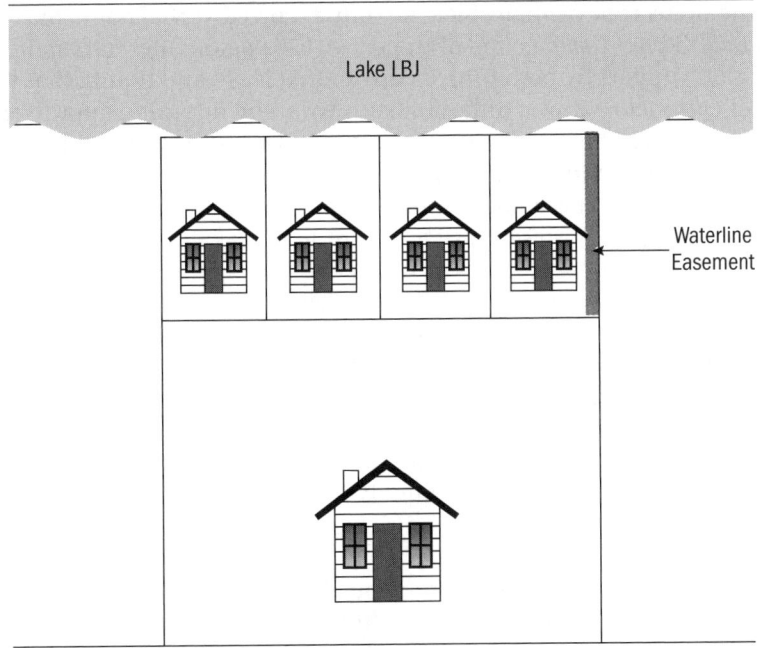

all on its own, but it is going to help the jury understand where the waterline easement is relative to other properties involved in the assignment. Anything you can do to create a better rapport with the jury will be beneficial.

## Additional Litigation Support Services

Often achieving success in a litigation assignment involves more than simply performing an appraisal and defending the value opinion persuasively on the witness stand. Many different kinds of litigation support services are common—and crucial—in the preparation for a deposition or trial.

When performing additional litigation support services, we often provide appraisal consulting services and sometimes function as investigators. In the previously mentioned Case Study 8.1, the author explains that he learned from the deposition of the opposing appraiser that the other appraiser had appraised the subject property at an earlier date but no longer had his file due to an office move. Ellis was able to locate a copy of that report, which contained information that was helpful to his client's position. This opposing appraiser also stated that, for one of his rent comparables, he only received verbal confirmation and did not have a copy of the lease. Ellis again offered beneficial litigation support by obtaining a copy of this lease and noting that the actual contract rent was different from what the opposing appraiser was reporting. The litigation environment is constantly changing, and your scope of services must also be able to change if you are expected to provide these types of additional litigation support services.

One commonly sought litigation support service is reviewing the work of the opposing appraiser. If you are performing an appraisal review—and you are allowed to do so even in situations where you have prepared your own appraisal in the case—it is important to understand and follow the USPAP requirements for this type of service, as set forth in Standard 3. Remember that an appraisal review is a critique of the work of another appraiser, not an attack on the appraiser who did the work. In other situations you may be asked to assist the attorney in a case as an advocate, for example, helping the attorney design the cross examination, which is not the same as acting as a reviewer. You may perform this service as long as you do not misrepresent your role. It must be clear to all parties that you are not participating as an appraiser, which would carry the expectation of being unbiased and independent. It is important to point out that you may not act as an advocate—that is, assisting the attorney as described above—and as an appraiser in the same case, as illustrated in Advisory Opinion 21 of USPAP (see the following page). To avoid any perception of advocacy, the parties in many larger litigation mat-

> **Litigation Support and Advocacy**
>
> In 2004, The Appraisal Foundation revised the illustrations in Advisory Opinion 21, USPAP Compliance. An example of litigation services was added that illustrates the fundamental separation that appraisers must maintain between acting as an appraiser and providing litigation support services in the same case:
>
> *Litigation Services*
>
> 4. Marie Vaughn has a diverse practice with a specialization in litigation services. She commonly aids attorneys in developing cross-examination strategies for expert witness testimony from appraisers. How does USPAP apply to Marie's "litigation services?"
>
>     Answer: In order to determine Marie's obligation, it is necessary to understand the nature of her role. If she is acting as an appraiser, her litigation services are part of appraisal practice and the ethics and competency requirements of USPAP apply. Marie must comply, at a minimum, with the portions of USPAP that apply generally to appraisal practice. These include the DEFINITIONS, PREAMBLE, the ETHICS RULE, the COMPETENCY RULE, and the JURISDICTIONAL EXCEPTION. As an appraiser, Marie cannot act as an advocate for any party or issue.
>
>     If Marie's services include providing an opinion of value, she must comply with the appropriate appraisal standards (STANDARDS 1 and 2, 7 and 8, or 9 and 10). If Marie's services include providing an opinion about the quality of another appraiser's work, the appraisal review requirements of STANDARD 3 apply. If the service includes providing analysis, recommendation, or an opinion to solve a real property problem where an opinion of value is a component of the analysis leading to the assignment results, then Marie must adhere to the appraisal consulting requirements of STANDARDS 4 and 5.
>
>     On the other hand, if Marie provides litigation services as an advocate, then she is providing a valuation service outside of appraisal practice. When performing services outside of appraisal practice, Marie can act as an advocate and accept contingent compensation. **The only USPAP obligation is that she not misrepresent her role.** She must use care to distinguish her role from other roles that would carry an expectation of being impartial, objective, and independent, i.e., acting as an appraiser.
>
>     Marie may provide litigation services by either acting as an appraiser or acting as an advocate for the client's cause; however, she must not perform both roles in the same case.
>
> Source: *Uniform Standards of Professional Appraisal Practice*, 2012-2013 ed.

ters will hire separate appraisers to review the appraisal made for the other side of the case and testify about that review.

In a litigation situation, no single individual produces a win or loss. In a litigation support role, the appraiser has much to offer the client beyond simply an opinion of value. The real estate appraiser is more familiar with the real estate market and the market participants than the attorney, so the appraiser is in a very good position to suggest other professionals who can offer needed expertise. There have been many times when my greatest contribution in a case was not my testimony but simply suggesting that a key witness who could testify in support of our valuation position should be hired.

# Chapter 3

# The Appraiser as an Expert Witness

*By Jeffrey A. Johnson, MAI, with Stephen J. Matonis, MAI, MRICS*

## The Real Estate Appraisal Expert Witness

Many years ago I was contacted by an out-of-town attorney who said he wanted to hire me to recommend a local appraiser for a particular litigation matter involving a hotel in the central business district of our city. I immediately went into a lengthy dissertation about the fellow professionals I knew who were more or less active in litigation cases within our community. He quickly stopped me and told me that that was not what he was looking for. He wanted me to tell him about the appraisers who were the most versed in hotel appraisals and those who were the most experienced in the downtown district. He wanted the appraiser who was the most experienced in terms of property type and location. He was looking for the most competent appraiser, and I had given him the most experienced witnesses. He also said that his job as the attorney was to make that top appraiser into a good witness. I will always remember that experience because it showed me what the marketplace was seeking and it also taught me that the way to be a better witness is to be a better appraiser.

Part of the role of the attorney you are working with is to make you into a better witness. You, of course, have a role in that process as well: being the best appraiser you can be and learning some of the things you can do to become a better witness.

Chapter 21 of the second edition of *Real Estate Valuation in Litigation* by J. D. Eaton and the documents cited in the extensive footnotes in that text provide a comprehensive discussion of the real estate appraiser serving as an expert witness. This chapter supplements that information, tying the theory provided in

> It is paradoxical that some of the best qualified appraisers make the worst value witnesses and some of the biggest rascals and rogues in the real estate business are the most effective witnesses. Condemnation law is not every lawyer's cup of tea, either. —Walstein Smith Jr., "The Value Witness in Condemnation," *The Real Estate Appraiser* (July-August 1970): 35, via Michael Y. Cannon, MAI, SRA, ASA, FRICS, CRE.

that text to real-life situations encountered by the authors and other appraisers on the witness stand.

Real estate appraisers may find themselves serving as expert witnesses in several different settings, some of which are

- A trial before a judge (sometimes referred to as a *bench trial*)
- A trial before a jury
- An administrative hearing before a court-appointed administrator or an appointed panel
- A mediation or arbitration proceeding
- A deposition
- A public forum such as a city zoning board meeting or other public agency panel

Regardless of the forum, there is a base of knowledge that can help the appraiser serve as a more effective witness. When an appraiser is hired for a litigation assignment, most clients share a common goal: they want their appraiser's opinion of value to prevail. We must not lose sight of the fact that we are in a client-oriented service business. The litigation setting is one that presents great opportunity to serve clients who are in positions of financial risk. While clients' needs are important, appraisers should never waiver from their obligation to adhere to ethical appraisal standards.

When I decided that I wanted to be more active as a real estate appraisal witness, I started viewing litigation cases. Many of these are open public events. You can learn a lot from simple observation. When I could not attend an interesting case, I talked with the par-

---

**Expert Witness Characteristics**

Regardless of their profession, expert witnesses have several characteristics in common. They are:
- well prepared
- thorough
- professional in attitude and appearance
- knowledgeable about the subject matter
- unbiased
- credible
- honest

Besides these characteristics, an expert appraisal witness is one who:
- ensures that the appraisal is accurate, thorough, complete, and unbiased ...
- informs the client's attorney of pertinent appraisal terminology, theory, and techniques
- furnishes the client's attorney with the questions the attorney should ask to ensure that the expert's appraisal is presented fairly and effectively ...
- knows and adheres to *Uniform Standards of Professional Appraisal Practice* (USPAP) requirements for the presentation of an oral report

— Richard Hoffman, "Preparing for Expert Testimony," *The Appraisal Journal* (October 2002): 381.

ticipants. Another of my training experiences was serving on court-appointed commissioner panels. In my area, the courts appoint a panel of three people to hear condemnation cases. I was appointed to serve on these panels after writing letters to the judges assigned to these types of eminent domain cases. I simply requested that they consider me to serve and told them of my appraisal experience. I heard many appraisers testify while serving on these panels. I was finally able to tell myself that I could do what these appraisers were doing.

> **expert witness.** A witness qualified by knowledge, skill, experience, training, or education to provide a scientific, technical, or other specialized opinion about the evidence or a fact issue. Also termed *skilled witness*. (*Black's Law Dictionary*, 9th ed.)

Teaching is another valuable experience. Being questioned by students who are trying to understand a concept is somewhat similar to being questioned in court; it teaches us to think on our feet. But ultimately you cannot learn to be an accomplished tap dancer solely by reading a book; at some point, you have got to get up on stage.

In any discussion about serving as a witness it is almost mandatory that we mention the oath, which is simply to "tell the truth, the whole truth, and nothing but the truth." Telling the truth is of prime importance. This cannot be stressed enough. But most people in our profession know that both facts and opinions are involved in developing our opinions of value. Some statements can be classified as true or false, such as the following:

- "The square footage of the subject building is 5,723 square feet."
- "The acreage of the land parcel that is referred to as Comparable Sale 2 is 2.734 acres."
- "The zoning classification of the subject parcel is B-4: Highway Business District."
- "The number of lanes of traffic on the street adjacent to the Comparable Sale 5 property is four."

The true or false character of each of these statements can be verified. Building square footage can be measured. Zoning classifications can be verified by the presentation of an official zoning map or letter from the city zoning staff.

In addition to all the verified facts presented in our evaluations, we present many intermediate opinions that are neither true nor false. These intermediate opinions vary greatly depending on the appraisal assignment, but some examples are as follows:

- The estimates of market rents for various spaces within the subject building

- The estimate of a vacancy rate that an investment buyer would use in a pro forma
- The appraiser's conclusion that a rezoning of the subject parcel is reasonably probable
- The appraiser's conclusion that a rezoning of the subject parcel is not likely

Opinions such as these are neither true nor false. Such opinions are either accepted or rejected by a judge or jury. When you read another professional's appraisal, you may accept some of that person's opinions and reject others. Your acceptance or rejection of these opinions is usually based on any prior experiences you have had with similar properties, any biases you may carry, or your evaluation of the support that the other person presents for his or her opinions. We can learn from our reviews of others' appraisals about how to present our own appraisals so that they are more readily accepted.

There is an old joke in our profession that goes something like this:
*Is appraisal a science or an art?*
*Answer: Well, it must be an art because we are often asked to paint a rosy picture.*
If this "joke" makes you laugh, you may not be well suited to being a witness because you do not look at the profession seriously. If this joke makes you cry, again you may not be well suited to the role because you take yourself too seriously. Remember that in our profession no single appraiser possesses a franchise on truth or the acceptance of his or her opinion. We deal with facts, and we also deal with lots of opinions. Many intermediate opinions go into forming a final appraisal opinion of value. Having your opinion prevail at a trial is a function of the support you have and how you present that support for all intermediate opinions leading to your final opinion of value.

Sometimes we have trouble identifying the weak points of our own appraisal opinions. However, a case will rarely go forward to

> Justice is an abstract concept in criminal law. Many restrictions have been provided to protect and preserve justice. The judge and the jury must make decisions based upon the logic and persuasiveness of lawyers and expert witnesses. Their decision is not necessarily right because a guilty man may be acquitted or an innocent man may be convicted. Value is an abstract concept in condemnation law. Who knows for certain that an easement will damage the remainder and if so, how much? Who knows for certain that a parcel of land will not ever be used for a much higher and better use than is forecasted? The qualified appraiser deals in probabilities based upon his education, training, experience, and judgment. His expertise is only as good as his qualifications and integrity. He may not be certain but he is more probable of being closer to the truth than an unqualified appraiser witness. —Walstein Smith Jr., "The Value Witness in Condemnation," *The Real Estate Appraiser* (July-August 1970): 42, via Michael Y. Cannon, MAI, SRA, ASA, FRICS, CRE.

trial or hearing without some weaknesses on both sides. As a result, identifying the weaknesses of your appraisal to the attorney you are working with will actually strengthen your case. The last place the attorney should discover those weaknesses is at the trial. You should never withhold information from the attorney you are working with because this is a form of lying, which is never a good policy.

As a witness in a valuation dispute, you must see the bigger picture: what the dispute is about, what positions the parties have taken, and what subject matter is to be covered at the trial. The client's attorney will likely be in a position to inform you of the dispute and positions prior to your engagement. It is very important to see both sides of the case. Remember that management of the case is in the hands of the attorney.

## Testifying at a Trial

Before we begin the discussion of important considerations for appraisers who testify at trials, we must note that many of these considerations pertain to all the other previously described testimony venues.

> Appraisers know that location is the most important aspect when estimating the value of a parcel of property. Similarly, preparation is critical to an expert witness's success on the stand. —Richard Hoffman, "Preparing for Expert Testimony," *The Appraisal Journal* (October 2002): 386.

In the courtroom, dress and appearance are very important. People form opinions based on first impressions, and they will have some opinion of you before you even speak. It is also a good idea to be well rested. Testimony can be tiring, and even the task of paying vigilant attention to the testimony of others can be tiring. Always be yourself on the witness stand. This is a good rule for many of life's situations, but it is very important in testifying. Many cases are decided based on who the jury liked better. Confidence and candor are the keys to a proper attitude. Do not, however, mistake arrogance for confidence: while the latter is essential, the former must be guarded against at all cost. Be prepared and have command of the facts and figures. Speak as if you are dictating a report—slowly enough for the listener to follow, clearly, and without using specialized real estate or appraisal terms. Some witnesses will try to testify as if they are explaining their analysis and opinion to a friend. Do not sit with others representing your client, and do not talk with others while in the court room. You are, and must be perceived to be, an independent, unbiased expert. Upon completion of your testimony and dismissal, thank the trier and quickly leave the court room. You should have no apparent interest in what happens after you have made your presentation.

It is the attorney's job to inform you about the judge, hearing administrator, or panel members. The attorney will inform you about what the audience for your testimony likes and doesn't like to hear.

This will help set the tone for the day and the manner of presentation. Testimony consists of the following:

1. Qualifying as an expert
2. Direct examination
3. Cross examination
4. Redirect and recross examinations

## Qualifying as an Expert

At trial, the process of qualifying as an expert is merely a question-and-answer session with the attorney in which you are asked questions about your appraisal training, education, and experience. Different court venues have different criteria for qualifying as an expert. Generally speaking, an expert witness is simply someone who is there to assist the jury in understanding a complicated or technical subject that is not within the common understanding of the average layperson.

> An appraiser may be qualified, but if his or her methodology is faulty the testimony may be thrown out by the judge or discounted by the jury. Likewise, an appraiser may have an acceptable methodology, but may not be qualified as an expert witness and as such, not allowed to testify. —Richard W. Hoyt, Robert J. Aalberts, and Percy Poon, "*Daubert* and Qualification of the Appraisal Expert Witness," *The Appraisal Journal* (Summer 2010):284.

As such, you are attempting to show the judge that you have the necessary expertise consisting of knowledge, skill, experience, training, and education. In federal court cases, a standard for qualifying and accepting an expert witness came out of the *Daubert* case, which may also have some applicability to qualifying as a real estate appraisal expert in some nonfederal court venues.[1] This case specifies that the court must consider the following:

1. Whether the theory has been or can be tested
2. Whether the theory has been subjected to peer review and publication
3. Whether or not there is a known rate of error
4. The general acceptance of the technique in question

Your attorney will be aware of the standard for the applicable court venue and will inform you of the questions he or she will ask you. This is part of preparing for the trial.

---

1. *Daubert v. Merrell Dow Pharmaceuticals, Inc.*, 509 US 579 (1993). For help in understanding this case and how it may apply to qualification as an expert witness, see www.bucklin.org/Daubert_History.htm and see also Richard W. Hoyt, Robert J. Aalberts, and Percy Poon, "*Daubert* and Qualification of the Appraisal Expert Witness," *The Appraisal Journal* (Summer 2010): 283-291.

If you are extremely well qualified, the other side of a case may waive your qualification so that the jury does not hear how qualified you are, which may contrast with a less-qualified appraiser on the other side. Qualification should not, as a general rule, be waived. State your qualifications in a matter-of-fact manner. Do not be boastful but do not shy away from any of your distinctions.

> **direct examination.** In a trial or other court proceeding, the initial questioning of a witness by the party who called the witness to testify. (*The Dictionary of Real Estate Appraisal*, 5th ed.)

## Direct Examination

*Direct examination* is the term used to describe the portion of the testimony in which the appraiser is questioned by the party who called him or her as a witness. It is usually performed as part of a trial to present responses in support of facts or opinions that satisfy a required element of a party's case. In direct examination, attorneys are generally prohibited from asking leading questions. This rule prevents an attorney from "feeding" the answers to a witness who is favorable to the attorney's case, so you will be asked questions that are not leading you to a desired response in any way.

As a witness, you will be asked questions by the attorney, but you should deliver your responses to the judge or the jury. The theory is that the answer should be delivered to the person (or people) you hope will be using it to decide the outcome of the case. In your direct examination testimony, you are trying to build a relationship of trust with the jury, and answering directly to them will help.

Nonverbal responses mean nothing. In everyday conversations, we often make nonverbal responses, and people understand them. However, at trial we are making a record, a formal transcript. Shaking your head in response to a question cannot be recorded to become part of the transcript. You should try to mention exhibit numbers when you are talking about specific exhibits. This will make the transcript of the trial easier to read. It is also important to identify the exhibit before explaining what you think it shows.

Exhibits such as photos, maps, charts, and graphs are great tools for conveying messages. For example, the graph on the following page appears in Case Study 1.4, "Partial Taking–Loss of Parking," by Douglas W. Nitzkorski, MAI, SR/WA. This exhibit provides a good example of how a graph can show the relationship between two variables in the real estate marketplace. Such a graph is very easy to explain to a jury. In this particular case study, the valuation question at hand is whether there is a relationship between the amount of on-site parking per 1,000 square feet of gross leasable area and the rent being paid for retail properties in this submarket. Such an exhibit

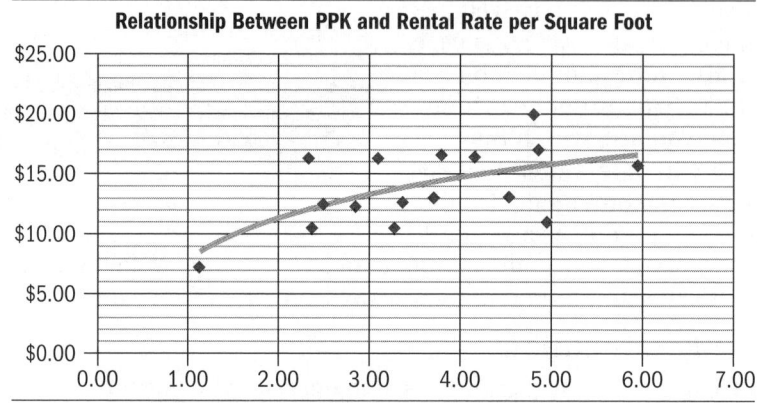

can be very helpful in showing any market relationship that you have found. When the relationship is compelling, as it is in this case, a visual aid can also help you explain your opinion.

When testifying, remember to speak slowly as you are being recorded. Pauses are not only acceptable, they can show thoughtfulness on behalf of the speaker.

Attorneys have many different courtroom styles. Some prefer to plan direct examinations in a question-by-question format, while others merely outline their direct examinations to make sure they cover all of the key points and then have more spontaneous interchanges with their witnesses. You should schedule preparation time with the attorney you are working with to give yourself a chance to learn what he or she plans to ask during the direct examination and to give the attorney a chance to learn what your responses to the specific questions will be. Testimony should not sound scripted or rehearsed.

Plan your testimony with the attorney you are working with so you can focus your time on the important points of the case. Every trial is a war consisting of many minor skirmishes, and you would ultimately like to prevail on each. Focus your direct testimony on the topics that are likely to contribute to the major differences in the two opposing valuations and those that have the greatest valuation impact.

Make sure you are well prepared to testify about your work. Sometimes you may be asked to testify years after you have completed an assignment. With this in mind, it is important to make a comprehensive review of your file and work product. Be very specific with respect to names, documents, facts, and figures. It is not a good idea to bring notes to the witness stand, as the opposing attorney has the right to see any documents you may bring.

Inexperienced witnesses often find the "hearsay rule" difficult to understand. You are generally not allowed to testify about what you were told by another person. That person is not available at the trial, and the court does not want to hear a one-sided recounting of that conversation. You might ask "Doesn't my appraisal opinion rest on a stronger base if I have talked to more market participants?" The answer is, of course, "yes." When presenting and answering questions about the scope of your appraisal work, make sure to itemize all the conversations you have had to show the jury that you have done your work. However, if you begin by saying something like, "Developer Smith told me . . . ," that will unfortunately be about as far as you'll get before the opposing attorney objects on the grounds of hearsay. The objection will be sustained, meaning that you cannot make or finish such a statement. On the other hand, if you say, "I have interviewed market participants including developer Smith, property manager Jones, and investor Johnstankowski, and based on those interviews and my experience as an appraiser and my analysis of the local market data, it is my opinion that the market vacancy rate for the subject property is 5%," there should not be a successful hearsay objection.

You may be asked—and should be prepared to testify—about the comparable sales used by the other side that were not included in your analysis. This gives you a chance to explain why you did not use those sales. Sometimes your side of the case may hire an appraiser to review and possibly comment on the appraisal made for the other side. If you are the one asked to comment, it is best to keep it very factual and not extend yourself so much that you appear to be an advocate for your side. It is easier to cross the advocacy line when you are commenting about the opposing appraisal. Once that line is crossed, a good measure of your credibility disappears.

## Cross Examination

Cross examination is the questioning of you by the attorney on the other side of the case. The purpose of cross examination is to bring out facts from the witness that are favorable to the other side of the case. Cross examination is a test of your credibility as a witness. It also serves to test the accuracy and resonableness of your direct testimony. The cross examiner is attempting to impeach your credibility so as to diminish the weight of any unfavorable testimony. Some cross-examining attorneys have an abrasive style. However, most experienced attorneys refrain from abrasive cross examination as they do not want to alienate members of the jury.

It has been said that cross examination is the art of examining crossly. The goal of cross

> **cross examination.** The process of questioning a witness whose direct testimony is adverse to the position of the party undertaking the questioning. The purpose of cross examination is to dilute, neutralize, or completely destroy the effect of the witness's direct testimony. (*The Dictionary of Real Estate Appraisal*, 5th ed.)

examination is to destroy the witness's direct testimony completely. That goal is rarely accomplished, but be aware that you will lose ground during cross examination. It is not a question of whether your testimony can be weakened, but rather by how much and in what manner.

Remember to always wait until the cross examination question is completed before responding. Take a deep breath. Avoid quick responses. This gives you time to fully appreciate the question, and it also gives the attorney you are working with a chance to object to the question.

In trial, the judge will not allow two people to speak at same time. This is not polite, and it is difficult or impossible for the court reporter to transcribe. Never lose your composure, even if the other side is hostile. It can work to your benefit and their detriment if you do not join in with their hostility.

Listen closely to the questions and focus on the precise wording. If there is any ambiguity in the question, do not hesitate to ask for a restatement or clarification of the question. Your answers should always be direct, accurate, and concise. Do not ignore the jury. They should be the focus of all your replies.

A common tactic I have seen is for a cross-examining attorney to ever-so-slightly misstate your earlier statements in a compound sentence asking a new question. Do not let that slide. It is acceptable for you to restate your exact recollection of your earlier response in the answer to the current question. This is why transcripts are kept at trial–to keep the participants honest.

I am sorry to inform you that you cannot outwit the opposing counsel. Don't even try to do this. Attorneys examine experts all the time. They are much more experienced in examinations than we are as occasional witnesses. Even though we know much more about the real estate market than they ever could, as we deal with that information every day, trying to outsmart the attorney rarely works very well. Think of how downright stupid the following exchange is:

*The cross-examining attorney says, "I like your tie."*

*The witness responds, "It's not for sale."*

This exchange is a little bit funny because parts are obviously missing from it. The two sentences do not go together very well. The missing parts are, of course, in the witness's head as he tries to outfox the attorney, who he is quite sure is out to buy his tie. This sort of maneuver is just as crazy when done in a real estate valuation trial. The best practice is to listen very carefully to the question being asked and to answer *only* that specific question. Do not speak to where you think the question is leading.

It is always best to answer emphatically and with no uncertainty. However, we are human, and the nature of our profession is that some opinions are more definitive than others. Some decisions we make are based on data from an actively traded, homogeneous market sector, and sometimes we must deal with a less-than-actively traded market. You can still be definite about a decision you have made in a thinly traded market. Some things we positively know, and some we are less certain of. A little humility goes a long way. Jurors do not generally identify with a know-it-all.

Another tactic of some cross examiners is to ask you a series of yes-or-no questions. They may even instruct you to answer only "yes" or "no." However, you may find that some of these questions are about situations that do not have definite yes or no answers. You can qualify your "yes" or "no" response. If the judge instructs you to simply answer "yes" or "no," do what the judge says. Remember that the attorney you are working with will come back to that question on redirect examination.

If you don't remember something, it is certainly acceptable to admit it. However, you should not use forgetfulness as an excuse to dodge a question you don't particularly like. It will be obvious to everyone in the courtroom that you are trying to use some type of self-created "free pass."

During cross examination, have trust in the attorney for your side. The attorney will see which points can be addressed on redirect and will do so. Your job is not to give long-winded answers to argue your case on each of the cross examination questions. If you do, you will definitely appear as an advocate.

If you have worked with a staff appraiser on your appraisal project, remember that you are responsible for all the work done. It never looks good to attribute an error to a staff person who is not present. The same holds true for any typographic errors in the report. You are responsible for all that is within your report. If there should happen to be any damaging admissions that you must make, make them in a very definite way. If you are wrong, say so. It happens sometimes. We are all human.

During cross examination you may be asked a question that would reasonably tend to explain, contradict, or discredit your direct testimony. It is not limited to only the material covered in your direct examination. The opposing counsel has the freedom to challenge the strength of your testimony. The limits on your cross examination would come from the trial judge, who would note any concerns about harassment, prejudice, confusion of issues, the witness's safety, or interrogation that is repetitive or only marginally relevant.

## Redirect and Recross Examinations

Redirect examinations and recross examinations are merely continuations of the direct and cross examinations. Redirect examination can only address topic areas covered on cross examination and cannot

> **redirect examination.** A second direct examination, after cross examination, the scope ordinarily being limited to matters covered during cross examination. Often shortened to *redirect*. Also termed (in England) *reexamination*.
>
> **recross examination.** A second cross examination, after redirect examination. Often shortened to *recross*.
>
> **advocacy.** 1. The work or profession of an advocate. 2. The act of pleading for or actively supporting a cause or proposal.
>
> (*Black's Law Dictionary*, 9th ed.)

expand past those boundaries; it does not give you a chance to bring up something that was forgotten on direct examination. Rather, redirect examination provides an opportunity to rebuild on any damaging testimony or correct any accusatory remarks of the opposing attorney during the cross examination. This is also your chance to expand and qualify those "yes" or "no" answers you were directed to make during cross examination.

During cross examination it may appear from questioning that you had omitted something in the direct examination. For example, you might be asked a leading cross examination question like the following: "Is it true that you did not include in your appraisal report the sale of the property located directly across the street from the subject property that closed only one month before the date of taking? Please answer 'yes' or 'no.'" It is always best to handle a situation like this in direct testimony rather than hope the cross examiner will not bring it up.

Planning ahead for possible cross examination questions and addressing them on your direct examination is a good strategy. But suppose you forgot to tell the attorney you are working with that the sort of situation described could become a question in the trial. You would now have to handle it with a redirect response like, "I did consider this sale in my analysis, but because it was between related parties it is not an arm's-length sale that we appraisers should use in our evaluations. It is part of my workfile, but it did not become part of my report." Similarly, recross examination is limited to only those topics addressed on redirect examination.

In the Appraisal Institute litigation classes that include the mock trial, the jurors are asked to critique the various witness participants. In all instances, "He or she appeared to be an advocate" has been a major criticism. This is a credibility killer.

## Rebuttal Testimony

After our direct, cross, redirect, and recross testimony, we may still not be done. We could be called to return to the stand to give rebuttal testimony. Rebuttal evidence is presented to contradict certain evidence presented by the other side of the case. After the other side has closed its case in chief, rebuttal testimony may then be allowed. The judge has the authority and discretion to limit the scope of any rebuttal testimony, if it is allowed at all. When allowed, such testimony is always limited to only the evidence that refutes or contradicts the evidence presented by the opposing side.

> **rebuttal testimony.** Testimony that is produced to refute the testimony presented by the opposition in a court case. (*The Dictionary of Real Estate Appraisal*, 5th ed.)

In real estate valuation cases, rebuttal evidence is usually limited to factual information rather than conflicting opinions. For example, you may be called to testify that you have reviewed market research reports prepared by the larger real estate brokerage firms in your community and that the range of reported office vacancy rates in this market was from 13.4% to 15.8%. This would directly rebut evidence presented by the other

---

**Testifying at a Deposition**

Although the focus of this chapter has been the appraiser's role as an expert witness at a trial, appraisers should prepare themselves just as carefully and thoroughly for expert testimony outside the courtroom, most commonly in depositions. A *deposition* is defined as any sworn testimony given at an event other than a courtroom trial. It is sworn testimony taken usually in a conference room with a court reporter present and making a transcript of the testimony. There may also be a video record made of the witness during the deposition. There are many functions of a deposition, including merely investigative inquiry seeking facts or appraisal opinions. But never forget that the transcript of a deposition can be used to impeach a witness if that person's testimony at trial is not consistent with the testimony at the deposition.

In a deposition, you are speaking to the record. You will be asked questions by the opposing attorney, but your response is to the record. The main function of a deposition is to make a record. This record may be read by parties who were not present at the time.

When being deposed, answer the questions as asked but do not volunteer information. Only give what is precisely asked of you.

Again, nonverbal responses are not acceptable. A head shake is not part of making a record. When you refer to exhibits, it is best to first identify the exhibit number and also provide a brief identification of the document. For example, if the document in question is a map, you could give a brief description of the geographic area of the map and explain which direction on the document indicates north before answering the question. By identifying the exhibit, you are helping the reader of the transcript follow the examination. Remember to wait for the entire question and pause before answering to give your attorney a chance to object to the question. In answering, speak slowly, as if you are dictating a report. This will help the court reporter make an accurate record. If you provide any names, spelling them out will help.

Deposition is taken without a judicial officer to rule on objections. You may be instructed not to answer. Remember that the attorney who is defending the deposition does not represent you; the attorney represents your client, or the attorney may be your client. You have to think for yourself and decide how you will respond.

> Whatever is brought out in deposition signals, for the most part, the relative strength or weakness of the appraiser's position, and many cases settle before trial based at least in part on these perspectives. This is reason enough for the appraiser to do well in deposition.
> —Paul Talmage, MAI, "Cross-examination at a Jury Trial," *The Appraisal Journal* (April 2003): 151.

side of the case that "the office market vacancy rate was about 8%." Rebuttal testimony should generally be short and factual. You may be asked to produce copies of those market studies.

As a rebuttal witness, you will be subject to cross examination. Don't worry, though. There is an end in sight. Rebuttal testimony is generally an expert witness's shortest shift on the witness stand.

## Postmortem

At the conclusion of the trial it is helpful to have a conversation with the attorney you are working with about what went well and what could have been better. This should be a candid discussion, not a back-slapping session. Sometimes the attorney will have the opportunity to interview members of the jury. This can be particularly valuable and surprising feedback. Learning from each experience is the best schooling for this occupation you can get. Take maximum advantage.

# Conclusion

At this point in the book, it should be clear that in many ways an appraisal for litigation purposes is both fundamentally the same as, but also more complicated than, a typical market value appraisal for a bank, property owner, or other traditional client. In a litigation appraisal assignment, negotiating the scope of work of appraisal services to be provided to the client, as discussed in Chapter 1, is often an involved process because of the client being served, the potential intended users of the appraisal, the timing of particular deliverables, and other considerations specific to litigation-related assignments. However, an appraisal that is intended for use in a court proceeding is still an appraisal like any other, subject to all the professional standards that ensure competent and credible appraisal practice, as discussed in Chapter 2. Accepted appraisal principles and techniques do not change simply because the appraiser's conclusions will be scrutinized and debated before a trier of fact. Nevertheless, delivering the appraisal product on the witness stand does create a host of concerns that are not present when the appraisal assignment is completed at the moment the appraiser hits "Send" to e-mail a written appraisal report to the waiting client. As shown in this chapter, credible expert witnesses are not born, but rather they are made by practice, by study, and by preparation for trial. Every appraiser who spends a good deal of time on the witness stand has a battle-tested style that he or she is comfortable with, and the remainder of this book gives readers a glimpse into the personal styles of experienced appraisers as they deal with real-life problems in litigation valuation.

In these three introductory chapters, we have discussed the practical matters appraisers must keep in mind at each of the major stages of an appraisal performed for litigation purposes. The case studies that follow illustrate how individual appraisers have handled the issues discussed so far in the context of their own appraisal assignments.

CASE STUDY 1.1

# Partial Taking–Corner Clip Road Project

*By Stephen J. Matonis, MAI, MRICS*

## The Assignment

The case study assignment is to estimate the market value of the fee simple interest in the larger parcel, the part taken, and damages to the remainder, if applicable. The case study includes a valuation summary for a before and after valuation analysis scenario.

The appraiser received a phone call from a local law firm for which the appraiser's firm had done substantial appraisal work. The attorney was representing a property owner who had land that the local expressway authority proposed to acquire for a highway project.

Through discussions with the client, we determined that the larger parcel contains approximately 40 acres of vacant land and is situated within an unincorporated rural area of the county. The site is located along Avalon Road, County Road (CR) 545. The area to be acquired (Parcel 219) consists of nearly three acres of land, and the attorney and his client believe that the taking may affect the future development of the property.

The attorney asked us to estimate the market value of the fee simple interest in the entire property. We were also asked to estimate the value of the part taken and damages to the remainder property, if applicable. Because this was a Florida case, the state rule was applicable.

We agreed to accept the assignment, and our client (the attorney) forwarded a copy of the construction plans and a legal description of the acquisition. He also provided the parcel identification number and a copy of the most recent warranty deed transferring ownership of the property.

## Scope of Work–Before the Taking

In this case study, the appraisal process in the before condition involved two steps:

1. Analyze the larger parcel and make a determination of the site's highest and best use.

2. Estimate the value of the property prior to the taking, ignoring the project for which the property is being taken. Since the site is a vacant parcel, the sales comparison approach was the only approach used in this appraisal.

### Course of Action–After the Taking

After the taking, the process is repeated to determine whether the property was damaged as a result of the acquisition and, if applicable, to estimate a cost to cure to mitigate (lessen) the damages. So after the taking, the steps would be

1. Analyze the remainder property and determine the highest and best use of the site after the taking (assuming that the road project will be completed).
2. Estimate the value of the remainder property.

If damages are indicated, the remainder property damages may or may not be curable. If a portion or all of the damages are curable, an estimate is required to determine the amount of damages that can be mitigated. A berm/sound wall or screening to mitigate the impact of an elevated right of way (ROW) for an area the size of the subject property has been estimated to cost $300,000.[1]

## Market Area Observations

We have recently seen a strong market for residential expansion, which has fostered a noticeable scarcity of land available for immediate development. According to two recently published articles in a reputable report, the pace of construction in homebuilding increased 28.4% over the previous year, with annual housing starts increasing by 10%. Data suggests that the single-unit inventory, including units under construction, finished vacant units, and model homes, equates to a 6.2-month supply. Vacant developed lot inventory has decreased 0.8% compared to the previous year, and industry analysts report a 19.6-month supply of lots, which is a decrease of 2.4 months from one year earlier. This suggests increased pressure on developers to deliver finished lots to keep pace with construction demand. Much of this current demand is fueled by low interest rates, affording many renters the opportunity to purchase their first homes.

Knowledgeable brokers estimated that farm or ranch land acreage prices had appreciated 7% to 12% per year for the past decade, and one developer reported that land selling five years earlier for $10,000 per acre was now selling for $25,000 to $30,000 per acre. Overall, homebuilders in this area are looking at land tracts farther

---

1. Regarding cost to cure, see J. D. Eaton, *Real Estate Valuation in Litigation*, 2nd ed. (Chicago: Appraisal Institute, 1995).

and farther away from the central business district (CBD) because of the shortage of "close in" sites.

As market conditions stabilize, we anticipate that more stable growth rates will follow. Due to the relative scarcity of comparable transactions, a market conditions (time) adjustment could not be quantified. However, given the dynamics of the residential market, the scarcity of residential land close to urban centers, and the decreasing lot inventory and low mortgage rates fueling demand, some type of annual market conditions adjustment is applicable.

In our discussions with the county utilities department, we found that water and sewer services were expected to be extended along Avalon Road in proximity to the subject site within two years.

When new roadway projects are constructed, the condemning authority often contracts with a local professional land planner to provide the contracted appraisers with a before and after land analysis of certain properties impacted by the project. This is generally accomplished when the highest and best use of a property could be an issue in the after condition, resulting in substantial impacts to the development potential of the remainder property.

## Description of the Project

State Road 429 (Western Beltway) is a beltway project around the west side of the metropolitan area. The subject is in the Part C development phase from the city of Ocoee south, and for the purposes of this appraisal we considered the subject phase to conclude at Seidel Road south of the subject property and two miles south of Schofield Road (see Exhibit 1).

For the purposes of this appraisal, the phase of the beltway between Seidel Road and Malcolm Road is considered to be ongoing, with construction beyond Malcolm Road south through the subject area to Seidel Road anticipated to be completed by year's end.

### Effects on the Roadways

Construction plans indicate that a diamond interchange is to be constructed at McKinney Road and also at Schofield Road. Land acquisition for a future interchange at Schofield Road is included in this phase of Part C.

The majority of the roads in the project area are minor collector east-west roadways, which include McKinney Road, Old YMCA Road, Malcolm Road, and Schofield Road. The following roads are considered to be more significant in terms of their effect on the project area:

- Avalon Road (CR 545) is a two-lane paved road extending from the city of Winter Garden south through southwest Orange County and continuing south to US Highway 192, approximately seven miles south of the project area.

**Exhibit 1**

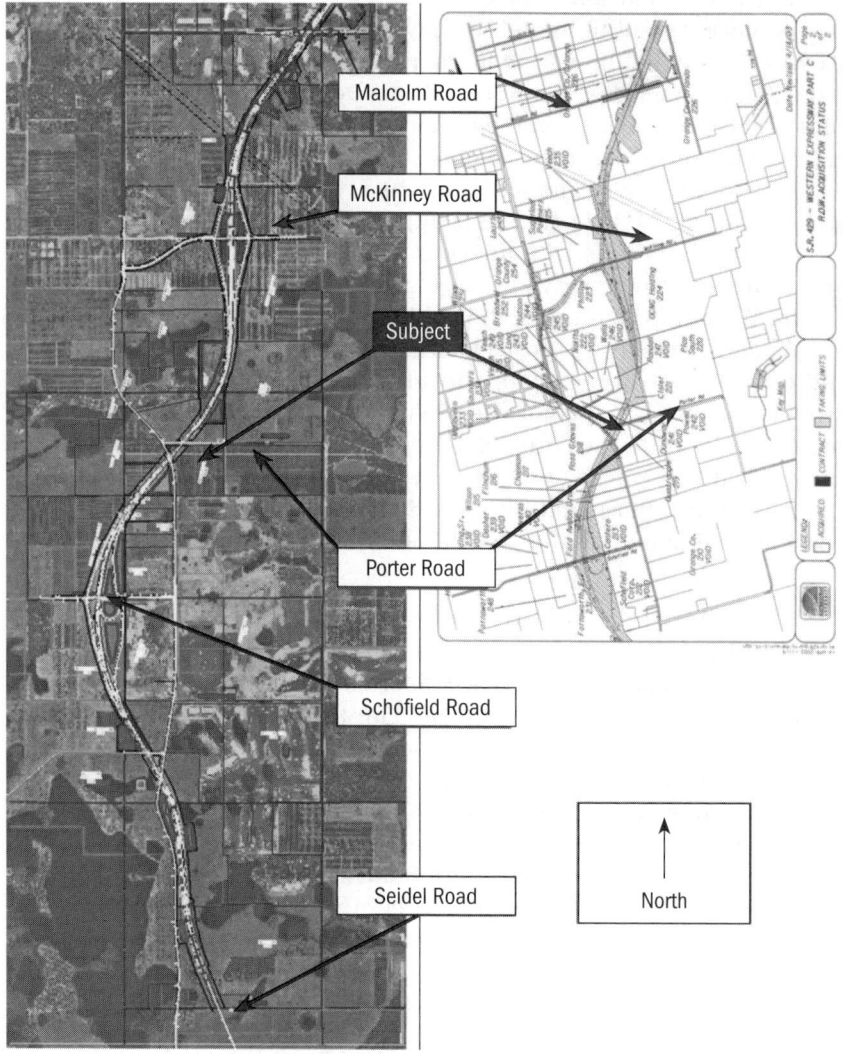

- Porter Road is primarily an east-west, paved, two-lane roadway commencing eastward from Avalon Road. This road varies in direction, winding through vast areas of citrus groves before connecting with Ficquette Road and, ultimately, Winter-Garden Vineland Road (CR 535). This roadway connects the rural area of Winter Garden with the communities of Windermere and Orlando to the east along with Bridgewater and Lakeside to the north via Ficquette Road.
- Seidel Road is another primarily east-west, paved, two-lane roadway commencing eastward from Avalon Road. This road also varies

in direction, becoming Lake Hancock Road and winding through vast areas of vacant acreage before connecting with Ficquette Road and, ultimately, Winter-Garden Vineland Road (CR 535).

## Impact on the Subject Property

The subject is located on the southeast corner of Avalon Road (CR 545) and Porter Road in unincorporated Orange County (see Exhibit 2). This places it at the western edge of the metropolitan area.

At the subject location, the limited-access Western Beltway will bridge over both Porter Road and Avalon Road. The beltway will be elevated approximately 23 feet at the centerline of Porter Road and 30 feet at the centerline of Avalon Road. These centerline points bracket the subject property (Parcel 219).

**Exhibit 2**

# Before the Taking

## Property Data

The site is located on the southeast corner of Avalon Road and Porter Road in unincorporated Orange County (see Exhibit 3). The site contains a total of 40.68 gross acres of vacant land that is slightly irregular in shape, with 1,310 feet of frontage on the east side of Avalon Road and 1,570 feet of frontage on the south side of Porter Road. Overall, the property is generally level and at or above road grade along Avalon Road and Porter Road. Avalon Road and Porter Road are two-lane, asphalt-paved rights of way with no sidewalks or turning lanes.

| | Physical Features |
|---|---|
| Land area (acres) | 40.68 gross acres |
| Configuration | Slightly irregular |
| Topography | Generally level; sloping in and around pond to eastern end of tract. The change in grade, however, is typical of properties in the area and is not considered a detriment to the development of the site. |
| Drainage | Appears adequate; on-site retention required. |
| Flood hazard | The subject property is located in Flood Zone C, an area of minimal flooding risk. |
| Road access (Avalon Rd.) | 1,310 feet of frontage, access, and exposure on the east side of Avalon Road. |
| Road access (Porter Rd.) | 1,570 feet of frontage, access, and exposure on the south side of Porter Road. Existing access onto the property is limited to a dirt path situated about midway along the site's frontage on Porter Road. |

### *Environmental Hazards*

An environmental assessment report was not provided for review, and environmental issues are beyond our scope of expertise. Our inspection of the site did not reveal any obvious signs of contaminants on or near the property. Because the site was historically agricultural, there may be environmental issues that need to be assessed. However, for this case study, we assumed that the subject is not adversely affected by environmental hazards.

### *Ground Stability*

A soil report was not provided for review. Based on our inspection of the property and observation of development on nearby sites, however, we assumed that the subject is not affected by any adverse soil conditions that would restrict it from being developed.

### *Utilities*

Water and sewer services are not readily available. The nearest service lines are approximately one mile to the north of the subject

Exhibit 3

*Partial Taking–Corner Clip Road Project*

property. Based on discussions with the county utility department, water and sewer services are expected to be extended along Avalon Road (CR 545) within two years, and adequate capacity is anticipated to serve the subject property.

| Utilities | |
|---|---|
| Water | None |
| Sewer | None |
| Electric | None |

## *Zoning*

Zoning and future land use classifications are established by Orange County. The current zoning is A-1, an agricultural zoning classification, and the future land use designation is R, rural. The A-1 zoning classification allows residential development of one dwelling unit per 10 acres of land area and is consistent with the future land use designation. Therefore, current uses allow maximum development of four dwelling units.

## *Easements, Encumbrances, and Restrictions*

A 35-foot-wide permanent pipeline easement traverses the property. The easement is for the purposes of reclaimed water distribution to the general area. In this area, it is common for this type of easement to be relocated at a nominal cost to the property owner.

## *Land Use*

In the immediate vicinity of the subject, land uses include a mix of rural residential and agriculture (pasture, citrus groves, and nurseries). The subject's immediate surrounding land uses are as follows:

| | |
|---|---|
| North | Vacant agricultural |
| South | Vacant agricultural |
| East | Vacant agricultural |
| West | Citrus groves |

## *Land Description Summary*

Overall, the physical characteristics of the site are suitable for agricultural or residential development. The subject site is adequate for uses such as those permitted by zoning.

## *Highest and Best Use*

The current use of the site is legally conforming to existing zoning. Zoning limits residential development to one dwelling unit per 10 acres of land and is consistent with the future land use. At a minimum, construction of a low-density residential development would be reasonable and would yield a maximum of four dwelling units.

Based on land development patterns in the immediate area, it appears likely that the site could achieve a more intense residential use at a density of three dwelling units per acre. Based on our discussions with the planning department, we concluded that it is reasonably probable that the site would be approved for single-unit development at the higher density. Four similar-sized sites on Avalon Road with agricultural zoning filed for rezoning to a more intense residential use and were recently approved. Therefore, only a residential use has been considered going forward.

Physically, the size, location, and configuration of the site would be suitable for a variety of uses. Economically, most uses allowed would produce a greater return to the land than an agricultural use. Market conditions indicate strong demand for residential development. Based on a higher density of three dwelling unit per acre the site size is sufficient to support a single-unit development containing a maximum of 120 dwelling units. Rezoning the site and changing the county's future land use plan would be required to achieve this density, and it would take nearly one year to obtain approvals. This could be completed concurrently with the extension of public water and sewer services within the expected two-year period.

*Conclusion*

Having considered what was legally permissible and physically possible, and based on our understanding of current economic conditions, we concluded that the maximally productive use and, therefore, the highest and best use of the property would be for future residential development. The site has been appraised "as is," assuming the reasonable probability that the property would be rezoned to a higher residential density at three dwelling units per acre and that public utilities would be readily available when the property is ready for development.

## Valuation of the Property

Much of the agricultural/citrus land in the market area is in transition to more intense use as growth expands into the area. As such, any income generated on an agricultural basis would contribute some value. However, land is being purchased in the immediate area based on speculation for a more intense nonagricultural uses. Accordingly, we have appraised the larger parcel at its highest and best use "as if vacant" and currently zoned for agricultural use with reasonable probability for rezoning to a more intense residential use.

Overall, we have considered that the subject property is well positioned for residential development. The size (40.68 acres), topography, shape, frontage, superior corner location, and exposure are considered good for development.

*Vacant Land Sales*

A search was made throughout western Orange County for land sales with characteristics similar to the subject tract. Our research produced multiple land sales considered relevant to the market area. These land sales are similar to the subject regarding the potential for rezoning, utilities, and other characteristics.

The sales were analyzed on a gross-acre basis. Each sale was adjusted upward for factors that were considered inferior to the subject and downward for factors that were considered superior to the subject. Characteristics considered for comparison included differences in market conditions, location, size, topography, access/frontage, zoning/future land use densities, and any other factors that might influence the value of the property.

The sales most comparable to the subject property are shown in Exhibit 4. The four properties ranged in price from $30,000 to $36,300 per gross acre and were sold within the past year. The sales, while "closed" within the past year, were negotiated (meeting of the minds) two years ago for Sales 1 and 2, one year ago for Sale 3, and six months ago for Sale 4.

Note that, in a litigation assignment, more analysis is obviously made of the comparable sales than indicated in this case study. See *The Appraisal of Real Estate*, 13th edition, for detailed examples of the application of sales comparison techniques.

*Conclusion*

Applying an estimated unit value of $35,000 per acre, which included sales the size of the subject site (40.68 acres), results in a fee simple value estimate of $1,423,800, rounded to $1,425,000 and calculated as follows:

$$40.68 \text{ acres} \times \$35,000 \text{ per acre} = \$1,425,000 \text{ (rounded)}$$

There are two schools of thought regarding rounding at this point in the assignment. Not rounding could imply a perfect market, but rounding could misstate damages or benefits.

## Description and Valuation of the Part Taken

The part taken, or the acquisition, is a triangle-shaped "corner clip" consisting of 2.829 total acres. The parcel to be acquired is numbered as Parcel 219 and Parcel 219 A, B, and C. Parcel 219 A, B, and C is dedicated for three ROW takings to be used for improvements to the local arterial frontage roads. The main acquisition, Parcel 219, is to be used for a limited-access right of way (L/A ROW) to be elevated over a portion of the subject property. Throughout this case study, the four parcels are considered in aggregate as Parcel 219 containing 2.829

**Exhibit 4**

**Land Sales Adjustment Grid**

| | Subject | Comparable 1 | Comparable 2 | Comparable 3 | Comparable 4 |
|---|---|---|---|---|---|
| Address | S/E/C of CR 545 and Porter Road | S/S Porter Road, E/O CR 545 | S/S Porter Road, E/O CR 545 | S/S Porter Road, E/O CR 545 | S/S Porter Road, E/O Scott Road |
| County | Orange | Orange | Orange | Orange | Orange |
| State | Florida | Florida | Florida | Florida | Florida |
| Sale date | | One year ago | One year ago | Six months ago | One month ago |
| Sale price | | $606,500 | $1,575,000 | $1,075,200 | $750,000 |
| Effective sale price | | $606,500 | $1,575,000 | $1,075,200 | $750,000 |
| Gross acres | 40.68 | 16.70 | 52.50 | 33.60 | 21.42 |
| Units | 0 | 0 | 0 | 0 | 0 |
| Price per gross acre | | $36,300 | $30,000 | $32,000 | $35,000 |
| Property rights | | Fee simple | Fee simple | Fee simple | Fee simple |
| Financing terms | | Cash to seller | Cash to seller | Cash to seller | Cash to seller |
| Conditions of sale | | Arm's length | Arm's length | Arm's length | Arm's length |
| Market conditions/time | | Inferior | Inferior | Similar | Similar |
| Location | | Similar | Similar | Similar | Superior |
| Physical characteristics | | Superior | Inferior | Similar | Similar |
| Utilities | | Similar | Similar | Similar | Similar |
| Zoning | | Similar | Similar | Inferior | Inferior |
| Overall comparison | | **Slt. superior** | **Inferior** | **Inferior** | **Similar** |
| Price range | | | $30,000–$36,300 | | |

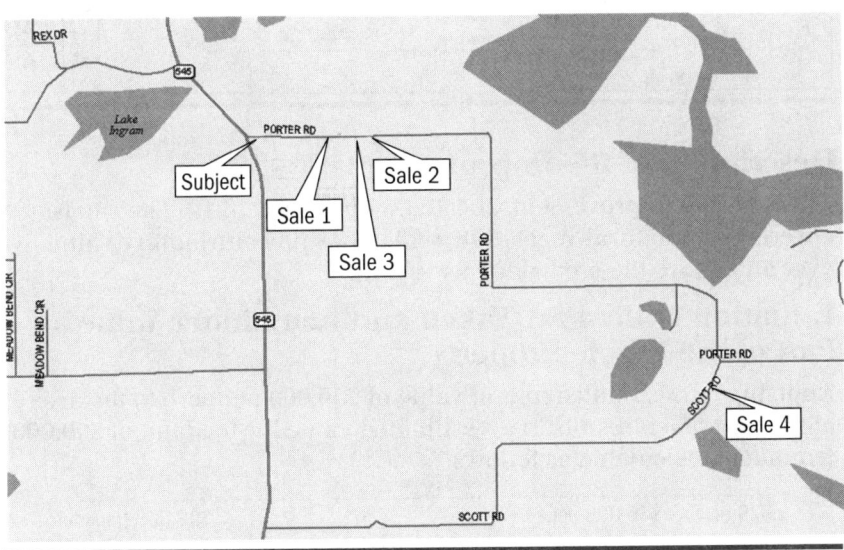

*Partial Taking–Corner Clip Road Project*

acres. The new limited-access highway is proposed as a toll roadway and as part of a bypass system around the metro area.

## Description of the Site

The part taken, Parcel 219, contains one limited-access right of way and three right-of-way takings, totaling 2.829 acres of land. The land area is a triangle-shaped tract that extends in a northeasterly-southwesterly direction in the northwest corner of the property. Exhibit 5 is a scanned map that depicts the L/A ROW.

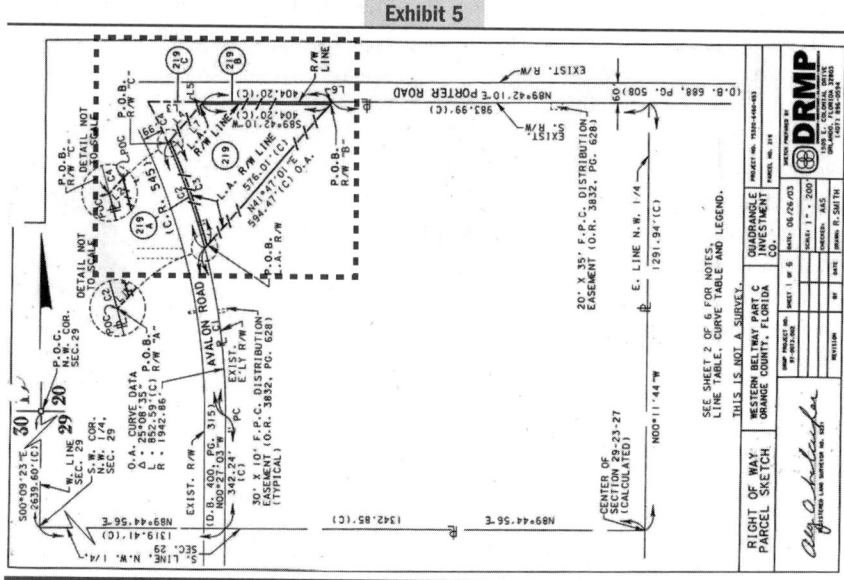

## Description of the Improvements

There are no improvements located within Parcel 219. The site is covered with natural vegetation, which has no contributory value over and above the land value as vacant.

## Valuation of the Part Taken and Remainder Value as Part of the Whole Property

Applying our estimated unit of value of $35,000 per acre to the area of the part taken results in an estimated value for the land of $99,000 (rounded), calculated as follows:

| | |
|---|---|
| 2.829 acres × $35,000 per acre = | $99,000 (rounded) |
| Estimated value of the whole property (larger parcel) | $1,425,000 |
| Less part taken—Parcel 219 (land value only) | − $99,000 |
| Remainder value as part of the whole property | $1,326,000 |

# After the Taking
## Property Observations
### Description of the Remainder Property
Exhibit 6 depicts the total ownership prior to the taking, the part taken, and the remaining ownership after the taking.

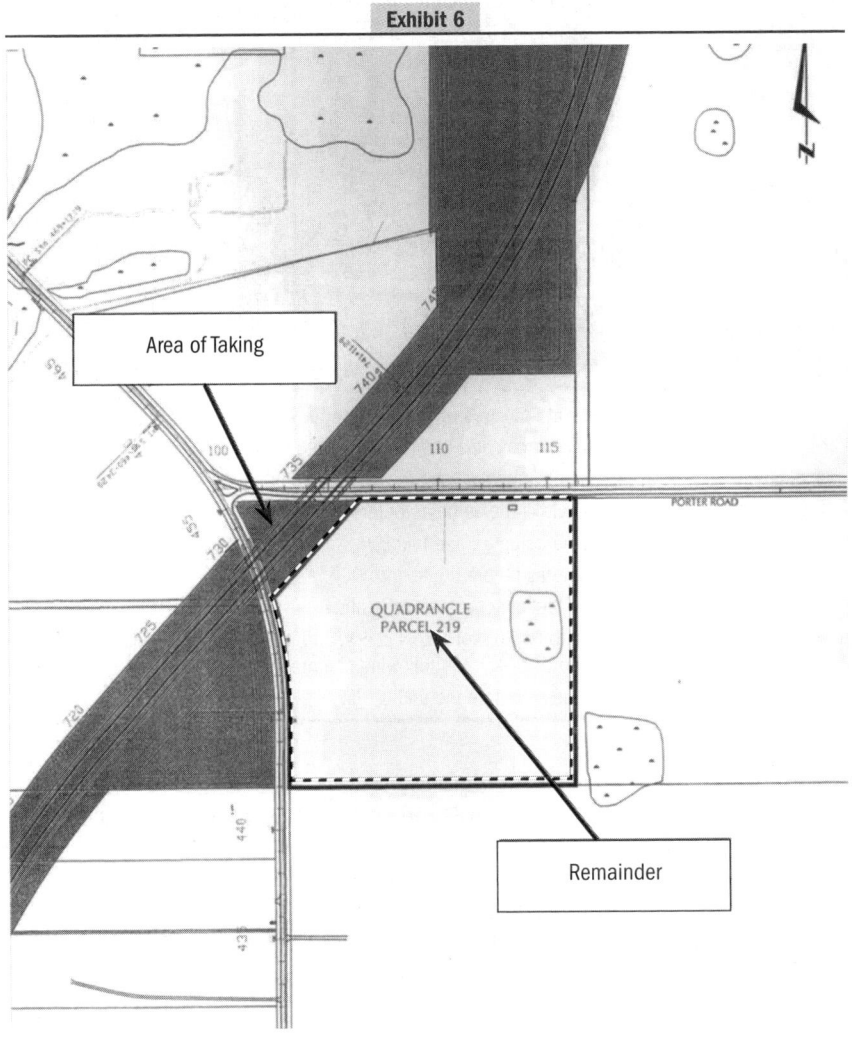

*Partial Taking–Corner Clip Road Project*

**Exhibit 6**
*(continued)*

**Physical Features of the Remainder Parcel**

| | |
|---|---|
| Land area (acres) | 37.85 gross acres—a reduction of 6.96% |
| Configuration | Slightly irregular—see the following comments |
| Topography | Generally the same as before the taking |
| Drainage | Same as before the taking |
| Flood hazard | Same as before the taking |
| Road access (Avalon Rd.) | 850 feet of frontage, access, and exposure on the east side of Avalon Rd. |
| Road access (Porter Rd.) | 1,000 feet of frontage, access, and exposure on the south side of Porter Rd.—see the following comments |
| Utilities | Same as before the taking |

## Access to the Remainder Parcel

The site's frontage along Avalon Road will be 850 feet, a reduction of 460 feet (1,310 feet − 460 feet = 850 feet), resulting in approximately 35% less frontage. As a result of the project, the property will have 600 feet of direct frontage along the southeast side of the L/A ROW. Frontage on Porter Road will be reduced by 570 feet, or 36%, from 1,570 feet to 1,000 feet. Exposure is affected substantially for southbound Avalon Road traffic. The limited-access right of way will be elevated approximately 23 feet to 30 feet above the pre-take grades of Porter Road and Avalon Road, respectively.

## Physical Configuration and Shape of the Remainder Parcel

The limited-access right of way will traverse the site at an angle, which creates an irregularly shaped remainder. Because of the zoning requirement for a 150-foot setback constraint along the expressway, any future development access roadway will need to be pushed southward along Avalon Road or eastward along Porter Road farther away from the L/A ROW boundary and the corner of Porter Road and Avalon Road.

*Land Description Summary*
Overall, the physical characteristics of the site remain suitable for agricultural or residential development. The subject site is adequate for uses such as those permitted by zoning.

*Highest and Best Use*
Before the taking, it was our opinion that the total ownership or larger parcel could be developed with a more intense, residential use. After the taking, the same legal considerations would apply to the remainder, and it is reasonably probable that the property could still be developed at a higher density of three dwelling units per acre, subject to rezoning.

The size of the site is reduced by the L/A ROW and ROW taking to 37.85 acres of land area, making up one remainder. The remainder will be irregular in shape, with frontage on the east side of Avalon Road reduced by 35%. Frontage along Porter Road will be reduced 36% by the taking, and ingress and egress to the remainder will remain basically the same as in the before condition.

Physically, the remainder property will abut the proposed elevated limited-access roadway at its reconfigured northwest property line. Based on construction plans, the subject property will have approximately 600 feet of frontage along the eastern boundary of the L/A ROW. Within this distance, a 150-foot setback requirement would be established from the ROW. The limited-access right of way will vary slightly in elevation ranging from 23 feet at the centerline of Porter Road to 30 feet at the centerline of Avalon Road. Porter Road is to be widened and improved within the acquisition Parcel 219 (in aggregate), and in our opinion this should not negatively affect the utility of the remainder.

As a result of the taking, the reduced size of 37.85 acres could be developed with 113 dwelling units (37.85 acres × 3 dwelling units per acre = 113). This is a reduction of seven units, or a 6% loss from conditions before the taking. Economic considerations are generally the same as in the before condition.

Based on the previously discussed legal, physical, and economic considerations, it is our opinion that the highest and best use of the remainder property would be for agricultural use until residential development is approved. This assumes that it is reasonably probable that the site would be rezoned and public utilities would be extended to the site. The uses generally are the same in the after condition but more restrictive than in the before condition for the reasons offered.

## Impact of the Taking on the Marketability of the Remainder Property

Since the highest and best use is for rezoning to a more intense residential development, we first considered that the acquisition of Parcel 219 would create the following negative impacts for a residential use along the western boundary of the site:

- The marketability of the remainder property may be diminished due to its proximity to the proposed limited-access roadway.
- Development costs on a per-lot or per-unit basis could be increased overall because the total costs would have to be spread over fewer potential lots.
- The limited-access right of way will be elevated approximately 23 feet to 30 feet along the property's L/A ROW frontage and may require buffering. This "buffer" would typically represent additional development costs, which would not have been incurred in the absence of the proposed road. Such buffering may include berms and privacy walls with landscaping.
- Also, based on topography and construction plans, the chain-link perimeter fencing required to secure the L/A ROW will create a visual eyesore and will not be considered compatible with residential developments typically found in the market area. The lighting and noise influences will encroach into the subject property, creating an overall nuisance for future development.

## Severance Damage Study

The purpose of completing a before-and-after analysis is to estimate damages, benefits (enhancement), or both. One method of estimating damages is to estimate the value of the remainder through the use of matched pairs of sales, if available, or through the completion of a detailed damage study. The analysis would basically consist of researching the market area for sales of properties having the same influences as the remainder property, which in this instance means attempting to locate residential land sales contiguous to limited-access rights of way, preferably elevated highways. The appraiser could then attempt to analyze matched pairs of sales to extract a damage estimate.

We conducted this type of damage study and found that residential properties in proximity to an elevated ROW in our area sold for less money per acre than those that did not. In our study, the difference in value range was from 15% to 30%, depending on distance, height, and other factors associated with an elevated expressway.

Based on this study, we are of the opinion the subject property was damaged 20% from the acquisition.

## Potential Cures to Mitigate the Damages

As indicated earlier, a buffer in the form of a berm or wall could be used to mitigate the damage. The cost of that "wall" was estimated to be $300,000. As shown in the following table, damages are $266,000, which is less than the cost to cure. We would not implement the cost to cure by rule because it is higher than our damage estimate.

## Value of the Remainder Property

The value of the remainder property is estimated to be $1,060,000 (rounded), calculated as follows:

$$37.85 \text{ acres} \times \$35,000 \text{ per acre} \times 0.80 = \$1,059,800$$
$$\text{Rounded to } \$1,060,000$$

| Summary of Value Conclusion | |
|---|---:|
| Value of larger parcel | $1,425,000 |
| Less: value of part taken | − $99,000 |
| Remainder value as part of the whole | $1,326,000 |
| Less: remainder value | − $1,060,000 |
| Damages | $266,000 |
| Cost to cure | $0 |
| **Summary** | |
| Value of part taken | $99,000 |
| Less: damages, as calculated above | − $266,000 |
| Total loss due to take area | $365,000 |

Under the federal rule, the following conclusion would be reached:

| | |
|---|---:|
| Before value | $1,425,000 |
| After value | $1,060,000 |
| Difference | $365,000 |

## Conclusions

In our appraisal assignment, we completed the following steps:

- We first estimated the value of the site as if vacant. This was accomplished to estimate the value of the land within the part taken. We used the sales comparison approach in this valuation scenario. The cost approach and income capitalization approach were not applicable in estimating the value of the property.
- We then performed a highest and best use analysis of the remainder property and considered the impact of the right-of-way project on the remainder property.
- We conducted a study of sales of large residential properties that were located on or in proximity to an elevated L/A ROW. We then compared them to properties that were not so impacted. This

"matched pairs" analysis showed that properties in proximity sold for less, implying damages to the remainder.
- Our final step in this case was to consider a possible "cure" to mitigate damages. In this instance, the cost to cure would exceed the damage estimate of $266,000. As such, we would not implement the cost to cure.

The acquisition of the land within the project area occurred in a high-growth period, and land values were appreciating at a rapid pace within the market area. The part taken (i.e., the corner clip) was also not typical because the acquisition cut across the corner of the tract of land at a roadway intersection, necessitating an elevated limited-access right of way that ranged from 23 to 30 feet in height.

This particular case was settled prior to trial, and the owner received compensation very close to the $365,000 conclusion discussed here.

CASE STUDY 1.2

# Partial Taking–Electric Transmission Line

*By Jeffrey A. Johnson, MAI*

## The Assignment

This case study includes selected sections from an appraisal report that was prepared for a condemnation hearing. In Minnesota, most condemnation cases are heard by a Commissioners Panel of three citizens appointed by the judge to decide on the case. Either side of the case can then appeal the Commissioners Panel's decision, which results in a district court trial.

This case study involves a partial taking condemnation case for an electrical transmission line project. The property subject to this partial taking is a two-story hotel located in Minnesota. Because it is a partial taking condemnation case, the valuation entailed estimating the compensable damages by using a before and after valuation approach.[1] We used a before-taking appraisal with the assumption that the appraisal was made independent of the then-proposed project and then conducted an after-taking appraisal to measure any and all damages resulting from the project.

Our client for this appraisal assignment was the power utility company, and we prepared an initial appraisal report to assist the client in making an offer to acquire the easement rights. Negotiations failed, and these property rights were acquired through condemnation.

When we initially met with the client about the proposed project, the client was not ready to start the appraisal component of the project, so we suggested that we begin the market research for the project. The client agreed. In the process of performing this market research task, we uncovered many electric transmission line easement-encumbered sales, which gave us a running start on the appraisals once we began this portion of the project.

Because the case was not settled, the hearing was held. We prepared the appraisal report for the hearing. As a result, this appraisal

---

1. Much has been written on this valuation method, so for this case study no preliminary explanation of the method will be presented other than to refer the reader to a very thorough presentation of the subject in J. D. Eaton, *Real Estate Valuation in Litigation*, 2nd ed. (Chicago: Appraisal Institute, 1995).

was made after the actual date of taking and with the benefit of seeing the finished construction project in place.

## The Subject Property

The subject property is a two-story, 149-room hotel built in 1973 that includes five whirlpool suites. The total gross building area is about 85,582 square feet. The typical rooms range in size from 237 square feet to approximately 263 square feet and are identified as queens, kings, or doubles. The five suites are adjacent to an indoor pool and water park. In addition to the 149-room hotel, the improvements contain a 385-seat restaurant and a 210-seat live production theater. The property contains banquet and meeting room facilities, with a total of seven meeting rooms for a combined area of approximately 5,061 square feet. The largest banquet room seats 250 and is adjacent to the restaurant. Other meeting rooms are situated on the first floor.

The property is located in a suburb of the Twin Cities in Minnesota. The site has an area of 331,945 square feet, or 7.62 acres, more or less. This parcel is zoned C-3, highway commercial, which allows for a hotel land use. There are 407 parking spaces on the site.

## Purpose, Property Rights, and Effective Date

The purpose of the appraisal is to develop an opinion of the diminution in the market value of the fee simple interest in the property resulting from the Great River Energy power line project as of the effective date of the appraisal, October 17, 2005. *Market value* is defined in the addenda to this report (not included in this case study). Unless otherwise stated, all factors pertinent to a determination of value are considered as of this date.

The appraisal report was prepared in October 2006, after the date of taking and the completion of the construction project. Because of this, the appraiser had the benefit of access to information on subsequent events in preparing this report for the hearing.

## Value Reconciliation—Before the Easement

Reconciliation involves the analysis of alternative value indications to determine a final value conclusion. Reconciliation is required because different value indications can result from the use of multiple approaches to value and within the application of a single approach. The values indicated by our analyses are as follows:

| | | |
|---|---|---|
| Cost approach: | $8,590,000 | $57,651 per room |
| Sales comparison approach: | $8,200,000 | $55,034 per room |
| Income capitalization approach: | $8,400,000 | $56,376 per room |

## Cost Approach

The cost approach is most reliable for newer properties that have no significant level of depreciation. The subject was constructed in 1973 and exhibits significant depreciation. Finally, purchasers of investment properties such as the subject do not typically rely on the cost approach. Accordingly, we did not rely on this approach in our analysis of the before situation. However, the results of the cost approach did support the value derived from the income capitalization approach.

## Sales Comparison Approach

The sales comparison approach is most reliable in an active market when sufficient numbers of sales are available for analysis. In this case, four sales were analyzed and adjusted. The reliability of this approach was reduced because significant adjustments were required to account for differences between the subject and the sales. As a result, the sales comparison approach was used primarily as support for the value derived from the income capitalization approach.

## Income Capitalization Approach

The income capitalization approach is usually given the greatest weight in valuing investment properties because it simulates the thought process of market participants in the investment property arena. The reliability of this approach is enhanced by the large quantity of market data available to develop estimates of occupancy levels, average rates, operating expenses, and capitalization rates. Therefore, we gave the income capitalization approach primary emphasis in our opinion of value.

## Conclusion of Value

Based on the preceding analysis and subject to the definitions, assumptions, and limiting conditions expressed herein, it is our opinion that the market value of the fee simple estate of the subject as of October 17, 2005, is $8,400,000.

# Valuation Analysis—After the Easement

The main valuation problem in an electrical transmission line easement valuation assignment is that parcels consisting of an easement alone very seldom sell in most markets. Most properties that have such an easement are much larger than the easement area alone, so when these properties do sell the easement is just one factor among many that the buyer is considering. As a result, when we evaluate any property that has an easement and that easement is a minor part of the total property, we are faced with the age-old appraisal problem of lack of market data. In this valuation project, we tried to address this issue by looking for vacant land parcels that were encumbered by rather large transmission line easements and comparing them to sales of similar land parcels that did not have easements. This application of the sales comparison approach helped us identify market pricing results due to the easement. We also tried to interview many buyers and sellers of easement-encumbered properties to identify pricing results due to the easement.

## The Project

Great River Energy provides electrical, energy, and related services to 28 member cooperatives, including Wright-Hennepin Cooperative Electric Association. To meet the growing electrical load in the Wright-Hennepin distribution area, Great River Energy needs to construct an approximately 14-mile-long, 115 kilovolt (kV) transmission line in the Plymouth and Maple Grove area of the Twin Cities. Wright-Hennepin provides electricity and related services to approximately 34,000 residential, commercial, and industrial customers, of which approximately 10,503 customers in the Plymouth-Maple Grove area benefit from the new high-voltage transmission line.

The project includes a new, approximately 4.25-mile, 115 kV transmission line from Xcel Energy's Parkers Lake Substation, which is located just south of County Road 6 and east of I-494, to Plymouth Substation, which is located just north of Schmidt Lake Road and west of I-494. The subject property is located on this stretch of the transmission line. Additionally, the project included the rebuilding of existing lines from the Plymouth Substation to the Bass Lake, Cedar Island, Arbor Lake, and Hennepin Substations. It also included the rebuilding and relocation of lines between a point near the intersection of Zachary Lane and County Road 81 to the Elm Creek Substation, located on County Road 81 at Fernbrook Lane. The date of taking was October 17, 2005.

## Easement Taking

This transmission line project has resulted in the need for a permanent transmission line easement on the westerly boundary of the subject site. The easement area will encumber 35,374.75 square feet of land area in a north-south direction along the west side of the subject property. The easement is approximately 70 feet wide. However, some of the easement area is outside the subject site. The width of the easement on the property varies and is generally 35 feet. The easement area was improved with three 75- to 90-foot-high transmission towers linked with an overhead 115 kV line.

The proposed transmission line easement includes a small area already encumbered by a parking easement that benefits the neighboring parcel to the south. The parking easement area, situated in the most southwestern portion of the property, contains 1,048.5 square feet.

## Access Easement

In addition to the easement described previously for the project transmission line, an access easement will also encumber the subject property as a result of the project. The access easement encumbers an area of 10,945 square feet and is a 20-foot-wide strip of land located in the southern portion of the subject, specifically in the existing drive lane between the most southerly parking bay adjacent to the southern elevation of the improvements. The access easement exists at the most southerly curb cut from Annapolis and is within the existing south driveway of the property. According to the easement document, the access easement will be used *only* when it is not practical to access the transmission line easement area from a public right of way.

## Easement Taking Summary

The unencumbered land area remaining after the easement taking is summarized as follows:

|  |  | Sq. Ft. |
|---|---|---|
| Gross land area before the taking |  | 331,945 |
| Less: Existing parking easement |  | – 1,049 |
| Net Land Area before the Taking |  | 330,896 |
| Easement rights taking |  |  |
| Transmission line (35,375 sq. ft. – 1,049 sq. ft.) | 34,326 |  |
| Access easement | 10,945 |  |
| Total Easement Rights Taking | 45,271 |  |
| Net Land Area after the Taking |  | 285,625 |

Exhibit 1 includes a legal description and a map of the taking.

# Property Changes and the Impact of the Taking

We have considered the changes to the subject property as a result of the power line easement that encumbers approximately 35 feet of the western site boundary. Before the taking, the easement area consisted of landscaped and sodded land and a portion of the westernmost parking bay. In our inspection, we noted that a total of seven mature deciduous trees existed within the power line easement area both before and after the taking.

Great River Energy plans to landscape the easement area, providing for replacement of the loss in trees. However, a proposed landscaping plan was not available. We addressed the loss of trees in the cost approach analysis after the taking.

To determine the impact of the electrical transmission line on the subject property, we considered the impact to the land and to the building. We considered all three approaches in the after-taking valuation and begin here with the cost approach.

## Exhibit 1
## Legal Description of the Taking

**Easement Area**

A strip of land lying thirty-five (35) feet on each side of the following described line: Commencing at the Southeast corner of the Southwest Quarter (SW1/4) of Section 22, Township 118 North, Range 22 West; thence South 89°47'42" West (assumed bearing) along the southerly line of said Southwest Quarter (SW1/4) of Section 22, Township 118 North, Range 22 West a distance of 1366.79 feet to the point of beginning; thence North 00°12'33" West a distance of 63.98 feet; thence North 17°33'43" East a distance of 405.19 feet; thence North 20°52'05" East a distance of 372.27 feet; thence North 10°05'13" East a distance of 89.0.3 feet more or less to a point of ending on the northwesterly extension of the most northerly line of the above described "Grantor's Property". The sidelines of said strip of land shall be shortened or extended to terminate at the property lines.

Subject to public road right of way.

The basis for the bearings shown is the southerly line of the Southwest Quarter (SW1/4) of Section 22, Township 118 North, Range 22 West, and is assumed to bear South 89°47'42" West.

**Access Easement Area**

For access purposes, all that part of the above described "Grantor's Property" lying ten (10) feet on each side of the following described lines:

A. Commencing at the southeast corner of said "Grantor's Property"; thence North 00°19'08" West (assumed bearing) along the east line thereof a distance of 63.38 feet to the point of beginning; thence South 89°34'16" West a distance of 485.16 feet and there ending.

B. Commencing at the southwest corner of said "Grantor's Property"; thence North 89°58'49" East (assumed bearing) along the south line thereof a distance of 192.00 feet to the point of beginning: thence North 00°06'58" East a distance of 62.07 feet and there ending.

**Exhibit 1**

**Map of the Taking**

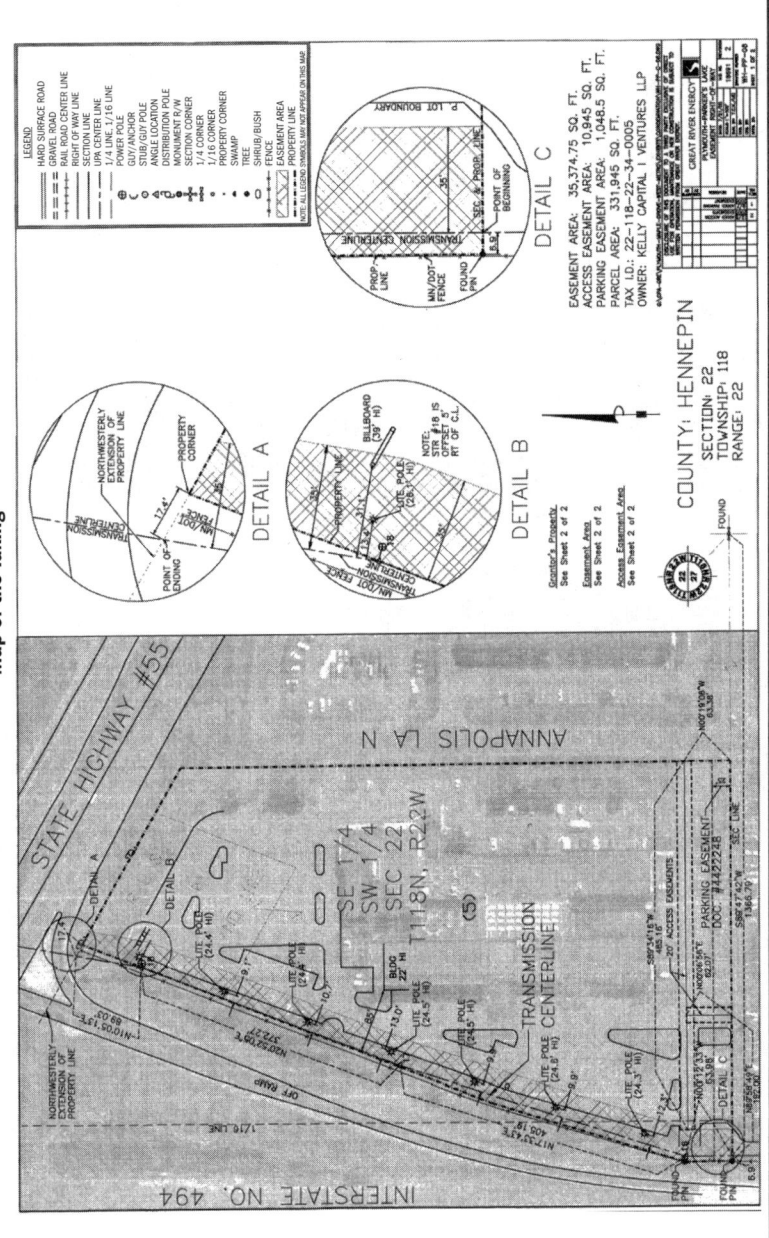

*Partial Taking–Electric Transmission Line*

The transmission line easement area after the taking

View of the west elevation, west parking area, and remaining landscaping of the subject property after the taking

The cost approach is a summation technique in which the various component parts are measured and added together to calculate a value for the total property. I find this particular approach to be helpful in the after valuation in partial taking appraisal assignments as it allows the appraiser to address each of the individual changes resulting from the partial taking. For a transmission line easement, an after-taking land valuation usually accounts for the easement rights taken, and a site improvements valuation will account for any landscaping or other site improvements lost to the project. Also, the cost approach allows an appraiser to address any additional depreciation or obsolescence that may be present in the after-taking condition. The income and sales comparison approaches also allow these issues to be addressed, but these approaches are more sweeping in their application.

## Cost Approach—After the Taking

The same land sales apply to this property in the after-taking configuration as in the before-taking analysis. We concluded that the market value of the unencumbered land is $12.50 per square foot in its after condition.

The subject property contains a total of 331,945 square feet of gross land area. A 25-foot parking easement exists on the southern site boundary. There is also a parking easement on the adjoining parcel providing parking for the subject parcel. The parties to this easement agreement are the subject property owner and the property owner to the south. This parking easement provides the subject property owner with the right to restrict access to the easement area from the adjoining property owner from 6 p.m. to 8 a.m. At all other times, the two parties grant and convey a nonexclusive easement for parking vehicles in this area. We concluded that the two parking easements favor the subject property owner, and we did not discount the value of this land for the parking easement area. The subject property also benefits from a parking easement on the adjoining property to the south. A small portion in the southwest corner of the subject and approximately 1,048.5 square feet of the parking easement will be encumbered by the new Great River electric transmission line easement.

To further define the rights of the Great River transmission line easement, an access easement was created in the after condition. This access easement is 20 feet wide and provides limited access to the power line easement along the western boundary. This 20-foot easement runs parallel with the southern boundary line. The access easement encumbers an area of 10,945 square feet and is located in the southern portion of the subject property, specifically in the existing drive lane between the southernmost parking bay and the parking bay adjacent to the southern elevation of the improvements. Based on a court order in the case, *Order Establishing the Scope of Easements*, it is our understanding that this access easement was established in the event that it would not be practical to access the electric transmission line easement area from the public right of way. The fee owner shall retain all rights in the access easement area except that this area can be used by the utility company for access only. We concluded that the access easement will rarely be needed to gain access to the transmission line easement area because it is adjacent to existing public right of way.

Also, we considered that our discount or loss in land value to the easement area land (determined as follows) accounted for not only the loss in land value for the easement rights taken in the easement area but also for the loss of access rights granting the power company access to this easement area. In our research and analysis of other transmission line easements, we concluded to discount percentages for the lands encumbered by easements that included not only the loss for the easement rights taken within the easement areas but also the loss resulting from the taking of access to the transmission line easement areas. As a result, we did not discount the underlying fee value for the presence of the easement that defines the access to the transmission line easement area.

We analyzed a number of land sales of properties that are encumbered by utility easements. Based on our analysis of these sales, we concluded that the market value in the area of the transmission line easement will be reduced by 33% of the fee simple land value, and 67% of the land value will remain with the owner.

## Land Value–After the Taking

In the report, we first presented our findings regarding the loss in value to the land. We analyzed a number of land sales that are encumbered by electrical transmission line easements. Our method of estimating the value loss due to those easements was to compare the encumbered land sales to similar yet unencumbered land sales. Exhibit 2 summarizes the findings. This chart is followed by a narrative

### Exhibit 2
#### Power Line Easement Impact on Value

| Comparable Land Sale | Property Location | Property Type | Total Land Area (Sq. Ft.) | Encumbered Land Area | Value Loss due to Encumbrance |
|---|---|---|---|---|---|
| 1 | Maple Grove | Hotel | 147,819 | 52,000 | 43.9% |
| 2 | Shakopee | Auto dealership | 248,244 | 94,098 | 30.5% |
| 3 | Lakeville | Restaurant | 54,272 | 13,725 | 25.2% |
| 4 | Lakeville | Bank | 60,750 | 20,000 | 70.9% |
| 5 | Lake Elmo | Office building | 585,961 | 98,270 | 50.3% |
| 6 | Oak Park Heights | Menard's store | 518,364 | 156,274 | 92.0% |
| 7 | Oak Park Heights | Car wash | 53,143 | 19,500 | 34.0% |
| Average % Value Loss | | | | | 49.6% |
| Median % Value Loss | | | | | 43.9% |

discussion of each market example of transmission line-encumbered land sales, which is then followed by a detailed analysis of each sale and the loss in value as a result of the transmission line.

Based on our analysis, we concluded that Comparable Land Sales 1, 3, and 5 are the most similar to the subject property. We also concluded that the appropriate value loss as a result of the transmission line easement-encumbered land area is 33%.

## Summary of Comparable Land Sales

Comparable Land Sale 1 is a 147,819-sq.-ft. commercial land parcel in Maple Grove that has been developed with a 120-room Hilton Garden Inn hotel. It is encumbered by an electrical transmission line easement along the eastern border. This parcel sold in March 2001 for $6.78 per square foot of land area. Its market value at the time was concluded to have been $8.00 per square foot, as if unencumbered. We concluded that the unencumbered area of this parcel sold at its market value and the value of the encumbered area was discounted 43.9%. There are no severance damages to the remainder parcel. This land has a 345 kV line compared to the subject property's 115 kV line. This comparable land parcel has a lattice tower compared to the single-pole structures at the subject parcel. The centerline of the transmission lines at this comparable property is about 60 feet from the rooms, while the centerline of the transmission lines at the subject property is about 205 feet from the south-end rooms and 85 feet from the north-end rooms (or an average of 145 feet). As a result, the indicated discount at this comparable property of about 44% must be adjusted downward for the subject property.

Comparable Land Sale 2 is a 248,244-sq.-ft. commercial land parcel in Shakopee that has been developed into Valley Apple Ford. It is encumbered by an electrical transmission line easement along its northern border. This parcel sold in December 2000 for $8.84 per square foot of land area. Its market value at that time was concluded to have been $10.00 per square foot, as if unencumbered. We concluded that the unencumbered area of this parcel sold at its market value and that the value of the encumbered area was discounted about 30%. There were no severance damages to the remainder parcel.

Comparable Land Sale 3 is a 54,272-sq.-ft. commercial land parcel in Lakeville that has been developed with an Applebee's restaurant. It is encumbered by an electrical transmission line easement that cuts through the parcel near its northwestern border. This parcel sold in June 2003 for $20.13 per square foot of land area. Its market value at that time was concluded to have been $21.50 per square foot, as if unencumbered. We concluded that the unencumbered area of this parcel sold at its market value and that the value of the encumbered area was discounted about 25%. There were no severance damages to the remainder parcel.

Comparable Land Sale 4 is a 60,750-sq.-ft. commercial land parcel in Lakeville, which has become a Citizens Bank. It is encumbered by an electrical transmission line easement that cuts through the parcel near its northwestern border. This parcel sold in December 2002 for $16.48 per square foot of land area. Its market value at that time was concluded to have been $21.50 per square foot, as if unencumbered. We concluded that the unencumbered area of this parcel sold at its market value and that the value of the encumbered area was discounted about 71%. There were no severance damages to the remainder parcel.

Comparable Land Sale 5 is a 13.45-acre industrial land parcel in Lake Elmo, which has been developed into an office building for Bremer Financial. It is encumbered by an electrical transmission line easement along its northern border. This parcel sold in April 2002 for $2.47 per square foot of land area. Its market value at that time was concluded to have been $2.70 per square foot, as if unencumbered. We concluded that the unencumbered area of this parcel sold at its market value and that the value of the encumbered area was discounted about 50%. There were no severance damages to the remainder parcel.

Comparable Land Sale 6 is a 12-acre commercial land parcel in Oak Park Heights, which has been improved with a Menard's store. It is encumbered by an electrical transmission line easement running east-west through the parking lot. This parcel sold in August 1995 for $3.37 per square foot of land area. Its market value at that time was concluded to have been $4.70 per square foot, as if unencumbered. We concluded that the unencumbered area of this parcel sold at its market value and that the value of the encumbered area was discounted about 92%. There were no severance damages to the remainder parcel.

Comparable Land Sale 7 is a 1.22-acre commercial land parcel in Oak Park Heights, which has been improved with a Pony Express auto wash. It is encumbered by an electrical transmission line easement along its southern border. This parcel sold in April 2001 for $6.11 per square foot of land area. Its market value at that time was concluded to have been $7.00 per square foot, as if unencumbered. We concluded that the unencumbered area of this parcel sold at its market value and that the value of the encumbered area was discounted about 34%. There were no severance damages to the remainder parcel.

Exhibit 3 provides information on Comparable Land Sale 1.

## Analysis of Comparable Land Sale 1

The entire width of the site's eastern border is encumbered with an electrical transmission line easement that is approximately 132 to 150 feet wide. We estimated that the encumbered area represents 35% of the total site, encumbering a total area of about 52,000 square feet.

This site has been developed into a Hilton Garden Inn hotel, with 120 rooms, an indoor pool, and an on-site restaurant and bar. We

**Exhibit 3**

**Comparable Land Sale 1**

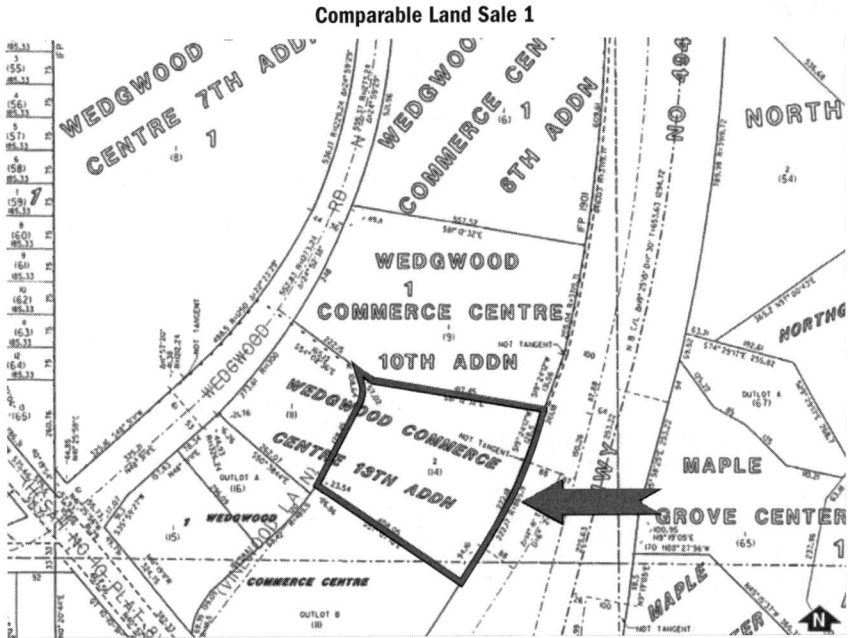

### General Information

| | |
|---|---|
| Code: | 110-03-60 |
| Source: | Personal inspection, site plan review, public records |
| Location: | 6350 Vinewood Lane North, Maple Grove, MN |
| Sale date: | March, 2001 |
| PID number: | 34-119-22-42-0014 |
| Intended use: | Construct Hilton Garden Inn hotel |

| Site Data | | Terms of Sale | |
|---|---|---|---|
| Parcel size: | 147,819 sq. ft., or 3.39 acres | Buyer: | Maple Grove Lodging Investors, LLC |
| Zoning: | PUD | | |
| Utilities: | All available | Seller: | TOLD Development Company |
| Topography: | Generally level | | |
| Soil conditions: | Assumed stable | Financing: | Cash sale |
| Visibility: | Good | Nominal price: | $1,000,000 |
| Access: | Average | Assumed specials: | 0 |
| | | Total price: | $1,000,000 |
| | | Price per unit: | $6.78 per sq. ft. |

**Remarks:** This site was purchased to build a Hilton Garden Inn hotel. The site has average access off Bass Lake Road and has good visibility to I-494 traffic.

*Partial Taking–Electric Transmission Line*

concluded that the following summarized sales are comparable to this power line easement-encumbered sale property (see Exhibit 4).

### Exhibit 4
#### Comparable Land Sale Summary

| Sale | Location | Sale Date | Land Area (Sq. Ft.) | Sale Price | Sale Price per Sq. Ft. |
|---|---|---|---|---|---|
| 1 | 6495 Sycamore Ct. N, Maple Grove, MN | Sep-05* | 214,459 | $1,668,552 | $7.78 |
| 2 | NWC Dunkirk Lane and Co. Rd. 30, Maple Grove, MN | Oct-99 | 61,420 | $635,976 | $10.35 |
| 3 | SWQ Co. Rd. 30 and I-94, Maple Grove, MN | Sep-99 | 133,958 | $812,720 | $6.07 |
| 4 | 9475 Garland Ave., Maple Grove, MN | Nov-02* | 140,220 | $1,157,000 | $8.25 |
| Easement-impaired sale site (Comparable Land Sale 1) | Hilton Garden Inn at 6360 Vinewood Lane North, Maple Grove, MN | Mar-01 | 147,819 | – | – |

\* Note that in some jurisdictions (such as federal court) appraisers are not allowed to use comparable sales that occurred after the date of valuation while in others the practice is acceptable. Appraisers should check with the attorney for guidance on whether comparable sales after the date of valuation are admissible evidence in the relevant jurisdiction.

We have adjusted the sales shown in Exhibit 4 to the power line easement-encumbered sale property (Comparable Land Sale 1), and its market value was concluded to be $8.00 per square foot, as if it were unencumbered.

View of the Hilton Inn and easement looking north along the eastern site boundary

Comparable Land Sale 1 sold in March 2001 for a price equivalent to $6.78 per square foot. We concluded, based on our analysis of comparable sales, that its market value as if unencumbered at that time was $8.00 per square foot. Exhibit 6 summarizes our conclusion that this easement reduced the land value in the encumbered area by 43.9%.

Our method of analysis was to start with the sale price of the entire property and subtract the estimated market value of the unencumbered area. The result is the contributing value of the easement-encumbered land area.

The value of the encumbered area was then estimated as if it were unencumbered. The ratio of these two values for the encumbered land shows the percentage loss of value due to the existing power line easement.

This valuation technique consists of evaluating Comparable Land Sale 1 in comparison to other noneasement land sales. Comparable Land Sales 2 through 7 will not be presented in this case study to save space, but those sales were analyzed in the same manner as Sale 1. This analysis resulted in the summary charts presented in Exhibits 2 and 7.

## Easement Loss Conclusion

The percentage of total land area encumbered by the electrical transmission line easement is 10.7%, compared to between 17% and 38%

View of the transmission tower looking northeast

### Exhibit 5
### Site Plan (Comparable Land Sale 1)

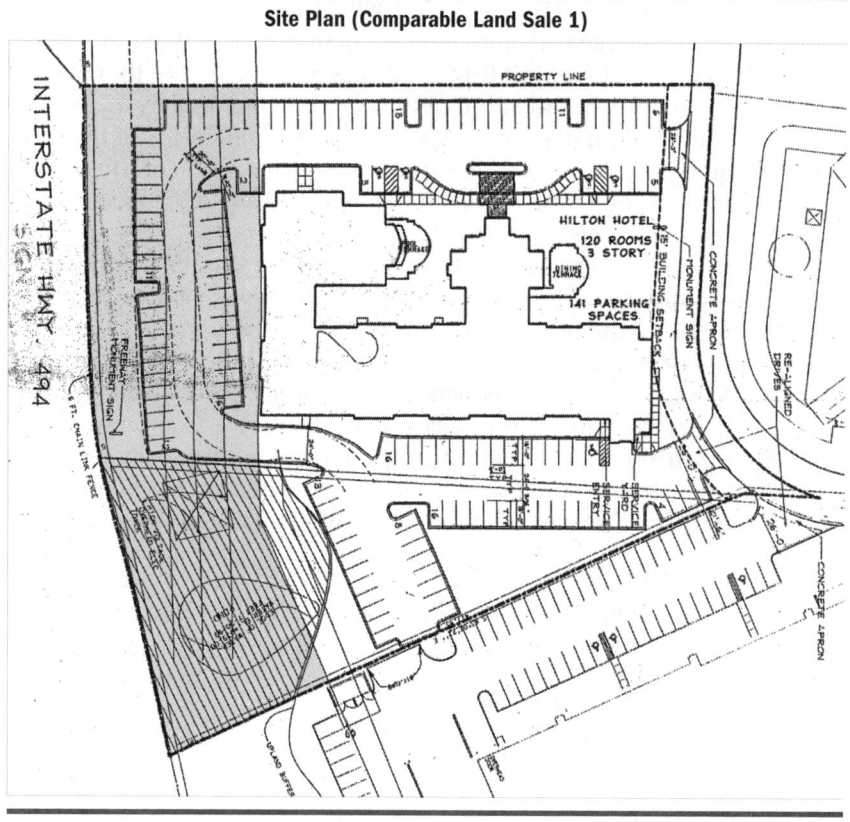

### Exhibit 6

| Verified sale price of property with encumbrance | | | | $1,000,000 |
|---|---|---|---|---|
| Less: Estimated market value of unencumbered land | | | | |
| **Unencumbered land area in square feet** | **Times** | **Estimated land value per sq. ft.** | **Equals** | **Indicated market value of unencumbered land** |
| 95,819 | × | $8.00 | = | $766,552 |
| Equals: Estimated contributing value of encumbered land | | | | $233,448 |
| Estimated market value of encumbered land, as if unencumbered | | | | |
| **Encumbered land area in square feet** | **Times** | **Estimated land value per sq. ft.** | **Equals** | **Indicated market value of land as if unencumbered** |
| 52,000 | × | $8.00 | = | $416,000 |
| Ratio of encumbered land value to unencumbered land value | | | | 56.1% |
| (233,448 / $416,000 = 56.1%) | | | | |
| **Estimated Value Percentage Loss Due to Encumbrance** | | | | 43.9% |
| **Estimated Severance Loss to Remainder for Encumbrance** | | | | None |

*Applications in Litigation Valuation: A Pragmatist's Guide*

**Exhibit 7**

**Summary of Power Line Easement-Encumbered Land Sales**

| Comparable Land Sale | Land Use/ Location | Estimated Value Loss in Encumbered Land Area | Location of Power Line Easement | Percentage of Total Land Area Encumbered | Width of Power Line Easement | Number of and Types of Towers | Power Line Easement Rights and Use at Sale | Access Rights Included in Easement |
|---|---|---|---|---|---|---|---|---|
| 1 | Hilton Garden Inn at 6360 Vinewood Lane North in Maple Grove, MN | 44% | at rear of property along border on freeway side of parcel | 35% | 132 to 150 feet | 1; lattice | unlimited; double circuit 345 kV | blanket easement |
| 2 | Valley Ford at 1624 Weston Court in Shakopee, MN | 31% | at side of property along border on freeway side of parcel | 38% | 159 to 168 feet | 1½; lattice | unlimited; single circuit 230 kV and part of double circuit 345 kV | blanket easement |
| 3 | Applebee's restaurant at 18404 Kenrick Ave. in Lakeville, MN | 25% | at front of property through interior of parcel | 25% | 75 feet | 1; H-frame | unlimited; single circuit 115 kV | blanket easement |
| 4 | Citizen's Bank at 18476 Kenrick Ave. in Lakeville, MN | 71% | at front of property through interior of parcel | 33% | 75 feet | 1; single pole | unlimited; single circuit 115 kV | blanket easement |
| 5 | Bremer Financial Service Center at 8555 Eagle Point Blvd. in Lake Elmo, MN | 50% | at side of property along border of parcel | 17% | 75 feet | 1; H-frame | unlimited; single circuit 115 kV | blanket easement |
| 6 | Menard's store at 5800 Krueger Lane in Oak Park Heights, MN | 92% | at front of property along border of parcel | 30% | 225 feet | 2; lattice | unlimited; double circuit 345 kV and single circuit 230 kV | blanket easement |
| 7 | Pony Express Auto Wash at 5970 Neal Avenue North in Oak Park Heights, MN | 34% | at front of property along border of parcel | 37% | 225 feet | none | unlimited; double circuit 345 kV and single circuit 230 kV | blanket easement |
| Subject | Kelly Inn at 2705 Annapolis Lane North in Plymouth, MN | 33% | at rear of property along border on freeway side of parcel | 10.7% | 20 to 42 feet all within required 50-foot front setback | 3; single pole | limited by scope of easement to 115 kV | limited by scope of easement |

for the transmission line-encumbered sales. Also, the width of the subject transmission line easement is significantly less than that of the comparables (75 feet to 225 feet for the comparables), and the subject easement width ranges from 42 feet at the south boundary to approximately 20 feet at the north boundary. Also, the entire easement area is all within the required 50-foot zoning code setback. The subject transmission line easement rights are limited to 115 kV as compared to the unlimited rights of the comparables. The subject easement access is limited by the *Order Establishing the Scope of Easements* document.

Based on our analysis of the previous land sales, we concluded that the appropriate value loss or discount is 33%. We also concluded from our analysis that the market value of the subject land–after the taking and based on a 33% discount to the encumbered transmission line easement area–is $4,000,000, calculated as shown in Exhibit 8.

### Exhibit 8

| Land Area in Sq. Ft. | Times | Estimated Land Value per Sq. Ft. | Equals | Indicated Market Value of Land |
|---|---|---|---|---|
| Unencumbered land: | | | | |
| 296,570 | × | $12.50 | = | $3,707,125 |
| Proposed GRE power line easement land: | | | | |
| 35,375 | × | $8.33 | = | 294,674 |
| | | | | $4,001,799 |
| | | | | rounded to |
| Indicated Market Value–After the Taking | | | | $4,000,000 |

## Replacement Cost Analysis–After the Taking

The next step in the cost analysis is estimating the replacement cost in the after condition. The new easement did not result in any loss in improvements, and we concluded that the presence of the easement does not result in any additional depreciation. (See the presentation of the obsolescence analysis and conclusions on pages 72-75.) As a result, our conclusion of depreciated replacement cost remains the same as in the before condition.

The only change to the improvements in the after condition is the loss in landscaping–i.e., the loss of seven mature trees within the transmission line easement area. The property owner has noted that the loss of the trees has created an increase in traffic noise, as the trees provided a sound buffer. The owner has expedited the capital improvement plan, which entailed the replacement of the 55 windows along the west elevation on the property.

We concluded that the loss of the seven trees does not substantially increase noise, as only four of the seven trees are in the area west of the guest rooms. Because the trees were mature deciduous trees with foliage only during the spring and summer, we are not of the opinion that the trees provide a noise buffer while dormant in late fall, winter, and early spring. Finally, numerous mature trees remain in the landscaped parking islands.

We apply a reduction in replacement cost as a result of the tree loss. Great River Energy plans on landscaping and replanting within the easement area. The landscaping plan has not been provided. We concluded that despite the new trees and landscaping within the easement area, the new plantings will not be of the size and scale of the mature trees that existed before the taking. As a result, we reduced landscaping costs in the after condition and concluded that the loss in seven trees reduces the landscaping cost by $10,000. The calculation of the replacement cost after the taking is summarized in Exhibit 9.

Next, we estimated depreciation in the after condition.

### Exhibit 9

**Base Cost**

| | | | |
|---|---|---|---|
| Source | Marshall Valuation | Base cost per sq. ft. | $63.50 |
| | Commercial Cost Manual | Sprinklers | 2.00 |
| Source reference | Section 12, page 9 | HVAC | 1.75 |
| Construction class | Commercial | Subtotal | $67.25 |
| Type | Motel | | |
| Quality | Average | Current cost multiplier | 1.110 |
| Year of construction | 1973 | Local cost multiplier | 1.150 |
| Actual age | 32 | Area/perimeter multiplier | 0.950 |
| Effective age | 25 | Story height multiplier | 1.000 |
| Economic life | 50 | | |
| | | Adjusted base cost | $81.55 |

**Building Improvements**

| | | |
|---|---|---|
| Main building | 85,582 sq. ft. @ $81.55 = | $6,979,212 |
| Swimming pool | | 275,000 |
| Fixtures and equipment | 149 rooms @ $4,000.00 = | 596,000 |
| Subtotal—Replacement Cost New | | $7,850,212 |
| Plus: Indirect cost | 5% | 392,511 |
| Subtotal | | $8,242,723 |
| Plus: Entrepreneurial incentive | 15% | 1,236,408 |
| Total Replacement Cost New | | $9,479,131 |

**Site Improvements**

| | | |
|---|---|---|
| Parking | | $450,000 |
| Lighting, landscaping | | 265,000 |
| Subtotal—Replacement Cost New | | $715,000 |
| Plus: Indirect cost | 5% | 35,750 |
| Subtotal | | $750,750 |
| Plus: Entrepreneurial incentive | 15% | 112,613 |
| Total Replacement Cost New | | $863,363 |

**Overall Property**

| | | |
|---|---|---|
| Replacement cost new—building improvements | | $7,850,212 |
| Replacement cost new—site improvements | | 715,000 |
| Subtotal—Total Replacement Cost New | | $8,565,212 |
| Indirect cost | 5% | 428,261 |
| Subtotal | | $8,993,473 |
| Entrepreneurial incentive | 15% | 1,349,021 |
| Total Replacement Cost New | | $10,342,494 |

## Physical Deterioration Estimate–After the Taking

No changes to the improvement resulted from the easement taking. As a result, we did not change our opinion of physical deterioration and concluded that a 50% physical deterioration is still applicable.

## Functional Obsolescence–After the Taking

As in the before condition, we concluded that 5% functional obsolescence exists. The taking did not affect the functional utility of the building.

## External Obsolescence–After the Taking

Finally, we considered whether the taking resulted in any external obsolescence. In our analysis of the impact of the transmission line on the improved property, we considered hotel sales that were encumbered by transmission line easements and surveyed the participants (buyer, seller, broker) about the impact of the power line on the sale of the property. All of the buyers or brokers of the hotel properties reported that the sale price was *not* affected by the presence of the transmission line easement.

In addition to hotel transactions, we also considered sales of commercial improved properties that are encumbered by transmission line easements. Again, based on our surveys with buyers, managers, and leasing agents, we found no impact on price or any impact on the rents or ability to lease the improvements.

Comparable Building Sales 2 through 7 will not be presented in this case study to save space. Comparable Building Sales 2 and 3 were hotels, and Sales 4 through 7 consisted of two office buildings, a multitenant office/warehouse, and a neighborhood shopping center. Those sales were analyzed in the same manner as Comparable Building Sale 1. Comparable Building Sale 1 was of a hotel, as were Sales 2 and 3, but in our market there were no other sales of hotels with electrical transmission line easements. We thought that it was important to have additional market data, so we included sales of other property types (Sales 4 through 7). This is, of course, less desirable than having all such sales being of similar hotel properties, but we were limited by the available market data.

The next section considers the impact of the transmission line easement on the improvements. The transmission line easement exists on the western boundary of the subject and is approximately 205 feet from the south end of the building. The centerline of the easement is approximately 85 feet from the north end of the building. The average distance is 145 feet. We ascertained that several hotel properties are encumbered by transmission line easements, some with easements within closer proximity to the improvements and others having easements well removed from the improvements.

**Exhibit 10**

## Comparable Building Sale 1

| | |
|---|---|
| Code/file: | 722-03-20 |
| Building name: | Former Holiday Inn Express |
| Location: | 814 American Boulevard East, Bloomington, MN |
| Legal description: | Lot 1, Block 1, Holiday Inn Express Addition |
| Property tax identification no.: | 02-027-24-21-0029 |
| Date of sale: | March 10, 2005 |
| Buyer: | BW Bloomington, LLC |
| Seller: | RFS Partnership, LP |
| Zoning: | FD-2 |
| Utilities: | All available |
| Topography/soil: | Generally level/assumed stable |
| Land area: | 95,201 square feet, or 2.19 acres |
| Gross building area: | 80,238 square feet |
| Number of rooms: | 142 |
| Year built: | 1986 |
| Sale price: | $5,475,000 |
| Assumed special assessments: | 0 |
| Total price: | $5,475,000 |
| Unit price: | $68.23 per sq. ft. of gross building area |
| | $38,556 per room |
| Estimated *NOI*: | $821,929 (2004, after 4% replacement allowances) |
| Indicated overall rate: | 15.01% |
| Estimated room revenue: | N/A |
| Revenue per available room (REVPAR): | N/A |

*Partial Taking–Electric Transmission Line*

---
**Exhibit 10**
---
*(continued)*

Remarks: The hotel originally opened as a Dillon Inn and was converted to a Holiday Inn Express in 1991. The Holiday Inn Express franchise terminated with the sale and could not be renewed. Therefore, the hotel sold as an independent hotel. The buyer subsequently put a Quality Inn flag on the property about nine months after the sale closed. The list price was $5,700,000, and the property was marketed by CB Richard Ellis Hotels. There were a number of bidders, and the property sold in approximately six months.

The site is an L-shaped parcel. It is set back behind a Denny's restaurant, but it still has I-494 visibility due to its signage and story height.

The property was built in 1986, and an indoor pool and whirlpool addition was constructed in about 2000. The room mix consists of 54 kings, 82 doubles, and six suites. According to the broker, the hotel received approximately $800,000 in capital expenditures over the three years prior to the sale, including granite bathroom countertops, renovation of six suites, purchase of new box springs and mattresses, and replacement of some guest room carpeting. Hotel amenities include an indoor pool, indoor whirlpool, exercise room, continental breakfast area, and two meeting rooms, totaling 1,461 square feet. The hotel is also attached by a breezeway to a Denny's restaurant.

A single-circuit 115 kV power line runs along the south side of the property. There is one single-pole tower structure on site near its southwest corner. The centerline of the power lines is about 100 feet from the south section rooms. **According to the broker, the presence of the power lines had no impact on the sale price. The broker stated that he wasn't sure that anyone knew they were there. This property had a previous lower offer, and this potential buyer attributed no value loss due to the power line.**

---

We surveyed fifteen hotel properties encumbered by a transmission line easement. **The survey respondents *all* stated that the power lines have *no* impact on occupancy rates and no negative impact on the average daily rate.** The results of this survey include a photo and description of each property, followed by the survey questions and responses.

Fifteen hotels located in the subject property county were found to have electrical transmission line easements. These properties were identified by driving the existing easement corridors. Representatives of all fifteen hotels participated in our survey. The presentation of the first of those interviews is provided in Exhibit 11. The remaining fourteen interviews are not presented here due to space limitations.

The survey responses were important for the presentation of this appraisal at the hearing because the owner's appraiser estimated a diminution in average room rate and occupancy resulting from the proposed transmission line, but these survey results did not support that conclusion. Some surveys are mere responses to how a market participant might react to a particular property feature. What people say they will do and what they actually do are sometimes different. For this reason I find these types of surveys to be less persuasive than actual market data. In the survey used in this appraisal, however, we asked property managers for the specific financial effects of electrical

**Exhibit 11**

**Survey Results of Hotels with Power Lines**

LeBourget Aero Suites
7770 Johnson Avenue South
Bloomington, MN

The LeBourget Aero Suites is a 160-suite hotel located on the north side of I-494 between France Avenue and Highway 100 in Bloomington.

This property has a double-circuit 115 kV power line along the north side of the property at the rear of the hotel. There are no structures on site. The power lines run over the rear parking lot, and the centerline of the power line is approximately 90 feet from the newer north addition.

**Survey Respondent:** ▉▉▉▉▉, General Manager (ph. ▉▉▉▉▉) on 9/12/06

| | |
|---|---|
| Do you ever have customers who complain about the power lines or ask to be moved to another room away from the lines? | Never |
| Do you think that there is any negative impact on occupancy rate due to the presence of the overhead power lines? | No |
| Do you think that there is any negative impact on average daily rate due to the presence of the overhead power lines? | No |

transmission line easements. I did find this survey to be credible in the analysis of the damages to this subject hotel property.

## Cost Approach–After the Taking: Conclusions

Based on the previously summarized survey and the examples of sales of hotel properties with transmission line easements, we concluded that external obsolescence is not present in the after condition as a result of the easement taking. As a result, we concluded that the value indication by the cost approach is $8,430,000, calculated as follows:

| Value Indication by Cost Approach—After the Taking | |
|---|---:|
| Replacement cost new | $10,342,494 |
| Less: Accrued depreciation | − 5,913,872 |
| Depreciated replacement cost | $4,428,622 |
| Land value | 4,000,000 |
| Indicated property value | $8,428,622 |
| Rounded: | $8,430,000 |

## Sales Comparison Approach—After the Taking

The same sales were used in the after analysis, and we considered the same adjustments in the after condition, as no changes occurred to the improvements as a result of the easement taking. We previously presented a number of transmission line easement-encumbered transactions, both of hotels and other commercial and office properties. Based on surveys about the impact of the transmission line on value, we concluded that no additional adjustments are warranted for the presence of the transmission line easement in the after condition other than its reduction on the land value component of the overall property. In the before analysis, we concluded that the market value conclusion via the sales comparison approach is $8,200,000.

Based on our analysis of transmission line-encumbered hotel and commercial building transactions as well as our survey of hotel managers, market evidence indicated that no diminution in value exists. We concluded that the market value of the land has suffered somewhat due to the presence of the transmission line easement even though there was no loss of land area. Considering all of our market data and analysis, we made a deduction for land value loss from the total property value.

Based on our before land value conclusion of $4,150,000 ($12.50 per square foot), we recognized that the improvements component had a market value in the before condition of $4,050,000.

In the after analysis, the overall land value is reduced due to the lower land value within the transmission line easement area. We concluded that the after land value is $4,000,000. Given that no change is made to the overall improvements, we concluded that the improvement value conclusion after deducting for the loss in trees is $4,040,000 and the land value is $4,000,000, resulting in an after-taking value conclusion of $8,040,000.

Sales Comparison Approach Conclusion—After the Taking: $8,040,000

## Income Capitalization Approach—After the Taking

Our research indicated that no loss to the average daily rate or decrease in occupancy is indicated as a result of the transmission line easement. We surveyed 15 hotel properties that are encumbered by a transmission line easement, and in no instance did on-site managers indicate that the average daily rate (ADR) or occupancy was affected as a result of the power line easement. As was explained in the previous section, we concluded from our surveys that no additional adjustments are warranted for the presence of the power line easement in the after condition other than its reduction on the land value component of the overall property, based on surveys about the impact of the transmission line on value.

Some market evidence indicated that no diminution in value exists and some showed minor losses. The analysis of land sales with transmission line easements showed a minor loss in land value. Our analysis of transmission line-encumbered hotel and commercial building transactions as well as our survey of hotel managers showed no diminution in value. It is our opinion that the market value of the land has suffered somewhat due to the presence of the transmission line easement even though there was no loss of land area. We have made a deduction for land value loss from the total property value.

In our after analysis, we concluded that the net operating income before replacement allowances is $926,831. We recognized that the net operating income is composed of the income attributable to the land and the income attributable to the improvements. In the before analysis, we concluded that the market value indication of the income capitalization approach is $8,400,000, with $4,150,000 allocated to the land. The before building value allocation is $4,250,000.

As in the application of the sales comparison approach, market evidence indicated that no diminution in value exists. However, we did find land sales showing a diminution for the existing transmission line easements, so we made a deduction for land value loss. As a result, we concluded that the after value is $8,240,000, with $4,000,000 allocated to the land value and $4,240,000 allocated to the improvements, after deducting for the loss in trees.

>Income Capitalization Approach Conclusion—After the Taking: $8,240,000

## Reconciliation—After the Taking

Reconciliation involves the analysis of alternative value indications to determine a final value conclusion. Reconciliation is required because different value indications may result from the use of multiple approaches and within the application of a single approach. The values indicated by our analyses are as follows:

| | | |
|---|---|---|
| Cost approach: | $8,430,000 | ($56,578 per room) |
| Sales comparison approach: | $8,040,000 | ($54,027 per room) |
| Income capitalization approach: | $8,240,000 | ($55,369 per room) |

## Conclusion of Value

Based on the preceding analysis and subject to the definitions, assumptions, and limiting conditions expressed herein, it is our opinion that the market value of the fee simple estate of the subject, after the easement taking as of October 17, 2005, is **$8,240,000**.

| Appraisal Summary | |
|---|---|
| Market value—before the taking | $8,400,000 |
| Market value—after the taking | − 8,240,000 |
| Diminution | $160,000 |

The allocation of the value loss is $150,000 for the easement rights and $10,000 for the loss in landscaping.

## Conclusions

In this appraisal, we analyzed land sales that had sold with electric transmission line easements. In effect, we appraised the comparable to see what it would have sold for if it had no easement. As a result, we were able to develop an opinion of how the easement affected its selling price.

To measure any damages, we looked to sales of commercial properties that sold and were encumbered by electrical transmission line easements. I was shocked to see how many such sale properties actually existed in our market. I was reminded of the old appraisal saying, "Look for the comps, you just might find some."

We also performed a survey of operators of hotels located within the subject county that have electrical transmission easements on their properties. We found this to be instructive in our analysis. It also helped because the landowner's appraiser concluded that the hotel room rate and the occupancy rate would drop after the electrical transmission line was constructed. At the hearing, the subject hotel operator did not present any actual subject property performance reports to show how the transmission line affected the operation of the hotel after its installation.

The most important lesson I learned in this assignment concerned advice I gave to my client's attorney. I was contacted prior to the hearing asking for my advice about accepting an offer to settle the case for $210,000. The negotiations had narrowed to an offer from the utility company of $200,000 and a counteroffer from the land owner of $210,000. My advice was to go to the hearing. But through this case

I learned the wisdom in a saying from another client who was also an attorney: "The worst settlement is still better than the unknown of a trial outcome." How true. After the hearing, the court-appointed commissioners ruled that the taking had damaged the market value of this property by $275,000.

> **Acknowledgments**
> The author of this case study would like to recognize the professional work of Lisa Olmen, senior analyst with the Minneapolis/St. Paul office of Integra Realty Resources. She, along with others in our firm, completed the appraisals and consulting work on numerous parcels for this electrical transmission line project. I am also thankful for the work of Pat Reilly, MAI, an independent fee appraiser who assisted our appraisal team with the survey of operators of hotel properties located on existing electrical transmission lines.

CASE STUDY 1.3

# Partial Taking– Petroleum Pipeline

*By Jeffrey A. Johnson, MAI*

## The Assignment

This case study includes selected sections from an appraisal report that was prepared for a scheduled condemnation hearing. In Minnesota, most condemnation cases are heard by a Commissioners Panel of three citizens who are appointed by the judge to decide on the case. Either side of the case can then appeal the Commissioners Panel's decision, which results in a district court trial.

This case study deals with a partial taking condemnation case (easement rights) for a petroleum pipeline project in Minnesota. The valuation entailed estimating the compensable damages by applying a before and after valuation approach to the larger parcel.[1] We used a before-taking appraisal with the assumption that the appraisal was made independently of the then-proposed pipeline project. The after-taking appraisal was made to measure any and all value diminutions resulting from the project.

Our client for this appraisal assignment was the pipeline company, and an initial appraisal report was prepared to assist the client in making an offer to acquire the easement rights. Negotiations failed, and these property rights were acquired through condemnation.

To measure the impact, if any, of the damages on the market value of the permanent petroleum pipeline easement, our appraisal team researched, confirmed, and analyzed sales of farms that had been sold with similar pipeline easements. This is a direct market measurement method that does not rely on secondary valuation methods to support the opinion of damages. The first such comparable sale was of a farm that was encumbered by an easement for the very same pipeline project. Between the date of the taking (September 2007) and the date of the scheduled hearing and preparation of the appraisal report (March 2009), one of the farm properties affected

---

1. Much has been written on this valuation method, so for this case study no preliminary explanation of the method will be presented other than to refer the reader to a very thorough presentation of the subject in J. D. Eaton, *Real Estate Valuation in Litigation*, 2nd ed. (Chicago: Appraisal Institute, 1995).

by the subject pipeline was sold. For that comparable, we not only interviewed the broker, who stated that the pipeline had no adverse impact on the price, but we also looked at similar farm sales to see if this comparable did sell for a reduced price or a price that was comparable to other farm sales that did not have such an easement.

As indicated earlier, the appraisal report was prepared on this property in anticipation of a hearing. However, the case was settled just prior to the hearing date for an amount of $13,500. This appraisal was made after the actual date of taking and with the benefit of seeing the finished construction project in place. In this case study the property description and the before-taking valuation section have been condensed, simply stating certain facts about the property and listing the comparable sales used in the before valuation.

## The Subject Property

The larger parcel is a 73.72-acre parcel of farmland. There are no structures on this property. The farming operations consist of corn and soybean crop rotation. The property is zoned AG, agricultural, which permits agricultural, single-unit residential, and supporting uses. There is one "potential building eligibility" with this parcel, meaning that if requested the county would approve a permit to construct one residence on the parcel. The property has frontage on State Highway 25 in Faxon Township of Sibley County, Minnesota. It is located about 15 miles northeast of Gaylord, the county seat, about 10 miles south of Norwood/Young America, and about 25 miles southwest of the Twin Cities of Minneapolis and St. Paul.

## Purpose, Property Rights, and Effective Date

The purpose of the appraisal is to develop an opinion of the market value, in the before condition, of the fee simple interest in the property as of the effective date of the appraisal, September 27, 2007. A hypothetical assumption was made upon request, as we also estimated the market value of the fee simple interest in the after condition as of September 27, 2007. Our appraisal firm, Integra Realty Resources–Minneapolis/St. Paul, had previously appraised the property in December 2006.

Our appraisal report was prepared in March 2009, after the date of taking and the completion of the construction project. As a result, we had the benefit of information on subsequent events in the preparation of this report.

# Sales Comparison Approach—Before the Easement

To apply the sales comparison approach, we searched for sale transactions most relevant to the subject in terms of location, size, highest and best use, and transaction date. Out of all the data reviewed in Sibley County, we selected the sales shown in Exhibit 1 as the best indicators of the subject's value. Four of the five comparable sales we used were listed for sale with real estate brokers through the multiple listing service, with an average exposure time of 90 days. The marketing time for the four sales ranged from 36 days to 154 days, indicating adequate exposure to achieve a maximum sale price. We chose price per gross acre as the most appropriate unit of comparison.

Note that we chose to include Sale 4, a parcel that was purchased for future rural residential lot development and that benefitted from part of its land being within the Conservation Reserve Program (CRP). The subject property, however, had only one residential housing eligibility. Sale 4 is not a very good comparable. However, as

### Exhibit 1

| Comparable Land Sale | Name/Address | Sale Date | Sale Price | Sq. Ft./ Acres | Zoning | $/Acre |
|---|---|---|---|---|---|---|
| 1 | Section 19 200XX 301st Ave. Faxon Twp. Sibley County | Jan-08 | $755,935 | 6,760,948/155.21 | Agricultural | $4,870 |
| 2 | Section 36 440XX 330th St. Sibley Twp. Sibley County | Aug-06 | $470,000 | 5,227,200/120.00 | Agricultural | $3,917 |
| 3 | Sections 31 & 36 Faxon Rd. & 314th Ave. Faxon Twp. Sibley County | Apr-06 | $358,000 | 3,905,154/89.65 | Agricultural | $4,000 |
| 4 | Section 35 25888 Scenic Byway Rd. Faxon Twp. Sibley County | Jan-07 | $715,000 | 3,512,243/80.63 | Agricultural | $8,868 |
| | Comments: | River bluff location; 30 acres in CRP until 2008; 30 acres tillable. Remaining land in ravine and flood plain. Primary use for residential subdivision with 2-acre rural lots. No utilities available. | | | | |
| 5 | Section 29 295XX State Highway 25 Faxon Twp. Sibley County | Jan-07 | $481,681 | 4,681,393/107.47 | Agricultural | $4,482 |

noted in Chapter 3 of this book, we sometimes include information in our report or our direct examination just so the other side cannot say that a particular sale was ignored.

## Land Value Conclusion

Prior to adjustments, the sales reflected a range of $3,917 to $8,868 per acre. After adjustments were made (as detailed in the original appraisal report but not in this case study due to space considerations), the range was narrowed to $5,041 to $5,906 per acre with an average of $5,419 per acre and a median of $5,368 per acre. No single sale was the most similar to the subject. We relied primarily on the average and median values, and concluded that the market value of the larger parcel was as follows:

| | |
|---|---:|
| Indicated value per acre | $5,400 |
| Subject acres | 73.72 |
| Indicated value | $398,088 |
| Rounded | $398,000 |

## Valuation Analysis—After the Easement

### Project Description and Impacts

The project consists of the construction of an underground crude oil pipeline from northern Minnesota at Clearbrook to the Flint Hills Refinery in Dakota County. The approximately 305-mile pipeline route goes through 13 counties, including Sibley, in which the subject property is located. Approximately 1,100 parcels will be crossed by the pipeline.

We estimated the diminution in market value of the subject property in fee simple interest for the purpose of measuring the market value diminution to the property resulting after the partial taking by the Minnesota Pipe Line Company (MPL) for the crude oil pipeline project.

The permanent taking is of certain land rights conveyed through an easement. The pipeline project requires an easement encumbering an area of 1.22 acres. The location of the pipeline easement taking is depicted in the survey shown in Exhibit 2.

In addition to the permanent pipeline easement land, a total of 1.39 acres of workspace area (temporary easements) is required. The location of the temporary workspace is also depicted on the map. The permanent easement area is 50 feet wide, with the temporary workspace area extending 25 feet on each side of the permanent easement.

The permanent easement will restrict any building over the 50-foot-wide area across the parcel. The construction phase of the pipeline will preclude any harvesting of crops for the 2008 season in the permanent easement area and also in the temporary workspace easement area.

The highest and best use of the subject to operate as cropland will not be permanently affected because the easement does not restrict agricultural uses within the permanent easement area. The language of the easement states that the Minnesota Pipe Line Company (or its successors and/or assigns) may enter onto the subject property for the purposes of surveying, maintaining, repairing, replacing, operating, updating, altering, removing, and abandoning an in-place pipeline and other appurtenances and equipment by persons, vehicles, machinery, equipment, devices, and materials. The subject property is unimproved. Therefore, no improvements are affected by the easement.

Note that in this type of litigation appraisal assignment, having more and better market data is always helpful. Because the farmland market in the subject area was relatively active at that time, we had sufficiently comparable recent sales data from which to estimate the market value before the taking. To estimate the market value after such a taking and quantify the market value diminution, appraisers generally:

- interview market participants,
- recall prior interviews with market participants,
- rely on their professional experience of reviewing sales with and without such easements, and
- analyze sales of similar properties that have similar pipeline easements.

It is always a challenge to find knowledgeable market participants to give those interviews greater meaning in our evaluations. An equal or greater challenge is finding market sales comparables to use in quantifying our after-taking adjustment for having a pipeline easement on the appraised property.

## Highest and Best Use Analysis–After the Easement

After the easement encumbrance, the highest and best use of the property will not change. The pipeline crosses the property within 79 feet of its western boundary line generally in a north to south line, entering at the west boundary line near the middle of the parcel, crossing diagonally for approximately 86 feet, turning due south for 998 feet, and then exiting the subject parcel at its south boundary line. Agricultural use remains the highest and best use of the subject, the same as in the before condition.

## Valuation Analysis

After the encumbrance of a property with a permanent easement, we typically value the property by identifying similarly encumbered properties that sold in the same or similar market areas as the subject. We researched sales throughout Sibley County, Carver County,

**Exhibit 2**

**Subject Certificate of Survey**

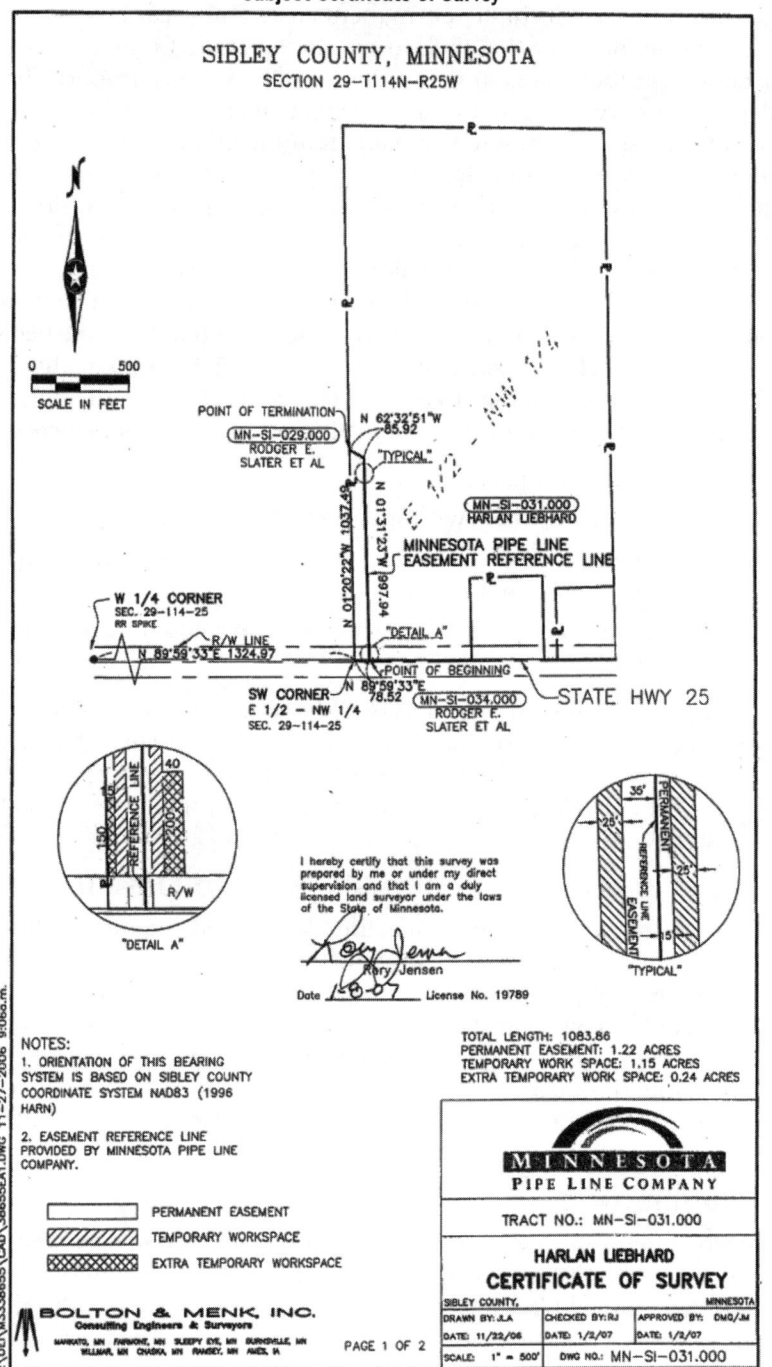

**Exhibit 2**

*(continued)*
**Legal Description of the Taking**

MN-SI-031.000
Harlan Liebhard                                                            Page 2 of 2

**Permanent Easement Description**
A 50.00 foot wide permanent easement, over, under, and across, that part of the East half of the Northwest quarter of Section 29, Township 114 North, range 25 West, Sibley County, Minnesota, said permanent easement being 15.00 feet Easterly and Northeasterly and 35.00 feet Westerly and Southwesterly of the following described reference line:

Commencing at the Southwest corner of the East half of the Northwest quarter of Section 29; thence North 89 degrees 59 minutes 33 seconds East (bearings based on the Sibley County coordinate system of NAD 83, 1996 adjustment) on the South line of the Northwest quarter of Section 29, a distance of 78.52 feet to the point of beginning of the reference line; thence North 01 degrees 31 minutes 23 seconds West, a distance of 997.94 feet; thence North 62 degrees 32 minutes 51 seconds west, a distance of 85.92 feet to the West line of the East half of the Northwest quarter of Section 29 and there terminating, said terminal point bears North 01 degrees 20 minutes 22 seconds west, a distance of 1037.49 feet from the Southwest corner of the East half of the Northwest quarter of Section 29. The sidelines of the 50.00 foot wide permanent easement are extended or shortened to terminate on the West line and South line of the East half of the Northwest quarter of Section 29.

Said permanent easement contains 1.22 acres of land.

**Temporary Work Space Description**
Two temporary work space easements. The first, a 25.00 foot wide strip of land, parallel with and adjoining the Westerly and Southwesterly line of the above described 50.00 foot wide permanent easement. The second, a 25.00 foot wide strip of land parallel with and adjoining the Easterly and Northeasterly line of the above described 50.00 foot wide permanent easement. The sidelines of the 25.00 foot wide temporary work space easements are extended or shortened to terminate on the West line of the East half of the northwest quarter of Section 29 and on the North right-of-way line of State Highway 25.

Said temporary work space easements contain 1.15 acres of land.

**Extra Temporary Work Space Description**
Two extra temporary work space easements. The first, a 15.00 foot wide by 150.00 feet in length (150.00 feet is the longest side in length) strip of land, contiguous to the North right-of-way line of State Highway 25, contiguous to and parallel with the Westerly line of the above described Westerly 25.00 foot wide temporary work space easement. The second, a 40.00 foot wide by 200.00 feet in length (200.00 feet is the shortest side in length) strip of land, contiguous to the North right-of-way line of State Highway 25, contiguous to and parallel with the Easterly line of the above described Easterly 25.00 foot wide temporary work space easement.

Said extra temporary work space easements contain 0.24 acres of land.

*Partial Taking–Petroleum Pipeline*

McLeod County, and other comparable rural areas for agricultural and semirural lands encumbered with pipeline easements. We identified more than 22 sales in which a party to the transaction had been consulted regarding any impact to the sale due to pipeline easements. In all cases, the buyers or agents indicated that pipeline easements had only minor or no influence on the prices they negotiated for the purchase of the properties. Similarly, the current or contemplated uses of the properties were not affected in any significant way, according to the buyers or agents.

We analyzed in greater detail the most comparable nine pipeline-encumbered land sales: one in Sibley County, three in Carver County, four in McLeod County, and one in Dakota County. Note that finding market sales of pipeline-encumbered properties is always a challenge. We decided to ask for help with this easement-encumbered sales search from two sources. Since the easements were acquired in September 2007 and this appraisal opinion was being prepared in March 2009, we asked the pipeline company if they were aware of any changes in the ownership of the larger parcels now encumbered by their easements. This led us to one sale that we have presented in this section of our report. Additionally, we went to the subject county geographic information system (GIS) officer and inquired about searching for sale properties with certain comparable specifications that also had pipeline easements.[2] We then did the same with surrounding counties. Now many counties post this information online and make it available to the public. With these successful GIS research results, our work was reduced to merely verifying these comparable sales with pipeline easements and analyzing the results. This research allowed us to use the valuation method that is presented in Exhibits 3 and 4.

Due to space considerations, Pipeline Easement Comparable Sales 3 through 9 will not be presented in this case study. More information was collected on Sale 1 than Sale 2 and the other pipeline easement sales analyzed in the original appraisal report because the parcel was sold just after the subject project placed a pipeline on it.

---

2. Receiving the summary printout was a personal breakthrough in my understanding of the power of GIS.

## Exhibit 3
## Comparable Sale 1

### General Information
| | |
|---|---|
| Source: | MLS and broker |
| Location: | Section 28, Faxon Township, Sibley County |
| Address: | 210XX 291st Avenue |
| Sale date: | November 3, 2008 |
| Legal description: | Lengthy, retained in file |
| PID number: | 13.2806.000 |
| Intended use: | Agricultural |

| Site Data | | Terms of Sale | |
|---|---|---|---|
| Parcel size: | 107.51 acres, 97.67 tillable | Buyer: | Dale and Laurie Otto Living Trust |
| Zoning: | AG, agricultural | Seller: | Malinda A. Schmid |
| Utilities | No municipal services | Nominal price: | $551,526 |
| Topography: | Gently rolling | Add'l consideration: | $0 |
| Access: | 291st Avenue | Total price: | $551,526 |
| | | Price per acre—gross/tillable: | $5,130/$5,647 |

**Remarks:** This property was vacant agricultural land at the time of sale. The property was listed for sale on the multiple listing service with a well-known real estate broker and was sold at auction 42 days after listing for $551,526. The land has a weighted average productivity rating of 82.5 from Surety Mapping/AgriData. The buyer purchased the property under a 1031 exchange for investment purposes and leased the land to an area farmer.

*Partial Taking–Petroleum Pipeline*

## Exhibit 3
*(continued)*
### Soils Map

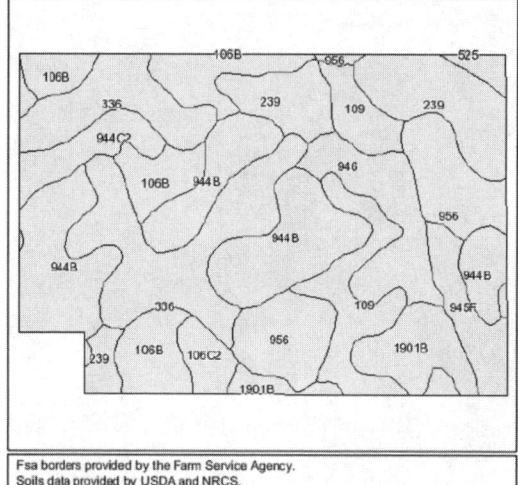

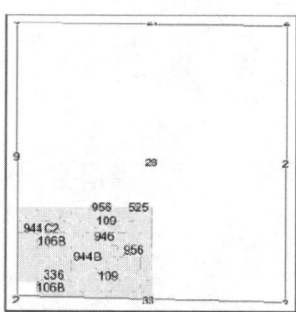

State: **Minnesota**
County: **Sibley**
Location: **028-114N-025W**
Township: **Faxon**
Acres: **107.58**

Maps provided by: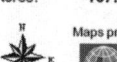

Fsa borders provided by the Farm Service Agency.
Soils data provided by USDA and NRCS.

| Code | Soil Description | Acres | Percent of field | Non-Irr Class | Productivity Index | Bromegrass alfalfa | Bromegrass alfalfa hay | Corn | Oats | Soybeans | Spring wheat |
|---|---|---|---|---|---|---|---|---|---|---|---|
| 944B | Lester-Hawick complex, 2 to 6 percent slopes | 22.2 | 20.7% | IIIs | 68 | 5.6 | 4.3 | 133 | 86 | 37 | 50 |
| 336 | Delft clay loam | 18.8 | 17.5% | IIw | 94 | 5.6 | 4.3 | 184 | 88 | 52 | 53 |
| 239 | Le Sueur clay loam | 12 | 11.1% | I | 98 | 6.2 | 4.8 | 192 | 92 | 54 | 55 |
| 106B | Lester loam, 2 to 6 percent slopes | 11.6 | 10.7% | IIe | 91 | 6.4 | 4.9 | 178 | 90 | 50 | 54 |
| 956 | Canisteo-Glencoe complex | 10.5 | 9.8% | IIw | 91 | 5.1 | 3.9 | 178 | 83 | 50 | 50 |
| 109 | Cordova clay loam | 9.1 | 8.5% | IIw | 87 | 5.6 | 4.3 | 171 | 88 | 48 | 53 |
| 946 | Nicollet-Linder complex | 6.8 | 6.3% | Is | 84 | 5.5 | 4.2 | 166 | 87 | 46 | 52 |
| 1901B | Lester-Le Sueur complex, 1 to 6 percent slopes | 5.8 | 5.4% | IIe | 95 | 6.2 | 4.8 | 186 | 91 | 52 | 55 |
| 945F | Lester-Storden complex, 18 to 65 percent slopes | 3.8 | 3.6% | VIIe | 6 | | | | | | |
| 944C2 | Lester-Hawick-Swanlake complex, 6 to 12 percent slopes, eroded | 3.7 | 3.4% | IIIs | 60 | 4.7 | 3.6 | 118 | 73 | 33 | 44 |
| 106C2 | Lester loam, 6 to 12 percent slopes, eroded | 2.4 | 2.2% | IIIe | 76 | 5.7 | 4.4 | 149 | 81 | 42 | 49 |
| 525 | Muskego muck | 0.9 | 0.8% | IIIw | 81 | 4.5 | 3.4 | 159 | 78 | 45 | 47 |
| | | | Weighted Average | | 82.5 | 5.5 | 4.2 | 161.1 | 83.9 | 45.2 | 50.1 |

**Pipeline Easement:** The property is encumbered with a 50-foot-wide MinnCAN crude oil pipeline easement that runs north to south through the midsection of the parcel. The published multiple listing information was explicit in disclosing the presence of the pipeline easement. The broker said that the buyer was aware of the pipeline but indicated that it did not play a role in the determination of the sale price or its use. The pipeline alignment aerial photo showing the placement of the easement on this property was shown previously.

### Exhibit 3
### (continued)

A summary of six comparable land sales in Sibley County, one encumbered with a MinnCAN pipeline easement and five unencumbered, illustrates and supports the conclusion that the pipeline easement had a minimal impact on the sale price of the encumbered property. These sales are summarized as follows:

#### Summary of Pipeline-Encumbered Land Sale vs. Comparable Unencumbered Sibley County Land Sales

| Comparable | PID/Address | Sale Date | Sale Price | Acres | $/Acre | % Tillable | Productivity Rating |
|---|---|---|---|---|---|---|---|
| | 13.2806.000 (Pipeline Encumbered)<br>210XX 291st Avenue<br>Section 29, Faxon Twp.<br>Sibley County, MN | Nov-08 | $551,526 | 107.51 | $5,130 | 91% | 82.5 |
| 1 | 13.1903.010<br>200XX 301st Avenue<br>Section 19, Faxon Twp.<br>Sibley County, MN | Jan-08 | $755,935 | 155.21 | $4,870 | 93% | 85.6 |
| 2 | 22.3601.000<br>440XX 330th Street<br>Section 36, Sibley Twp.<br>Sibley County, MN | Aug-06 | $470,000 | 120.00 | $3,917 | 95% | 94.1 |
| 3 | 13.3105.010 & 13.0601.010<br>314th Avenue & Faxon Road<br>Sections 6 & 31, Faxon Twp.<br>Sibley County, MN | Apr-06 | $358,000 | 89.65 | $4,000 | 78% | 85.4 |
| 4 | 13.3506.000<br>25888 Scenic Byway Road<br>Section 35, Faxon Twp.<br>Sibley County, MN | Jan-07 | $715,000 | 80.63 | $8,868 | 37% | 73.0 |
| 5 | 13.2905.030<br>295XX State Highway 25<br>Section 29, Faxon Twp.<br>Sibley County, MN | Jan-07 | $481,681 | 107.47 | $4,482 | 97% | 90.5 |
| | | | Comparable Average | | $5,227 | | |
| | | | Comparable Median | | $4,482 | | |

The summarized unencumbered comparable Sibley County sales range in sale dates from April 2006 to January 2008. After accounting for changing market conditions over time, soil productivity, percent tillable acreage, parcel size, and use, the comparable sale most similar to the MinnCAN pipeline-encumbered sale is Comparable 1, which was sold for $4,870 per acre. This compares to the MinnCAN pipeline-encumbered sale at $5,130 per acre. These two sales are most proximate in time (November 2008 versus January 2008), they are both located in Faxon Township, they have similar soil productivity (82.5 versus 85.6), and they are both mostly tillable acreage (91% versus 93%). A comparison of these unencumbered sales with this pipeline-encumbered sale confirms the remarks made by the broker that the presence of this pipeline easement on the sale parcel did not adversely influence the price of this sale comparable.

**Exhibit 4**

## Comparable Sale 2

### General Information

Source: Buyer and public records
Location: Section 6, Benton Township, Carver County
Address: 13760 114th Street, Benton Township
Sale date: July 1, 2004
Legal description: Lengthy, retained in file
PID number: 01-006-0600
Intended use: Agricultural

| Site Data | | Terms of Sale | |
|---|---|---|---|
| Parcel size: | 48.33 acres, 36 tillable | Buyer: | Richard M. Gorra |
| Zoning: | AG, agricultural | Seller: | Norman Schwich |
| Utilities: | No municipal services | Nominal price: | $540,000 |
| Topography: | Moderately rolling | Add'l consideration: | $0 |
| Access: | 114th Street | Total price: | $540,000 |
| | | Price per acre—gross/tillable: | $11,173/ $15,000 |

**Remarks:** This property includes both land and improvements. The property was not listed for sale, and the buyer knew the seller. The seller had originally asked for $550,000. Due to a necessary mound septic system, negotiations resulted in a sale price of $540,000. The land has a weighted average productivity rating of 80 from Surety Mapping/AgriData.

**Exhibit 4**

*(continued)*

## Soils Map

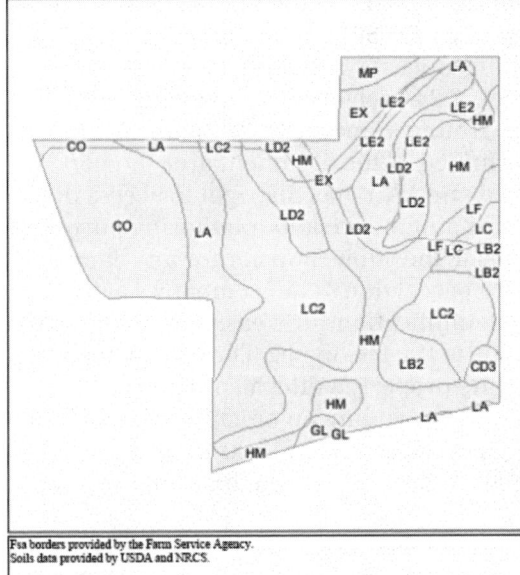

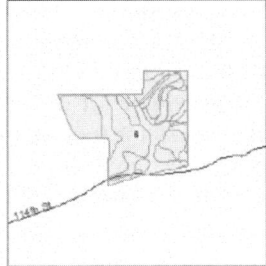

State: **MN**
County: **Carver**
Location: **6-115N-25W**
Township: **Benton**
Acres: **43.6**

© 2008 AgriData, Inc.
www.AgriDataInc.com

Fsa borders provided by the Farm Service Agency.
Soils data provided by USDA and NRCS.

| Code | Soil Description | Acres | Percent of field | Non-Irr Class | Productivity Index | Alfalfa hay | Barley | Corn | Oats | Soybeans | Spring wheat |
|---|---|---|---|---|---|---|---|---|---|---|---|
| LC2 | Lester loam, 6 to 12 percent slopes, eroded | 10.3 | 23.6% | IIIe | 82 | 4.3 | 75 | 161 | 75 | 45 | 48 |
| HM | Hamel loam | 10.0 | 22.9% | IIw | 94 | 0 | 90 | 184 | 90 | 52 | 56 |
| CO | Cordova clay loam | 6.5 | 14.9% | IIw | 87 | 0 | 90 | 171 | 90 | 48 | 55 |
| LA | Le Sueur-Lester loams, 1 to 4 percent slopes | 5.4 | 12.4% | Ie | 95 | 4.6 | 90 | 186 | 90 | 52 | 57 |
| LD2 | Lester loam, 12 to 18 percent slopes, eroded | 3.0 | 6.9% | IVe | 67 | 3.3 | 60 | 131 | 55 | 37 | 40 |
| LE2 | Lester loam, 18 to 25 percent slopes, eroded | 2.5 | 5.7% | VIe | 34 | 0 | 0 | 0 | 0 | 0 | 0 |
| LB2 | Lester loam, 2 to 6 percent slopes | 2.1 | 4.8% | IIe | 91 | 4.5 | 85 | 178 | 85 | 50 | 55 |
| EX | Essexville sandy loam | 1.4 | 3.2% | Vw | 30 | 0 | 60 | 0 | 55 | 0 | 40 |
| LF | Lester loam, 25 to 40 percent slopes | 0.6 | 1.4% | VIIe | 15 | 0 | 0 | 0 | 0 | 0 | 0 |
| MP | Klossner and Muskego soils, ponded | 0.6 | 1.4% | VIIIw | 5 | 0 | 0 | 0 | 0 | 0 | 0 |
| LC | Lester loam, 6 to 12 percent slopes | 0.5 | 1.1% | IIIe | 82 | 4.3 | 80 | 161 | 80 | 45 | 50 |
| CD3 | Lester clay loam, 12 to 18 percent slopes, severely eroded | 0.4 | 0.9% | IVe | 67 | 3.2 | 60 | 131 | 57 | 37 | 38 |
| GL | Glencoe clay loam | 0.3 | 0.7% | IIIw | 86 | 0 | 75 | 169 | 80 | 47 | 50 |
| | Weighted Average | | | | 80 | 2.1 | 75 | 150 | 74 | 42 | 47 |

**Pipeline Easement:** The property is encumbered with a Northern Natural Gas pipeline easement that runs diagonally across the tillable acreage from the northwest to the southeast. The buyer was aware of the pipeline but indicated that it did not play a role in the determination of the sale price or its use. The buyer indicated that the tillable acreage is leased, the tenant "loves" the land, and the pipeline has no impact on the agricultural use. The buyer indicated that the pipeline and easement may have an impact in the future if or when the property is developed.

## Permanent Easement Valuation

After the easement encumbrance and completion of the project, the subject property has a 50-foot-wide permanent easement area that crosses primarily north to south, entering at the middle of its west boundary line, crossing diagonally for 86 feet, and then turning due south for 998 feet before exiting at its south boundary line near the southwest corner of the parcel. A 24-inch crude oil pipeline is buried at least 4½ feet below the ground's surface in this area. While agricultural activities are permitted in the easement area, no permanent structures are allowed and MPL has the right to access the permanent easement area for maintenance and monitoring purposes. However, MPL must compensate the subject owner for any damage or loss anywhere on the entire parcel due to the company's activities.

Despite this and other indemnifications, the easement represents a certain loss of property rights to the fee owner. The easement, as a permanent encumbrance on the property's title, also represents a loss of certain less quantifiable rights, including an ongoing relationship with MPL (or its successors), perceived risk of leaks or spills, and the right of MPL to place above-ground structures such as bulk valves within the easement area.

Market evidence demonstrated that most buyers assigned little, if any, impact to the value or use of agricultural land due to underground pipeline easements. However, we acknowledge that most buyers—when presented with a choice between otherwise equal properties, one with an easement and one without—would prefer the property without an easement. This raised the question of why the market indicated neither a willingness to pay significantly more for an unencumbered property nor an insistence on paying significantly less for an encumbered property. This clearly and repeatedly demonstrated market behavior may be attributed to the following factors:

- Supply and demand
  The current market for agricultural properties is weighted more toward the demand side, with more buyers than available properties. In this environment, property attributes that are only relatively less desirable have minimal or no impact on marketability or price.

- Farmers as entrepreneurs
  Farmers are constantly evaluating the risks associated with changing conditions, such as weather, crop pricing, and costs for supplies and fuel. These factors may work for or against farmers, but they are unavoidable and accepted as part of farming. Against this risk-taking background, farmers perceive underground pipelines as a relatively minor risk.

- Underground pipelines are not rare
  Many farms and other property types have been encumbered with pipeline easements for decades. Farmers share experiences, including those associated with pipelines, with each other. Through these shared experiences, farmers realize that underground pipelines minimally affect their properties. History has shown that negative incidents associated with underground pipelines are infrequent, and occurrences have generally been well managed with no long-term impacts.

Given the loss of certain property rights with an easement encumbrance, we made a judgment as to the extent of damages based on the permanent easement's placement and configuration on the property and the amount of land encumbered.

An easement that closely follows a property's boundary line and does not extend into the usable or buildable area is considered to have less impact than an easement that might cross a parcel's midsection at an odd angle. For the subject property, the easement crosses the parcel, closely following its west boundary line from north to south before exiting near its southwest corner. In contrast, an easement that bisects a property's midsection and extends into the usable or buildable area is considered to have greater impact. The easement affecting the subject crosses the subject primarily within 79 feet of its west boundary line, from north to south, for a total of 1,084 feet.

The amount of the subject larger parcel land encumbered may be a factor in the consideration of any damage and diminution of market value to the remainder parcel. The subject property larger parcel contains 73.72 gross acres. Relative to the permanent easement area of 1.22 acres, this is 1.7% of the total area. Given the relatively small portion of the subject encumbered and the remaining rights of the fee owner to use the property in essentially the same manner as before the easement, we did not assign any damage due to the easement. Market evidence also supported the conclusion that there was no damage, as buyers in the market did not value properties with pipeline easements any differently than they valued properties without easements. Therefore, we estimated the value of the subject parcel in the after condition at $5,400 per acre, the same as in the before condition.

We estimated that the placement of the permanent easement on the subject property so that it follows the west boundary line of the parcel within 79 feet diminished the value of the permanent easement area by 80%. As a result, the landowner–who can farm this easement area–retained 20% of the land value, or about $1,080 per acre ($5,400 per acre × 20% = $1,080 per acre). The after-taking market value was calculated as shown in Exhibit 5.

### Exhibit 5

| Land Area in Acres | Times | Estimated Land Value per Acre | Equals | Indicated Market Value of Land |
|---|---|---|---|---|
| Unencumbered land: | | | | |
| 72.50 | × | $5,400 | = | $391,500 |
| Encumbered land: Proposed MinnCan pipeline easement land | | | | |
| 1.22 | × | $1,080 | = | $1,318 |
| Total land area: | | | | |
| 73.72 | | | | $392,818 |
| | | | | Rounded to |
| Indicated Market Value of Land—After the Taking: | | | | $393,000 |

The indication of value shown in Exhibit 5 does not account for the temporary easement, nor does it account for any crop loss within the permanent easement area.

### Temporary Easement Valuation

The larger parcel has a temporary construction easement encumbrance that encompasses 25 feet on either side of the 50-foot permanent easement, or 1.15 acres. The subject also has an extra temporary work space easements of 0.24 acre, which together with 1.15 acres of temporary easement equal a total of 1.39 acres in temporary easements. The temporary easements will be in place for approximately 15 months, from September 27, 2007, through December 31, 2008. We used the crop loss valuation method to estimate the value of the temporary easement.

For this particular pipeline project, an approved agricultural impact mitigation plan document provided for crop losses to be paid. The evaluation used to determine the temporary workspace easement value is not presented in this case study because it was specific to this project.

## Appraisal Summary

The total market value diminution due to the owner as a result of the partial taking of the permanent and temporary easements is summarized in Exhibit 6.

## Conclusions

The scope of this appraisal assignment included an inspection of the subject property and an interview with the owners regarding their concerns about the pipeline and easement. We also

- Interviewed real estate brokers active in this market
- Interviewed area assessors about their views on pricing and as-

### Exhibit 6

**Appraisal Summary: Brian Liebhard Property**
**297XX State Highway 25, Section 29, Faxon Twp., Sibley County**

|  | Indicated Market Value Before the Taking | Indicated Market Value After the Taking |
|---|---|---|
| Cost approach | N/A | N/A |
| Income approach | N/A | N/A |
| Sales comparison approach | $398,000 | $393,000 |
| Estimated market value | $398,000 | $393,000 |
| Diminution |  | $5,000 |
| Temporary easement/crop yield loss |  | $3,000 |
| **Indicated Just Compensation** |  | **$8,000** |

sessments of pipeline-encumbered parcels
- Interviewed buyers of similar parcels
- Viewed all phases of the construction of the subject pipeline
- Reviewed materials about the construction practices to be followed in this pipeline construction
- Interviewed buyers of pipeline-encumbered parcels for their views on the pricing impact of pipelines
- Performed a comparative analysis of a farm parcel that sold just after being encumbered by the subject project pipeline easement

Finally, one important lesson that I learned in the valuation process on this pipeline project was the power of geographic information systems, or GIS. When we received the lists of farm parcels that had sold and were encumbered by pipeline easements from the GIS officers, we were elevated from mere researchers to valuation analysts. Our work then became focused on confirming those sales, learning what we could from the market participants, and performing appraisal analysis of those sales. We found this sales data and the comments of the buyers and brokers involved in those pipeline-encumbered sales to be quite informative and persuasive.

## Paired Sales Showing Damages From Pipeline Easements

In this case study, analysis of the sales of comparable properties available for direct comparison with the farmland in Sibley County did not support a conclusion that the subject property suffered from substantial damages as a result of the presence of a pipeline easement on the property. However, data may lead an appraiser to an entirely different conclusion in another market at another time. For example, the two pairs of sales analyzed in this supplimental section of the case study illustrate other markets in the vicinity of the Twin Cities in which the presence of a pipeline easement substantially affected the market value of the parcels encumbered by the easement.

## Adjacent Nonurban Service Lot Comparison

These two single-unit, nonmunicipal service lots shown here are the same shape and size, are situated next to each other, and sold within seven months of each other. The two properties are very similar, except Sale 1B is encumbered by a natural gas transmission pipeline easement 43 feet in width that crosses the western portion of the parcel in a north-south direction. When we compared the sale prices of the two lots ($115,000 and $125,000), we saw that the pipeline-encumbered lot sold for about 8% less than the noneasement lot ($115,000 ÷ $125,000 = 0.9200, restated as -8.0%). The indicated discount before any adjustments for the pipeline easement was 8.0%. Note that this natural gas transmission pipeline easement was reopened in 2009 and a second pipeline was added within the original easement area.

### Sale 1A

| | |
|---|---|
| Location: | 11736 44th Str. Ln., Lake Elmo, MN |
| Sale date: | November 9, 2000 |
| Buyer: | Mary Miller |
| Parcel PID No.: | 12-029-21-42-0015 |
| Legal Desc.: | Lot 17, Block 1, The Fields of St. Croix, 2nd Addition in Washington County |
| Zoning: | Residential |
| Land area: | 0.9 acre |
| Utilities: | No municipal water or sewer |
| Sale price: | $125,000 |
| Sale price/acre: | $138,888 |

Remarks: Parcel has access off of 44th Street Lane North in Lake Elmo. Parcel has small natural gas transmission pipeline easement at very northwest corner, past the pond.

We also compared these two sales by making adjustments for any significant differences other than the natural gas transmission pipeline easement. There was a difference in sale dates of about seven months. Analyzing other market data, we concluded that Sale 1B, which sold in May 2001, should be adjusted for its later sale date when compared to Sale 1A, which sold in November 2000. We used an annual rate of price appreciation of 5% per year, which brings the sale price of Sale 1B to $112,125, as if it had sold on the same sale date as Sale 1A. Sale 1B is adjacent to an open space parcel to its west. (Half of the pipeline easement is on the open space parcel.) This adjacent open space adds value to this parcel, and we adjusted this sale price down 5% for the adjacent city-owned open space. As a result, Sale 1B as adjusted for market conditions (time adjustment) and proximity to city-owned open space indicates an adjusted sale price of $106,519. On its north boundary, Sale 1A is adjacent to privately owned, currently undeveloped land. This neighboring land to the north has future development potential. No other adjustments are considered necessary, as the parcels are the same size and have similar exposure, topography, and shape.

### Sale 1B

| | |
|---|---|
| Location: | 11730 44th Str. Ln., Lake Elmo, MN |
| Sale date: | May 18, 2001 |
| Buyer: | James/Tracy Bauer |
| Parcel PID No.: | 12-029-21-42-0016 |
| Legal Desc.: | Lot 18, Block 1, The Fields of St. Croix, 2nd Addition in Washington County |
| Zoning: | Residential |
| Land area: | 0.9 acre |
| Utilities: | No municipal water or sewer |
| Sale price: | $115,000 |
| Sale price/acre: | $127,777 |

Remarks: Parcel has access off of 44th Street Lane North in Lake Elmo. Parcel has a natural gas transmission pipeline easement that is 43 feet wide (part of 86-foot total pipeline easement) crossing in a north-south direction on the westerly part of the lot. The area to the west of the parcel is common area within this development.

The adjusted sale price of Sale 1B was $106,519, or about 14.8% less than the otherwise similar lot that only has this natural gas transmission easement at its extreme corner ($106,519 ÷ $125,000 = 0.8522, rounded and restated as 14.8%). After all adjustments, the estimated discount for the natural gas transmission pipeline easement was **14.8%**.

## Large Tract Parcels for Single-Unit Residential Subdivision Uses Comparison

The properties described below are both located in Monticello about one mile apart, south of interstate highway I-94, in very similar neighborhoods. They were purchased for development with single-unit residential subdivisions of 63 and 43 units. The two properties are very similar, except that Sale 2B is encumbered by a natural gas transmission pipeline easement that crosses diagonally through the western portion of the parcel in a northeast-southwest direction. When we compared the prices of the two parcels on a per-acre basis ($27,993 and $34,797), we saw that the pipeline-encumbered parcel sold for a price that was about 19.6% less than the noneasement parcel ($27,993 ÷ $34,797 = 0.8045, rounded to and restated as -19.6%). The indicated discount before any adjustments for the pipeline easement was 19.6%.

### Sale 2A

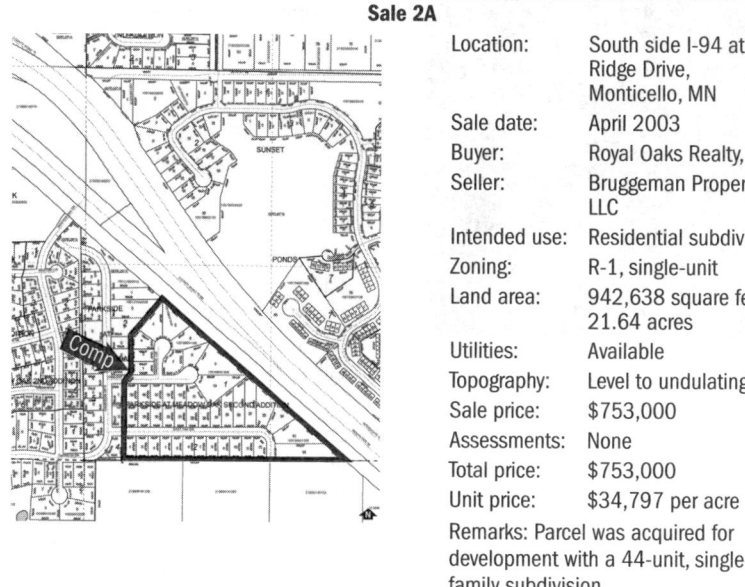

| | |
|---|---|
| Location: | South side I-94 at Oak Ridge Drive, Monticello, MN |
| Sale date: | April 2003 |
| Buyer: | Royal Oaks Realty, Inc. |
| Seller: | Bruggeman Properties, LLC |
| Intended use: | Residential subdivision |
| Zoning: | R-1, single-unit |
| Land area: | 942,638 square feet or 21.64 acres |
| Utilities: | Available |
| Topography: | Level to undulating |
| Sale price: | $753,000 |
| Assessments: | None |
| Total price: | $753,000 |
| Unit price: | $34,797 per acre |

Remarks: Parcel was acquired for development with a 44-unit, single-family subdivision.

Additionally, we compared these two sales by making adjustments for any significant differences other than the natural gas transmission pipeline easement. No adjustment for general location differences was warranted, nor was any adjustment needed for zoning, parcel size, or amenities. We did adjust for market conditions over time at an annual rate of 12%, based on an analysis of other market data. Sale 2A occurred in April 2003 and Sale 2B in September 2003. The market conditions (time) adjustment brought Sale 2A to $36,537 per acre, as if it had sold on the same date as Sale 2B. We also adjusted Sale 2A up 10% for its proximity to interstate freeway I-94, which caused the lots closest to the highway to be larger to provide some buffer. If the property had not been adjacent to I-94, another four to six lots would have been developable in that area. These two adjustments brought Sale 2A to $40,191 per acre, as if its location were identical to that of Sale 2B and it sold on the same date. The other significant difference was that Sale 2B is encumbered with an underground natural gas transmission pipeline easement running diagonally through the site, while Sale 2A has no such encumbrance. The effect of the pipeline easement according to the developer was

### Sale 2B

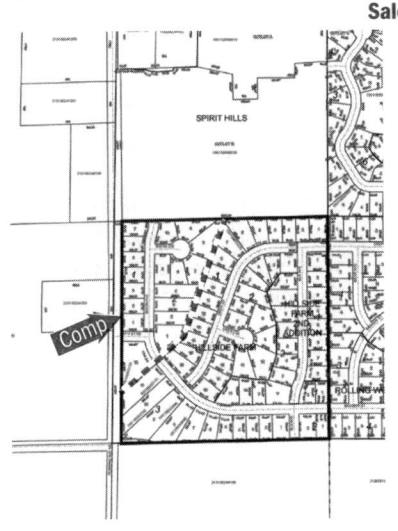

| | |
|---|---|
| Location: | East side Fenning Ave., Monticello, MN |
| Sale date: | September 2003 |
| Buyer: | Trison Development, Inc. |
| Seller: | James & Tarra Schultz |
| Intended use: | Residential subdivision |
| Zoning: | R-1, single-unit |
| Land area: | 1,742,400 square feet, or 40.00 acres |
| Utilities: | Available |
| Topography: | Level to undulating |
| Sale price: | $1,119,728 |
| Assessments: | None |
| Total price: | $1,119,728 |
| Unit price: | $27,993 per acre |

Remarks: Parcel was acquired for development with a 63-unit, single-family subdivision. Site is encumbered with an underground natural gas transmission pipeline easement running diagonally through the midsection of the parcel.

a reduction in the number of possible lots. The estimated price differential between the two sales was 30.4% ($27,993 ÷ $40,191 = 0.696, restated as -30.4%).

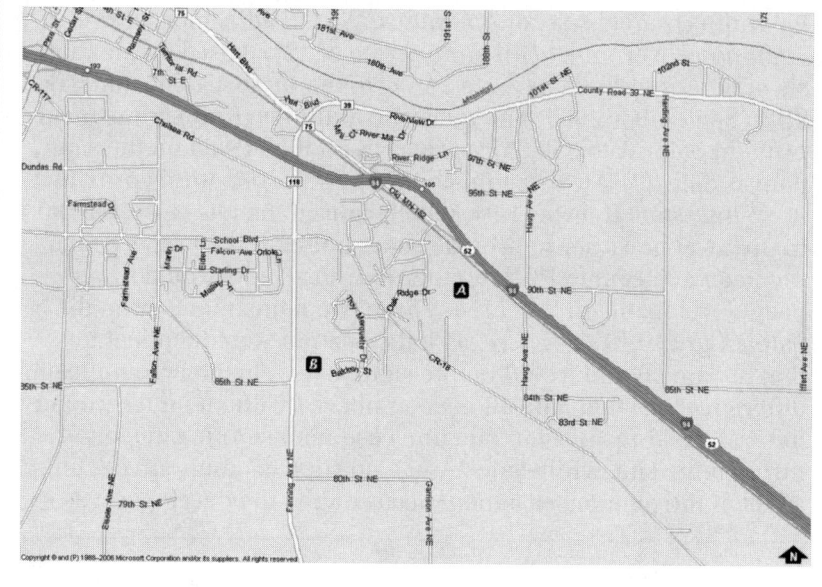

## Acknowledgments

The author of this case study would like to recognize the professional work of Warren Czaia, senior analyst with the Minneapolis/St. Paul office of Integra Realty Resources. He, along with others in our firm, completed the appraisals and consulting work on numerous parcels for this pipeline project.

CASE STUDY 1.4

# Partial Taking– Loss of Parking

*By Douglas W. Nitzkorski, MAI, SR/WA*

## The Assignment

This case study includes selected sections from an appraisal report that was prepared for an eminent domain project and a proposed partial acquisition for a street-widening project in Denver, Colorado. Colorado's constitution mandates that just compensation be paid for both the "taking and damaging" of property. The steps we took for this assignment were as follows:

1. Estimate the value of the total property (the larger parcel), ignoring the effect of the proposed project.
2. Estimate the value of the part taken as it contributes to the larger parcel.
3. Estimate the value of the remainder as part of the whole, ignoring the effect of the proposed project.
4. Estimate the value of the remainder after the acquisition, considering the effect of the project.
5. Determine damages or special benefits to the remainder based on the difference between items 3 and 4.

The client for this appraisal assignment was the property owner, and the condemning agency was the city and county of Denver. With federal funding involved, the Colorado Department of Transportation (CDOT) provided project oversight, including plan approval and appraisal review. The appraisal and report were prepared in conformity with the Uniform Relocation Assistance and Real Property Acquisition Policies Act of 1970, as amended.

## The Subject Market

The street-widening project for which the acquisition was required was located along a portion of Federal Boulevard in Denver, Colorado. The principal arterial in this neighborhood, Federal Blvd. (State Highway 88), extends for 20 miles, north to south, along the west side of the Denver metropolitan area. Roughly 43,000 vehicles a day were using this route at the time of the acquisition.

The area was considered a well-established commercial corridor made up of largely homogeneous properties. Building improvements were typically one-story commercial buildings that were 30 to 60 years old. Several properties were single-family units that had long since been converted to commercial uses. Some buildings were dated and obsolete. However, others received major rehabilitation, and a few were removed and replaced with modern structures.

The subject property was typical for the neighborhood. In this neighborhood, most properties included land areas of two to six lots (6,250 to 18,750 square feet), and building sizes ranged from about 1,200 to 8,000 square feet. Land value was relatively high and typically represented 40% to 50% of the total property value (even higher for the subject).

The neighborhood properties included a diverse range of retail uses. In addition to restaurants, small offices, retail stores, and beauty salons, other establishments included glass stores, auto repair and service, auto accessories and sound system sales, tire sales, and gas stations. These businesses served local transit-dependent residents as well as residents throughout the city.

Regardless of the type of business, this particular market accepted a very modest level of finish in commercial buildings. As a result, buildings were easily and commonly converted from one use to another with minimal renovation required to accommodate new tenants.

Because no street parking was available along Federal Blvd., vehicle access and parking were especially important to these local businesses. Many curb cuts allowed for direct access to the properties and secondary access through the alleys. However, the sidewalks in this commercial corridor were narrow and not considered to be pedestrian friendly because they were adjacent to the traveled roadway. Not only were the pedestrian crossings limited, they were also spaced nearly a half mile apart.

Most of the properties along this corridor had limited off-street parking, and what limited parking there was could often be found at the front of the property. With limited spaces available on side streets, the off-street parking was very valuable to property owners in the neighborhood. Any loss in the number of already limited parking spaces could result in a loss in property value. While a quick glance at the project plans revealed that the subject would lose only four parking spaces, this could present a problem for the remainder after the acquisition in this particular market.

# The Subject Property–Larger Parcel (Before)

In eminent domain, three conditions provide guidance in establishing the larger parcel for the consideration of compensable damages and special benefits:

- Unity of ownership
- Physical contiguity
- Unity of use

In this case, identification of the larger parcel was very clear and included the entire property.

The subject site was rectangular and located in the middle of the block. The site was level, with 100 feet of frontage along the east side of South Federal Blvd., and had a total land area of 14,369 square feet. The site was zoned B-4, general commercial district, a desirable zoning classification that allows for a wide range of commercial uses.

The site is improved with a 3,840-sq.-ft., one-story building and a small, detached utility/storage building at the rear of the property. The primary building was 35 years old at the time of appraisal. The building was an L-shaped steel structure that included a sale and display area as well as a shop area (accessed from the rear alley). The property was used for the sale and installation of automobile accessories.

The property had a land-to-building area ratio of 3.74:1 and a total of 12 off-street parking spaces–including nine located in front of and along the side of the building and three more, located behind the L-shaped building for employees. For this analysis, the unit of comparison we used was parking spaces per 1,000 square feet of building area, or PPK. The subject property before the taking had a parking ratio of 3.12 PPK ((12 spaces/3,840 square feet) × 1,000).

# Purpose, Property Rights, and Effective Date

The purpose of this appraisal was to develop an estimate of the total value lost due to the taking, which would comprise the following:

1. The reasonable market value of the property actually taken
2. Compensable damages, if any, to the remainder parcel after the taking
3. Special benefits, if any, to the remainder parcel after the taking

The real property interest in the subject larger parcel before the taking, the part taken, and the remainder after the taking were valued as fee simple title. The effective date of value was April 30, 2009, and the date of the appraisal report was May 10, 2009.

## Highest and Best Use–Larger Parcel (Before)

The highest and best use of the subject land as if vacant was judged to be for commercial development, conforming to zoning regulations and similar to surrounding land uses. This conclusion provided a basis for the selection of land sales to be used for direct comparison with the subject site. The highest and best use of the property as improved was judged to be for continued use of the building under its current, or a similar, use.

## Value Reconciliation–Larger Parcel (Before)

Three approaches were used to value the larger parcel, and befor value indications from each approach were developed:

| | |
|---|---|
| Cost approach: | $516,300 |
| Sales comparison approach: | $499,200 |
| Income capitalization approach: | $503,300 |

### Land Valuation

Eight land sales along Federal Blvd. with the same zoning as the subject provided a solid basis for estimating the value of the subject land. The raw land sales data included unit values ranging from about $21 to $35 per square foot. Adjustments were made, and the land value was estimated at $27 per square foot, or $388,000.

### Cost Approach

The subject building was 35 years old and the total estimated depreciation was quite high, which is often a good reason to omit the cost approach. However, the land value estimate was very well supported with eight sales along Federal Blvd., and land value represented more than 75% of the total property value. Therefore, the value indication by the cost approach was considered and provided support for the other two approaches.

### Sales Comparison Approach

Five improved sales were selected for direct comparison with the subject property. Relatively modest adjustments adequately reflected the differences between the sales and the subject. As a result, the sales comparison approach provided a meaningful indicator of value. The indicated value by the sales comparison approach was $130 per square foot, or $499,200.

### Income Capitalization Approach

On the date of value, the subject property was leased to a tenant who used the building for the sale and installation of automotive accessories. The property had been leased to the same tenant for 10 years, with no adjustment in the rental rate. As a result, the contract rent was well below the estimated market rent.

Five comparable rental properties were selected for analysis to estimate the market rent ($13 per square foot) for the subject, and actual expenses were available. The resulting estimated net operating income was well supported. Overall capitalization rates were extracted from five sold properties to provide a basis for estimating the appropriate capitalization rate for the subject. The indicated value by the income capitalization approach was $503,300.

### Conclusion of Value

The sales comparison and income capitalization approaches were considered to be the most meaningful. Our opinion of the market value of the larger parcel before the taking as of April 30, 2009, was $500,000. The total estimated value was allocated as follows:

| | |
|---|---|
| Land value: | $388,000 |
| Improvements value: | $112,000 |

## The Project

This $30 million roadway improvement project involves improvements to Federal Blvd. from Alameda Avenue to West Sixth Avenue in the western portion of Denver. A third northbound lane will be added, resulting in a total of three 11-foot-wide traffic lanes in each direction. A 16-foot-wide raised median will also be constructed (see Exhibit 1).

While the median will be open at many intersections, the removal of the existing center turn lane will prevent traffic from directly accessing many businesses. Access will generally become more restrictive, resulting in new local travel patterns. In Colorado, as in many jurisdictions, a change in access is not a compensable loss unless the change meets the threshold of "substantial impairment of access." The change in access to the subject property did not meet that threshold.

Eight-foot-wide pedestrian amenity zones will be built on each side of Federal Blvd., adjacent to the traffic lanes. These will include a three-foot buffer strip and a five-foot sidewalk. A cross section of the proposed improvement is shown in Exhibit 2.

## The Acquisition

Identified on the right-of-way plans as Parcel 9, the acquisition from the subject property was a fee taking of a strip along the front of the site (Federal Blvd. frontage). The parcel taken was a near rectangle, about 8.5 feet deep, along the entire 100-foot front of the property. The total land area of Parcel 9 was 868 square feet. Site improvements

Exhibit 1

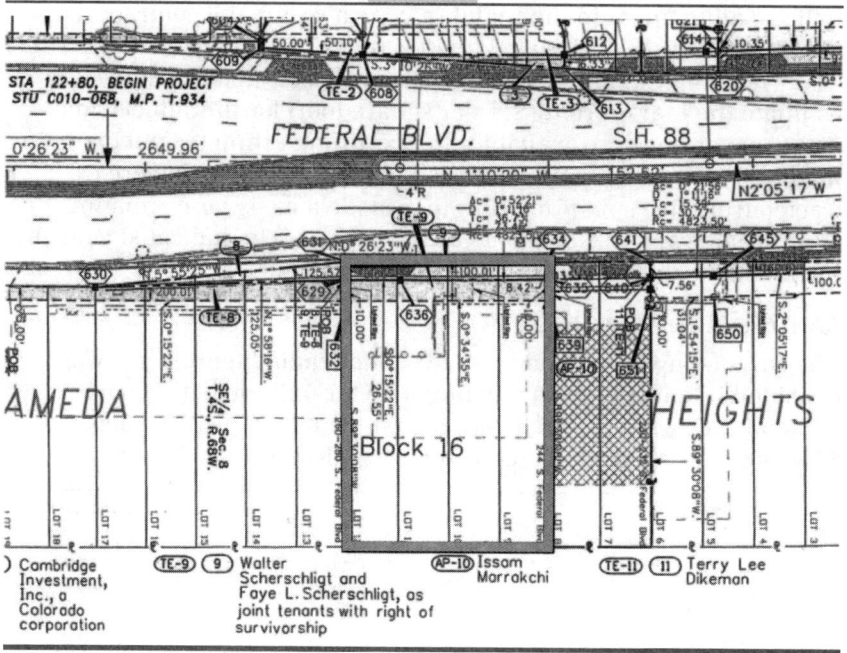

Exhibit 2

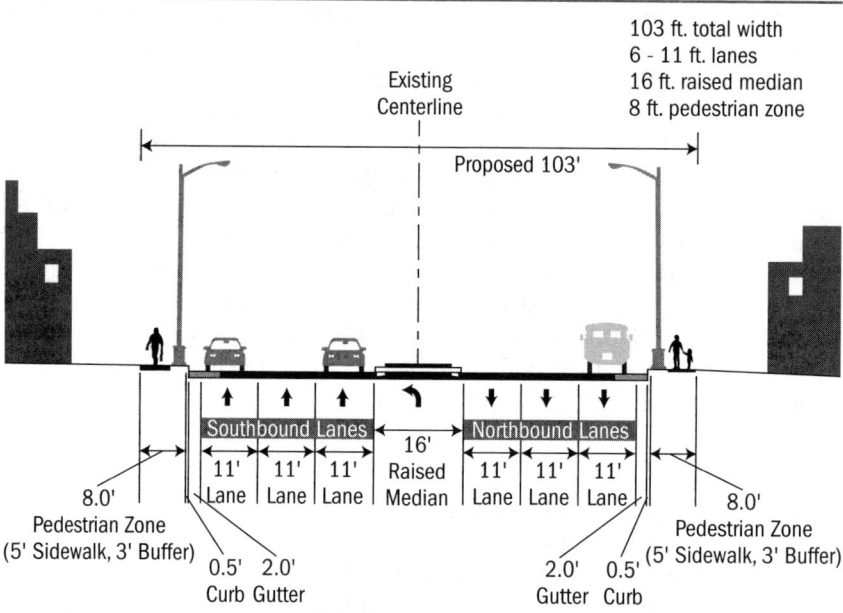

located within the area taken included concrete and asphalt paving as well as an on-premises sign.

## Allocation Between the Part Taken and the Remainder (Before)

### Land Value of the Part Taken

The subject larger parcel land was valued at $27 per square foot. The part to be acquired contributed on a pro rata basis. Therefore, the portion of the land to be acquired in fee was also valued at $27 per square foot.

> Estimated value of land taken: 868 square feet @ $27 = $23,400

### Improvements' Contributory Value of the Part Taken

The improvements within the taking were valued at a total of $7,500: $3,500 for the concrete and asphalt paving and $4,000 for the on-premises sign. (In Colorado, an on-premises sign is considered real property.) The contributory value of the affected improvements was estimated by use of depreciated costs and by consultation with a professional sign company.

> Estimated value of the improvements taken: $7,500

### Total Value of the Part Taken

The total value of the part taken is as follows:

> Land: $23,400
> Improvements: 7,500
> Total value of the part taken: $30,900

## Value of the Remainder (Before)

The next step in allocating the total value of the larger parcel between the part taken and the remainder is calculating the value of the remainder before the taking. This step is simple:

> Larger parcel value: $500,000
> Less value of part taken: − 30,900
> Value of the remainder (before): $469,100

## Description of the Subject Property– Remainder (After)

As a result of the acquisition, the land area of the subject property will be reduced by about 6%, from 14,369 to 13,501 square feet. The building setback will be reduced from about 20 feet to about 11.5 feet. By itself, the change in proximity to the street will not impair the building's use or value. The rental and sales data collected for this assignment relate to properties with wide-ranging setbacks, from near zero to over 50 feet. However, no apparent relationship between proximity and values or rents exists.

Before the acquisition, the property had 12 parking spaces for a parking ratio of 3.12 PPK. After the acquisition, the number of parking spaces will be reduced to eight. The resulting parking ratio is 2.08 PPK. The acquisition will eliminate head-in parking. After the acquisition, only one space directly in front of the building and four spaces in the "nook" of the L-shaped building will remain. The three parking spaces behind the building will not be affected.

The function, use, and value of the building will be affected by the project because of the reduction in parking. The magnitude of that loss is based on a parking analysis used in the valuation of the remainder (after).

## Highest and Best Use–Remainder Parcel (After)

Before the acquisition, the highest and best use of the property was continued use for the sale and installation of automotive accessories. In the after condition, the highest and best use remains the same but the reduction in off-street parking at the property will reduce its appeal and marketability. The City and County of Denver have a long-standing policy stating that if a property, as a result of eminent domain action, becomes nonconforming, the property may continue to operate as a legal, nonconforming use. Only upon redevelopment will the property have to comply with zoning requirements existing at that time. Therefore, continued use of the property was allowed. Numerous examples of similar legal, nonconforming uses were evident in the neighborhood.

## Value of the Remainder (After)

While a quick glance at the project plans revealed that the subject would lose only four parking spaces, this actually reflects a loss of one-third of the existing spaces for this property, which could present a problem.

The key to the valuation of the subject remainder property was to judge the diminution, if any, to the remaining property as a result of the acquisition and the reduction in parking in particular. In order to analyze the impact of reduced parking, a study was undertaken to learn if any correlation between parking ratios and unit prices or rental rates existed.

### Market Norm for Parking

At certain levels of parking availability, adding or losing a space may have no diminution whatsoever to the remaining property. However, the property value may be affected significantly when there are severe space limitations.

For this analysis, the unit of comparison was based on the number of parking spaces relative to the size of the building. The number of parking spaces per 1,000 square feet of building area (PPK) was used for comparative purposes.

Parking requirements are typically established by city zoning regulations and represent the minimum parking requirements. To establish a starting point, we consulted Denver zoning regulations. The minimum parking requirements were established for developing new commercial property in the B-4 zoned neighborhood.

The requirements usually vary depending on the use of the property. For example, the parking requirements for retail properties are one space for every 200 square feet of gross building area. This equates to 5 PPK ($1/200 \times 1,000$). In comparison, the parking requirement for auto repair facilities is one space per 300 square feet of gross building area, or 3.3 PPK. For office use, the requirement is one space per 500 square feet of gross building area, or 2 PPK.

However, this particular area was unique despite the parking requirements established. Because the subject neighborhood included a variety of retail, office, and service structures and because it was not uncommon for buildings to be converted from one use to another between tenant occupancies, there was no clear trend regarding parking availability and current use. As a result, no distinction was made among the various uses relative to the market's acceptance of parking.

A sample of properties in the neighborhood revealed typical parking ratios for existing properties. After the extremes were eliminated, most properties had parking ratios between 2 and 7 PPK. Properties exceeding a parking ratio of 7 generally included small buildings or relatively large land areas. A parking ratio of 7 clearly exceeded the highest requirement of 5 PPK that was established by zoning.

After careful analysis, we concluded that a parking ratio of 5 PPK was adequate for any use within that neighborhood and additional parking beyond 5 PPK would not add significant incremental value. This conclusion was also supported by an analysis of the relationship between PPK and rental rates or sale prices per square foot. In any event, the subject parking ratio was less than 5 PPK both before and after the acquisition.

## The Data

In order to analyze the relationship between parking ratios and values, both rental rates and sale prices were measured relative to the PPK for each property and adjusted for market conditions to the date of valuation. The rental rates were further adjusted for lease terms. Sold or leased properties with unusually large or small land or building areas were eliminated, along with properties with parking ratios that exceeded 6 PPK. While many factors influenced rental rates and sale prices, the comparable data available were filtered to include the 16 rental comparables and 16 sales comparables that were most similar, which were then plotted on graphs.

These data were not adjusted for noted property differences, such as age, condition, quality, or size. If modest judgmental adjustments had been made for such elements, the trend lines would not be materially affected but the data would be less dispersed. For the purpose of this discussion, we will use the raw data, adjusted only for time and lease terms. The relationships between unit prices and PPK and rental rates and PPK were quite similar, as shown in the two charts in Exhibit 3.

## The Market Evidence

The graphs in Exhibit 3 illustrate that changes in parking availability have a very similar impact on prices and rental rates. Of particular interest is the consistency of the trend line reflecting the impact on values and rents when the parking ratio falls between 1 and 5 PPK. The data in these graphs allows the measurement of changes in values and rents as parking ratios are reduced or increased. Exhibit 4 summarizes the observed changes in rental rates and unit prices as PPK is reduced below 5.

As parking ratios fall below 5 PPK, the diminution in value is measurable. When PPK is reduced from 5 to 4 (a 20% decrease in parking), rental rates decline by 8% and prices decline by 7%. When PPK is reduced from 4 to 3 (a 25% decrease in parking), rental rates decline by 10% and prices decline by 9%. The rate of decline in price and rental rate increases as parking nears zero. When the parking ratio is reduced from 5 spaces to 1 space per 1,000 square feet of building area, rental rates are reduced by 49% and the unit prices are reduced by 51%.

In essence, it becomes very difficult to find a tenant if a property has less than one parking space per 1,000 square feet of building area. With a reduction in parking from adequate (5 PPK) to almost none (1 PPK), the indicated diminution in property value is about 50%. With land value representing 50% or more of property value in the neighborhood, this study suggests that the contributory value of the improvements may be reduced to near zero as the number of parking spaces approaches zero. A clear relationship between off-street parking and value is indicated by this analysis.

## Anecdotal Evidence

Recently, when faced with very limited parking (1.6 PPK), one of the local property owners within this project area chose to demolish a portion of his building when the only resulting benefit was to increase the amount of off-street parking at the property. The building included

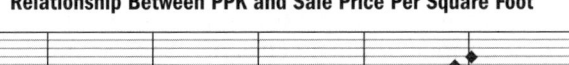

### Exhibit 3

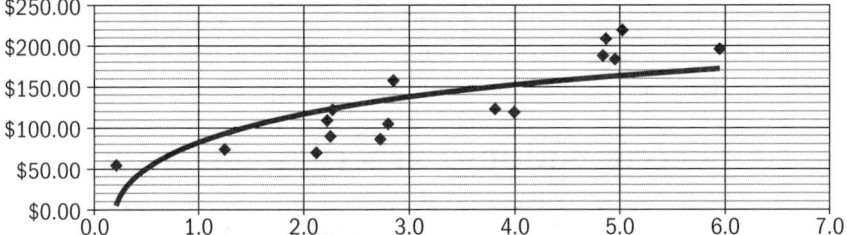

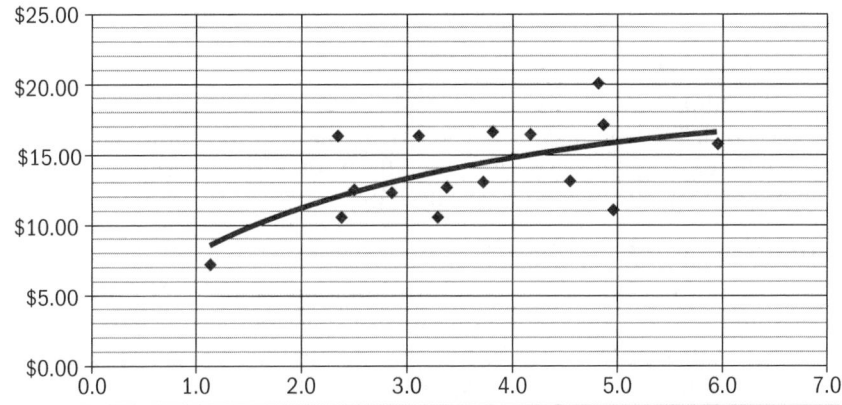

### Exhibit 4

| Parking Change | | | Rental Rate Change | | | Unit Price Change | | |
| --- | --- | --- | --- | --- | --- | --- | --- | --- |
| From | to | as % | From | to | as % | From | to | as % |
| 5.0 | 4.0 | -20% | $15.80 | $14.60 | -8% | $162 | $150 | -7% |
| 4.0 | 3.0 | -25% | $14.60 | $13.20 | -10% | $150 | $137 | -9% |
| 3.0 | 2.0 | -33% | $13.20 | $11.30 | -14% | $137 | $117 | -15% |
| 2.0 | 1.0 | -50% | $11.30 | $8.00 | -29% | $117 | $80 | -32% |

both retail and office space, with a total building area of 2,527 square feet. By removing the front 417 square feet of the office portion of the property, parking was increased from 1.6 PPK to 2.8 PPK.

The loss of 17% of the building area, plus the cost of demolition, was seen as a fair price to pay to increase off-street parking from 1.6 PPK to 2.8 PPK. The owner's opinion that his property value would be enhanced is supported by the data, which suggests that the unit value of his property may have increased from about $100 per square foot for the original 2,527 square feet with 1.6 PPK to about $130 per square foot for his smaller building of 2,110 square feet with 2.8 PPK.

In researching the market data within this particular project area, we had discussions with many property owners, buyers, sellers, tenants, and brokers. Almost universally, the topic of parking was prominently mentioned while discussing property attributes. Parking issues in this neighborhood clearly influence decisions regarding purchase, tenancy, renovation, and new developments.

## Value Reconciliation–Larger Parcel (After)

Two approaches were used to value the remainder parcel after the taking, and value indications from each approach were developed:

| | |
|---|---|
| Sales comparison approach: | $430,000 |
| Income capitalization approach: | $430,300 |

### Land Valuation

The 6% reduction in land size did not result in a different unit value for the land. The remainder parcel was valued at the same $27 per square foot as the larger land parcel. Remainder land value was estimated at $27 per square foot, or $364,500.

### Cost Approach

The cost approach was not used in valuing the remainder property. A functional obsolescence adjustment would be required because of the parking shortage. This loss was best measured by the sales comparison and income capitalization approaches.

### Sales Comparison Approach

The same five improved sales used to value the larger parcel were again used to value the remainder after the taking. The parking analysis provided a solid basis for adjusting the sales for parking adequacy. The trend lines in the graphs indicate a reduction in unit price from about $138.56 to $118.60 (about -14%), as the parking ratio is reduced from 3.12 to 2.08. The adjustment for parking ratio was changed to reflect this difference. The sales comparison approach indicated a unit value of $112 per square foot of building, or $430,000.

### Income Capitalization Approach

In the income capitalization approach, market rent for the remainder was estimated at $11.50 per square foot, based on rental comparables with parking ratios between 2 and 2.5 PPK, which were deemed most comparable to the subject. Market rent had been estimated for the larger parcel at $13 per square foot, based on rental comparables with parking ratios between 2.5 and 3.7 PPK. The indicated value of the remainder after the acquisition by the income capitalization approach was $430,300.

## Conclusion of Value

The value indications by the sales comparison and income capitalization approaches were nearly identical. Our opinion of the market value of the remainder property after the taking as of April 30, 2009, was $430,000.

The total estimated value was allocated as follows:

| | |
|---|---|
| Land value: | $364,500 |
| Value of improvements: | $65,500 |

## Indicated Damages to the Remainder

A comparison between the value of the remainder property before the taking and the value of the remainder property after the taking provides a measure of the damages to the remainder property:

| | |
|---|---|
| Estimated value of the remainder before the taking: | $469,100 |
| Estimated value of the remainder after the taking: | $430,000 |
| **Indicated damages to the remainder:** | **$39,100** |

## Conclusions

The value conclusions are summarized as follows:

**Valuation Summary**

| | |
|---|---|
| Larger parcel before the taking | $500,000 |
| Part taken | $30,900 |
| Remainder value before the taking | $469,100 |
| Remainder value after the taking | $430,000 |
| Indicated damages to the remainder | $39,100 |

This appraisal required a method of analyzing the relationship between off-street parking and unit values. Nearly all of the comparable data reflected parking ratios between 2 and 5 PPK. The subject property also fell within that range, both before and after the acquisition.

The data provided a reasonable basis for adjusting comparable sales and comparable rents for differences in parking ratios, both for the larger parcel before the taking and for the remainder property after the taking. The difference between the value of the remainder parcel before and the value of the remainder parcel after represented the damages to the remainder resulting from the acquisition and particularly from the reduction in parking.

The sales data and rental data analyses provided evidence of a clear correlation between parking ratios and values. As parking ratios declined, particularly below 5 PPK, a value decline was evident. The credibility of these results is bolstered by the case study wherein a property owner chose to demolish a portion of his building with the sole intent of creating more parking spaces and increasing his overall property value. Discussions with many market participants offered further support for the notion that parking is very important in this neighborhood and drives value to some degree.

It is nearly impossible to isolate the parking ratio as a lone variable to measure the value difference between any two properties. While these data do not provide a perfect fit, the trend lines between prices and rents are quite consistent and provide persuasive evidence of a diminution in value attributed to diminished parking. This type of analysis can provide an appraiser with a reasoned basis for estimating the degree of value diminution attributed to lost parking.

The total value reduction supported by the parking study was $18 per square foot (about -14%). This total reduction in value included both the part taken and the severance damages to the remainder. In this case, the acquiring agency reviewed our appraisal and offered the property owner compensation based upon our conclusions. The case settled quickly.

### Acknowledgments
The author of this case study would like to recognize the professional work of John F. Derungs, MAI. Mr. Derungs contributed to the preparation of the appraisal that served as the basis for this case study.

### CASE STUDY 1.5

# Permanent Easement– Access

*By L. Burl Wilson Jr., MAI*

This case study involves estimating the market value of a permanent easement acquired to provide access to a commercial condominium adjacent to a replacement bridge that is to be constructed on the island of Venice in Sarasota County, Florida. The condemning authority contacted our firm requesting a second appraisal of the parcel for litigation purposes.

The easement had already been acquired through an order of taking, but settlement negotiations were futile.[1] The Florida Department of Transportation (FDOT) had wanted to provide sloped driveway access to the original parking lot in a temporary construction easement (TCE). However, the owners' attorney filed a motion petitioning the court to rule that the taking was a permanent easement because permanent improvements were to be installed in the easement area. The presiding judge ruled in their favor. Ancillary to this petition was that business damages are limited in a TCE but not in a permanent taking under Florida law (*Wiggles Banana Boat v. FDOT*).

After discussions with the client, we determined that we could meet the court-mandated deadlines and agreed to accept the assignment.

## Description of the Subject Property

Through information provided by the client, public record research, and information provided through discovery, we learned that the larger parcel was a recorded condominium called Hamilton Square containing eleven units in two buildings, with a parking area between the buildings. Units A to E were in the south building, while Units F to K were in the north building. All units were part of the larger parcel. Exhibit 1 shows a floor plan of the property, and Exhibit 2 breaks down the square footage of each unit. Several photographs of the property are also provided.

---

1. The Florida Department of Transportation can take title and possession in advance of a final judgment by filing a declaration of taking based on the approved estimate of value and depositing that amount into the court. This is commonly called a "quick taking." See J. D. Eaton, *Real Estate Valuation in Litigation*, 2nd ed. (Chicago: Appraisal Institute, 1995) for more information on larger parcel issues.

### Exhibit 1

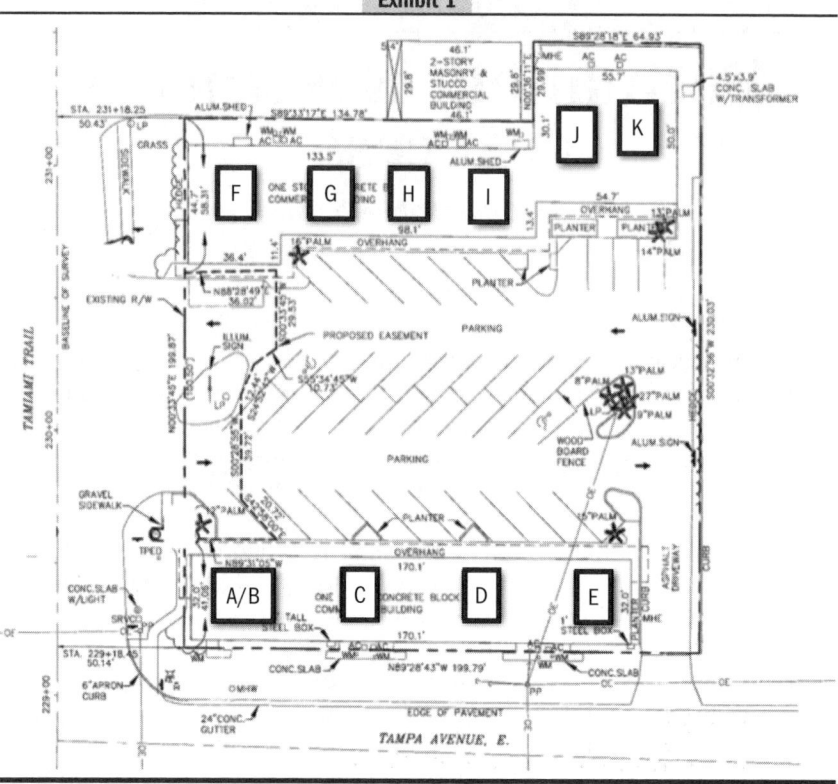

### Exhibit 2

| South Building | Size (Interior) | North Building | Size (Interior) |
|---|---|---|---|
| Unit A/B | 2,058 sq. ft. | Unit F | 1,504 sq. ft. |
| Unit C | 1,026 sq. ft. | Unit G | 1,049 sq. ft. |
| Unit D* | 1,031 sq. ft. | Unit H | 1,033 sq. ft. |
| Unit E* | 1,017 sq. ft. | Unit I* | 1,021 sq. ft. |
| Total | 5,132 sq. ft. | Unit J | 1,318 sq. ft. |
| | | Unit K | 1,313 sq. ft. |
| | | Total | 7,238 sq. ft. |

\* Indicates units that were no longer part of the lawsuit but were included in the valuation of the larger parcel.

*Permanent Easement–Access*

The larger parcel's site area was determined to be 41,897 square feet, with a taking of 2,832 square feet in the form of a permanent easement. All of the units were appraised inclusive of the common area. However, the owners of three units had settled with the condemning authority and were no longer part of the suit, although the units remained part of the larger parcel. These owners were not entitled to additional compensation regardless of the lawsuit's results.

Two of the units (A and B) had been combined into a single unit under the same ownership. In some instances multiple units were under the same ownership but were not combined. Even though some of the unit owners had settled with the condemning authority, it was considered necessary to value all of the units in the larger parcel prior to the allocation of value to the units involved in the suit.

The existing parking prior to the acquisition consisted of 41 angled parking spaces. The number of spaces required by code was dependent on the use. The code requirements for the most likely uses in the center are shown in the following table:

| Site Use | Parking Requirements |
|---|---|
| Office | 1 space per 200 sq. ft. of nonstorage area |
| Medical office | 1 space per 150 sq. ft. of nonstorage area |
| Commercial/service | 1 space per 400 sq. ft. of nonstorage area plus one space for each vehicle based at the site |
| Retail | 1 space per 300 sq. ft. |

The center generally met the requirements for the number of parking spaces given this broad range of required parking, although the parking was nonconforming due to the required parking circulation into the existing right of way and substandard handicap spaces. Circulation issues were considered to create a functional problem. (See Exhibit 1.) This functional problem was considered curable, with the cure costing an estimated $4,023. It required deletion of one parking space, leaving a remainder of 40 parking spaces for the center. The resulting parking ratio of one space per 309 square feet of interior building area was considered substandard based on the current zoning code and uses on the site. This was considered in the appraisal.

The overall market in the Sarasota County area was somewhat stratified. Sales of properties on the barrier islands typically indicated values higher than those found elsewhere in the county. Properties sold in the city of Sarasota generally indicated higher values than those in other inland areas. Sales in the city of Venice indicated values slightly below those in the city of Sarasota.

The property was located at the outskirts of the Venice central business district (CBD). Uses in the area included those oriented towards tourism, including gift shops, clothing stores, and restaurants.

There was also a commercial office presence and various cultural amenities reflective of the coastal area. Land values were strong in the area, recognizing the absorption of most of the available vacant land in the nearby CBD. Few substitute properties were available in the area. The typical range of value for such land was $10 to $16 per square foot. The value of a specific property was dependent on location, size, access, and shape. All typical utilities were available on the island.

The values indicated by the sales of commercial improved properties followed the same stratification as the land sales. Vacancies were generally low. The indicated sale price per square foot for similar commercial properties ranged from $56 to $109.80 per square foot, depending on the age and condition of each property. Most similar properties indicated a range in value from $56 to $85 per square foot of building area. Location was an important component in the prices paid for such properties. Other factors influencing value were access and exposure, building quality and age, parking, and finish.

Leases in the area indicated rents ranging from $9 to $14.75 per square foot for competing properties, with higher rates paid in the Sarasota CBD. These rents were primarily on an adjusted gross basis, with tenants paying for utilities and normal interior maintenance. This is considered a gross rent in the central Florida area because all outside maintenance, major repairs (such as air-conditioning units and plumbing), real estate taxes, insurance, and management are paid by the landlord. The quality of interior unit finish affected the rent rates, as did the unit size, the location of the unit within the center, and the location of the center itself. Because the property was a condominium, the bulk of the other expenses were charged as a condominium association maintenance (CAM) fee.

The general market area showed a wide variety of vacancy rates, with the subject at 9% vacancy as of the date of value. The project was anticipated to be of general benefit to the neighborhood because it would ease traffic congestion in the area by decreasing the number of bridge openings obstructing traffic. Traffic in the before condition was a particular problem during the high season winter months. The anticipation of decreased traffic congestion resulted in a value enhancement to the prop-

> **state rule.** The process of determining just compensation by estimating the value of the portion to be acquired as a part of the whole property plus the net severance damages; may be referred to as a *taking plus damages rule.* (*The Dictionary of Real Estate Appraisal*, 5th ed.)
>
> **general benefits.** The benefits that accrue to the community at large as a result of the new public work and the increased general prosperity that accompanies development. (*The Dictionary of Real Estate Appraisal*, 5th ed.)
>
> In Florida, **special benefits** are generally interpreted to be benefits to a specific property due to a project. They may be used to offset damages.

erty.[2] This was applied as the property was being appraised under the state rule.

The project's perceived general benefit to the property was a higher occupancy rate after completion. Therefore, a 5% rate was considered reasonable for the property. This was not a special benefit. The commercial market was considered generally strong in the area, with some variance based on location.

## Description of the Project

The proposed road project was intended to improve the section of US 41 north of Tampa Avenue to include four driving lanes, including an extension over the Hatchett Creek Bridge. There was to be a concrete center median extending from just north of Tampa Avenue to just north of the bridge. Along the US 41 frontage of the subject property, concrete curbing and gutters with drop curbs defining two one-way driveways would be installed. There was also to be a concrete sidewalk located between the subject property line and the edge of the pavement on US 41. Hatchett Creek Bridge was to be raised to approximately 30 feet, decreasing the frequency of openings for boat traffic. There would be a striped center turning lane south of the bridge for shared east-west egress from US 41. In addition to the two northbound and southbound lanes, the portions of US 41 at the intersection of Tampa Avenue and US 41 South would have appropriate turning lanes similar to what existed as of the date of value. Exhibit 3 provides an aerial view of Sarasota County showing the completed project area. Exhibit 4 shows the project plans for the property.

The change in road elevations at the front of the property would be approximately 0.7 feet at the south end of the property, rising to approximately 8.8 feet at the extreme north end of the property, past the northernmost building. North of the driveways, a mechanically stabilized earthwork would begin approximately 10 feet inside the right of way (R/W) line. At the R/W line, the north drive would be about 3.2 feet above existing grade. The south drive would be about 2 feet above existing grade. Both would slope at 10%. The length of the new drives was to be about 17.8 feet on the south driveway and 32.7 feet on the north driveway. The two drives would be at a 10% grade, with a drainage inlet within the easement area accepting the site's stormwater. Between the drives would be a sodded area at a 12% slope. This slope was to be mowable by conventional methods. No gravity walls would be built between these drives. The condemning authority would do all the needed construction within the easement

---

2. Under the typical interpretation of Florida law, any benefit to a property that occurs prior to the date of filing of the resolution authorizing condemnation of a property should be considered in the valuation of the property.

**Exhibit 3**

**Exhibit 4**

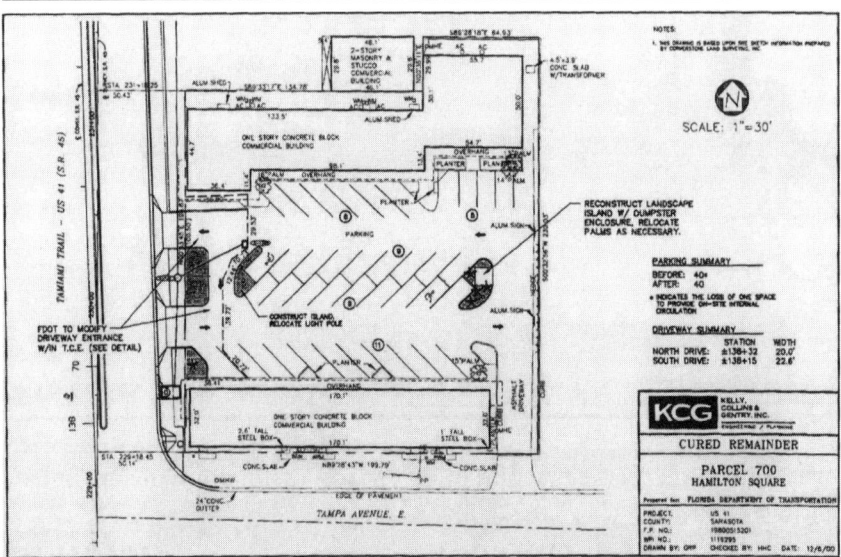

*Permanent Easement–Access*

**Exhibit 4**

*(continued)*

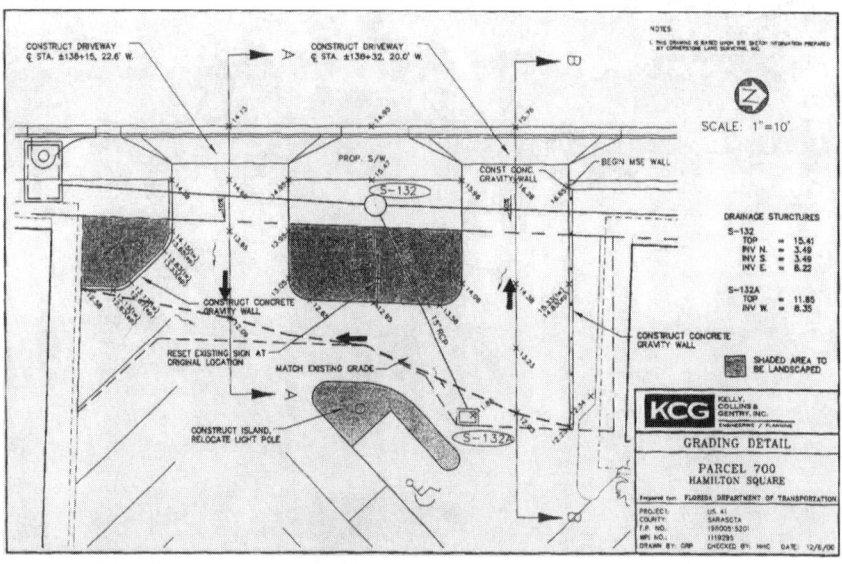

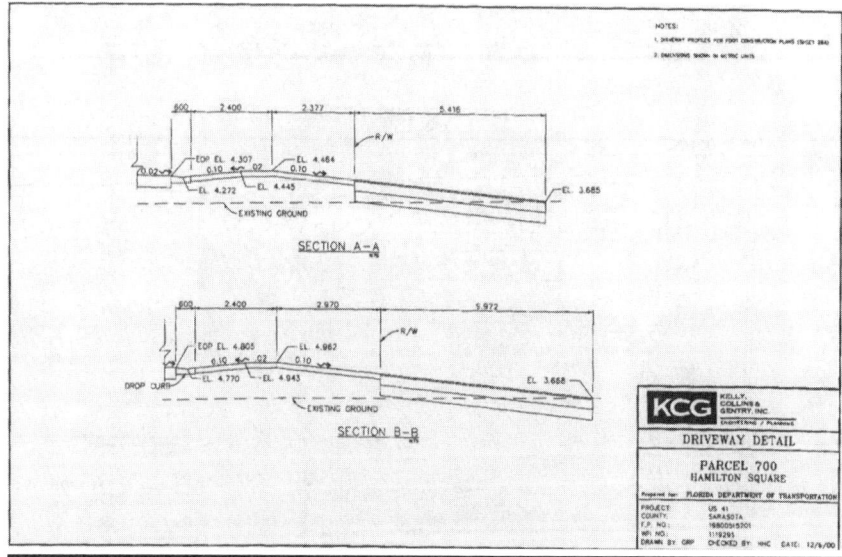

area, including reconstruction of the drives, installation of sod, and similar work.

## Description of the Part Taken

The part taken was roughly rectangular and was intended to provide a right of access to restore the driveways to the subject property during the adjacent road project. It contained a total of 2,832 square feet. The rights acquired were for the right of access to the property for a period of 75 months. No permanent right of use was to be acquired other than the provision for stormwater to travel across the drive and back into the road drainage system, which was the reason for the original intention to acquire the property as a TCE.

Improvements in the acquired area consisted of the following:

| Item | Units |
|---|---|
| Asphalt paving | 1,986 sq. ft. |
| Landscaping (palm tree, gravel, misc.) | 1 LS |
| Concrete curbing | 28 linear ft. |
| Business sign | 1 LS |
| Light pole | 1 LS |
| Concrete sidewalk | 67 sq. ft. |

Easements such as this are rarely bought and sold on the open market, requiring the appraiser to estimate the percentage of rights actually acquired. Analyses of the dominant and servient estates are necessary because the impact on the latter is the determinant for the valuation. Part of the consideration is of the impact on the subsurface, surface, and air rights intrinsic in the fee value of the property. In the case of the subject property, the area acquired for the easement was used for access prior to the acquisition and would be used for access after the acquisition. Parking would also be in the easement area after the project.

A drain grate was to be installed at the easterly edge of the easement to accept stormwater from the subject property. Some stormwater would flow onto the easement area to be collected by this drain and flow back out onto the right of way.

Several factors were considered to determine the percentage of rights acquired. The same general uses for the property would be possible both before and after the easement was acquired. However, there would be stormwater flowing into this easement before flowing back out into the right of way. Therefore, it is considered intrusive upon the uses to which the owner can put this particular part of the property. In addition, the term of the easement (75 months) was considered to consist of about 30% of the remaining economic life of the improvements. Taking into consideration the possible percentage of the bundle of rights acquired as well as the previously mentioned factors, 75% was considered to be a reasonable percentage for the value acquired.

## Description of the Remainder Property

The size of the remainder property stayed the same as it was prior to the taking, but the remainder was encumbered by a permanent easement. The potential for actual uses of the site was unchanged. The site improvements remained the same on the subject property, with the exception of some minor landscaping and other site improvements contained within the easement area. The business sign and light pole within the easement area was to be relocated as necessary.

## Impact on the Subject Property

The utility of the subject land was not detrimentally affected by the acquisition, given the provision for access provided by the condemning authority. As improved and prior to the cure, the project would leave the property lacking one to two parking spaces and adequate parking circulation. This created a functional problem requiring a cure. The signage and light pole were to be relocated as necessary by the condemning authority, although the business sign did not require relocation.

The cost to cure the curable functional problems resulting from the acquisition was $23,100. This cost included redesign of the front island and parking area as well as the rear landscaped island to remedy the functional condition. There was no entrepreneurial profit added to this amount, as there was not considered to be any risk or additional costs to the owner to implement the cure. Prior to the cure, the parking loss and site circulation problem was considered to reduce the overall value of the property.

All of the functional problems resulting from the acquisition that involved the site improvements were considered curable, with the exception of a nominal increased maintenance cost to the site due to the acquisition.

After the take, a small amount of additional wall area would require painting. Further, a drain inlet within the easement area would occasionally require clearing, depending upon what debris might be washed into it. This additional maintenance would be taken care of in normal site maintenance activities. Consideration of these potential annual costs as well as an allowance for some miscellaneous costs that may occur would indicate an annual potential increased maintenance cost of about $100. This expense would be charged as part of the CAM fee to the individual units. It resulted in minor damage to the units.

All the vertical units on the site were considered largely unaffected by the acquisition, with the exception of Unit F. In the before situation, this unit was accorded a premium of 5% to reflect its better exposure to US 41, as was also accorded to Unit A/B. After the project, Unit A/B was still considered to have this benefit. However, Unit F's visibility to motorists turning into the center was limited because of the project, with the increasing grade in front of this particular unit. Although the current use was not considered impacted, as it was a destination-oriented use, in the remainder the alternate potential uses for this unit were considered slightly less than would have been possible prior to the acquisition. As a result, this unit was not afforded the 5% premium in the remainder that was given in the before analysis.

## Scope of Work

Following the state rule under which this property was valued, the procedure for determining the value for acquisition involved the following steps:

1. We first estimated the land value of the property, as this was necessary to estimate the value of the acquisition.
2. We valued each of the condominium units based on two approaches to value and allocated the total value of each to its components.
3. We determined the value of the acquisition itself based on the allocation of each unit's before value.
4. We determined the factors potentially impacting the remainder value from both a physical and a market perspective.
5. The impacts from these factors were determined by several methods, including
    - a paired sales analysis of an after sale to the subject's before values
    - studies based on interviews with market participants
    - reliance on costs and analyses generated by other experts
6. The resulting conclusions were incorporated into a valuation of each unit as uncured.
7. A cost to cure was determined and incorporated into the valuation.
8. A cured value was derived for each unit to determine incurable damages.
9. A summary was presented to illustrate the market value of the acquisition for each unit.

In each step, any value indications were rounded based on the requirements of the condemning authority; that is, the value indications were rounded to the nearest "50" as appropriate.

This summary of work was accomplished through the following steps:

1. Valuation before the taking
   The valuation before the taking followed the standard steps in the valuation process described in *The Appraisal of Real Estate*.[3] The intended use of the appraisal was to provide a basis for the con-

---

3. *The Appraisal of Real Estate*, 13th ed. (Chicago: Appraisal Institute, 2008), 131.

demning authority to establish recommended compensation. In the application of the approaches to value, the sales comparison and income capitalization approaches were considered appropriate. The cost approach was not considered appropriate due to the type of improvements involved (condominiums) and their age (over 20 years old at date of value).

2. Valuation of the part taken
   The valuation of the part taken was based on an allocation from the components valued before the taking. The easement was valued based on the per-unit land value established and the percentage of fee rights acquired. The improvements acquired were based on an allocation of the value of these improvements as part of the whole property.

3. Value of the remainder as part of the whole
   This value was derived by subtracting the value of the part taken from the before value. The resulting value is the basis from which the damage was determined.

4. Value of the remainder before the cure
   This value is determined to establish damages. The property was valued without a cure. The resulting value indication was subtracted from the remainder value as part of the whole to establish total damages, both curable and incurable. This value considers the impact of the taking, which includes

   - loss of exposure
   - impact on access
   - the slope of US 41 access (10%)
   - loss of parking
   - parking circulation
   - additional maintenance costs
   - adequacy of the acquired area for constructing the access ramp and drainage structure

   The process used to determine the impacts included consultation with the other previously identified experts as well as additional research work in the local market. The local market work included interviews with market participants that had physical locations similar to the subject's location after the project. Three bridges connected Venice to the mainland, and there were sufficient commercial uses near these bridges to allow for interviews of the users. These results were used to determine and support our conclusions of impact on the property due to the new bridge.

   To determine the impact of the sloped driveway, we conducted a survey in various areas of Sarasota County where sloped drives were created by older road projects. The occupants of these properties were interviewed to determine if the purchase prices of the properties or rents paid differed from those without sloped drives. Also, the engineer for the assignment was given the locations of each property used in the study and calculated the slope for each of the parcel's driveways to avoid being struck by the court for lack of expertise. In addition, two of the subject units sold after the taking and were used as after sales to support a minor loss in value for each unit. They were purchased after the grantor's settlement with the condemning authority.

5. Establishment of a cost to cure
   This cost to cure is the cost estimate plus contingencies and entrepreneurial profit to repair, replace, or rehabilitate any items damaged or in need of rehabilitation due to the taking. If the net cost of this cure is less than the damages cured, it is considered feasible.

   The proposed cure for the property primarily involved harmonization of the grade change and reconfiguration of the parking. All cure items were outside of the acquired area, as the condemning authority would construct all necessary cure items in the easement area.[4]

6. Value of the remainder after the cure
   This value is established after the cure and is the basis, after subtraction from the remainder value as part of the whole, for incurable damages. This value considers any mitigation or offset of damages due to a cure.

## Valuation Before the Taking
### Highest and Best Use

The subject has a land use designation and zoning designation that allows for commercial development. The principal uses allowed in the zoning district are most types of commercial or office uses. The subject site has a total size of 41,897 square feet, a desirable characteristic under its legal restrictions for use. There are no physical impediments to commercial development. Access is adequate, and the corner location is generally considered a benefit to commercial development because it provides better access and exposure than an interior site. Commercial use is the predominant use in the immediate area. The examined sales and occupancies of existing properties indicate that such a use is financially feasible.

The legal, physically possible, and financially feasible use for the property that returns the highest net present value is considered the

---

4. For additional discussion of cost to cure, see *Real Estate Valuation in Litigation*, 2nd ed., 296-301.

maximally productive use of the property. No alternate use would return a higher value to the site than commercial development.

The existing use of the site is a legal nonconforming use in relation to setback and access requirements. The setback of the buildings from the road frontage is not in conformity with existing zoning requirements, but it has been "grandfathered in" and would be allowed to remain. However, if the buildings were substantially destroyed, any new construction would likely be required to meet current requirements. Also, the mansard roof at the property's US 41 frontage appears to encroach within the existing right of way. However, this condition appears to have been in existence for some time and allowed to remain. Such nonconformity is not unusual for older buildings in the area. Therefore, this is also considered a legal nonconforming use having no significant impact on the value of the property.

The traffic circulation on the site is illegal. Using internal circulation around the main parking area requires exiting into the existing right of way, crossing across traffic flow, and returning to the parking area. This is a functional design problem because it is an illegal traffic pattern, but it is curable. The estimated cost to cure this functional problem is $4,023. This cost includes the work necessary to create a circular pattern for the traffic and results in the elimination of one parking space.

With the cure of the functional problem, the available parking on the subject site is 40 spaces. This indicates a parking ratio of 1 space per 309 square feet of building area. This is a marginal ratio of parking for the center in general, but it is not considered to have a substantial impact on the value of the property because parking for many of the commercial buildings in the Venice area is relatively minimal.

The improvements are considered to be of average quality overall and in average to average-fair condition. They contribute substantially to the value of the property. The general benefit to the island area because of the new bridge project was considered in the before valuation. Therefore, with this condition, the property is considered to be in an area with reasonably good exposure and no substantial traffic congestion problems beyond those that would normally be experienced in the overall area.

Analysis of the parcel indicated that the existing improvements substantially contribute to the value of the property over and above the value of the site. Given their continued contribution to the property, they are considered feasible. Analysis indicated a residual to the building–after the extraction of the value of the land and site improvements–that is less than would be anticipated for a new center with a functional layout. However, no alternate use would justify the removal of the improvements. The buildings remained a commercial establishment with reasonable access and exposure. As a result, the improvements were considered the maximally productive use of the site.

## Vacant Land Analysis

Four sales were found to be suitable for analysis after a search of the market area. The subject was considered to be in a good corner location in a commercial district. Because the condemning authority requires a quantitative analysis, this method was presented in the report. However, the sales are also analyzed based on a qualitative analysis and a ranking basis because these methods are more familiar to a layperson on a jury. The comparison grid for the vacant land analysis is shown in Exhibit 5.

### Exhibit 5

|  | Subject | Sale 1 | Sale 2 | Sale 3 | Sale 4 |
|---|---|---|---|---|---|
| Sale price |  | $630,000 | $110,000 | $750,000 | $525,000 |
| Property rights |  | Fee simple | Fee simple | Fee simple | Fee simple |
| Financing |  | Cash | Cash | Cash | Cash |
| Conditions of sale |  | Arm's-length | Arm's-length/ assemblage, no exposure | Arm's-length | Arm's-length |
| Expenditures after purchase |  | None | None | None | None |
| Date of sale |  | Similar | Similar | Similar | Similar |
| Price per unit |  | $9.46 | $10.85 | $15.99 | $15.00 |
| Size | 41,897 sq. ft. | 66,600 | 10,140 | 46,895 | 35,002 |
| Comparison |  | Inferior | Superior | Similar | Similar |
| Location | Bus. 41 S. Hatchet Crk. | Similar | Similar | Superior | Superior |
| Physical characteristics |  | Inferior | Inferior | Superior | Superior |
| Utilities | Trash, electric, water, sewer | Similar | Similar | Similar | Similar |
| Land use/zoning | Common/CG | Similar | Similar | Similar | Similar |
| Overall comparison |  | Inferior | Inferior | Superior | Superior |

The range of indicated values is $9.46 per square foot to $15.99 per square foot. In ranking the value indications, we considered the subject superior to Sales 1 and 2 and inferior to Sales 3 and 4. Our value conclusion is $13 per square foot, or $544,700:

$$41,897 \text{ sq. ft.} @ \$13.00 = \$544,661$$
$$= \$544,700 \text{ (rounded)}$$

## Sales Comparison Approach

Five sales were found to be suitable for comparison in the before analysis of the larger parcel. These sales are considered to indicate an appropriate range for a value conclusion for each of the subject's condominium units. Because of the basic similarity of most of these units, a base unit was selected to establish a base value. From this base value, consideration was given to differences in each of the other units. In this manner, an individual value was derived for each of the subject units. The comparison grid for the improved sales is shown in Exhibit 6.

### Exhibit 6

|  | Subject | Sale 5 | Sale 6 | Sale 7 | Sale 8 | Sale 9 |
|---|---|---|---|---|---|---|
| Sale price |  | $140,000 | $120,700 | $225,000 | $145,000 | $325,000 |
| Property rights |  | Fee simple | Fee simple | Fee simple | Fee simple | Fee simple |
| Financing |  | Cash | Cash | Market | Cash | Market |
| Conditions of sale |  | Arm's-length | Arm's-length | Arm's-length | Arm's-length | Arm's-length |
| Expenditures after purchase |  | None | None | None | None | None |
| Date of sale |  | Similar | Similar | Similar | Similar | Similar |
| Price per unit |  | $109.80 | $66.06 | $56.92 | $85.55 | $56.28 |
| Unit size | 1,033 sq. ft. | Similar | Similar | Inferior | Similar | Inferior |
| Effective age | 20 | Similar | Similar | Similar | Similar | Similar |
| Location | Bus. 41, Venice | Superior | Similar | Similar | Superior | Similar |
| Physical comparisons |  | Slightly superior | Similar | Inferior | Slightly superior | Inferior |
| Parking ratio | 1:309 | Slightly superior | Similar | Slightly inferior | Similar | Slightly inferior |
| Comparison |  | Superior | Similar | Inferior | Superior | Inferior |

The comparison of each of the sales to the base unit of the subject indicates a value ranging between $56.28 per square foot and $109.80 per square foot. In ranking the sales and the subject, we considered Sales 5 and 8 superior, while Sale 6 is generally similar. Sales 7 and 9 are inferior. Our final value conclusion is $68 per square foot, or $70,250:

$$1,033 \text{ sq. ft.} @ \$68.00 = \$70,244$$
$$= \$70,250 \text{ (rounded)}$$

After determining the base unit value, adjustments were made recognizing differences between the base unit and each of the other units. Differences included street exposure, unit finish, and additional plumbing and electric distribution. The value of the common area is included in the overall unit value. It is apportioned based on the condominium documents. Based on market recognition of these factors, the values indicated for each unit are shown in Exhibit 7. These indicated values for each unit cannot be summed to indicate a value for a bulk purchase of the entire property.

## Income Capitalization Approach

Five rentals were examined to determine a market rent for the base unit. Differences between the base unit and upgraded units were then considered to determine a market rent for each subject unit. Rentals

### Exhibit 7

| Units | Square Feet | Base Value/ Sq. Ft. | Adjusted Value/Sq. Ft. | Pro Rata Share to Cure Functional Obsolescence | Final Value (Rounded) |
|---|---|---|---|---|---|
| A/B | 2,058 | $68.00 | $71.40 | <$667.01> | $146,270 |
| C | 1,026 | $68.00 | $73.00 | <$333.51> | $74,560 |
| D | 1,031 | $68.00 | $73.00 | <$333.51> | $74,930 |
| E | 1,017 | $68.00 | $68.00 | <$333.51> | $68,820 |
| F | 1,504 | $68.00 | $81.40 | <$491.61> | $121,930 |
| G | 1,049 | $68.00 | $68.00 | <$333.91> | $71,000 |
| H | 1,033 | $68.00 | $68.00 | <$333.91> | $69,910 |
| I | 1,021 | $68.00 | $73.00 | <$333.51> | $74,200 |
| J | 1,318 | $68.00 | $68.00 | <$431.27> | $89,190 |
| K | 1,313 | $68.00 | $68.00 | <$431.27> | $88,850 |

in the subject were not used due to concerns regarding condemnation blight.[5] An allowance for vacancy and collection loss and other expenses were subtracted from the gross rent to reach a net operating income for each unit. Finally, a market-derived overall rate was used to reach a value for each unit by this approach.

### Gross Income

The comparable rent range was from $9 to $14.75 per square foot. The market tends to negotiate gross rents with minimal pass-throughs. The final gross rent conclusion for a base unit was determined to be $10.75 per square foot. The comparable rental grid is shown in Exhibit 8.

### Exhibit 8

| | Subject | Rent 1 | Rent 2 | Rent 3 | Rent 4 | Rent 5 |
|---|---|---|---|---|---|---|
| Annual rent | | $11,820 | $18,000 | $14,400 | $9,600 | $8,997 |
| Tenant expenses | | Trash, electric | Electric | Trash, electric, water, sewer | Utilities | $25 CAM for utilities |
| Finish allowance | | None | None | None | None | None |
| Pass-throughs | | None | None | None | None | None |
| Amount | | Similar | Similar | Similar | Similar | Similar |
| Rent per sq. ft. | | $13.49 | $14.75 | $9.00 | $9.60 | $9.47 |
| Unit size | 1,033 sq. ft. | Similar | Similar | Similar | Similar | Similar |
| Physical comparisons | | Superior | Superior | Inferior | Inferior | Inferior |
| Location | Bus. 41, Venice | Superior | Superior | Similar | Similar | Similar |
| Parking ratio | 1:309 | Slightly superior | Slightly superior | Similar | Slightly superior | Similar |
| Comparison | | Superior | Superior | Similar | Slightly superior | Slightly superior |

5. For additional information on condemnation blight, see *Real Estate Valuation in Litigation*, 2nd ed., 118-124.

After determining a base rent, we considered adjustments to the individual units, which included adjustments to Units A/B and F for exposure and adjustments to Units C, F, and I for better finish. The final gross rent for each unit was derived with the adjustments for differing amenities as shown in Exhibit 9.

| | | | Exhibit 9 | | |
|---|---|---|---|---|---|
| Units | Square Footage | Base Gross Rent/Sq. Ft. | Adjustment | Adjusted Rent/Sq. Ft. | Indicated Gross Rent |
| A/B | 2,058 | $10.75 | $0.54 | $11.29 | $23,235 |
| C | 1,026 | $10.75 | $0.71 | $11.46 | $11,758 |
| D | 1,031 | $10.75 | $0.71 | $11.46 | $11,815 |
| E | 1,017 | $10.75 | Base | $10.75 | $10,933 |
| F | 1,504 | $10.75 | $1.96 | $12.71 | $19,116 |
| G | 1,049 | $10.75 | Base | $10.75 | $11,277 |
| H | 1,033 | $10.75 | Base | $10.75 | $11,105 |
| I | 1,021 | $10.75 | $0.71 | $11.46 | $11,701 |
| J | 1,318 | $10.75 | Base | $10.75 | $14,169 |
| K | 1,313 | $10.75 | Base | $10.75 | $14,115 |

### *Vacancy and Collection Loss*

The actual vacancy rate in the subject was 9%. However, part of this could be inferred to occur due to condemnation blight. Based on the general market, a reasonable vacancy and collection loss was estimated at 5%. This amount was subtracted from the gross rent for each unit to indicate the effective gross income for each unit, as shown in Exhibit 10.

| | | Exhibit 10 | |
|---|---|---|---|
| Unit | Gross Rent | Vacancy and Collection Loss @ 5% | Effective Gross Income |
| A/B | $23,235 | $1,162 | $22,073 |
| C | $11,758 | $588 | $11,170 |
| D | $11,815 | $591 | $11,224 |
| E | $10,933 | $547 | $10,386 |
| F | $19,116 | $956 | $18,160 |
| G | $11,277 | $564 | $10,713 |
| H | $11,105 | $555 | $10,550 |
| I | $11,701 | $585 | $11,116 |
| J | $14,169 | $708 | $13,461 |
| K | $14,115 | $706 | $13,409 |

### *Expenses*

The CAM covered most of the subject's expenses, so the only additional expenses were taxes and a management fee. The CAM used in the analysis was based on actual costs provided by the owner. They were in line with market expenses for the items, including exterior maintenance, lawn work, and normal operational costs. The taxes were based on actual taxes. The management fee was determined to be 6%, based on typical charges in the area.

*Capitalization Rate*

Three methods were used to determine a capitalization rate for each unit. These included looking at market sales and applying band of investment and debt coverage ratio techniques. Two sales indicated overall rates. In addition, two sales not used in direct analysis were found from which an overall rate could be extracted:

| | Market |
|---|---|
| Sale 8 | 18.8% |
| Sale 9 | 10.76% |
| Sale document number | Rate |
| 000027576 | 8.24% |
| 99104876 | 9.80% |

For the other two approaches, local market indications for mortgage rates were found as follows:

| | |
|---|---|
| Loan-to-value ratio | 70% to 80% |
| Amortization term | 15 years maximum |
| Debt coverage | 1.15 to 1.5 |
| Interest rate | 8.5% to 10% |

After examining the alternatives, a reasonable loan for the subject was considered to be 70% of value, at a 15-year term, with a 1.25 debt coverage ratio. The interest rate would be about 8.5%, indicating a loan constant of 0.1182.

The equity component consisted of the remaining value (30%) plus an equity capitalization rate. Insufficient information was available to derive this rate from comparable data, but the equity component was considered to be riskier than the mortgage component and therefore should be higher than the mortgage capitalization rate. However, this rate will be closer to the mortgage rate for owner/user properties. From an owner's perspective, less risk is involved than for a pure income property. Based on this reasoning and the available information, a reasonable rate is estimated to be 12%. With these components, indications for an overall capitalization rate from a band of investment and debt coverage ratio analysis were calculated as shown in Exhibit 11.

From these three approaches, a reasonable overall capitalization rate for each unit was determined to be 10.2%, with slightly more

### Exhibit 11

**Debt Coverage Ratio**

| 1.25 (DCR) | × | 0.1182 ($R_M$) | × | 0.7 (L-to-V) | = | 10.34% |
|---|---|---|---|---|---|---|

**Band of Investment**

| 0.1182 ($R_M$) | × | 0.7 (L-to-V) | = | 0.08274 |
|---|---|---|---|---|
| 0.12 ($R_E$) | × | 0.3 (E) | = | 0.036 |
| | $R_o$ | | = | 11.87% |

consideration given to the sale indications and the general benefits accruing from the bridge project.

With the components of the income capitalization approach established, a value indication for each unit was derived. This process entailed establishing a gross income for each unit, subtracting the vacancy, collection loss, and expenses, and capitalizing the resulting net income by the derived overall capitalization rate. Finally, a pro rata amount of the established cost to cure the parking functional problem was subtracted from each unit's value, leaving the resulting values for each unit by this approach:

| Unit | Value Indication (Rounded) |
|---|---|
| A/B | $154,680 |
| C | $78,600 |
| D | $80,740 |
| E | $73,130 |
| F | $131,530 |
| G | $74,190 |
| H | $72,820 |
| I | $78,150 |
| J | $89,700 |
| K | $89,220 |

## Reconciliation

From the value indications derived from the sales comparison approach and the income capitalization approach, a final before value was reconciled for each unit. Each unit value was further broken into components of land, site improvements, and vertical structure value for later analysis of the part taken. The vertical unit value is the extracted value of the actual unit, within each unit's walls. This is the square footage of actual rentable area. The pro rata value of land and site improvements allocated to each unit was based on the apportionment of values in the condominium documents, as shown in Exhibit 12. Based on these percentages, the before values and allocations are shown in Exhibit 13.

### Exhibit 12

| Units | Square Feet | % of Common Area |
|---|---|---|
| A/B | 2,058 | 16.58% |
| C | 1,026 | 8.29% |
| D | 1,031 | 8.29% |
| E | 1,017 | 8.29% |
| F | 1,504 | 12.22% |
| G | 1,049 | 8.30% |
| H | 1,033 | 8.30% |
| I | 1,021 | 8.29% |
| J | 1,318 | 10.72% |
| K | 1,313 | 10.72% |
| Totals | 12,370 | 100.00% |

### Exhibit 13

| Unit | Final Value Estimate | Less Pro Rata Land | Less Pro Rata Site Improvements | Vertical Unit Value |
|---|---|---|---|---|
| A/B | $153,000 | $90,311 | $10,617 | $52,072 |
| C | $77,500 | $45,156 | $5,309 | $27,035 |
| D | $77,800 | $45,156 | $5,309 | $27,335 |
| E | $70,900 | $45,156 | $5,309 | $20,435 |
| F | $130,500 | $66,562 | $7,825 | $56,113 |
| G | $73,500 | $45,210 | $5,315 | $22,975 |
| H | $72,000 | $45,210 | $5,315 | $21,475 |
| I | $77,000 | $45,156 | $5,309 | $26,535 |
| J | $89,500 | $58,392 | $6,865 | $24,243 |
| K | $88,900 | $58,392 | $6,865 | $23,643 |
| Total | | $544,701 | $64,038 | |

## Valuation of the Part Taken

Using the derived per unit land value of the before analysis and the derived percentage of rights acquired, we can calculate a value for the land acquired as follows:

> Fee value: 2,832 sq. ft. @ $13.00 = $36,816
> Percent of fee acquired: 75% = $27,612
> = $27,625 (rounded)

The value of the improvements in the taking was calculated from allocation as part of the before analysis.

All of these improvements disturbed during the harmonizing of the driveway to the new road grade were to be reestablished by FDOT with equal utility to that which was originally on site. The improvements would be removed and replaced as needed. The business sign and light pole would be relocated as necessary, even though the business sign would not likely require relocation. The remaining minor site improvements, although they were replaced with items of equal utility, were within the area of acquisition. As a result, it was considered reasonable to pay for these fixed improvements. The value of each item was established in the before value based on its perceived contributory value to the larger parcel. Considerations included estimated cost, condition, and overall utility to the property. The improvements contained within Parcel 700 are listed in Exhibit 14.

### Exhibit 14

| Item | Units | $/Unit | Total |
|---|---|---|---|
| Asphalt paving | 1,986 sq. ft. | $2.00 | $3,972 |
| Landscaping (palm tree, gravel, misc.) | 1 LS | $733.00 | 733 |
| Concrete curbing | 28 linear ft. | $6.00 | 168 |
| Concrete sidewalk | 67 sq. ft. | $2.85 | 191 |
| Business sign | 1 each | Relocate if necessary | |
| Light pole | 1 each | Relocated | |
| | | | $5,064 |

As part of this assignment, we calculated a value for the easement as a temporary construction easement for proffer in the event of an appeal of the verdict. That value was included in the addenda of the report and proffered outside of the jury's presence:

| Total Value of the Easement | | Rounded |
|---|---|---|
| Easement land | $27,612 | $27,625 |
| Easement improvements | 5,064 | 5,075 |
| | $32,676 | $32,700 |

The value of the remainder as a part of the whole was calculated as the difference between the before value and the value of the part taken. This calculation was used in the determination of damages and a cost to cure as follows:

| | |
|---|---|
| Value before | $910,600 |
| Less taken | 32,700 |
| Remainder | $877,900 |

# Valuation After the Taking: The Remainder Uncured

## Highest and Best Use

The subject property as vacant was subject to the same considerations as in the before analysis. As previously discussed, commercial development was acceptable for the property from a legal perspective. The subject remained suitable from a physically possible standpoint for commercial development, which was considered to be its financially feasible and maximally productive use. The acquisition was not considered to have affected the land value because the condemning authority still provided access from US 41. Therefore, commercial development was considered to meet the four tests for highest and best use as vacant.

As improved, the subject was considered to have the same characteristics and potential for use as in the before analysis. However, the property now suffered from curable functional problems resulting from the installation of the ramps. Interior site circulation was no longer possible as it would have been after the cure of the functional problem in the before analysis. Further, some parking was lost prior to consideration of a cure. As a result, the highest and best use as improved was still considered to be its existing use as discussed in the before analysis but with the curable functional problems as detailed later in the analysis. Additional incurable damages were indicated. These did not change the highest and best use as improved of the subject units.

## Land Valuation

The valuation of the uncured remainder in the after condition was substantially similar to the before analysis. The land value was affected only by the loss of a portion of the fee rights acquired in the acquisition, leaving a remainder value of $517,000:

```
       41,897 sq. ft. @ $13.00 = $544,661
       Less: Fee rights acquired    27,625
                                  $517,036
                                  $517,000 (rounded)
```

## Sales Comparison Approach

The same process was used as in the before analysis with the inclusion of an after sale involving the subject property. This sale (Sale 10) was the purchase of Units D and E of Hamilton Square. It was purchased after the original owner had settled with the condemning authority. These units were no longer under the threat of eminent domain. Verification with the purchaser indicated that he was aware of the project and its impact on the subject and that this knowledge was reflected in the purchase price. In the analysis, this sale required acknowledgement of size, as it was a double unit. The factors involved in this sale are shown in Exhibit 15.

The value conclusion, considering Sale 10 and prior to consideration of a cure, was $65 per square foot for the base unit. The value of each unit prior to consideration of a cure was then determined as shown in Exhibit 16.

## Exhibit 15

|  | Subject | Sale 10 |
|---|---|---|
| Sale price |  | $130,000 |
| Grantor |  | Dussault |
| Grantee |  | Kirton |
| Property rights |  | Fee simple |
| Financing |  | Market |
| Conditions of sale |  | Arm's-length |
| Expenditures after purchase |  | None |
| Date of sale |  | Similar |
| Price per unit |  | $63.48 |
| Unit size | 1,033 sq. ft. | Slightly inferior |
| Effective age | 20 years | Similar |
| Location | Bus. 41, Venice | Similar |
| Physical factors |  | Similar |
| Parking ratio | 1:309 | Similar |
|  |  | Similar |
| Comparison |  | Slightly inferior |

## Exhibit 16

| Units | Square Footage | Base Unit Value | Adjustments | Adjusted Value/ Sq. Ft. | Indicated Value before Functional Obsolescence | Pro Rata of Curable Functional Obsolescence (based on percentage of common area) | Pro Rata of Parking Loss | Indicated Value Less Functional Obsolescence | Rounded |
|---|---|---|---|---|---|---|---|---|---|
| A/B | 2,058 | $65.00 | $3.25 | $68.25 | $140,459 | <$5,521.14> | <$5,207> | $129,731 | $129,730 |
| C | 1,026 | $65.00 | $5.00 | $70.00 | $71,820 | <$2,760.57> | <$2,704> | $66,355 | $66,360 |
| D | 1,031 | $65.00 | $5.00 | $70.00 | $72,170 | <$2,760.57> | <$2,734> | $66,675 | $66,680 |
| E | 1,017 | $65.00 | Base | $65.00 | $66,105 | <$2,760.57> | <$2,044> | $61,300 | $61,300 |
| F | 1,504 | $65.00 | $10.00 | $75.00 | $112,800 | <$4,069.26> | <$5,611> | $103,120 | $103,120 |
| G | 1,049 | $65.00 | Base | $65.00 | $68,185 | <$2,763.90> | <$2,298> | $63,123 | $63,120 |
| H | 1,033 | $65.00 | Base | $65.00 | $67,145 | <$2,763.90> | <$2,148> | $62,233 | $62,230 |
| I | 1,021 | $65.00 | $5.00 | $70.00 | $71,470 | <$2,760.57> | <$2,654> | $66,055 | $66,060 |
| J | 1,318 | $65.00 | Base | $65.00 | $85,670 | <$3,569.76> | <$2,424> | $79,676 | $79,680 |
| K | 1,313 | $65.00 | Base | $65.00 | $85,345 | <$3,569.76> | <$2,364> | $79,411 | $79,410 |

## Income Capitalization Approach

Using Sale 10 as a basis, the potential rent impact due to the acquisition was determined and used in the income capitalization approach. The before base unit value was $68 per square foot. The comparison of Sale 10 to the before base unit value indicated a decrease in value of 6.6%. However, Sale 10 also included a more finished unit. Using the same finish adjustment as in the before analysis would increase the before value used for comparison to $73 per square foot, indicating a higher change in value. Based on the concept that rents and value are directly related, the after rent should be decreased.

Because the grantee of Sale 10 indicated that the interior partitioning of Unit D was given little value in the decision to purchase (it was an overimprovement for his purposes) and the base sale price included both a base and partitioned unit, a reasonable adjustment was considered to be towards the lower end of the range. Therefore, the after base rent was estimated at $10.25. For Unit F, with the loss of the premium for exposure, the adjustment from the base rent for this unit was $1.42 per square foot, which was the return on and of the extra cost of the finish. Exhibit 17 indicates the gross rents for each individual unit.

### Exhibit 17

| Units | Square Footage | Base Rent | Adjustment | Adjusted Rent | Indicated Gross Rent |
|---|---|---|---|---|---|
| A/B | 2,058 | $10.25 | $0.51 | $10.76 | $22,144 |
| C | 1,026 | $10.25 | $0.71 | $10.96 | $11,245 |
| D | 1,031 | $10.25 | $0.71 | $10.96 | $11,300 |
| E | 1,017 | $10.25 | Base | $10.25 | $10,424 |
| F | 1,504 | $10.25 | $1.42 | $11.67 | $17,552 |
| G | 1,049 | $10.25 | Base | $10.25 | $10,752 |
| H | 1,033 | $10.25 | Base | $10.25 | $10,588 |
| I | 1,021 | $10.25 | $0.71 | $10.96 | $11,190 |
| J | 1,318 | $10.25 | Base | $10.25 | $13,510 |
| K | 1,313 | $10.25 | Base | $10.25 | $13,458 |

The vacancy and collection loss was increased to 15% before the cure due to the loss of site circulation and parking. This increase was based on studies indicating that a reduction in parking has an impact on occupancy.

The expenses were about the same even though the management fee was slightly reduced (because of the lower effective gross income) and the CAM was slightly increased (to reflect higher maintenance costs to maintain improvements installed by the condemning authority). The overall capitalization rate was considered unchanged. With these considerations, the value of each unit by the income capitalization approach was derived as detailed earlier in this case study:

| Unit | Value Indication |
|---|---|
| A/B | $119,700 |
| C | $61,240 |
| D | $63,310 |
| E | $56,550 |
| F | $97,970 |
| G | $57,180 |
| H | $56,030 |
| I | $60,850 |
| J | $68,220 |
| K | $67,820 |

## Reconciliation

The value conclusion prior to the cure is presented in Exhibit 18. The allocation of land and site improvements was again based on the percentages for each unit of the common area.

### Exhibit 18

| Unit | Approach | Final Value Estimate | Less Pro Rata Land | Less Pro Rata Site Improvements | Vertical Unit Value |
|---|---|---|---|---|---|
| A/B | Sales comp: $129,730<br>Income cap: $119,700 | $125,000 | $85,719 | $9,777 | $29,504 |
| C | Sales comp: $66,360<br>Income cap: $61,240 | $64,000 | $42,859 | $4,889 | $16,252 |
| D | Sales comp: $66,680<br>Income cap: $63,310 | $65,000 | $42,859 | $4,889 | $17,252 |
| E | Sales comp: $61,300<br>Income cap: $56,550 | $59,000 | $42,859 | $4,889 | $11,252 |
| F | Sales comp: $103,120<br>Income cap: $97,970 | $101,000 | $63,177 | $7,206 | $30,617 |
| G | Sales comp: $63,120<br>Income cap: $57,180 | $60,400 | $42,911 | $4,895 | $12,594 |
| H | Sales comp: $62,230<br>Income cap: $56,030 | $59,300 | $42,911 | $4,895 | $11,494 |
| I | Sales comp: $66,060<br>Income cap: $60,850 | $63,500 | $42,859 | $4,889 | $15,752 |
| J | Sales comp: $79,680<br>Income cap: $68,220 | $74,000 | $55,422 | $6,322 | $12,256 |
| K | Sales comp: $79,410<br>Income cap: $67,820 | $73,500 | $55,422 | $6,322 | $11,756 |
| Total* | | | $516,998 | $58,973 | |

* Rounding causes a slight difference in these totals in relation to the derived values.

## Damages

The overall damages to the subject are calculated as follows. Each unit suffers a part of this damage based on its pro rata share of the common area of the property:

| | |
|---|---:|
| Remainder value (as part of whole) | $877,900 |
| Remainder (appraised uncured) | 744,700 |
| Damages (total uncured) | $133,200 |

These damages were a result of curable functional problems brought about by the acquisition as well as damages due to parking loss and site circulation. The bulk of these damages were considered curable. There was no damage to the land. The light pole and business sign were within the easement area and were relocated by the condemning authority, with no damages accruing from this source. The marketability of the remainder was considered unchanged from its marketability prior to the acquisition, with provision for the damages as illustrated previously.

Analysis of the property after the take, considering the benefits of the project in the before analysis, indicated some damages to each unit. The total amount of incurable damage, to be segregated later, was $34,900.

## Cost to Cure

The bulk of the damages to the subject were considered curable. Based on analysis and input by the engineer, the proposed cure provided for harmonizing of the grade change by way of entrance ramps from US 41 into the interior of the subject property. The south ramp will be the shorter of the two because the road grade at that point has minimal difference from the existing grade. The access point at the north end of the parking lot will be somewhat higher due to the increasing elevation of US 41 at that point. Other provisions of the cure included relocation of the light pole on the west end of the parking lot as well as relocation of the sign, if needed. Parts of the cure outside of the easement area included reconfiguration of the landscaped islands and parking area to allow interior circulation within the site, as well as the regaining of parking spaces lost due to the acquisition.

The cost-to-cure damages were for required cure items *outside* of Parcel 700. The condemning authority provided information indicating that it would construct and pay for all cure items contained within the easement area. Therefore, the owner would only have to pay to restore parking and traffic circulation outside of the acquisition area.

Alternate cure scenarios were also examined, including a provision for a single access point with ingress and egress. This cure plan afforded 41 parking spaces, whereas in the before analysis there were only 40 spaces after fixing the illegal traffic circulation. However, because the subject's US 41 driveway was divided in the before situation, the proposed cure was executed in a manner identical to what was available prior to the acquisition, even though the single-access point cure was considered more beneficial to the subject remainder. All of the cure items were outside of the take area and were not considered replacements for any items paid for in the acquisition. As a result, no items paid for in the take would be subtracted from the cost to cure, leaving the total cost of the cure as the net cost to cure. The cost to cure is calculated in Exhibit 19.

### Exhibit 19

| Item | Quantity | Unit | Price per Unit | Total | |
|---|---|---|---|---|---|
| Front landscaped island/parking | 1 | LS | $7,035.75 | $7,035.75 | |
| Rear landscaped island | 1 | LS | $20,385.50 | $20,385.50 | |
| Installed drainage inlet | 1 | LS | $1,500.00 | $1,500.00 | |
| Easement area improvements | 1 | LS | FDOT | $0.00 | |
| | | | | $28,921.25 | $28,950 |
| | | | Less: Paid in take | | 0 |
| | | | Net cost to cure | | $28,950 |

Note. Calculations do not include items paid for in the taking that the condemning authority would restore.

## Valuation After the Taking: The Remainder Cured

After the cure, the remainder was restored to essentially its before condition, with the exception of the loss of the visibility to Unit F and the minor increase in maintenance costs to the remaining units. The latter is reflected in slightly higher CAM costs. Also, based on comparison of the before values of the units to the after sale of Units D and E, some minor damages due to the acquisition were indicated. These appeared to occur not so much because of any specific change in physical factors, such as the sloped entry or bridge proximity, but due to the perceived overall impact of the project on the parcel. In the before analysis there was an anticipation of relieved traffic congestion, a general benefit to the area that was reflected in the value. In the valuation of the remainder cured, this benefit is offset slightly by the actual impact of the project on the property itself. The interior site circulation and parking were restored.

The effect of the acquisition on the remainder cured was minimal. The cure leaving the divided driveway on US 41 did not result in any lost parking. The subject remainder cured was essentially the same as the subject prior to the acquisition, with the exception of the loss of exposure to Unit F and slightly higher CAM charges. The increased grade of US 41 approaching the Hatchett Creek Bridge did not have any direct impact on the subject that can be quantified by observation of similar properties. However, Unit F did suffer some direct damages due to the perceived loss of visibility from the entry to the subject after the project. The overall impact was some nonspecific damages to all of the units.

## Highest and Best Use

The highest and best use of the subject property as vacant was the same as discussed in the Valuation After the Taking: The Remainder Uncured section of this case study. The highest and best use as vacant was considered to be commercial development.

As improved, the highest and best use of the subject was considered to be its existing use, with minor diminishment in value to all units as previously discussed. Specific impacts were to Unit F due to a loss in visibility and a minor diminishment in value to all units because of the increased CAM charges that resulted from the higher maintenance costs. An alternate cure plan provided additional parking beyond what existed before the acquisition. However, as the subject had a divided driveway on US 41 for ingress and egress prior to the acquisition, the cure leaving the same type of ingress and egress was used.

The subject experienced no other curable functional problems. It had the same remaining economic life as discussed earlier. The only change in the highest and best use as improved was for the incurable damage that was discussed previously. This is quantified in the analysis.

## Land Valuation

The land valuation procedure remained unchanged from the uncured analysis:

```
41,897 sq. ft. @ $13.00 =   $544,661 (rounded)
Less: Fee rights acquired  −  27,625
                            $517,036
                            $517,000 (rounded)
```

## Sales Comparison Approach

The sales comparison approach was substantially the same as the valuation uncured, with acknowledgement of the cure. The valuation reflected the increased CAM charges, loss in value due to the easement acquisition, minor impact due to the project, and the impact on Unit F due to the loss of exposure. The conclusion of value for each unit by this approach is shown in Exhibit 20.

### Exhibit 20

| Units | Square Footage | Base Unit Value | Adjustment | Adjusted Value | Indicated Value | Rounded |
|---|---|---|---|---|---|---|
| A/B | 2,058 | $65.00 | $3.25 | $68.25 | $140,459 | $140,500 |
| C | 1,026 | $65.00 | $5.00 | $70.00 | $71,820 | $71,800 |
| D | 1,031 | $65.00 | $5.00 | $70.00 | $72,170 | $72,200 |
| E | 1,017 | $65.00 | Base | $65.00 | $66,105 | $66,100 |
| F | 1,504 | $65.00 | $10.00 | $75.00 | $112,800 | $112,800 |
| G | 1,049 | $65.00 | Base | $65.00 | $68,185 | $68,200 |
| H | 1,033 | $65.00 | Base | $65.00 | $67,145 | $67,100 |
| I | 1,021 | $65.00 | $5.00 | $70.00 | $71,470 | $71,500 |
| J | 1,318 | $65.00 | Base | $65.00 | $85,670 | $85,700 |
| K | 1,313 | $65.00 | Base | $65.00 | $85,345 | $85,300 |

## Income Capitalization Approach

The same technique was used in the income capitalization approach for the remainder cured as in the previous valuations. The gross rent was adjusted to reflect the minor loss in gross rent for each unit. The rent for Unit F was adjusted to reflect its loss in visibility. The vacancy and collection loss was estimated at 5% after the cure due to the restoration of those physical characteristics that affected the uncured value.

The expenses for the subject were considered unchanged, with the exception of the CAM charge. The minor take of the easement area was not considered to have any measurable impact on property taxes or the management fee percentage. The only changes from these factors were for Unit F, for which the management fee would be reflected in a slightly lower effective gross income. The CAM charge was increased slightly for each unit to reflect the added maintenance costs for the improvements installed for the subject property's benefit by the condemning authority. This additional charge was based on the pro rata share of the expenses afforded each unit and is reflected in the tables at the end of this section.

The overall capitalization rate for the cured valuation was the same as in the before analysis. The anticipated return of and on capital was unchanged from the previous analysis. The indication of value for each unit is shown in the following table:

| Unit | Value Indication (Rounded) |
|---|---|
| A/B | $145,630 |
| C | $74,360 |
| D | $76,480 |
| E | $68,930 |
| F | $118,220 |
| G | $69,840 |
| H | $68,550 |
| I | $73,920 |
| J | $84,250 |
| K | $83,790 |

## Reconciliation

The reconciliation process after the cure mirrored the previous reconciliation. The values for each unit are calculated in Exhibit 21. Keep in mind that the sum of these values is *not* the value to a single buyer.

### Exhibit 21

| Unit | Approach | Final Value Estimate | Less Pro Rata Land | Less Pro Rata Site Improvements | Vertical Unit Value |
|---|---|---|---|---|---|
| A/B | Sales comp: $140,500<br>Income cap: $145,630 | $141,000 | $85,719 | $9,777 | $45,504 |
| C | Sales comp: $71,800<br>Income cap: $74,360 | $72,000 | $42,859 | $4,889 | $24,252 |
| D | Sales comp: $72,200<br>Income cap: $76,480 | $73,000 | $42,859 | $4,889 | $25,252 |
| E | Sales comp: $66,100<br>Income cap: $68,930 | $66,500 | $42,859 | $4,889 | $18,752 |
| F | Sales comp: $112,800<br>Income cap: $118,220 | $113,000 | $63,177 | $7,206 | $42,617 |
| G | Sales comp: $68,200<br>Income cap: $69,840 | $68,500 | $42,911 | $4,895 | $20,694 |
| H | Sales comp: $67,100<br>Income cap: $68,550 | $67,400 | $42,911 | $4,895 | $19,594 |
| I | Sales comp: $71,500<br>Income cap: $73,920 | $72,200 | $42,859 | $4,889 | $24,452 |
| J | Sales comp: $85,700<br>Income cap: $84,250 | $85,000 | $55,422 | $6,322 | $23,256 |
| K | Sales comp: $85,300<br>Income cap: $83,790 | $84,400 | $55,422 | $6,322 | $22,656 |

## Special Benefits

There were no special benefits to the subject due to the project.

## Summary of Values

Exhibit 22 shows the calculations on the "gross" value of the acquisition. It is the sum of the unit values and is presented for condemning authority purposes. Following the summary, the value of the take for the individual units is shown in Exhibit 23. The source for this summary is the components of the valuation.

## Exhibit 22

| | | |
|---|---|---|
| 1 | Before property | $910,600 |
| 2 | Part acquired (land and improvements) | 32,700 |
| 3 | Remainder value (as part of whole) ([1] – [2]) | $877,900 |
| 4 | Remainder (appraised uncured) | 744,700 |
| 5 | Damages (total uncured) ([3] – [4]) | $133,200 |
| 6 | Special benefits | 0 |
| 7 | Damages ([5] – [6]) | $133,200 |
| **Feasibility of Cost to Cure Damages:** | | |
| 8 | Remainder (appraised as cured) (or [3] is less) | $843,000 |
| 9 | Remainder (appraised, uncured) ([4]) | 744,700 |
| 10 | Damages, curable ([8] – [9]) | $98,300 |
| 11 | Damages, incurable ([7] – [10]) | $34,900 |
| 12 | Cost to cure (or reestablish) | $28,950 |
| 13 | Improvements cured but paid for in [2] | 0 |
| 14 | Net cost to cure ([12] – [13]) | $28,950 |

**Summary of Total Compensation:**

| | |
|---|---|
| Part taken | |
| Land | $27,625 |
| Improvements | 5,075 |
| Damages, uncured | 34,900 |
| Net cost to cure | 28,950 |
| Total compensation | $96,550 |

## Exhibit 23

| Unit | A/B | C | D | E | F |
|---|---|---|---|---|---|
| Before value | $153,000 | $77,500 | $77,800 | $70,900 | $130,500 |
| Percent of common area | 16.58% | 8.29% | 8.29% | 8.29% | 12.22% |
| Percent of take | $5,421.66 | $2,710.83 | $2,710.83 | $2,710.83 | $3,995.94 |
| Remainder as part of whole | $147,578 | $74,789 | $75,089 | $68,189 | $126,504 |
| Value before cure | $125,000 | $64,000 | $65,000 | $59,000 | $101,000 |
| Damages | $22,578 | $10,789 | $10,089 | $9,189 | $25,504 |
| Value after cure | $141,000 | $72,000 | $73,000 | $66,500 | $113,000 |
| Curable damages | $16,000 | $8,000 | $8,000 | $7,500 | $12,000 |
| Incurable damages | $6,578 | $2,789 | $2,089 | $1,689 | $13,504 |
| Pro rata of net cost to cure | $4,799.91 | $2,399.96 | $2,399.96 | $2,399.96 | $3,537.69 |
| Total per unit | $16,799.57 | $7,899.79 | $7,199.79 | $6,799.79 | $21,037.63 |

| Unit | G | H | I | J | K | Totals |
|---|---|---|---|---|---|---|
| Before value | $73,500 | $72,000 | $77,000 | $89,500 | $88,900 | $910,600 |
| Percent of common area | 8.30% | 8.30% | 8.29% | 10.72% | 10.72% | 100% |
| Percent of take | $2,714.10 | $2,714.10 | $2,710.83 | $3,505.44 | $3,505.44 | $32,700 |
| Remainder as part of whole | $70,786 | $69,286 | $74,289 | $85,995 | $85,395 | $877,900 |
| Value before cure | $60,400 | $59,300 | $63,500 | $74,000 | $73,500 | $744,700 |
| Damages | $10,386 | $9,986 | $10,789 | $11,995 | $11,895 | $133,200 |
| Value after cure | $68,500 | $67,400 | $72,200 | $85,000 | $84,400 | $843,000 |
| Curable damages | $8,100 | $8,100 | $8,700 | $11,000 | $10,900 | $98,300 |
| Incurable damages | $2,286 | $1,886 | $2,089 | $995 | $995 | $34,900 |
| Pro rata of net cost to cure | $2,402.85 | $2,402.85 | $2,399.96 | $3,103.44 | $3,103.44 | $28,950 |
| Total per unit | $7,402.95 | $7,002.95 | $7,199.79 | $7,603.88 | $7,603.88 | $96,550 |

## Conclusions

This particular case was the subject of two trials. The first trial resulted in a mistrial after a lengthy *voir dire* (preliminary examination) of the appraiser. The mistrial was granted due to time constraints as insufficient time had been scheduled given the complicated nature of the case. The second trial covered a two-week trial block and occurred about nine months later. The property owner's appraiser estimated damages at $925,000, inclusive of business damages.

Our business damage expert testified to a range of damage from $0 to $33,000, giving us a range of total value, inclusive of business damages, up to about $111,000.

The final verdict was $115,468, inclusive of business damages. The defendants had refused an offer of over $250,000 from the FDOT while the jury was deliberating and only a few minutes later received less than half that amount by verdict.

### Acknowledgments
The author would like to thank Rodney C. Wade, Esq., for providing input on legal issues involved in this case study.

CASE STUDY 1.6

# Special Benefits

*By Lori E. Safer, MAI, MRICS*

## The Assignment

We were hired by the state attorney general's office, which had filed a condemnation action against the property owner. The state required the property as part of a road-widening and improvement project and had been unable to negotiate with the property owner. The case was ultimately settled under confidential terms.

This case occurred in the state of Washington, which follows the federal rule that special benefits can be offset against both the damages to the remainder and the value of the land taken. It should be noted that only 18 states follow this rule.[1] As will be seen in this case, the purpose of the federal rule is to ensure that property owners are in the same monetary position in the after condition as they were in the before condition.

In this case study, we concluded that although the project itself did not produce a special benefit, the acquisition of a portion of the property that included the existing septic system produced a special benefit to the property because of a preexisting failure of a separate septic system that needed to be replaced. The acquisition and subsequent damages to the property produced a special benefit to the subject property that partially offset the market value of the take and related damages.

Our methodology first required estimating the market value of the fee simple interest in the entire property and then estimating the market value of the remainder. Then, through further analysis, the difference between the two values was allocated between the value of the real property acquired and the value of the damages and special benefits to the remaining real property and property rights.

## The Subject Property

The property consists of a 68,704-sq.-ft. (1.578-acre) rural parcel improved with a 4,286-sq.-ft., wood-frame restaurant constructed in

---

1. J. D. Eaton, *Real Estate Valuation in Litigation*, 2nd ed. (Chicago: Appraisal Institute, 1995), 326-333.

1916. An apartment is located on the second floor, and there is an attached garage.

The site is zoned for neighborhood business (NB). This type of zoning allows for a variety of commercial uses, including the existing restaurant use. Parking requirements under the county zoning code call for one stall per 75 feet of dining or lounge area. In this case, 2,099 square feet divided by 75 equals 28 required stalls. The current parking area consists of gravel. The property is considered to be in conformance with current zoning, even though the parking area is not striped. The site coverage is 6.27%, well below that of more urban properties but not atypical for a rural commercial site due to the site requirements for on-site drain fields for septic systems.

Available utilities include public water, power, and telephone. The site is served by two separate septic systems:

1. A black water system, which handles sewage, located on the east side of the improvements (fronting the highway)
2. A gray water system, which handles kitchen and sink wastewater, located to the north of the improvements

The gray water system is failing, and the property owner has been cited by the county health department on several occasions. The gray water system needs to be replaced because it has exceeded its holding capacity.

The existing building has been inventoried by the county as a historical site but has not been designated as a historical landmark.

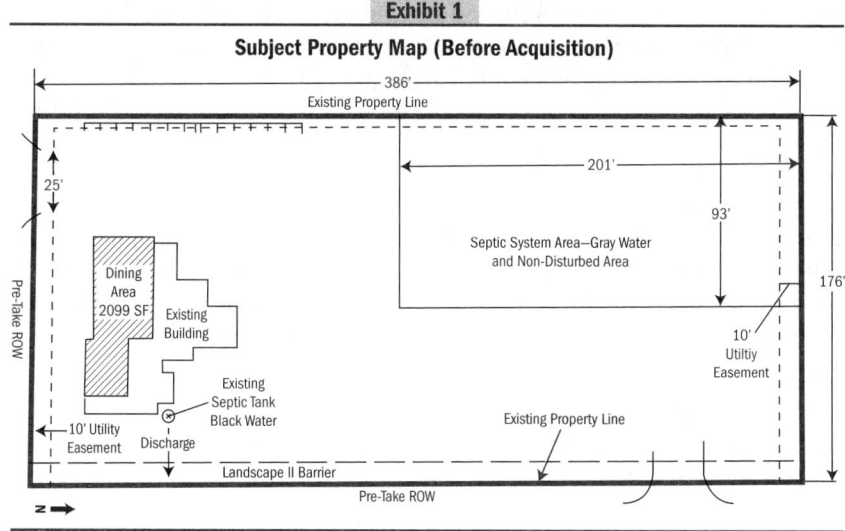

**Exhibit 1**

**Subject Property Map (Before Acquisition)**

Changes to the building would need to be reviewed by the county and would require special permit action.

## The Appraisal Problem

The state needs to acquire 8,848 square feet along the south and east sides of the subject property. The proposed acquisition will affect the site and improvements as follows:

- The site area will be reduced from 68,704 square feet to 59,856 square feet.
- The existing septic tank (black water) will discharge to the east across the proposed acquisition area and will need to be relocated elsewhere on the site.
- The garage will be too close to the right of way in the after condition, and the door will need to be relocated to another side of the building.

In the before condition, the property has a failing gray water system that needs to be replaced. Because of the proposed acquisition, the existing black water septic system, which is within the road-widening strip being acquired, will need to be relocated on the site.

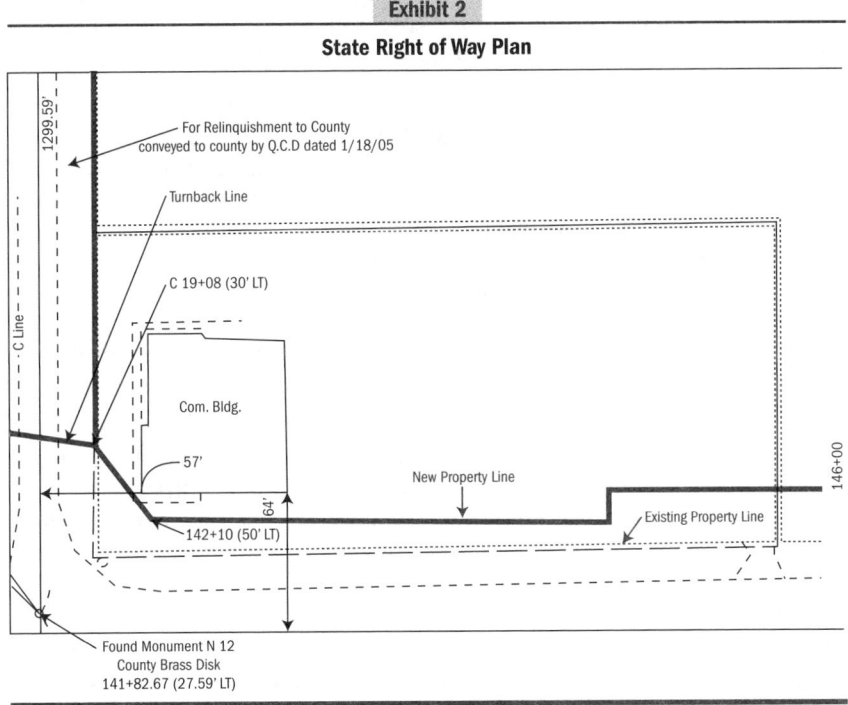

Exhibit 2
State Right of Way Plan

There is no room for relocating the black water system unless a new combined black water and gray water system can be constructed on the reserve drain field.

### Special Benefits

*Special benefits* pertain to any value accruing to the remainder of a property by reason of acquisition and use by the state of a portion of such property where such value is special to said remainder and not enjoyed by the general public (*Washington State Right of Way Manual, Appraisal Report Guide,* September 2004).

## Valuation of the Property in the Before Condition

### Highest and Best Use in the Before Condition

The highest and best use of the property as vacant is for development of a commercial use consistent with current zoning. The highest and best use of the property as improved is the continuation of the current use as a restaurant with the gray water system replaced.

### Land Valuation–Before

The land sales shown in Exhibit 3 were used in the analysis to estimate the underlying land value for the subject property in the before condition. The subject property land was valued appropriately at $5 per square foot as of the date of the take, or $343,520, rounded to $345,000.

#### Exhibit 3

| Sale | Location | Date | Sale Price | Lot Size (sq. ft.) | Price/Sq. Ft. |
|---|---|---|---|---|---|
| 1 | 747 Boeing St. | May 2011 | $200,000 | 43,566 | $4.59 |
| 2 | 623 Sherlock Ave. | Apr. 2011 | $175,000 | 30,056 | $5.82 |
| 3 | 852 Stevens St. | Dec. 2010 | $535,740 | 126,398 | $4.24 |
| 4 | 907 Coal St. | June 2010 | $442,500 | 75,056 | $5.90 |
|   | Subject property |   |   | 68,700 |   |

### Valuation of the Improved Property–Before

All three approaches to value were used to value the property. However, only the sales comparison approach is presented in this case study.

The improved sales listed in Exhibit 4 were used in this analysis to estimate the overall value of the property as improved in the before condition.

The subject has a fairly low site coverage ratio because of the presence of the two septic systems, which is not unusual for rural commercial properties. We therefore searched for improved sales that

### Exhibit 4

| Sale | Location | Date | Sale Price | Bldg. Size (sq. ft.) | Lot Size (sq. ft.) | Coverage | Price/ Sq. Ft. Bldg. |
|---|---|---|---|---|---|---|---|
| 1 | 1404 Coal St. | May 2011 | $875,000 | 6,000 | 85,714 | 7% | $145.83 |
| 2 | 1502 S. Train St. | Jan. 2011 | $750,000 | 5,000 | 15,152 | 33% | $150.00 |
| 3 | 635 F Ave. | Nov. 2010 | $1,422,744 | 12,816 | 69,139 | 19% | $111.01 |
| 4 | 102 E. Main St. | July 2010 | $600,900 | 3,960 | 19,800 | 20% | $151.74 |
| | Subject property | | | 4,286 | 68,700 | 6% | |

were most similar to the subject in terms of site coverage, improvement size, and overall site area. Without considering the replacement of the gray water system mandated by the health department, we concluded that the property is most appropriately valued at $145 per square foot of building area, or $621,470, rounded to $620,000.

## Deferred Maintenance—Repair of the Septic System

In the before condition, the subject property suffered from a failing gray water septic system. We contacted a construction company and a septic specialist to obtain cost estimates to replace or repair the gray water system. Because the gray water system has exceeded its holding capacity, it will need to be replaced at a cost of $40,000.

## Before Value Conclusion

We deducted the cost to replace the failing gray water septic system from our before value conclusion as follows:

| | |
|---|---|
| Market value potential of property | $620,000 |
| Less cost to replace gray water septic system | − 40,000 |
| "As is" value of property in the before condition | $580,000 |

Subtracting the value of the underlying land at $5 per square foot, or $345,000, the implied portion attributable to the building is $235,000, as shown below.

| | |
|---|---|
| Total value | $580,000 |
| Land contribution | − 345,000 |
| Implied improvement value | $235,000 |

# Description of the Property—After Condition
## Description of the Acquisition

The state is acquiring 8,848 square feet along the east and south frontages of the subject property. The site's frontage and visibility remain the same in the after condition.

## Impact of the Proposed Acquisition

In the after condition, the land area will be reduced to 59,856 square feet (from 68,704 square feet in the before condition). The site area will be reduced, and the shape of the property will change. However, access to the site will remain the same as in the before condition. Additionally, there would still be adequate site area to construct a variety of improvements consistent with current zoning, if the site were vacant. Therefore, we concluded that the per-square-foot value of the site remains the same in the after condition.

The black water septic system is located within the proposed acquisition area and will need to be relocated elsewhere on the site. The construction company and septic specialist concluded that in order to meet county health department regulations, a new septic system will need to be constructed on the subject reserve drain field. This new system will be a combined gray and black water system due to the lack of site area to replace both the black and gray water systems with separate drain fields (as configured in the before condition). The contractor estimated that the cost to replace the failing gray water system with a combined gray and black water system will be $100,000, which can be allocated as $40,000 to replace the gray water system and $60,000 to replace the black water system.

Current county regulations require building setbacks of 60 feet from a highway right of way. We concluded that there are no proximity damages. However, the location of the new right of way is close enough to the non-restaurant portion of the building (the garage) to require a physical change to the improvements. This will be discussed later in this case study in the section on cost to cure.

## After Value Analysis
### Highest and Best Use as Though Vacant

We concluded that the highest and best use of the site as though vacant remains the same as in the before condition: development with a rural commercial use that is consistent with current zoning.

### Highest and Best Use as Improved

As stated previously, the subject in the before condition is improved with a restaurant building that was constructed in 1916. This structure is consistent with the highest and best use of the site as though vacant and, while it lies within the setbacks of the proposed right of way, it is considered to be a legal, nonconforming use. However, access to the east side of the building (the non-restaurant/garage portion of the improvements) will be affected by the proximity of the new right of way. We obtained a cost-to-cure estimate to move the garage door to the north side of the building to maintain similar access and utility.

The highest and best use is concluded to be the same as in the before condition: continued use of the existing building (which will require relocating the garage door and replacing the septic system). Although the property is now a legal nonconforming use because of its location within the required road setbacks, we concluded that there are no proximity damages.

## Land Valuation–After Condition

In the after condition, the subject property as though vacant has characteristics that are essentially the same as they were in the before condition. The same land sales used in the before valuation analysis are used in the after valuation. After comparing and contrasting the comparable land sales with the subject, we estimated that the subject as though vacant and in the after condition would have the same value per square foot as in the before condition. Based on the after land area of the site, the concluded land value is $299,280, rounded to $300,000.

## Improvement Value–After Condition

Based on the concluded value in the before condition, the implied value of the improvements in the after condition is $150,000, as shown below.

| | |
|---|---|
| Improvement value | $275,000 |
| Less cost to cure garage | − 25,000 |
| Less cost to replace black and gray water septic systems | − 100,000 |
| Improvement value–after condition | $150,000 |

## Damages, Benefits, and Cost to Cure

The proposed right of way is relatively close to the eastern side of the building, and the garage area will no longer be accessible in the after condition. A contractor was hired to provide a cost estimate to relocate the garage door to the north side of the building. The cost to cure the garage is estimated at $25,000, which includes direct and indirect costs (plans, permits, taxes, etc.).

In addition to the garage door, the black water septic system is located within the proposed right of way and will need to be relocated to the northern portion of the site. The cost to construct the new septic system is $100,000, which can be broken out as $60,000 to replace the black water system and $40,000 to replace the failing gray water system. Because the property owner had to replace the failing gray water system in the before condition, $40,000 of the overall $100,000 combined septic system cost is considered to be a special benefit to the property.

The following chart illustrates the after value of the subject property:

| | |
|---|---|
| Building | $150,000 |
| Plus land value | 300,000 |
| Total | $450,000 |

This value reflects the damages to the building as they relate to the cost to cure and the benefits to the property overall from replacing the failing gray water septic system.

## Conclusions

The difference between the before and after values is summarized below.

| | |
|---|---|
| Value of the property in the before condition | $580,000 |
| Value of the property in the after condition | − 450,000 |
| Difference | $130,000 |
| | |
| Allocation: | |
| Acquisition of site area | $45,000 |
| Damages to garage | 25,000 |
| Replacement of black and gray water septic systems | 100,000 |
| Less special benefit to improvements | − 40,000 |
| Total | $130,000 |

In this appraisal assignment, the property suffered from deferred maintenance because of the failing gray water system in the before condition. In the after condition, the state paid the property owner for a combined black and gray water system at a cost that is much greater than what the $40,000 cost would have been to replace only the gray water system in the before condition. The special benefit is *not* the cost of the combined new system. This is a common error. The special benefit is reflected in the difference between the value of the property with a failing gray water system and the value of the property with a replaced gray water system, rather than the total cost to replace both systems. The black water system had to be replaced only because of the state's action. The gray water drain field needed to be replaced in the before condition regardless of the state's action, and therefore the replacement of the gray water system is considered to be a special benefit to the property. We did consider whether the property value in the after condition would be higher because of the new system but concluded that the market did not recognize such an enhancement in value.

This case occurred in the state of Washington, where the rule that special benefits are offset against both the acquisition and damages to the property applies. As a result, the just compensation to be paid to the property owner was concluded to be $130,000 rather than $170,000 (the sum of the acquisition at $45,000, plus the damages to the building at $25,000, plus the full cost to replace the black and gray water septic systems at $100,000). Another way to consider the offset of the special benefits against the acquisition and the damages to the building is to consider that the property owner has to pay $40,000 to replace the gray water system no matter what. If the system had been replaced the year before, the owner would have been paid the full $170,000. However, the net to the property owner would still be $130,000, considering the payment made the prior year.

Exhibit 5 shows the case study data in a tabulation form that is used by the state of Washington for all appraisal assignments. While it is not indicative of appraisal methodology, it presents all of the relevant components and allows the appraiser and reviewer to quickly grasp the appraisal problem and valuation issues.

## Exhibit 5
## RURAL RESTAURANT PROPERTY
(Accounting tabulation--NOT indicative of appraisal method employed)

**INDICATED VALUE BEFORE ACQUISITION**
Highest and best use before: commercial

| Land value | Area | Unit Value | | |
|---|---|---|---|---|
| | 68,704 | $5.00 | $345,000 (rounded) | |
| Total land value | | | | $345,000 |
| Improvements | | | | |
| Restaurant | | | $275,000 (rounded) | |
| Less cost to replace gray water septic system | | | -$40,000 | |
| Total improvement value | | | | $235,000 |
| **TOTAL INDICATED VALUE BEFORE** | | | | **$580,000** |

**INDICATED VALUE OF REMAINDER**
Highest and best use: commercial

| Land value | Area | Unit Value | | |
|---|---|---|---|---|
| | 59,856 | $5.00 | $300,000 (rounded) | |
| Total land value | | | | $300,000 |
| Improvements | | | | |
| Restaurant | | | $275,000 | |
| Less cost to relocate garage door | | | -$25,000 | |
| Less cost to replace black and gray water septic systems | | | -$100,000 | |
| Total improvement value | | | | $150,000 |
| **TOTAL INDICATED VALUE AFTER** | | | | **$450,000** |

**BREAKDOWN OF ACQUISITION**

| Land value | Area | Unit Value | | |
|---|---|---|---|---|
| Unencumbered | 8,848 | $5.00 | $45,000 (rounded) | |
| Total land value | | | | $45,000 |
| Improvements | | | | |
| Total improvement value | | | | $0 |
| Damages (cost to cure) | | | | |
| Garage portion of building | | | $25,000 | |
| Replace black and gray water septic systems | | | $100,000 | |
| Benefits | | | | |
| Replaced gray water system | | | -$40,000 | |
| Total damages and benefits | | | | $85,000 |
| **Total acquisition value** | | | | **$130,000** |
| Difference between the before and after values | | | | $130,000 |

## Case Study 2.1

# Missing Waterline Easement–Water Rights

*By Randy A. Williams, MAI, SR/WA, FRICS*

This case study is concerned with a title company and an easement that was missed in the title search. The assignment was to provide a diminution in value appraisal, which would calculate the insured's actual loss as defined in the policy. The assignment called for the estimation of two values: the market value of the property without the easement and the market value of the property with the easement in place.

The assignment began when the appraiser received a phone call from an attorney representing a title company. A property owner had purchased a house with an undisclosed waterline easement across an adjacent property. The title insurance company insured the existence of the easement. A house was built on the adjacent property that the waterline ran through and the waterline was severed (see Exhibit 1). The owner of the subject property discovered that the waterline easement was not conveyed. The owner of the adjacent property would not allow a waterline easement or replacement of the existing waterline. The title company had to compensate the owner of the subject property for the loss of the waterline easement.

Municipal water is available in this neighborhood, but at a very high cost. The subject lot is more than one acre in size, and it is very expensive to water with municipal water.

## Scope of Work

As will be discussed later, the appraiser was able to find a cure for the lost easement. The waterline had not been in place long enough for the subject owner to claim a prescriptive easement. Therefore, the cost of this cure will reflect the difference in the value of the property after the missing waterline easement was discovered.

### Course of Action

This problem calls for a before and after analysis. First, the property value is estimated with the easement. Then the valuation process is repeated without the easement across the neighboring lot in place.

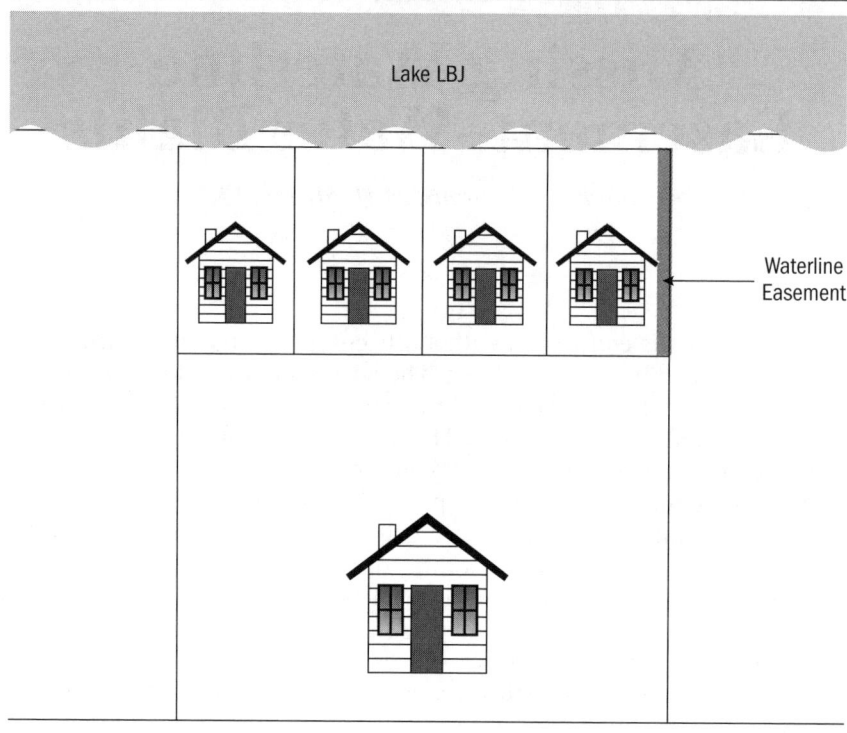

This is done to ascertain if there was any diminishment or damage to the property due to the loss of the easement.

## Surrounding Area Analysis
### Location

The subject neighborhood and market area are defined as the Highland Lakes region of Central Texas, located in the south and western portions of Burnet County and the eastern portion of Llano County. The neighborhood is influenced by the Highland Lake system, a series of lakes situated along the course of the Colorado River. The lakes nearest the subject are Lake Lyndon B. Johnson (Lake LBJ), Lake Marble Falls, Inks Lake, Lake Buchanan, and the northernmost section of Lake Travis.

There are several resort communities to the south and east of the market area. The communities of Meadowlakes, Horseshoe Bay, Granite Shoals, Highland Haven, and Sunrise Beach Village are situated along two of the lakes formed by the Colorado River. Located on either side of Lake Marble Falls and Lake LBJ, these communities have private shorefront properties available and several points of public access to the lakes. Additionally, Meadowlakes, Horseshoe Bay, and Kingsland have golf courses associated with the developments.

The neighborhood's terrain is rolling to steeply hilly, which is characteristic of the hill country west of Austin. The areas around Kingsland are rural and most of the land outside the city limits is used for agriculture, primarily for livestock ranching. In addition, many vineyards have been planted recently. The hilly topography and shallow, rocky topsoil limit crop farming. The area's lakes are popular boating and fishing destinations, and the countryside is famed throughout Texas for superb hunting.

The subject neighborhood is about 85% built up, with a number of vacant parcels available for development. The predominant land use is single-family residential and most homes are of older, frame construction.

## Outlook and Conclusions

The subject neighborhood is in a steady, moderate growth stage with noticeable revitalization of the older residential buildings. Single-family residential developments are scattered throughout the area and are reached by feeder streets connected to the primary roadways. Multifamily properties are also found throughout the area, on the larger residential feeder streets within the city limits of Kingsland and Marble Falls. Most of the city's commercial (retail and office) properties are on the primary highways. Western and northern Marble Falls have considerable new commercial development on the city's two main traffic arteries, West FM 1431 (east/west) and US 281 (north/south). These trends are projected to continue in the near future.

# Description and Analysis of the Land

The following description is based on our inspection of the property, analysis of the legal description, and experience in the market area:

| Land Description | |
|---|---|
| Land area | 1.07 acres; 46,661 sq. ft. |
| Land area (usable) | 1.07 acres; 46,661 sq. ft. |
| Source of land area | CAD |
| Primary street frontage | Lakeview Dr. |
| Shape | Irregular |
| Corner | Yes |
| Topography | Level and sloping |
| Drainage | Adequate |
| Environmental hazards | None reported or observed |
| Ground stability | No problems reported or observed |
| Flood area panel number | 481531000B |
| Date | September 27, 1991 |
| Zone | X |
| Description | Outside of 500-yr. floodplain |
| Insurance required? | No |
| **Zoning: Other Regulations** | |
| Zoning jurisdiction | Sunset Beach |
| Zoning designation | SF |
| Description | Single family |
| Legally conforming? | Yes |
| Zoning change likely | No |
| Permitted uses | Single family |
| **Utilities** | |
| **Service** | **Provider** |
| Water | LCRA |
| Sewer | Private septic |
| Electricity | Pedernales |
| Natural gas | N/A |
| Local phone | Verizon |

## Easements, Encroachments and Restrictions

We are not aware of any easements, encumbrances, or restrictions that would adversely affect the use of the site. We were not provided with a survey, but an inspection of the site revealed no apparent encroachments. It is assumed that the property is free and clear of encroachments.

## Other Land Use Regulations

We are not aware of any land use regulations other than zoning that would affect the property, nor are we aware of any moratoriums on development. The property is in the Sunset Beach zoning district.

## Summary of Land Description

Overall, the physical characteristics of the site are suitable for the uses permitted by zoning. Most factors, including its topography, location, accessibility, and availability of utilities, are positive attributes. In comparison to other residential sites in the region, we rate the subject as follows:

| Attribute Ratings | |
|---|---|
| View | Average |
| Utilities | Average |
| Shape and contour | Average |
| Land available for future development | Average |
| Landscaping | Average |

# Improvements Description and Analysis

The subject property includes a 1,925-sq.-ft. single-family residence with a 155-sq.-ft. enclosed porch with no air-conditioning and a 585-sq.-ft., attached two-car garage, all of which were constructed in 1980. The subject residence has a concrete slab foundation. The pitched roofs of the residence and the garage are of composition shingle. The pitched roof of the covered concrete patio is metal. The exterior of the subject residence has brick masonry/masonite siding, a covered concrete patio, and a chain link yard fence. The driveway for the subject is paved asphalt. The subject property also includes a 736-sq.-ft. metal outbuilding with a concrete slab foundation.

# Highest and Best Use Analysis

## Highest and Best Use as if Vacant

The only uses permitted under the zoning that are consistent with prevailing land use patterns in the area are residential uses. There are no physical limitations that would prohibit development of a residential use on the site.

Based on our analysis of the market, there is currently adequate demand for residential uses in the subject area. A newly developed residence on the site would have a value commensurate with its cost. Therefore, residential use is considered to be financially feasible.

There does not appear to be any reasonably probable use of the site that would generate a higher residual land value than residential use. Residential use is the only use of the site that meets the four tests of highest and best use so it is concluded to be the highest and best use of the property as if vacant.

## As Improved

Currently, the subject property is developed with a single-family residence, which is considered to add substantial contributory value to the site. For this reason, it is the appraisers' opinion that the highest and best use of the property as improved is continued use as a single-family residence.

## Most Probable Buyer

The most probable buyer is an owner-user.

# Valuation Analysis

## Valuation Methodology

Appraisers usually consider three approaches in estimating the market value of real property: the cost approach, the sales comparison approach, and the income capitalization approach. The subject is a 25-year-old, single-family residence in a neighborhood that is predominantly owner occupied. As such, the cost and income approaches were not considered applicable.

The purpose of this analysis was to estimate the impact on value (if any) of the loss of a waterline easement across an adjacent property. As the appraisers will explain later in the analysis, there is a cure for the loss of this waterline easement. The subject property as improved will be valued via the sales comparison approach, and the cost to cure will be deducted from this value.

## Sales Comparison Approach

The sales comparison approach is a set of procedures in which a value indication is developed by comparing the subject to similar properties that have recently been sold. The steps taken to apply the sales comparison approach were

- Research recent sales of comparable properties.
- Select sales most similar to the subject and assemble pertinent data.
- Compare the sales to the subject with regard to various elements of comparison and adjust the sale prices to compensate for all differences that affect value.
- Reconcile the adjusted prices of the sales into a value indication for the subject property.

First, we conducted a search of public records and proprietary data sources to identify recent improved residential sales in proximity to the subject with a similar highest and best use. From all the data reviewed, we selected the sales shown in Exhibits 2 and 3 as the best indicators of the subject's value. We chose price per square foot as the most appropriate unit of comparison because market participants typically compare sale prices and land values on this basis.

## Exhibit 2
### Summary of Improved Sales

| No. | Address | Sale Date | Sale Price | Sq. Ft. |
|---|---|---|---|---|
| 1 | 303 Circle Dr.<br>Sunrise Beach<br>Llano, TX | 03/05/04 | $98,300 | 1,578 |
| 2 | 123 Winding Way<br>Sunrise Beach<br>Llano, TX | 04/09/04 | $117,000 | 1,437 |
| 3 | 240 Overstreet Dr.<br>Sunrise Beach<br>Llano, TX | 08/30/04 | $75,000 | 1,224 |
| 4 | 604 Sandy Mountain Dr.<br>Sunrise Beach<br>Llano, TX | 11/15/04 | $185,000 | 1,325 |
| 5 | 106 Stribling Dr.<br>Sunrise Beach<br>Llano, TX | 03/14/05 | $110,000 | 2,088 |
| | Subject | | | 1,925 |

## Exhibit 3
### Comparable Sales Map

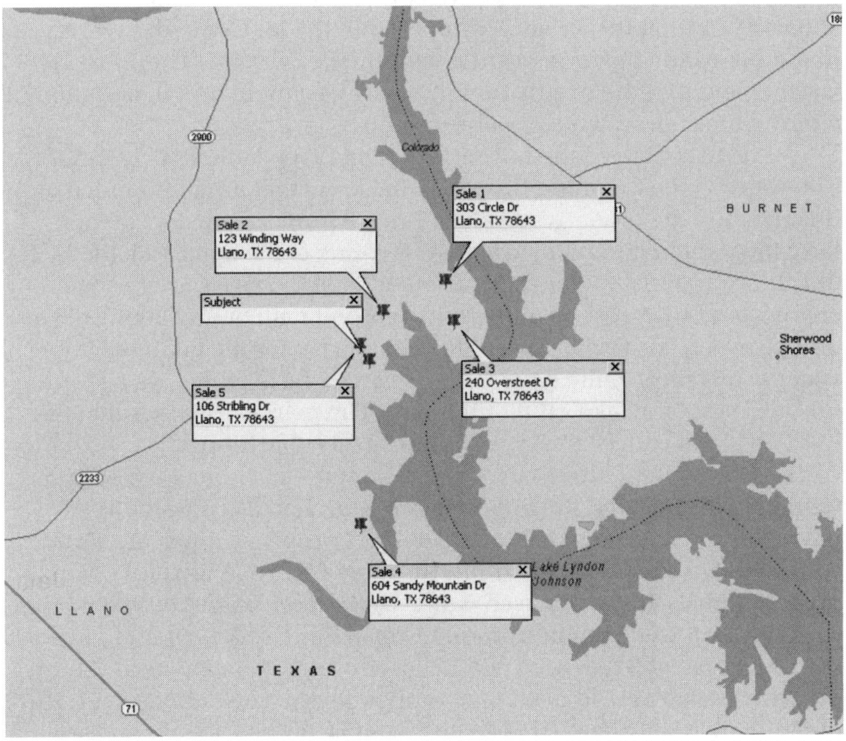

## Reconciliation and Conclusion of Value

The five comparable sales ranged in size from 1,224 to 2,088 square feet. All of the comparable sales either had access to lake water or to a well. After making minor adjustments to the unit prices of the comparable sales for size, age and condition, quality of construction, and other factors, we reconciled the value indications of the comparable sales to a unit price of $80 per square foot. As a result, we estimated the market value of the subject property as improved and subject to the hypothetical condition that the property had access to lake water to be $154,000.

## Exposure and Marketing Times

We estimated the exposure time for the property to be 12 months. The estimated marketing times was also 12 months.

## Diminution in Value

To analyze the diminution in value, we considered the feasibility of a new easement and waterline to access the waters of Lake LBJ and examined another alternative for the replacement of the waterline and the easement.

To research the feasibility of a new easement and waterline to access the waters of Lake LBJ, we contacted the owners of properties situated between the subject property and the lake. We discovered that none would agree to grant a waterline easement. Therefore, it was evident that the acquisition of a new easement and installation of a new waterline was not a viable option.

Next we contacted the Lower Colorado River Authority (LCRA). The water in the Colorado River and the lakes that are impounded on this river are the property of LCRA. Private property owners do not have the right to pump this water. At the time of the appraisal, the LCRA did allow property owners to take water from the river or lakes without charge, but LCRA reserved the right to prohibit all or any taking of river or lake waters for private use or to charge a fee for the taking of this water at any time in the future. Homeowners have pulled water from this lake since the lake's impoundment. The market assumes that the LCRA will not restrict this right in the foreseeable future.

In search of an alternative way to supply the subject property with irrigation water, the appraisers researched the possibility of having a water well drilled on the subject property. A private water well is legally permissible within the city of Sunrise Beach Village. To accomplish this, a licensed water well driller would be retained to apply for a well permit from the City of Sunrise Beach and pay the permit fee of $100. Also, the licensed water well driller and the property owner would need to comply with the regulations set forth in Ordinance Number 201, Articles I and II, of the City of Sunrise

Beach Village. Note that no underground water district controlled the drilling and pumping of water in Llano County, and at the time there were no pumping restrictions for private wells. Therefore, with the installation of a private water well, the property owners could have an unlimited supply of water to irrigate the subject property.

After discussions with four licensed water well drilling companies operating in the market area, we learned that the subject property was situated within a local aquifer of varying quantity and quality. However, because the subject was in proximity to Lake LBJ, the probability of drilling a water well that would produce sufficient water quantity and quality was extremely high. Therefore, the drilling of a private water well on the subject property was a viable alternative and was considered by the appraisers to be the cost to cure.

The interviews with the well drilling companies had revealed that the subject lot was not large enough to be granted a well permit by the city. After we interviewed city officials and the mayor and explained the circumstances, however, the city agreed that a variance to allow the well would be granted if the owner applied for the permit. As a result, our conclusions were subject to the extraordinary assumption that there was a high probability of the permit being granted.

The appraiser obtained verbal estimates from four licensed water well drilling companies familiar with the problems associated with installing a water well in the subject area. The cost to drill as well as the cost of set casing, the well pump, pipe, the pressure tank, electrical wiring and connections, and any other work or materials necessary ranged from $2,500 to $4,500, including the $100 permit fee. Because of the difficulties of installing a water well in this area, the appraisers felt that the highest estimate should be used. Therefore, the cost to cure was considered to be $4,500. In comparison, the cost of municipal water to irrigate the lot was estimated to be $400 per month during the summer and fall. Given this cost of approximately $2,000 per year, the well was the most feasible solution. The costs of pumping from a well versus pumping from the easement were similar. While the well would ultimately require more maintenance than a buried waterline, this factor was offset by the assurance that water from the well could not be cut off.

Based on the analyses and conclusions in the accompanying report and subject to the definitions, assumptions, and limiting conditions expressed herein, it was our opinion that the market value of the fee simple estate of the subject as of June 28, 2005, was:

| Diminution Value/Cost to Cure | |
|---|---:|
| Concluded value of the subject property excluding diminishment | $154,000 |
| Diminution value/cost to cure | − $4,500 |
| Diminished value of the subject property | $149,500 |

## Conclusions

In this assignment, the property owner wanted to have his access to inexpensive irrigation water restored. The simple solution would have been to reestablish an easement to the lake. However, the lakefront lots were being developed with large, expensive homes, and there was no way to legally compel these owners to grant an easement. An investigation in the neighborhood showed that many of the older non-waterfront homes had wells for irrigation. The well drillers we interviewed were certain they would be successful in drilling for water. One problem to be overcome was that the subject lot was not large enough to be allowed a private well under current restrictions. By contacting and explaining the circumstances to the City of Sunrise Beach, we were able to overcome this problem and make the homeowner whole. The case was settled based on the cost to cure.

# Case Study 2.2

# Missing Waterline Easement–Property Boundary

*By Shawn Wilson, MAI*

Central Florida is home to many "ski lakes." These are typically small to medium-sized freshwater lakes with boat access and water conditions conducive to waterskiing. The subject of this case study is a property located on a ski lake in a quiet residential neighborhood in a medium-sized town. The lake has clear water and a sandy bottom, which are prized attributes in a residential market area with dozens of lakes to choose from. Most of the lots on this lake have long been developed with single-unit homes. Most of these homes have boat docks, many with covered sitting areas, boat lifts, or both.

The north side of the lake adjoins an arterial roadway. As a result, several commercial uses, including a new hotel, have rear lot water frontage on the lake's north side. Public water has long been available in the neighborhood, but public sewer service is restricted to lots on or near the arterial roadway. The other properties around the lake use on-site septic systems with drain fields.

The subject property is a 1.04-acre vacant lot with a metes and bounds legal description. It has paved road frontage and good lake frontage, and it faces west for spectacular sunset views. Its south boundary adjoins a "creek," now a channelized canal, that provides drainage and flood control in the area (see Exhibit 1). The creek is not navigable because a flood control structure (similar to a concrete dam) was installed near the intersection of the creek and the lake decades earlier.

The topography of the lot is mounded, with the center of the site well above the grade of the adjoining roadway and the lake's shoreline. The legal description of the site includes land beneath the waters of both the lake and creek, so the size of the upland portion of the 1.04-acre lot is not readily evident. Note also that the observed upland size would be larger in times of drought and smaller in times of heavy rain.

The owners of the property made a claim on their title insurance policy because it did not reflect the existence of a permanent easement for the creek. When the owners became aware of the easement, they felt that the value of the land was severely diminished. A lawsuit was filed. The attorney for the title insurance company ordered an appraisal.

## Exhibit 1

*Applications in Litigation Valuation: A Pragmatist's Guide*

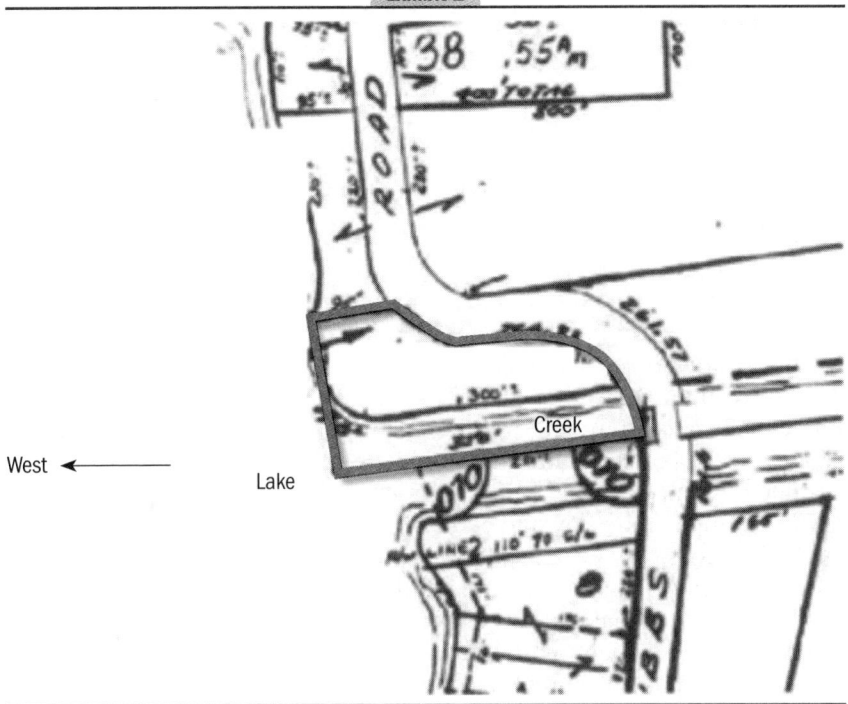

**Exhibit 2**

The easement area includes the channelized creek and flood control structure, but it also extends 110 feet north of the centerline of the creek into the lot (see Exhibit 2). From tax maps and visual inspection, the easement could encumber 50% or more of the upland area of the waterfront lot. Structural improvements cannot be built within the area of the easement.

In order to complete the appraisal assignment, the following actions were necessary:

1. Identify the location of the easement on the subject property.
2. Determine the rights and restrictions associated with the easement.
3. Analyze the zoning, future land use, and building regulations that govern the lot.
4. Identify any entitlements or special rights available to the property.
5. Identify the upland area beyond required setbacks from the lake and creek.
6. Determine the highest and best use of the lot without the permanent easement.

7. Determine the highest and best use of the lot with the permanent easement in place.
8. Determine land value with and without the easement.

A recent survey of the property was not available to the appraiser. An older tax map depicted the general shape and characteristics of the site and indicated a total land area of 1.12 acres. A newer GIS tax map depicted a similar shape but a somewhat different location of the waters' edge for the lake and creek.

The easement document, dating back to 1966, was located after a long search of the county engineering office's historic maps relating to the channelization of the creek. A notation on one of those maps led to the official record book and page citation for the easement. That document states that the areas encumbered by the easement are for "construction to include spoil placement, widening, deepening, straightening, and installation of appurtenant structures; for or in connection with the operation, maintenance, and inspection of such channel; and for the flowage of any waters in, over, upon, or through such channel."

The subject property has residential zoning and future residential land use. Both the lake and the creek are classified by the county as "surface water bodies," which triggers special permitting and setback requirements for development on adjoining land. The applicable section of the land development regulations states that the required setback is "the lesser of 50 feet or 40% of the average depth of the site as perpendicularly measured from the mean high waterline." Other restrictions of note are:

- The minimum floor area of the dwelling is 1,000 square feet.
- The minimum ground floor area of the dwelling is 750 square feet excluding carports, porches, patios, storage, and utility rooms.
- Septic systems must be set back at least 75 feet from the creek and lake.
- A septic system cannot be located under a structure or driveway.

The subject property is a waterfront lot, so development regulations pertaining to boat docks were also researched. In that county, a dock or boathouse can only be built as an accessory to a dwelling on the same site or within 150 feet of a property under the same ownership with residential occupancy. The 150 feet is measured as a straight-line distance between the closest corners of the two properties. As a result, the legally permissible use of the site could only be a house, with or without a dock. The site could not be developed with only a dock or boathouse. Note that the only properties within 150 feet of the subject property already have a boat dock or are used for nonresidential purposes and therefore do not qualify for a boat dock on the effective date of value.

The age of the easement and the long history of continuous ownership before purchase by the current property owner suggested that the subject site may have existed in its present configuration before the onset of zoning and other modern land use regulations. Another trip to the county planning department confirmed that this was the case. Because the lot had existed in its current configuration prior to January 1, 1971, the subject property was designated as a nonconforming lot of record in that county.

The development regulations set forth special entitlements for such lots of record, with the right to construct residential dwellings and customary accessory buildings "even though such lot fails to meet the requirements for area or width, or both, that are generally applicable in the district, provided that yard dimensions and other requirements not involving area or width, or both, of the lot, shall conform to the Regulations."

The width and area of the site did not appear to be as problematic for legally permissible development as did the waterfront setback requirements. However, additional research with county representatives and the various land development regulations indicated that even lots of record must conform to setback requirements for environmentally sensitive land, such as the lake and creek. Hardship variances are available from the county in some circumstances, but they are not applicable to environmental setbacks.

Because of the poor maps and the knowledge that legal permissibility for development of the site depends on setbacks of "the lesser of 50 feet or 40% of the average depth of the site as perpendicularly measured from the mean high waterline," the entire analysis hinges upon accurate identification of that mean high waterline. This means that the appraiser needs assistance from a really, really good surveyor.

A conversation with the most highly recommended local surveyor did not inspire confidence. The appraiser then called an exceptionally intelligent and experienced surveyor friend, inconveniently located 100 miles away from the subject property, to ask for a referral. The appraiser learned the bad news: there is no such thing as a mean high waterline on a lake, which has a normal pool. However, the good news was that it is not uncommon for surveyors to cover a wide geographical area, so the exceptionally intelligent surveyor could handle the assignment himself.

The surveyor provided a bid for services to retaining counsel, a contract was signed, and the survey effort began. The appraiser provided a copy of the legal description, the easement, and the land development regulations relating to setbacks from the water. The surveyor explained that the term *mean high waterline* relates to saltwater bodies and that freshwater bodies instead have a normal pool, or safe upland line. Other names for the applicable water level used by market participants in that area include *ordinary high waterline*, *mean water level*, *high waterline*, and *mean high waterline*.

The surveyor explained that the flood control structure adjoining the subject property would likely have a measuring device for the water level, so he would research the appropriate agency records. He also used historical aerial photography, environmental maps, and government water management records to establish a normal pool, or safe upland line, at 102.7 feet above sea level. That line as well as other lines relating to the lake and creek are shown in his survey (Exhibit 3). The surveyor also found that the 1.12-acre size reported in the tax records was in reality only 1.04 acres.

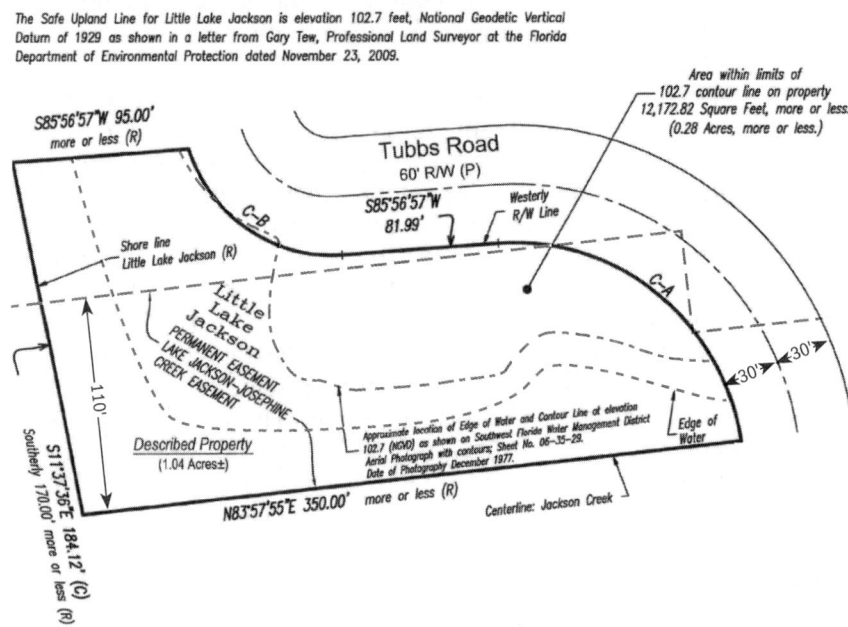

**Exhibit 3**

The Safe Upland Line for Little Lake Jackson is elevation 102.7 feet, National Geodetic Vertical Datum of 1929 as shown in a letter from Gary Tew, Professional Land Surveyor at the Florida Department of Environmental Protection dated November 23, 2009.

Pertinent land areas were calculated by the surveyor as follows:

| | |
|---|---|
| Total area in legal description | 1.04 acres |
| Area above the 102.7 contour line | 0.28 acres |
| Area below the 102.7 contour line | 0.76 acres |
| Area within the permanent easement | 0.84 acres |
| Area outside the permanent easement | 0.20 acres |
| Area landward of shoreline | 0.62 acres |
| Area below the water | 0.42 acres |

The highest and best use analysis was dependent on the setback distance from the 102.7 contour line or safe upland line (also described as the *mean high waterline* in county regulations). The actual edge of the water is currently below the 102.7 contour line due to drought conditions. However, the search for and analysis of comparable sales were also dependent on the upland areas of the property, considered both with and without the easement. The upland areas of the site are those landward of the edge of the water. As stated previously, the water's edge of a freshwater lake changes over time, depending on the season, rainfall, water table, and even the phases of the moon. The surveyor located the edge of the water using various maps and governmental indices and calculated the land areas as 0.62 acres landward of the shoreline (uplands) and 0.42 acres below the shoreline (wetlands).

Note that the water's edge depicted on the survey is situated well inland of the current water level (edge of water) line depicted on the survey. This is due to mild drought conditions that had persisted for a period of several years prior to the analysis. The physical shoreline can change frequently, while the water's edge is a more fixed analytical boundary.

The survey indicates that the land above the 102.7 contour line—the line at which building setbacks must begin—is almost entirely located within the permanent easement. Half of the analysis of legally permissible uses is now easy. With the easement in place, the lot is not buildable. A house cannot be built, and therefore a dock cannot be built. As a result, the highest and best use of the lot as encumbered by the easement is sale to an adjoining property owner or one within 150 feet as measured by the closest corners of the two properties.

The highest and best use as unencumbered by the easement is more complicated. Recall that the requirements for a house are a minimum ground floor footprint of 750 square feet along with a septic system that must be set back 75 feet from the creek and lake and cannot be built under the structure or driveway. The 75-foot setback from the creek pushes any possible location for the septic system towards the roadway in the same general vicinity of the only place to construct a driveway.

Many site plan possibilities were sketched out, but no workable combination was found. This inability to site a home with a related septic system and driveway above the 102.7 contour line was confirmed with government representatives in the planning and health departments. It was also double-checked by the surveyor. The highest and best use without the easement is the same as the highest and best use with the easement. In both scenarios, the lot is unbuildable.

A hypothetical condition was used to value the subject property as if it were not encumbered by the permanent easement that was the subject of the title insurance claim. This is the value "as insured."

A search for comparable sales yielded two recent sales of lakefront lots that were unbuildable due to their shape or size. Both had been purchased by adjoining landowners. The sales were analyzed using price per front foot, price per square foot, and overall sale price. Data summaries for these two sales follow.

## Sale 1. Property along Lake Damon

| | |
|---|---|
| Sale price | $3,000 |
| Size | 0.2116 acres or 9,218 sq. ft. (net of road) |
| Unit price | $0.33 per sq. ft. |
| | $38.96 per front ft. on lake |
| Comments | North Lake Damon Road divides this property into two sections. The larger portion of the site has frontage on Lake Damon. The front footage on Lake Damon is estimated to be 77 feet, based on an analysis of maps and the legal description. |

## Sale 2. Property along Lake Istokpoga

| | |
|---|---|
| Sale price | $20,000 |
| Size | 4.05 acres or 176,314 square feet |
| Unit Price | $0.11 per square foot |
| | $56.34 per front foot on lake |
| Comments | This site has canal and lake frontage along Lake Istokpoga. The front footage on Lake Istokpoga is estimated to be 355 feet, based on an analysis of maps and the legal description. The western 35 feet of the site is encumbered by a permanent easement. |

Application of the sales comparison approach is shown in Exhibit 4.

| | | Exhibit 4 | |
|---|---|---|---|
| Sale | Subject | 1929/871 Lake Damon | 1823/734 Lake Istokpoga |
| Date of sale | 1/17/2006 | 11/16/2005 | 1/30/2005 |
| Sale price | | $3,000 | $20,000 |
| Land area (acres) | 1.0400 | 0.2116 | 4.0500 |
| Lake frontage (front ft.) | 140 | 77 | 355 |
| Sale price/sq. ft. | | $0.33 | $0.11 |
| Sale price/front ft. | | $38.96 | $56.34 |
| **Element of Comparison** | | Adjustment | Adjustment |
| Land area (acres) | 1.0400 | 0.2116 | 4.0500 |
| | 0.62 uplands | Similar | Inferior |
| Zoning/FLU | R-1A/medium-density residential | AU/AU<br>Similar | AU/AU<br>Similar |
| Location | 3337 Tubbs Rd.<br>Urban | N. Lk. Damon Rd.<br>Suburban<br>Similar | CR 621<br>Rural<br>Inferior |
| Access/road frontage | Adequate | Adequate<br>Similar | Adequate<br>Similar |
| Utilities (telephone, electric, water, sewer) | TEW | TEW<br>Similar | TEW<br>Similar |
| Development potential | Unbuildable | Unbuildable | Purchased for mitigation |
| Lake | Little Lake Jackson | Lake Damon<br>Similar | Lake Istokpoga<br>Superior |
| Misc. | Adjoins canal | | Adjoins canal |
| **Composite comparison** | | Similar | Inferior |

The unadjusted range of unit prices among the comparable sales was between $0.11 and $0.33 per square foot. The unadjusted sale prices for the two comparables range from $3,000 to $20,000. The estimated prices per front foot range from $38.96 per front foot to $56.34 per front foot.

The most weight was given to the Lake Damon sale because it is more similar to the subject property in terms of size. The subject property is considered to be slightly superior to the Lake Damon property because it has more adjoining landowners within 150 feet who may be interested in the potential waterfront amenities of the site. The Lake Damon sale adjoins one single-unit home and a developed condominium complex, with only the single-unit home neighbor having reasonable expectations for beneficial use of the site.

The survey shown in Exhibit 3 was used for the purposes of calculating the front footage of the subject property. The distance from the north boundary to the south edge of the water is approximately 140 feet. This distance is tested using the front footage value indications shown below.

| | |
|---|---|
| Lake Damon | 140 front feet × $38.96 per front foot = $5,454 |
| Lake Istokpoga | 140 front feet × $56.34 per front foot = $7,888 |

The square foot prices for the properties were also tested for use in the analysis. The subject property has an upland area of 0.62 acres (1.04 acres minus 0.42 acres), or approximately 27,000 square feet. This land area is used to calculate value indications based on the comparable sales as follows:

| | |
|---|---|
| Lake Damon | 27,000 square feet × $0.33 per square foot = $8,910 |
| Lake Istokpoga | 27,000 square feet × $0.11 per square foot = $2,970 |

This analysis was given the least weight because of the difficulty of estimating upland area for the Lake Istokpoga sale.

Equal weight was given to the analysis using front-foot calculations and the overall sale price, with the market value estimated to be a rounded $10,000. When considering the subject property as encumbered by the permanent easement, the same effective date of value is used. No hypothetical condition is required. This is the value estimate "subject to the defect," or subject to the condition at issue in the title insurance claim ("as is"). The highest and best use, comparable sales, analysis of the sales, and potential purchasers for the site are identical to those for the property as unencumbered by the easement.

However, if given the choice between two identical properties in which all characteristics are equal except for a large area encumbered by a permanent easement, a well-informed potential buyer would choose the property without the easement. Because of this, a value differential is considered to exist. The quantity and quality of the sales of unbuildable waterfront properties were insufficient to extract a precise adjustment for the difference. The similarities between the two valuation scenarios, however, indicate that the value difference is small.

If the permanent easement had caused a change in highest and best use for the subject property whereby the lot was buildable without the easement and unbuildable with the easement, the value differential would be very large. Because the easement could encumber so many of the rights within the small area of land that lies above the 102.7 contour line, such an easement would be expected to have an impact of between 80% and 90% of the fee simple value of that land.

Instead, the presence of the easement on the subject property has no impact on the highest and best use of the site or the pool of potential purchasers who constitute the market for the subject property. For this reason, the easement is estimated to have a relatively small impact on the fee simple value. For an easement such as this, with a negligible impact on the fee simple land, an easement valuation of 5% to 25% is considered to be typical.

The low end of the range for easement valuation is most reasonable based on the highest and best use analysis with and without the easement. A nominal 10% valuation for the easement was selected and tested for reasonableness. The calculations are as follows:

| | |
|---|---|
| Value without the easement | $10,000 |
| Rights encumbered by the easement | 10% |
| Diminution in value attributable to the easement | $1,000 |
| Value of the site as encumbered by the easement | $9,000 |

The resulting market value of $9,000 was within the range of comparable sales using the front foot, square foot, and overall sale price analyses. Even though the easement encumbers much of the upland area of the property, it does not impact the highest and best use of the site. The diminution in value is estimated to be as follows:

| | |
|---|---|
| Value as insured (no easement) | $10,000 |
| Value subject to the defect (with easement) | $9,000 |
| Diminution in value attributable to the easement | $1,000 |

The appraisal report was submitted to opposing counsel. Several questions regarding the surveyor's analysis and the appraiser's highest and best use analysis using the survey were received and answered. The case settled immediately thereafter. Exhibit 5 shows the full survey of the subject property.

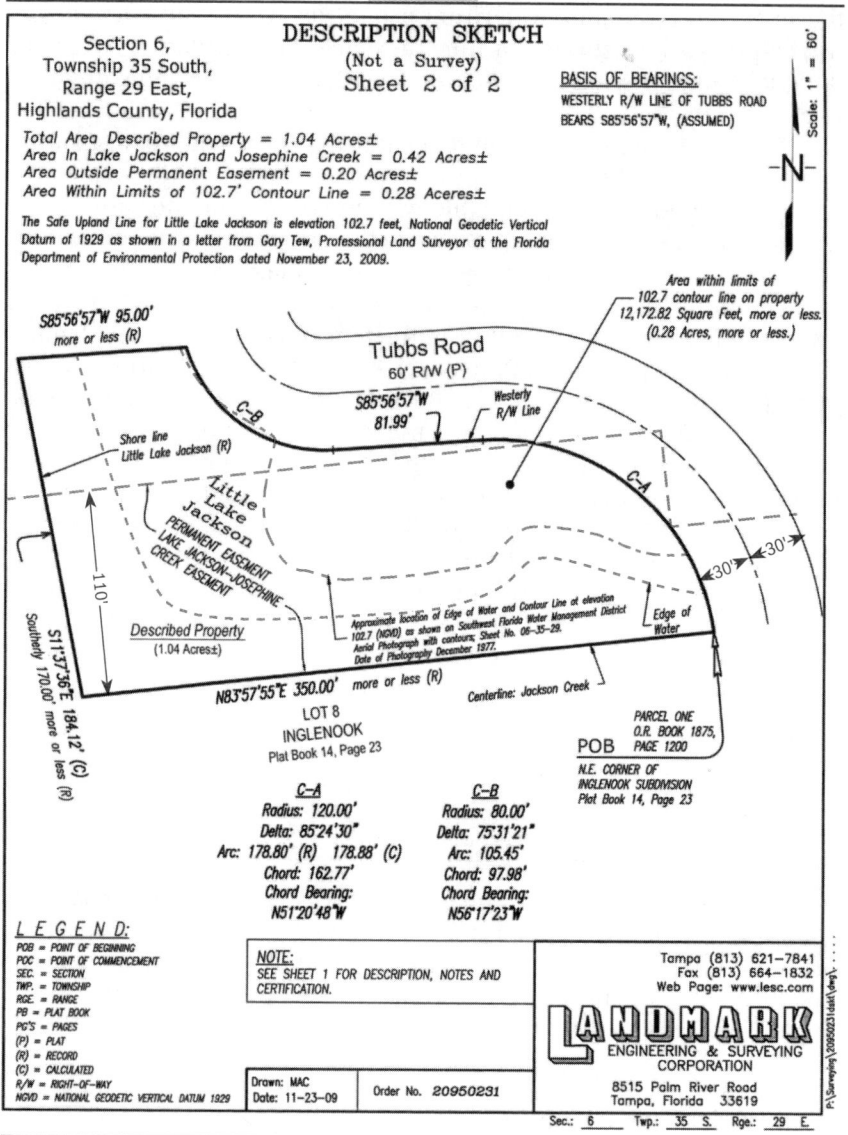

CASE STUDY 2.3

# Missing Utility Corridor Easement–Valuing Grandmother's Oak

*By Shawn Wilson, MAI*

A large, handsome oak tree is located in the front yard of a three-bedroom, two-bathroom, ranch-style home. The home is located on Maple Avenue in a neighborhood of similar residences, all built in the early 1950s. The home is typical for the neighborhood in terms of size and style, while the tree is particularly large and attractive when compared to others in the area.

The homeowners are very attached to the tree, as it was planted by the mother of the current owner on the occasion of his birth. His children spent many happy years climbing the tree, which they refer to as "Grandmother's Oak." The home was purchased five years prior to the assignment, in conjunction with probate proceedings. The sale price for the home was based on an appraisal, and the buyers obtained a survey and title insurance to secure a mortgage for the home.

The tree appears to be healthy, and the owners use a licensed arborist to perform periodic pruning and maintenance. The trunk of the oak tree is situated approximately 18 feet from the front property line. The canopy of the tree shades much of the home's front yard.

A scrivener's error on the subdivision plat resulted in the utility easements along Maple Avenue being marked as 10 feet wide, when they were in fact 20 feet wide. The correct easement width was noted elsewhere in the subdivision documents.

## A New Utility Project

The local water management authority announced plans to construct a significant water transmission line in the area to connect a nearby river to a new man-made reservoir structure. The reservoir was designed to store excess fresh water during the rainy season, rather than allowing it to flow to the sea.

Construction plans for the reservoir project call for the installation of a large water transmission line along the east side of Maple Avenue, within the existing 20-foot utility easement. When survey crews began placing stakes along the route, it was obvious that Grandmother's Oak would be in the path of construction, as shown in the following diagram.

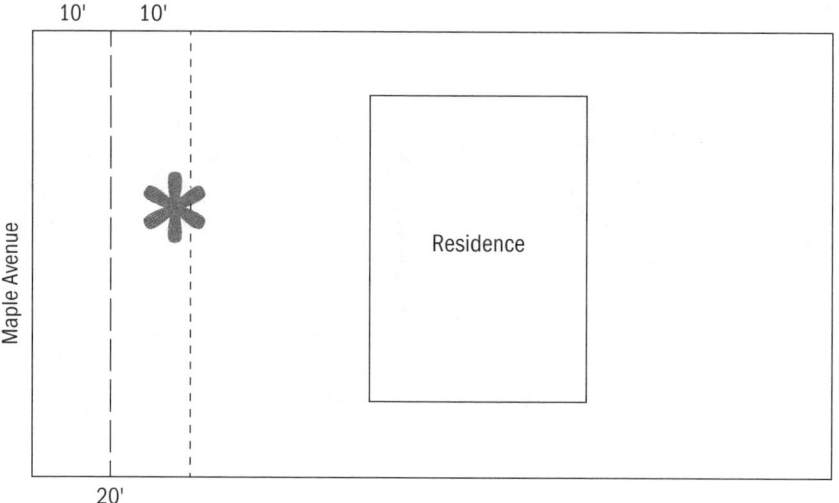

The proposed construction was not problematic for most homeowners on the area because they did not have significant improvements on the strip of land located 10 to 20 feet from the roadway. The owners of the subject property decided to make a claim on their title insurance policy because the easement was identified on the survey as being only 10 feet in depth rather than 20 feet. The homeowners contacted their arborist, and their attorney hired a real estate appraiser.

## Scope of Work

The most significant difference between a 10-foot easement and the 20-foot easement is the loss of the large oak tree that will inevitably result. When considering a tree as real property attached and appurtenant to the real estate, the appropriate valuation method is generally the before-and-after technique, which measures the diminution of overall property value attributable to the loss of the tree. In some areas of the country, this is also known as the *diminution-in-value technique*. The appraiser consulted with the attorney in this case, who advised that the legally applicable test for measuring damages was valuing the overall property with and without the tree.

After reviewing information related to the case and consulting with the attorney, the appraiser determined the appropriate scope of work as follows:

- Appraise the subject property using a before-and-after analysis considering the additional 10 feet of easement area.
- Determine the value of the home with the 10-foot easement, including the tree, using typical appraisal techniques.
- Determine the value of the home with a 20-foot easement, assuming removal of the tree, using typical appraisal techniques.
- Conduct additional market research and observation regarding the contributory value of the tree, if needed.

The existing home represents the highest and best use of the subject property. The appraiser gathered appropriate research and comparable sales to value the home assuming a 10-foot easement with the tree intact (the "value as insured"). Note that this valuation scenario requires the use of a hypothetical condition because the easement is actually 20 feet wide. Three good, recent comparable sales of similar homes are available. All have above-average trees and landscaping. The market value as insured, using typical appraisal techniques, is estimated to be $150,000.

A review of the project maps and plans indicates that construction of the water transmission line for the reservoir will encompass the entire 20-foot easement area across the front property boundary. The setback between the home and road is unaffected; it will remain typical for the neighborhood. The plans indicate that the tree will be removed as part of the construction project.

The appraiser requested an interview with the project engineer to determine the physical characteristics of the site after construction was complete. The engineer explained that the proposed underground pipe is six feet in diameter, buried 15 feet below ground.

There will be no evidence of the pipe above ground (i.e., no valves or control structures). After construction, the project contractor will replace sod in the area. Driveway connections will be reconstructed with asphalt driveway aprons as in the before condition.

The subject property has minor landscaping near the home, but none near the road. The improvements within the taking are sod (to be replaced by the contractor), the driveway (to be replaced by the contractor), and the large oak tree.

The appraiser's research indicated that, within the area encumbered by the easement:

- Driveways and parking pads can remain or be installed.
- Fencing can remain or be installed.
- Sod and minor landscaping can remain.
- Trees and large shrubs cannot be planted within the easement (roots could damage the pipe).
- Improvements with deep foundations (such as a swimming pool or large flag pole) cannot be built within the easement.

## Valuing the Property Subject to the Defect

The appraiser used a hypothetical condition to describe the physical characteristics of the home as if the project were complete, using the same effective date of value as before. The home is essentially the same in both valuation scenarios, with the exception of the large tree that will be removed. In the 20-foot easement scenario, a replacement tree or trees cannot be planted in the area of the easement.

In order to appraise under this hypothetical condition, the appraiser must search for sales of homes without above-average trees or landscaping that are otherwise similar to the subject property. If sufficient data of this type is available, the appraiser will use typical valuation methods to estimate the value of the home without the tree.

If an insufficient number of comparable sales of houses that lack a similar tree are available for the sales comparison approach, other types of analyses must be used. Examples of such analyses are paired sales research, market observation, and interviews with market participants.

For this assignment, only one comparable sale was found of a home with below-average trees and landscaping that was otherwise similar to the subject. After analyzing the transaction and making minor adjustments as necessary, the value difference attributable to the trees and landscaping was 5%. The estimate of market value in the 10-foot easement scenario was $150,000, so a 5% diminution in value would equate to $7,500. The appraiser also found two paired sales for newer homes in a similar neighborhood. Those paired sales indicated a value premium for mature trees ranging from 3% to 10%.

The appraiser analyzed lot sales in a nearby subdivision. Lots with extra amenities such as mature trees or views of a conservation area commanded premiums ranging from 10% to 20%. Additional market observations, including interviews with local realtors and developers, were completed. After considering all the data gathered, the appraiser estimated a 5% to 10% premium for homes similar to the subject, attributable to above-average trees and landscaping in the front yard.

The market value of the home in the before condition was estimated to be $150,000. Loss of the 5% to 10% premium would suggest a diminution in value of $7,500 to $15,000. The resulting value of the home, considering a 20-foot easement and the loss of Grandmother's Oak, would range from $135,000 to $142,500.

The appraiser considered sales and listings of similar homes in the market area to check the reasonableness of the range of value. He found that three-bedroom, two-bath homes in the area rarely sold for less than $140,000, even with below-average landscaping or other detrimental conditions. As a result, the upper end of the range of diminution in value was not supported by market evidence.

The difference in curb appeal related to the loss of the large tree was considered to be dramatic, so the appraiser reconciled the value to $140,000, at the bottom of the range supported by sales and listings. This reflects a diminution in value of approximately 7%, which was supported by additional market research such as paired sales analysis. The loss in value attributable to the loss of Grandmother's Oak was therefore estimated to be $150,000 minus $140,000, or $10,000.

## Defending the Market Value Estimate

The appraiser delivered his report to the homeowners' attorney. The attorney, and later the homeowners, expressed dismay over the market value estimate. The homeowners' arborist, who was familiar with the tree and had provided periodic maintenance for it over a period of 20 years, had provided them with a written value estimate of $35,000 for Grandmother's Oak.

Arborists and other green industry professionals provide valuation services for a variety of reasons, including casualty loss claims, business valuations for plant and tree nurseries, valuations of orchards and groves, tree removal for development purposes, and timber valuation. They use a variety of industry-approved methods for valuation, including the tree trunk formula, replacement cost, inch-for-inch replacement cost, net prospective value, and tree ordinance value.

The homeowners' arborist used the tree trunk formula method to arrive at his $35,000 value estimate. As with many of the industry-approved methods that arborists and green professionals use for valuing trees, this application of the tree trunk formula considered the subject tree as personal property rather than real property appurtenant to the overall site. Because confusion regarding this distinction is common, it was essential for the appraiser to ask the attorney to provide the appropriate foundation for a legally correct analysis.

The arborist reported that the subject tree is large, healthy, and of a variety popular in the market area for aesthetic appeal and longevity. He assigned a condition rating of 85%. The condition rating used by arborists is the inverse of the depreciation estimated by real estate appraisers. Grandmother's Oak, with an 85% condition rating, is therefore considered to be in above-average condition. In real estate appraisal terms, the tree is 15% depreciated.

The appraiser met with the homeowners and their attorney and explained that his market value estimate reflected the contributory value of Grandmother's Oak to the real property, rather than a value in use or the tree's value as a separate and independent element of personal property. In *The Dictionary of Real Estate Appraisal*, fifth edition, *contributory value* is defined as "the change in the value of a property as a whole, whether positive or negative, resulting from the addition or deletion of a property component."

The appraiser illustrated that a $35,000 value for the tree could not be supported as reasonable because the estimate of market value for the whole property, less Grandmother's Oak, would be calculated as $150,000 minus $35,000, or $115,000. The majority of three-bedroom, two-bathroom homes in the market area sell for at least $140,000, so a market value estimate for the home and lot of $115,000 was not plausible.

While the attorney and homeowners preferred the $35,000 value estimate provided by the arborist, they realized that good faith negotiations could only occur if they presented a defensible argument. Although the arborist used a well-known tree valuation technique, his value estimate was not applicable because it exceeded the contributory value of the tree.

## Case Study 3.1

# Leaking Underground Storage Tank–Former Gasoline Service Station

*By Thomas O. Jackson, PhD, MAI, AICP, CRE, FRICS, and Stephanie Norwood*

## The Assignment

This case study involved a lawsuit by the owner of a former gasoline service station site in Naples, Florida, against a major oil company to recover the alleged diminution in market value resulting from groundwater contamination from a leaking underground storage tank (LUST). The site had been vacated by the oil company 10 years prior to the date of value. As of the date of value, it was leased to a luxury car dealership. Although contamination still exists beneath the site, it ranks as a low priority in the state's program for LUST sites, and no additional remediation was required as of the date of value. Previously, there had been extensive remediation.

The assignment focuses on estimating any property value diminution attributable to the contamination. Of interest would be the effects, if any, of past contamination that was remediated as well as any environmental stigma due to the previous contamination, the property's current environmental condition, and the remaining contamination. To address these issues, a highest and best use analysis was conducted to determine any effects on the use of the property given its environmental condition. Three methods were employed to determine value diminution for the subject property:

1. A paired sales analysis was conducted and showed no market evidence that buyers required a discount for former UST sites because of their environmental condition.

2. Market interviews were conducted with local lenders to determine their perceptions about lending on the subject property. The mortgage lenders expressed some reluctance to provide a loan, but indicated that time and remediation efforts could increase their willingness to lend.

3. A lease and lost income analysis was conducted and showed minimal loss due to the property's environmental condition.

Diminution in value can be attributed to increased environmental risk (risk effects), limits on site usability (use effects), or the costs of remediation (cost effects) if such costs are to be borne by a prospective purchaser. In estimating diminution, the following formula may be used:

> Impaired Value = Unimpaired Value − Cost Effects (Remediation and Related Costs)
> − Use Effects (Effects on Site Usability)
> − Risk Effects (Environmental Risk/Stigma)

## Definitions

Specific definitions related to the valuation of environmentally impacted properties are relevant to this discussion. The following definitions are contained in the Appraisal Standards Board's Advisory Opinion 9: The Appraisal of Real Property That May Be Impacted by Environmental Contamination, published with the Uniform Standards of Professional Appraisal Practice (USPAP).

| | |
|---|---|
| **Diminution in Value (Property Value Diminution)** | The difference between the unimpaired and impaired values of the property being appraised. This difference can be due to the increased risk and/or costs attributable to the property's environmental condition. |
| **Environmental Contamination** | Adverse environmental conditions resulting from the release of hazardous substances into the air, surface water, groundwater or soil. Generally, the concentrations of these substances would exceed regulatory limits established by the appropriate federal, state and/or local agencies. |
| **Environmental Risk** | The additional or incremental risk of investing in, financing, buying and/or owning property attributable to its environmental condition. This risk is derived from perceived uncertainties concerning: (1) the nature and extent of the contamination; (2) estimates of future remediation costs and their timing; (3) potential for changes in regulatory requirements; (4) liabilities for cleanup (buyer, seller, third party); (5) potential for off-site impacts; and (6) other environmental risk factors, as may be relevant. |
| **Environmental Stigma** | An adverse effect on property value produced by the market's perception of increased environmental risk due to contamination. (See Environmental Risk, above.) |
| **Impaired Value** | The market value of the property being appraised with full consideration of the effects of its environmental condition and the presence of environmental contamination on, adjacent to, or proximate to the property. Conceptually, this could be considered the "as-is" value of a contaminated property. |
| **Remediation Cost** | The cost to cleanup (or remediate) a contaminated property to the appropriate regulatory standards. These costs can be for the cleanup of on-site contamination as well as mitigation of off-site impacts due to migrating contamination. |

| | |
|---|---|
| **Remediation Lifecycle** | A cycle consisting of three stages of cleanup of a contaminated site: before remediation or cleanup; during remediation; and after remediation. A contaminated property's remediation lifecycle stage is an important determinant of the risk associated with environmental contamination. Environmental risk can be expected to vary with the remediation lifecycle stage of the property. |
| **Source, Non-source, Adjacent and Proximate Sites** | Source sites are the sites on which contamination is, or has been, generated. Non-source sites are sites onto which contamination, generated from a source site, has migrated. An adjacent site is not contaminated, but shares a common property line with a source site. Proximate sites are not contaminated and not adjacent to a source site, but are in close proximity to the source site. |
| **Unimpaired Value** | The market value of a contaminated property developed under the hypothetical condition that the property is not contaminated. |

## Subject Property

The subject property consists of a rectangular site of approximately 30,000 square feet at the corner of a major, six-lane divided highway (US 41) and a paved, two-lane road in Naples, Florida. Access is provided via curb cuts from both roads. The site has 200 feet of frontage along the six-lane highway, with good visibility to passing traffic 150 feet along the two-lane road. The surrounding neighborhood consists of commercial highway-oriented development, and the market in the immediate area appears strong. The site is improved with asphalt paving, planters, and fencing and, at the time of this appraisal, functioned as part of a luxury car dealership. The owner of the site leased it to the car dealer, who owned the adjoining parcels, which were improved with showroom space and additional car lot area. The site had been under lease since 1993, and current renewals extended the lease arrangement through 2004. As clearly stated in the lease agreement, the lessee had agreed that future rent payments would not be affected by any remediation activities.

## Purpose, Property Rights, and Effective Date

The purpose of this appraisal was to analyze the diminution in market value, if any, of the fee simple interest in the subject property attributable to groundwater contamination from a leaking underground storage tank (LUST). In addition, potential rent loss due to the property's condition during previous remediation has been analyzed. The effective date of valuation was April 11, 2001.

# Environmental History and Condition

A major oil company leased the subject property from 1970 to 1990, during which time it was used as a gasoline service station. In 1988 petroleum hydrocarbon contamination was discovered in the soils at the property. In May and June 1990, underground storage tanks (USTs) and approximately 1,691 tons of contaminated soil were removed from the site. The excavation remained open until April 1991 to allow volatilization of some residual contamination. In 1991 the backfilled area was re-excavated and backfilled with wash rock for better compaction. An additional 800 tons of contaminated soil was also excavated at that time and treated on site. The soil was removed from the site in September 1992. A 5-inch diameter groundwater recovery well was also installed in 1992.

A contamination assessment report (CAR) was submitted in 1993. A CAR addendum (CARA) and a second CAR addendum were submitted in 1993 and 1994, respectively. The CAR reports, approved by Florida DER in May 1994, established the presence of hydrocarbon compounds in groundwater at the site encompassing an area of about 125 feet by 250 feet. A remedial action plan (RAP) was submitted to the State of Florida Department of Environmental Protection in 1995. The RAP included groundwater recovery, treatment via an air stripper tower, and on-site reinjection. Natural attenuation was recommended for residual soil contamination. Annual monitoring of all on-site monitoring wells was also proposed. Based on the size of contaminant plume, the time required to clean up the groundwater was estimated to be 18 months. Currently, consultants estimate $160,000 in clean-up costs for an air sparging and soil vapor extraction system to be operating for 18 months. However, no additional remediation systems have been activated to date.

In Florida, owners of underground petroleum tanks with suspected contamination that were reported to the Department of Environmental Protection between June 30, 1986, and December 31, 1988, were eligible for either state-contracted cleanup or reimbursement of costs for a privately managed cleanup. A critical component of this Early Detection Incentive (EDI) program was the creation of a "grace period" or exemption from departmental enforcement actions for sites that were reported.[1]

The subject site was accepted into the Florida EDI program in 1989 and received partial reimbursement for expenses incurred during the initial remedial action program. However, the site ranking was not high enough to warrant further funding for proposed

---

1. Source: Florida Dept. of Environmental Protection: www.dep.state.fl.us/waste/categories/pcp/pages/edi.htm/.

remedial activities through the EDI program from 1995 to 2000. Subsequently, Florida's program was extended to sites whose priority ranking had previously been too low for clean-up funding. Accordingly, the property is now eligible to receive funding for additional remediation. In the event that Florida EDI approved only partial reimbursement of future costs, then the balance would be financed by the major oil company that had previously leased the site from its current owner, assuming such remediation is required by the state and the oil company is permitted to oversee site cleanup. As of the date of value, proposals were being sought for additional soil investigation and submission of a site assessment report (SAR) that will summarize current site conditions and recommend the next appropriate course of action. The estimated remediation costs may be revised following submission of the SAR.

## Highest and Best Use

This highest and best use of the subject property is analyzed considering its environmental history as described above. Highest and best use may be defined as "the reasonably probable and legal use of vacant land or an improved property that is physically possible, appropriately supported, and financially feasible, and that results in the highest value."[2]

Legally permissible uses of this property are not limited by land development regulations such as zoning or comprehensive plan restrictions. Existing and future commercial/retail uses would be allowable under these regulations and planning requirements. And, according to representatives of the Florida petroleum cleanup (EDI) program administered by Collier County, there would be no legal restrictions on the use, development, or redevelopment of the subject due to its environmental condition and participation in this program.

Thus, the physically possible uses of the subject site for commercial/retail purposes would not be limited. The site is a rectangular, 30,000-sq.-ft. parcel with access on a major roadway and a secondary street. The potential remediation could involve a shallow air sparging system. According to specialists knowledgeable about this type of system and familiar with the subject site, the property could be developed or redeveloped for any market-supported commercial/retail use with such a system in place or in conjunction with the installation of this system. Trenching and pipes for the system would fit under the slab of a new building or under the existing improvements at the property. A vapor barrier would likely be installed under the slab. A small shed could be located at the rear of the property in an unobtrusive place.

---

2. *The Appraisal of Real Estate*, 13th ed. (Chicago: Appraisal Institute, 2008), 277-278.

The only possible limitation or effect would be the additional costs, but these would be borne by the EDI program or the oil company. The site would not be suitable for residential uses from a market or environmental perspective. In addition, it is possible that, given the length of time since the USTs were removed, the extensive soil remediation, and other factors, active remediation of the site may not be required at all. In this situation, natural attenuation with ongoing monitoring through the existing system of monitoring wells may be all that is required, and this would not impede any form of future development.

As noted, the market in the area surrounding the subject property is primarily commercial/retail and highway-oriented. The predominant development pattern along US 41 has been strip commercial development with small retail centers. A resort located west and across US 41 from the subject provides an upscale atmosphere for the location. Nevertheless, for small, 30,000-sq. ft. sites like the subject located along US 41 at a corner, the market-supported highest and best is for some type of commercial/retail development. The current configuration of the subject as part of the auto dealership supports the site's economic viability where such an assemblage is possible. Indeed, as improved and considering the property's current function as part of an auto dealership, its continued use as part of a larger commercial property assemblage is logical. So, given the character of the area, the subject's location, the existing use, and likely market conditions, a commercial/retail use is the only financially feasible and maximally productive use for the site. Residential and industrial uses would not be appropriate or reasonable for the site, regardless of the property's environmental condition. Therefore, it is my opinion that the highest and best use of this property as if vacant and as improved is for commercial/retail development as supported by existing and likely future market demand and conditions.

## Paired Sales Analyses

The first approach to analyzing the diminution in property value, as noted, is through paired sales analysis in which sales of unimpaired properties are matched and compared to sales of impaired properties with environmental conditions similar to the subject. The objective of this analysis is to determine if the observed impaired prices of the properties are supported by the prices of otherwise similar, unimpaired properties. Two impaired property sales have been selected for this purpose.

### Impaired Sale 1. Former Gasoline Service Station Site

This is the sale of a 0.59-acre parcel (25,596 square feet) on the same major highway. The property was a former gasoline service station and had a leaking underground storage tank, which had been previously removed. The site was purchased in July 1999 for $768,000, or $30.00 per square foot. According to documentation in the files of the county pollution control department, which administers the Florida petroleum cleanup program under a contract with the Florida DEP, no further assessment was required as of December 1999. This site is located several blocks south of the subject property. The unit price for this property is within the market range for comparable properties without environmental issues.

## Comparison with Unimpaired Sales

Three unimpaired comparable sales were also analyzed. The first (Unimpaired Sale 1-1) was the December 1999 sale of 1.015 acres (44,200 square feet) for $1,330,000, or $30.09 per square foot. This property is north of Impaired Sale 1. With a larger size (inferior) and a corner location (superior), this property was determined to be similar to the impaired sale site. The second unimpaired comparable (Unimpaired Sale 1-2) is the sale of 2.28 acres in May 1998 for $2.5 million, or $25.17 per square foot. This property is larger (inferior), triangular (inferior), and further north from the central business district (inferior) compared to Impaired Sale 1, which accounts for its lower unit price. The third unimpaired comparable (Unimpaired Sale 1-3) is the March 1999 sale of 0.56 acres for a unit price of $34.35 per square foot. This property is close to the CBD (superior location) and south of the property in Impaired Sale 1, accounting for its higher unit price. So, the market range of $25.17 to $34.35 tightly brackets the sale price for Impaired Sale 1 of $30.00 per square foot, indicating a market transaction price for the site with a leaking UST. In addition, the impaired sale property was reported to be under contract for a price near $1.0 million in 2001, a significant increase over its 1999 price of $768,000.

These sales can be summarized in a relative comparison array as follows:

| Sale | Unit Price | Net Comparison (Comment) |
|---|---|---|
| Unimpaired Sale 1-3 | $34.35 | Superior (location closer to CBD, rectangular) |
| Unimpaired Sale 1-1 | $30.09 | Similar (inferior size but superior corner location) |
| Impaired Sale 1 | $30.00 | Former UST site |
| Unimpaired Sale 1-2 | $25.17 | Inferior (larger, triangular, and further north) |

## Impaired Sale 2. Former Gasoline Service Station Site

Impaired Sale 2 is a site of 4.66 acres, or 202,990 square feet, with frontage on the same road as the subject. The property, a former gasoline service station with a leaking UST, was sold in 1998 for $3.5 million, or $17.24 per square foot. The site was purchased for development with a drugstore. As confirmed with parties to the transaction, there was ongoing remediation at the site when it sold and during its redevelopment. There were no reported indemnifications for future environmental liabilities. In addition, documents for the site indicate that there were "areas of hydrocarbon impact in groundwater at the site," as well as "excessively contaminated soil, as defined in Chapter 62-770, F.A.C." Despite these seemingly adverse environmental conditions and the fact that the site was not fully remediated at the time of sale, its sale price of $17.24 per square foot is well bracketed by the market data on unimpaired sales and appears to have been unaffected by the contamination.

## Comparison with Unimpaired Sales

The value conclusion is based on a comparison with four otherwise similar unimpaired sales. The first (Unimpaired Sale 2-1) was the sale of a 2.67-acre parcel, also for development as a drugstore. The site is located on the same major highway and was sold in December 2000 for $975,000, or $8.38 per square foot. Although similar in use and purpose, this sale's lower unit price reflects its slightly inferior exposure and location relative to Impaired Sale 2, which has good exposure and access from two highways. The second comparable (Unimpaired Sale 2-2) is the sale of 1.93 acres in February 1999 for a unit price of $21.41 per square feet. This site is located in an upscale area to the south of Impaired Sale 2. This site was also purchased for development as a drugstore. Its higher price reflects the superior location. The third comparable (Unimpaired Sale 2-3) was the sale of 5.5 acres across a major highway from Impaired Sale 2. This site was acquired by its current owner in June 2000 for $5.50 per square foot. Its lower unit price reflects its secondary corner location (inferior). However, its location in the immediate vicinity of Impaired Sale 2 and lower price provides a further indication of the lack of any discounts in the sale price of Impaired Sale 2. Lastly, the fourth comparable (Unimpaired Sale 2-4) is the sale of 1.925 acres in September 1998 for $11.51 per square foot. The commercial/retail site was subsequently developed for a branch bank and an auto service facility. The lower price relative to Impaired Sale 2 can be attributed to its inferior corner location and the fact that the road on which it is located is not a through street.

The sales are summarized in a relative comparison array as follows:

| Sale | Unit Price | Net Comparison (Comment) |
|---|---|---|
| Unimpaired Sale 2-2 | $21.41 | Superior (upscale area) |
| **Impaired Sale 2** | **$17.24** | **Former UST site** |
| Unimpaired Sale 2-4 | $11.51 | Inferior (weaker intersection) |
| Unimpaired Sale 2-1 | $8.38 | Inferior (secondary location, not on main intersection) |
| Unimpaired Sale 2-3 | $5.50 | Inferior (secondary corner, not at main intersection) |

As can be seen, the unit price for Impaired Sale 2 is bracketed by unimpaired market transaction data and prices. There is no market evidence that the price paid for this former UST site was discounted or reduced due to its environmental condition. Indeed, its price is above the price paid for sites in its immediate vicinity and for another site to be similarly developed as a drugstore.

## Conclusion

These analyses of impaired property sales involving former gasoline service station sites with leaking underground storage tanks indicate that their sale prices were consistent with market level pricing. No discounts were observed or are evident in this data. The impaired property sale prices are well supported by market comparables that did not involve leaking tanks. The findings do not show any effect on sale prices as a result of previous contamination from leaking USTs. There was simply no sale price evidence that the properties with leaking USTs had been adversely affected.

# Market Interviews

Several interviews were conducted in April 2001 to assess the perceptions of mortgage lenders with respect to the specific environmental condition and history of the subject property. After reviewing information concerning the property (similar to what was provided in the subject property and environmental history and condition sections of this case study), four lenders were asked whether the environmental condition described in the case study would deter them from making a loan secured by the property. If the subject property's environmental condition was perceived as detrimental, then the lender was asked about the specific credit underwriting adjustments necessary to compensate for any increased risks. The lenders were asked to assume that the prospective borrower was otherwise creditworthy. The borrower's creditworthiness was important to all of the lenders. The questionnaire used in the interviews is presented in Appendix A and the results are summarized below.

## Lender A

The first lender is a commercial loan officer with a local Naples bank that has a primary business base in commercial real estate lending. This lender reviewed the case study with a senior vice president at the bank who has over 30 years of experience. Thus, the responses from this lender reflect the perceptions of both individuals. Over the previous 12 months, this bank had closed more than 100 commercial real estate loans, and these loans represent about 80% to 85% of their total business. This active commercial real estate lender also indicated that the bank had previously made a loan on a contaminated convenience store property in the Naples area. The lender's initial reaction to the subject property and its condition was that a loan would be contingent on the completion of the planned remediation, which he referred to as "a timing issue." However, after considering that the buyer/borrower would not be responsible for clean-up costs and that the existing lease income would continue during remediation, the lender indicated that a loan could be made, but perhaps at a reduced loan-to-value (LTV) ratio, which would require additional equity or other collateral from the borrower. The lender concluded by noting that they "haven't walked away from 'dirty' sites (in the past)."

## Lender B

The second lender is a senior vice president with a smaller, locally based Naples bank. This lender has 22 years of experience and his institution made more than $400 million in commercial real estate loans in the previous year, representing about 40% of their total lending business. With respect to the subject property and its environmental condition, this lender said he would prefer to wait 18 months until the remediation described in the case study was complete. However, the lender would be willing to consider a mortgage loan on the property now, with a firm estimate of the clean-up costs and with these costs placed in escrow. Alternatively, if the Florida DEP would approve of natural attenuation and monitoring as an appropriate remediation strategy, then a market loan could be made now. Current commercial property loan rates and terms would be an interest rate of prime to prime plus ½ (about 7.5%), a 15-year amortization period, and a three-year term.

## Lender C

The third lender respondent is with a major Southeast regional financial institution that had previously held a mortgage on a property adjoining the subject. The local loan officer for this bank reviewed the environmental case study for the subject property and responded that, given the EDI program and the agreement by the oil company to provide for any balance of the cleanup costs, the environmental issues would not preclude lending on the property–i.e., the lender "can get over it (environmental risks)." However, the loan officer indicated that all loans involving environmental issues at this bank are reviewed by an environmental policy officer in Birmingham, so the case study was sent to that individual and a second interview was conducted.

When asked whether the subject property's environmental condition would deter financing, the environmental specialist responded "No, absolutely not," and indicated that the bank could "mitigate risks/concerns." This individual was very familiar with the Florida EDI system, its rankings, and similar sites. The policy officer also had previous experience with the oil company and believed the company to be very responsible in their cleanup of other leaking UST sites. The officer said that the bank "would be absolutely interested" in loaning on this property and that they "have done contaminated property loans" in the past. The officer also noted that the use of the site for commercial purposes was important, and that it would probably not be appropriate for residential use given its condition. In addition, the officer was interested in seeing recent groundwater sampling data from the site, and said that the contamination in such an old plume had "probably degraded." The lender also mentioned various environmental insurance products that are available to mitigate environmental risks.

## Lender D

The fourth lender is a vice president with the Naples office of a major national financial institution. The lender's initial reaction to the environmental case study on the subject property was that they would not be interested in providing mortgage financing until the property was remediated. However, the lender "may take a look" at the property in its current status. There was concern that the environmental testing data on the subject was old and a current assessment such as the SAR described in the case study would be required. Once the remediation was complete in 18 months, the lender would not be deterred from making a mortgage loan secured by the subject property. In addition, if a passive, natural attenuation plan was approved by the Florida DEP, that would reduce the lender's risks so that current market financing would be available. In the meantime, other collateral would be required.

## Conclusion

In summary, the results of the market interviews present a mixed picture for the subject property. The property would not be treated the same as a comparable uncontaminated property, but the lenders indicated that, with some adjustments, there were ways to mitigate the risks and provide financing for the property in its current condition. One of the four lenders, the one with the most experience with these issues, was confident that a solution could be found to provide a mortgage loan on the property in its current condition by including additional steps to mitigate risks. The lenders agreed, though, that an approved passive remediation strategy would remove these risks now. They also agreed that the property could be financed at the conclusion of the 18-month remediation period. Thus, the issue at this point is timing and the additional effort needed to obtain a current environmental assessment and remediation plan.

## Estimate of Property Value Diminution

The property value diminution of the subject property is the difference between its unimpaired and impaired market values. The unimpaired value for the subject property was estimated by experienced local appraisers. The impaired value was then estimated using the unimpaired value as a baseline and adjusting for any value reductions or risk perceptions observed in the marketplace. The analyses underlying these adjustments, as presented in the preceding pages, include paired sales analyses involving former gasoline service stations with previous leaking USTs and a set of case study market interviews that provided mortgage lenders with a detailed description of the environmental history and condition of the subject property.

The sales data did not show any tendency of the market to reduce prices for former gasoline service station sites with previous leaking USTs, whether or not they had been fully remediated prior to sale. The only issue that arose was the need for some additional environmental investigatory work to secure a mortgage loan. The lenders showed no hesitancy to provide an unadjusted market loan on the property in its prospective condition in 18 months, or at the conclusion of the remediation period. The lender with the greatest knowledge of UST environmental issues was confident that the property could be financed in its current condition and all existing risks could be entirely mitigated.

Given these findings, and particularly the sale price data, it is reasonable to conclude that the property could be sold at its unimpaired value in its current condition. Therefore, as of the April 11, 2001 date of value, there is no evidence of any property value diminution at the subject property and its unimpaired and impaired values would be the same.

| | |
|---|---:|
| Unimpaired Property Value as of April 11, 2001: | $900,000 |
| Impaired Property Value as of April 11, 2001: | $900,000 |
| Indicated Property Value Diminution as of April 11, 2001: | $0 |

## Lease and Lost Income Analysis

As explained in the environmental history section at the beginning of this case study, there was extensive soil remediation of the subject property after the previous lessee, a major oil company, vacated the property in 1990 and before the current lessee, a luxury auto dealer, began leasing it in 1993. As part of the soil remediation activities, the site was left with a large "open pit" area for a period of approximately one year. The commercial real estate market was slow during this period, and these on-site activities may have further limited the owner's ability to market the site to another lessee or to a purchaser. Marketing times during this period, which has been characterized a "real estate depression," were quite long, and a marketing period of one to two years was not uncommon in Florida commercial real estate markets. Lending institutions adopted the concept of "fair value" to reflect discounts due to these excessive marketing periods. Thus, in assessing the owner's ability to market the site to a prospective owner or lessee, it is difficult to separate the effect of the property's condition during remediation from the adverse general market conditions. Considering all these factors, the remediation activities on site during this time may have resulted in six months of lost income.

The unimpaired value of the subject property as of 1990 has been estimated at $450,000. The potential annual income that a property with this value could generate can be estimated with an appropriate land capitalization rate ($R_L$). Reportedly, land leases in the Naples area are not common. Most users would prefer to purchase a site before improving it with a structure or another development. The leases that are executed are usually on a long-term basis of 15 to 20 years, as confirmed by a representative of a major convenience store franchise real estate operations office.

Information on two leases was obtained during the research for this assignment. The first was the lease of a portion of the excess land of Impaired Sale 2. This 1.07-acre (46,609 square foot) site was leased by 7-Eleven on a triple-net basis for a reported annual rent of $80,000. With an estimated value for the leased parcel of $975,000, this lease rate equates to an $R_L$ of 8.2%. For comparison, a second lease for a 2.0-acre site with no reported environmental issues, located on the same road as the subject, had an asking rate of $2.50 per square foot (triple net). With an estimated site value of $30.00 per square foot, this equates to an $R_L$ of 8.3%. The consistency of these two income rates (8.2% and 8.3%) provides further evidence of the negligible impact on return requirements of environmental conditions associated with leaking USTs. Applying the 8.2% $R_L$ to the subject's value in 1990 of $450,000 indicates an income potential of $36,900 per year. Thus, six months of lost income, or $18,450, can be attributed to the remediation of the site in 1990. This amount could be compounded forward at a judicially defined interest rate to obtain its present value for purposes of the litigation. However, this rate and the results from it would not be considered in the determination of the 2001 property value diminution.

## Conclusions

The three analyses–paired sales analysis, lender interviews, and the lost income analysis–all pointed to a nearly negligible impact from the contamination as of the date of value. However, while the paired sales analyses involving sales of former gasoline station sites indicated no diminution in value, the lenders did indicate some reluctance to provide financing when asked about the specifics of the subject site. This inconsistency underscores the difficulty of using interview and survey information to estimate property value diminution. There is often a discrepancy between how market participants may react to a hypothetical situation and their actions in real transactions. While interviews and surveys can be quite informative in developing an understanding of an environmental situation, value and impacts on value should be estimated with transactional data. The "hypothetical bias" of survey-based techniques for estimating property value diminution has been noted in several recent articles in *The Appraisal Journal.*

Another issue in this case study was the date of value and the environmental status of the subject property. There was some disagreement about this during the litigation. The plaintiff's expert wanted to use an earlier date, closer to the time when the contamination was first discovered. At that point in time, some 10 years prior to the date used in our report, the risk would have been greater and marketability would have been limited. A prospective buyer would have been faced with uncertainties concerning the initial remediation. Indeed, the property was not leasable at that time. As of the more recent date, the property was largely remediated and part of the Florida EDI program, where it was listed as a low-priority site with no remediation required. While this did not indicate regulatory closure, the risks and uncertainties had been reduced to the point at which the market was comfortable and no discounts were evident in the sales of other properties in similar condition.

## Appendix A

### Sample Lender Questionnaire

Assume that you are contemplating providing an acquisition or refinance loan with the subject property as collateral, and assume that the applicant is creditworthy.

I. **Lending Opportunity**

   1) In general, (as of the date of value) assuming no history or existence of contamination:

      (i) What interest rate or range would you charge for financing the purchase of the property described in the case study? _____

      (ii) Would you require the buyer to pay any points? _____

      (iii) What would be the required loan-to-value ratio? _____

      (iv) What would be your minimum required debt coverage ratio? _____

      (v) Over what period would the loan be amortized? _____

      (vi) What would be the term of the loan? _____

   2) What type of due diligence would you require on the subject property? _____

   3) As of (the date of value):

      (i) Would the environmental history and condition of this property prevent you from committing to acquisition financing? _____

      (ii) If yes, why? _____

      (iii) If no, would the environmental history and condition of this property impact the terms of the mortgage? Why? _____

      (iv) If yes, which of the following would change?

      Interest rate _____    Discount points _____

      Amortization period _____    Term _____

      Debt coverage ratio _____    LTV ratio _____

II. **Company Policy**

   1) (i) Does your bank have a policy with regard to contaminated properties? If so, briefly describe what it is and how long it has been in place. _____

      (ii) If not, what guidelines do you use to evaluate contaminated real estate? _____

   2) (i) Are you familiar with any loans that your bank has considered for acquisition financing of environmentally contaminated property? If so, when were they considered? _____

      (ii) Did you extend or deny the loans? Why? _____

   3) What is your title? _____

   4) What are your general responsibilities? _____

III. **Lending Characteristics**

   1) During the past 12 months, approximately how many loans has your bank made on properties similar to the subject for acquisition financing? _____

   2) What percentage of your real estate loans are made on property in, or competitive with, the market area of the subject property? _____

## Case Study 3.2

# Environmental Contamination and Proximity

*By Michael V. Sanders, MAI, SRA*

## The Assignment

This litigation was certified as a class action involving two tracts of homes adjacent to Wyle Laboratories, a large and rather secretive testing facility in Southern California that was ultimately found to have significant environmental issues. We were engaged as appraisal experts on behalf of one of the defendant developers who faced allegations of inadequate or incomplete disclosure of issues relating to Wyle Laboratories, among other things. Even though the counsel for the other developer elected to retain their own experts, there was discussion of joint retention on behalf of both developers, which is not uncommon when the interests of the codefendants are closely aligned. The task was to evaluate claims of value diminution associated with the disclosure issues and adjacent environmental disamenities and to critique the opinions of the opposing appraisal expert. The case was filed in the California Superior Court, but the parties agreed to use judicial reference in lieu of a jury trial, settling after expert depositions were completed.[1]

## Class Action Litigation

A class action is "a lawsuit in which a single person or a small group of people represents the interests of a larger group."[2] The purported advantage of a class action is to avoid a multiplicity of lawsuits in situations involving a large number of potential plaintiffs, aggregating individual claims into a single representational lawsuit. Among the requirements to maintain a class action are commonality with respect to legal and factual issues and a presumption that the claims of the class representatives are typical of the class in general. Members of a proposed class are automatically included, unless they affirmatively make a decision to opt out. Class action lawsuits brought in fed-

---

1. At the request of the client, specific information regarding the identities of the parties and properties has not been disclosed.
2. Bryan A. Garner, ed. *Black's Law Dictionary*, 2nd pocket ed. (St. Paul, MN: West Group, 2001), 103.

eral district courts are governed by the Federal Rules of Civil Procedure, which also govern class actions in some states (not California). Other states prohibit or limit the types of claims that may be brought as class actions. In general, class litigation is relatively uncommon in real estate matters and is vigorously opposed by defense counsel because of the potential damages involved.

## The Subject Properties

The subject project is a low-density residential community encompassing approximately 217 homes. The topography is rolling. Lot sizes range upwards from about 20,000 square feet, although pad areas are typically smaller. Some sites enjoy average to good area views. The project was built between 1999 and 2001 and includes three product types, with floor plans ranging from 2,400 to 3,900 square feet. The product is relatively comparable to other homes of similar size and recent vintage in the general area. Initial builder sales took place over a time period from March 2000 through March 2002, with a large number of subsequent resale transactions. As part of each original sale transaction, buyers were provided with the following disclosures:

- Nearby property is zoned commercial. Developer makes no representation as to what type of business or businesses will be built on this site, or when such development may occur.
- This subdivision is located adjacent to Wiley [sic] Labs, an industrial research facility. All inquiries regarding Wiley Labs and the nature of any activities conducted at the facility should be addressed to Wiley Labs.

## Wyle Laboratories

Wyle Laboratories is a 429-acre site located adjacent to the subject project. The facility opened in 1957 and has performed physical tests on a variety of military and aerospace components as well as consumer products, typically under extreme conditions. The nature of these activities was not well known, leading to a listing on the California Abandoned Site List in 1983 due to a lack of information and the high level of security that limited access to the property. A preliminary assessment by the California Department of Health Services (DHS) in 1988 recommended no further action by the California Environmental Protection Agency (EPA), and a 1988 assessment by the US EPA concluded that no further action was necessary.

The only item of concern on the Wyle property noted in a Phase I environmental site assessment in connection with development of the subject project was a leaking underground storage tank (LUST) identified on the state LUST database, which had reportedly received case closure. Soil and groundwater tests in 1999, however, revealed on-site contamination with trichloroethylene (TCE) and other volatile organic compounds (VOCs). A joint investigation by the local Regional Water Quality Control Board (RWQCB) and the California Department of Toxic Substances Control (DTSC) in 2001 indicated the need for further soil and groundwater characterization, leading to the subsequent discovery of several contaminants, including dichloroethylene (DCE), vinyl chloride, perchloroethylene (PCE), perchlorate, lead, benzene, polychlorinated biphenyls (PCBs), N-Nitrosodimethylamine (NDMA), and hydrazine. A California RWQCB memorandum in July 2003 noted that VOCs were the primary contaminants of concern, present in concentrations of concern in a few isolated source areas of the site. On-site contamination was also confirmed after a preliminary assessment and site inspection by the US EPA in November 2003, which was made available to the public by mid-2004.

The closure of the Wyle facility was announced in January 2002, at roughly the same time the lawsuits were filed against the developers of the adjacent homes. The property was sold for residential development in November 2002, although Wyle is believed to have continued operations for a period thereafter, with the facility reportedly closed in 2004.

Concerns over contamination at Wyle Laboratories began to mount, with the city adding a Wyle link to its website in May 2003 and presenting extensive reports at city council meetings during May through July of 2003. Agency testing performed on water exiting an ephemeral stream on the Wyle property near the boundary of the subject project in 2003 reported low concentrations of VOCs in surface water (below maximum contaminant levels for drinking water), consistent with samples from Wyle dating back to 1999, and noted that the contaminants evaporated to nondetectable levels a very short distance from the site.

Wyle submitted a work plan for the investigation and remediation of soil and groundwater in June 2003. The DTSC signed an order with Wyle and its successor-in-interest in October 2003 for full characterization and cleanup, with a groundwater treatment system in operation since 2004. Testing in mid- to late 2004 confirmed the off-site migration of contamination from the Wyle property to adjacent residential neighborhoods on the opposite side of the facility (away from the subject project), and vapor extraction systems were installed to supplement on-site cleanup efforts.

There was extensive media coverage of Wyle Laboratories in the local press. The coverage began with the lawsuits filed against the subject and adjacent developer in early 2002 and spiked in mid-2003 and again in the second quarter of 2004, coinciding with the city's response to a grand jury report about Wyle Labs and tests confirming the off-site migration of contamination from the property. This media coverage is graphed in Exhibit 1.

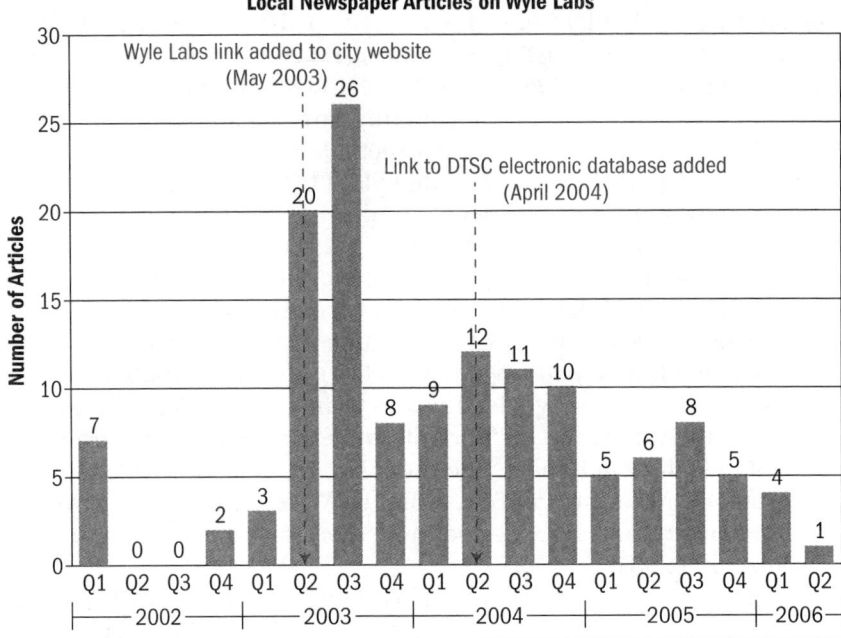

## The Complaint

The complaint in this matter was filed in early 2002, along with a similar lawsuit against the developer of the adjacent project. The three major issues identified in the complaint were as follows:

1. Deceptive disclosure about Wyle Labs
2. Failure to disclose anything about an adjacent battery disposal site
3. Deceptive disclosure about future development

### Deceptive Disclosure about Wyle Labs

The complaint stated that

- The Wyle site is "designed primarily for testing various hazardous and dangerous substances, systems, and munitions, including ordnance systems, weapon systems, remediation, and environmental matters."
- "Wyle Labs is identified by the EPA as a 'large quantity generator' of hazardous waste."
- "Wyle Labs is located in [an area] zoned for heavy industrial use ... [with] potential harmful environmental conditions resulting from this industrial usage."

- "The soil and water on or near the . . . Wyle Property has been contaminated by multiple toxic chemicals."
- "Wyle Labs is a potential noise nuisance."
- "The Homes are located in a fire hazardous area."
- "Wyle is *not* spelled 'Wiley.'"

## Failure to Disclose Anything about an Adjacent Battery Disposal Site

According to the complaint, the adjacent battery disposal site had been designated as a Superfund site by the EPA.[3] "Although the Superfund 'clean-up' was completed in 1988, highly toxic and hazardous battery chemicals . . . remain buried at the site encased in treated soil and concrete."

## Deceptive Disclosure about Future Development

The complaint stated that while disclosures were made regarding potential future developments in the immediate area, there was "no reference to any potential extension of [a major roadway]" and "no reference to a large [drugstore] that would soon be built as the anchor store in what would become a large commercial site adjacent."[4]

## Certification as Class Action

The case was filed as a class action. The class was ultimately certified, despite defense motions to decertify the class. Instead of a jury trial, the parties elected to use judicial reference, an alternative to litigation in California whereby a referee (a retired judge, in this case) effectively hears the case and renders a statement of decision to the trial court, which becomes the judgment of the court. Although the procedure has some similarities to arbitration (another method of alternative dispute resolution), there are significant differences. Referees are judicial officers who are required to follow the law and rules of evidence, and decisions made by judicial reference are subject to review (appeal), like other court decisions. Interestingly, the companion case involving the adjacent tract of homes with nearly identical allegations was not certified as a class action, and the court declined an order of reference in lieu of trial by jury. So much for predictable results.

---

3. *Superfund* refers to the US EPA's program for addressing abandoned hazardous waste sites. It is also the name of the fund established by the Comprehensive Environmental Response, Compensation and Liability Act of 1980. This law allows the EPA to clean up such sites and compel the responsible parties to perform cleanups or reimburse the government for such cleanups.
4. An order by the judicial referee subsequently dismissed claims relating to the alleged nondisclosure or concealment of the adjacent commercial development, including road extensions.

# Market Data Analysis

A comprehensive summary of sale transactions within the subject project was assembled using data from public records and other sources. This data was used to construct a time series analysis of square foot prices from March 2000 through April 2006. There were 28 initial closings in March 2000 at prices ranging from $100-$145 per square foot. Unit prices generally showed little overall change during 2000 and 2001, averaging about $118 per square foot. Since January 2002, when the developer's marketing program was nearly complete, price trending showed an increase of nearly 142% through April 2006. This data is depicted in Exhibit 2, including an overlay showing the volume of Wyle media coverage in the local newspaper over the time period in question. Although this coverage was almost uniformly negative, there was no apparent impact on the sales velocity or rate of appreciation.

Of particular interest is whether prices in the subject project behaved differently from the market as a whole. An additional time series shown in Exhibit 3 depicts the same data for the subject project, along with monthly median square foot prices for existing homes in the county, the subject city, and an adjacent city from January 2000 through April 2006.[5] While the trend lines for both cities are above the line for the subject project because the subject homes are larger and

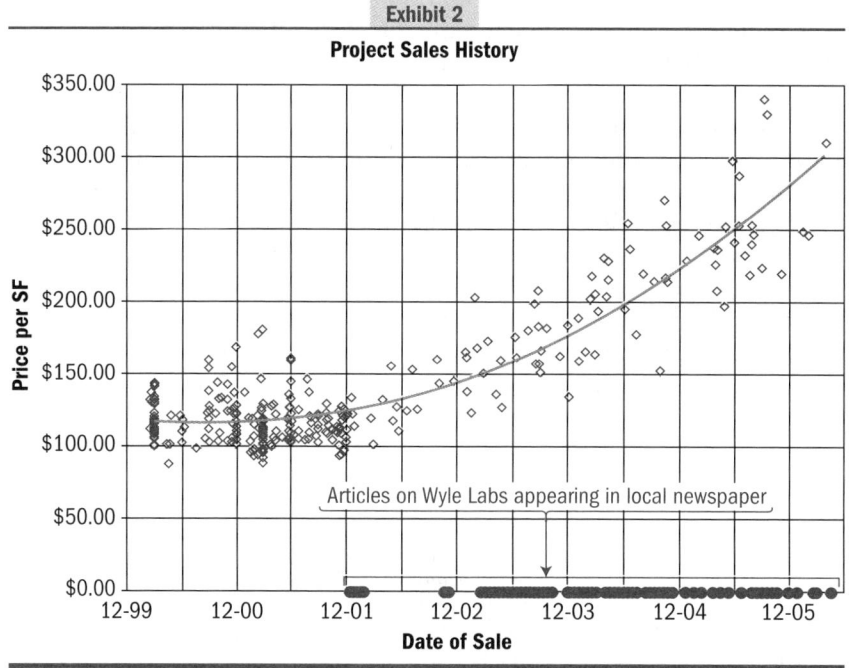

5. The subject project is located in City 1 but is adjacent to the city limits of City 2.

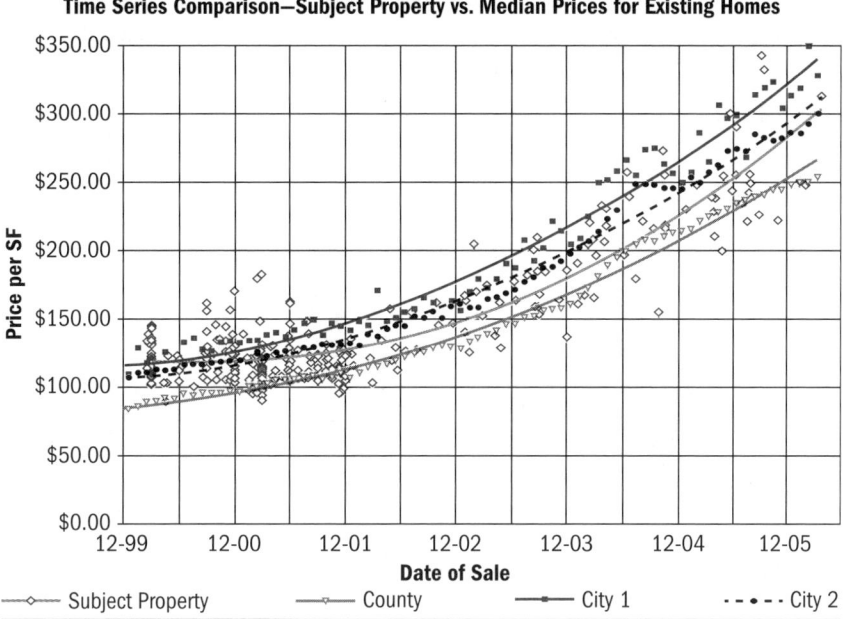

**Exhibit 3**

**Time Series Comparison—Subject Property vs. Median Prices for Existing Homes**

more expensive as compared to the broader market, all three trend lines track fairly closely with the subject project since early 2002.

Exhibit 4 depicts a similar time series analysis, comparing the subject project to the adjacent project (also in litigation with similar allegations) and three other developments. Project 1 is a competitive project located in the same city but distant from Wyle Labs or the former battery recycling site. Projects 2 and 3 are further away but were selected for comparison because both were identified in the declaration of one of the class representatives as being alternatives considered in conjunction with their purchase of a home in the subject project. In this case, the product is generally comparable in terms of size and overall appeal. All projects reflect price trends that track closely with the subject from January 2002 through April 2006.

Exhibit 5 shows comparative appreciation rates for the subject project relative to median monthly prices for the county and two cities between January 2002 and April 2006. Exhibit 6 compares appreciation rates for the adjacent project and other comparable projects in the same period. The subject's total appreciation over this time period is 141.9%, reflecting the top end of the range in comparison to the balance of the data.

Evidence suggests that resale disclosure statements in the subject project have varied widely. Nineteen homeowners were dismissed

**Exhibit 4**

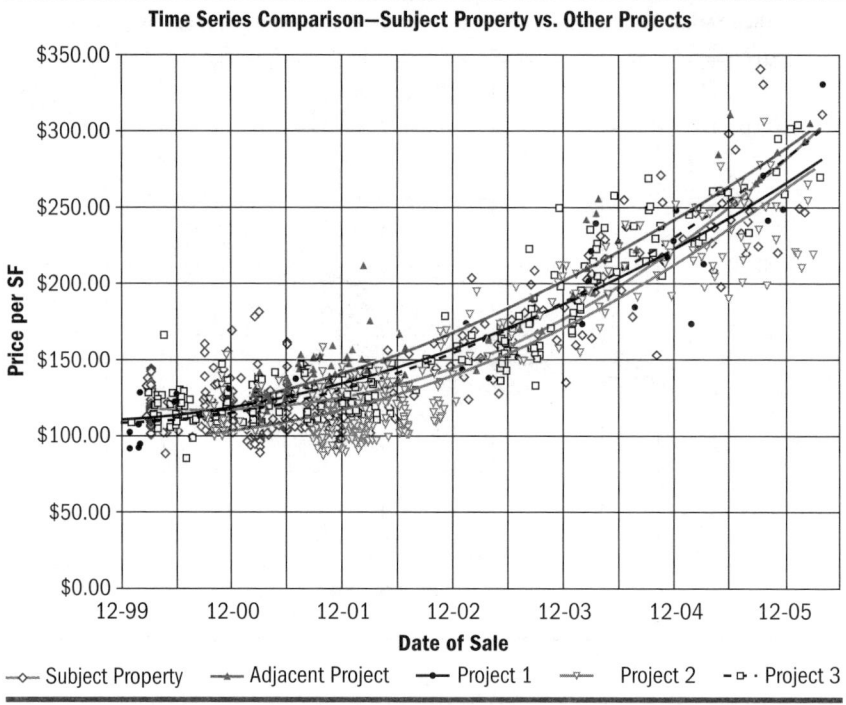

**Exhibit 5**

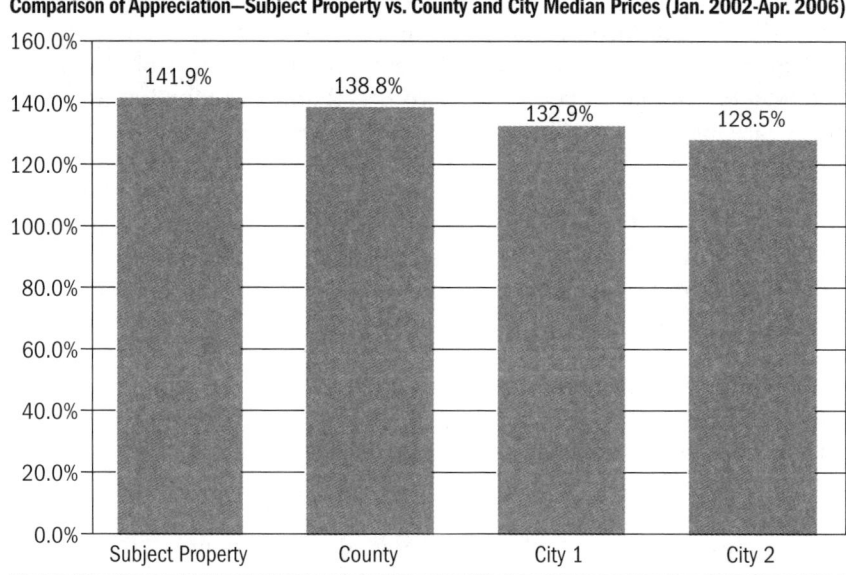

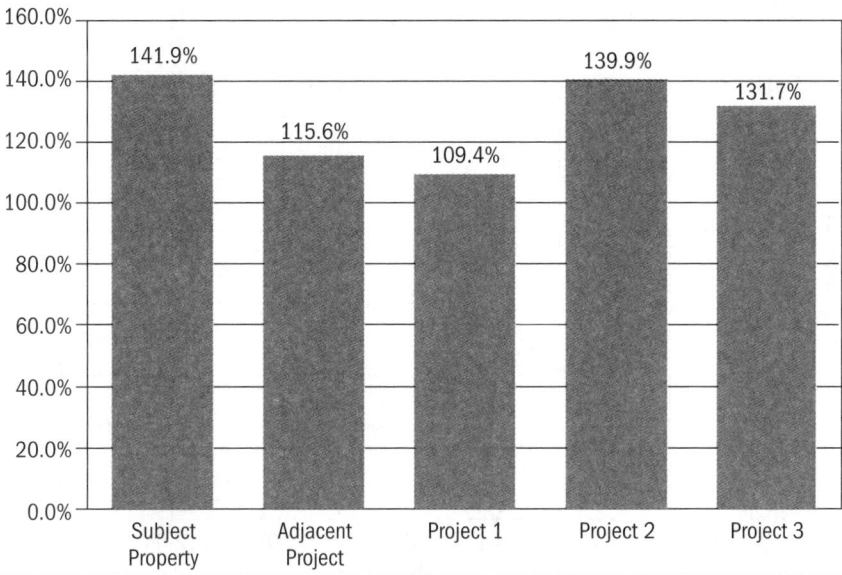

**Exhibit 6**

**Comparison of Appreciation—Subject Property vs. Other Projects (Jan. 2002-Apr. 2006)**

- Subject Property: 141.9%
- Adjacent Project: 115.6%
- Project 1: 109.4%
- Project 2: 139.9%
- Project 3: 131.7%

from the class by order of the judicial referee in May 2005 for failing to make proper written disclosures to subsequent buyers regarding the issues in the lawsuit, including Wyle Labs or the battery recycling facility. We were, however, provided with written disclosures by six original homeowners that were acknowledged and signed by subsequent purchasers. These resales were plotted on the original time series, shown in Exhibit 7. The location of these data points relative to other sales transactions and the trend line does not indicate that such disclosures materially affected the prices paid for the properties, nor do aggregate marketing times or sale-to-list price ratios suggest a significant variance from the market.

A similar analysis was performed for sales of properties abutting Wyle Laboratories and the former battery recycling site, one of which also included a written and signed disclosure on resale. The transactions noted are well distributed throughout the data range, indicating no material impact on the prices paid for such properties (see Exhibit 8).

Additional analyses were performed using a citywide database of MLS sales with the following characteristics:

- Minimum lot size of 15,000 square feet
- Built between 1990 and 2004
- Gross living area of 2,000 to 5,000 square feet
- Sold between January 2004 and early September 2005

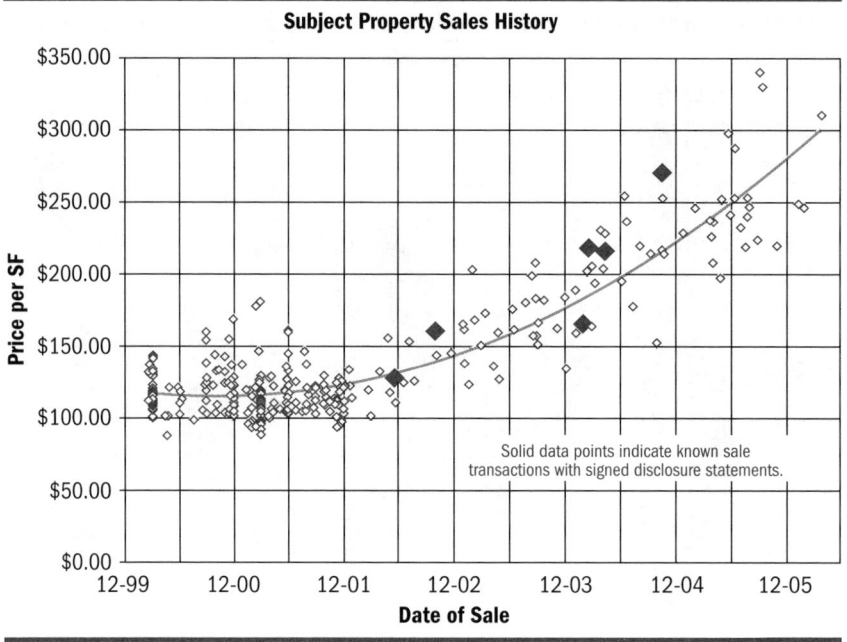

**Exhibit 7**
**Subject Property Sales History**

Solid data points indicate known sale transactions with signed disclosure statements.

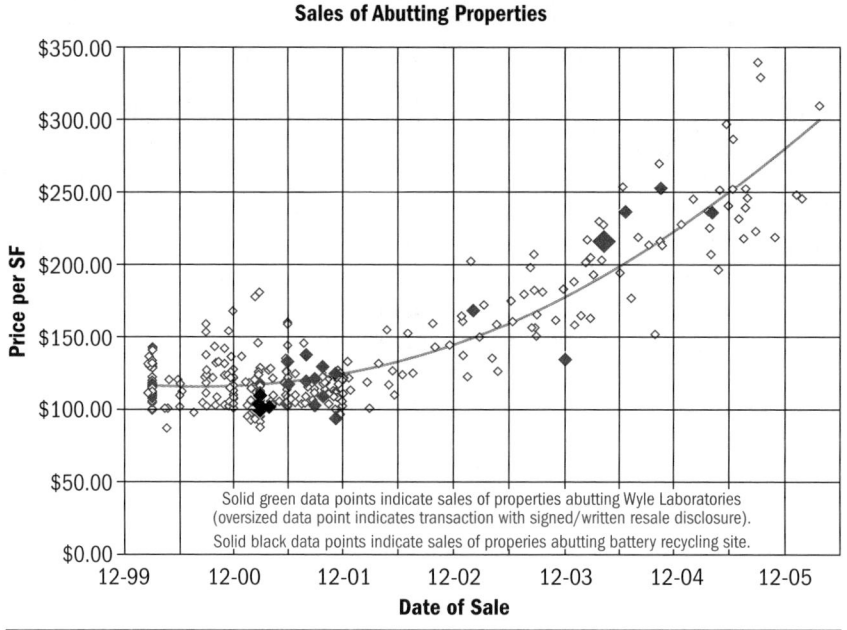

**Exhibit 8**
**Sales of Abutting Properties**

Solid green data points indicate sales of properties abutting Wyle Laboratories (oversized data point indicates transaction with signed/written resale disclosure).
Solid black data points indicate sales of properies abutting battery recycling site.

*Applications in Litigation Valuation: A Pragmatist's Guide*

A total of 138 sales transactions were assembled. Four of these were ultimately discarded because three could not be verified with public records and one resold immediately for a significantly higher price.[6] Descriptive statistics do not indicate that homes in the subject or adjacent projects sell for markedly different prices compared to the broad market, nor is there any apparent negative impact on marketing time or sale-to-list price ratio (see Exhibit 9).

### Exhibit 9

| No. | Location | Lot (sq. ft.) | Built | GLA | Garage | List Price | Sold Price | COE | Price/ Sq. Ft. | DOM | Sale/ List |
|---|---|---|---|---|---|---|---|---|---|---|---|
| 45 | Subject Project Adjacent Project | 33,184 | 2001 | 3,374 | 3.467 | $764,673 | $755,511 | 10/06/04 | $225.85 | 60 | 98.8% |
| 89 | Other Properties | 26,665 | 2001 | 3,212 | 3.303 | $734,666 | $718,904 | 01/23/05 | $227.38 | 63 | 97.9% |

This same data was used for multiple regression analysis (see Exhibit 10), with consideration of the following independent variables and their impact on selling price:

- Date of sale (measured in months from January 2004)

### Exhibit 10

**SUMMARY OUTPUT**

**Regression Statistics**

| | |
|---|---|
| Multiple R | 0.791550260 |
| R Square | 0.626551814 |
| Adjusted R Square | 0.602651130 |
| Standard Error | 74,060.68 |
| Observations | 134 |

**ANOVA**

| | df | SS | MS | F | Significance F |
|---|---|---|---|---|---|
| Regression | 8 | 1.1503E+12 | 1.43788E+11 | 26.21480692 | 2.07957E-23 |
| Residual | 125 | 6.85623E+11 | 5484984409 | | |
| Total | 133 | 1.83593E+12 | | | |

| | Coefficients | Standard Error | t Stat | P-Value | Lower 95% | Upper 95% |
|---|---|---|---|---|---|---|
| Intercept | 191,846.07 | 51,144.90 | 3.751030521 | 0.000268193 | 90,623.97 | 293,068.17 |
| Sale Month (from January 2004) | 9,378.72 | 1,187.56 | 7.897454284 | 1.25322E-12 | 7,028.38 | 11,729.05 |
| Lot Size (square feet) | 1.13 | 0.38 | 2.998991913 | 0.003269453 | 0.38 | 1.87 |
| View | 22,905.16 | 15,144.84 | 1.512406883 | 0.132954548 | -7,068.36 | 52,878.67 |
| Age (years) | -1,941.95 | 1,984.39 | -0.978616426 | 0.329659745 | -5,869.30 | 1,985.39 |
| Gross Living Area (square feet) | 99.58 | 13.64 | 7.299948490 | 2.94257E-11 | 72.58 | 126.57 |
| Garage (spaces) | 11,335.63 | 10,102.36 | 1.122077957 | 0.263980069 | -8,658.19 | 31,329.46 |
| Pool | 86,076.88 | 17,104.22 | 5.032492757 | 1.64471E-06 | 52,225.50 | 119,928.26 |
| Location (WPH/Centex) | 19,783.39 | 15,255.65 | 1.296791176 | 0.197091734 | -10,409.43 | 49,976.22 |

6. This transaction also reflected the lowest listed and sold prices among the data considered.

- Lot size (square feet)
- View (yes or no)
- Age (years)
- Gross living area (square feet)
- Garage (number of spaces)
- Pool (yes or no)
- Location within the subject or adjacent projects (yes or no)

The coefficient of determination ($r^2$) is approximately 63%, indicating a significant amount of unexplained variation in the model. This is not necessarily unexpected because there are a number of factors—upgrades, condition, landscaping, other site improvements, and so on—that were not included as additional independent variables for practical purposes. Importantly, the $F$ statistic, which measures the strength of the relationship between the dependent variable (price) and the independent variables, is highly significant. Coefficients for the independent variables have expected values and signs, although coefficients for the date of sale, lot size, gross living area, and pool are the only ones significant at better than the 10% level.[7] Although it is not considered statistically significant, the item of interest is the coefficient for location, indicating a *positive* value of nearly $20,000 for homes in the subject and adjacent projects.

A report was ultimately prepared documenting opinions and conclusions. As part of the discovery process, this report and the accompanying workfile were produced in advance of deposition, which followed the depositions of the plaintiffs' expert witnesses.

## Opinions of Opposing Experts

The plaintiffs' case regarding damages relied on two experts. The primary expert was a real estate appraiser, whose opinions also incorporated a contingent valuation survey performed by a market research consultant. Documents were deposited in advance of deposition, giving us an opportunity to review the opposing expert's material and draft proposed deposition questions. Although the opposing appraisal expert signed several declarations attesting to certain opinions, no formal report was actually prepared. As a result, the opinions expressed in deposition were effectively considered an oral report under USPAP Standards Rule 2-4.

The plaintiffs' appraisal expert required three separate sessions, the third of which we attended in person in an effort to focus attention on important questions for which there were still no concrete

---

7. All are significant at better than the 1% level. While eliminating other variables results in an improved $F$ statistic, the coefficient of determination ($r^2$) and coefficients for remaining independent variables show relatively little change.

answers. Following completion of the final deposition session and review of the transcripts and file documents, an appraisal review report was prepared under Standard 3 of USPAP, which supplemented the report documenting our affirmative opinions and conclusions.

The plaintiffs' major claim was that class members overpaid for their properties, based on the allegation of insufficient disclosure of nearby environmental nuisances by the developer. Some of the appraisal opinions and related issues identified were as follows:

- To calculate lost appreciation, the appraiser for the plaintiff compared appreciation rates for the subject project and other properties (control group) over differing time periods that did not have consistent growth rates. The appraiser then extrapolated the difference over an anticipated holding period. The data and analysis were riddled with errors, and when analyzed carefully, the data actually demonstrated that properties in the subject project *outperformed* properties in the control group.

- Opinions were offered regarding a "stigma impact" based on a review of articles that were contained in the appraiser's file. In deposition, it was clear that the appraiser knew little about the articles, many of which did not support the appraiser's opinions.

- Reliance was placed on a consumer survey performed by the expert market research consultant. The appraiser did not quote the results of the survey accurately, had no apparent knowledge of the technique employed (contingent valuation), and did not even have a copy of the survey in the workfile. The use of survey methodology in lieu of empirical market data was a significant criticism.[8]

- The appraiser misrepresented having experience in appraising homes in the geographic area of the subject project and was forced to acknowledge as much in the deposition.

- The plaintiff's counsel asked the appraiser to assume that original disclosures were inadequate or incomplete, without the appraiser reviewing the actual disclosures or environmental data available at the time, and without employing an extraordinary assumption regarding the inadequacy of such disclosures and the potential impact on opinions or conclusions if found to be false.

- The appraiser further stated the opinion that the disclosures were inadequate but acknowledged having no specific training with respect to disclosure duties, effectively offering opinions well outside the appraiser's area of expertise.

---

8. Although the court accepted the contingent valuation testimony of the plaintiffs' market research consultant in an opposition to motion for summary judgment, the court ultimately granted a motion in limine precluding this expert from testifying at trial.

- While commenting that class members overpaid for their properties, the appraiser did not value the class representatives' properties at the time of purchase and could not even identify them on an aerial photograph of the project during deposition.
- The appraiser testified that because the assignment did not involve a federally related transaction, USPAP did not apply. This statement is clearly contrary to the California Business and Professions Code, which states that "the Uniform Standards of Professional Appraisal Practice constitute the minimum standard of conduct and performance for a licensee *in any work or service performed that is addressed by those standards* [emphasis added].

## Case Disposition

Notwithstanding the environmental nature of the case, the plaintiffs' damage claims did not include health impacts or even allegations that their properties were contaminated, instead they related only to loss of property value from proximity impacts. Mediation claims and settlement offers are confidential and will not be discussed here. The ultimate opinion of the plaintiffs' appraisal expert, using flawed analysis, was approximately $157,000 per home for "lost appreciation," or slightly over $34 million.

After the completion of expert depositions in mid-2006, a $700,000 settlement was reached and finalized in late 2006. The plaintiffs' attorneys reportedly worked on the case for more than 6,000 hours, settling for $210,000 in attorney fees (30% of the settlement amount) plus approximately $150,000 for the reimbursement of costs. Allocated over the 185 class members remaining at the conclusion of the litigation, the average recovery per homeowner was slightly over $1,800. In addition to the primary payment of $700,000 on behalf of the class members, it was agreed that defendants would also pay expenses associated with the settlement.

As a side note, the plaintiffs' counsel subsequently proposed to publish our report and related documents on their public website. This was presumably to help their clients understand the reasons for the settlement, although such information was not restricted to these clients. It was in the interest of our client as well to have plaintiff class members understand and consent to the settlement. However, this was clearly not consistent with standard assumptions and limiting conditions that restrict the rights of publication or dissemination without prior written consent. A potential problem was that our retention (including standard assumptions and limiting conditions) was a contract with our client, not with the opposing counsel or their clients. An agreement was ultimately reached with the plaintiff counsel requiring removal of our report and related documents from their website but granting permission to provide a copy of our report to plaintiff class members upon request, contingent upon their signature of an acknowledgement and release drafted by our attorney.

CASE STUDY 3.3

# Radioactive Contamination of Nuclear Weapons Test Site

*By Randall Bell, MAI*

## Overview

On March 1, 1954, the United States' "Shrimp" thermonuclear device was detonated at Bikini Atoll, in the Marshall archipelago of the Pacific Ocean. This test was known as "Castle Bravo." Several hours prior to the detonation, the winds shifted from the usual northwesterly direction to an easterly direction. Several hours after the Bravo test, radioactive fallout blanketed vast areas, including the subject atolls of Rongelap, Rongerik, and Ailinginae in the Republic of the Marshall Islands. The subject atolls contain a gross combined land area of approximately 3,156.9 acres: 1,946.1 acres for Rongelap, 457.5 acres for Rongerik, and 753.3 acres for Ailinginae.[1]

The assignment was to complete an appraisal report estimating the loss in use value for the Rongelap, Rongerik, and Ailinginae Atolls for the periods of loss of full and safe use resulting from the contamination caused by the US Nuclear Testing Program. The subject properties were occupied by claimants during a portion of the periods of lost use and were directly exposed to nuclear fallout.

The purpose of this assignment was to provide the Marshall Islands Nuclear Claims Tribunal with a loss in use value conclusion as well as supporting property and market data upon which compensation-related decisions could be based. The loss-in-use value conclusion reflects a loss in use to the people of the subject atolls for the period that use of this land had been denied or for which the radioactivity level had exceeded the US Government/Nuclear Claims Tribunal standard (15 millirems). The value conclusions address additional claim issues including future loss in use but do not consider remediation, physical and emotional suffering, hardship, or any other consequential damages.

The scope of this assignment included

1. Physically inspecting Rongelap Atoll and the surrounding vicinity
2. Reviewing documents provided by the client

---

1. An *atoll* is "a coral island consisting of a reef surrounding a lagoon." *Merriam-Webster's Collegiate Dictionary*, 11th ed. (Springfield, MA: Merriam-Webster, 2005), 78.

3. Collecting and analyzing market data related to the radioactive environmental issues
4. Conducting a loss-of-use analysis

Portions of this case study were derived from appraisal reports for the Nuclear Claims Tribunal submitted jointly by Randall Bell, MAI, and Nicholas Captain, MAI. Statistical calculations were performed by William T. Woodard, PhD. The reports in this case were voluminous, and this case study reflects a portion that illustrates the loss-of-use valuation techniques used for a five-year period from January 1, 1996, to December 31, 2000. This case study illustrates the use and importance of "project delay" and "loss-of-use" economic models for damaged real estate.

## Nuclear Claims Tribunal

This case was performed for the Marshall Islands Nuclear Claims Tribunal in an effort to determine the just compensation of landowners for the loss of use to their properties as a result of contamination with nuclear fallout.

The Nuclear Claims Tribunal Act, enacted by the Marshall Islands, and the Agreement for Implementation of Section 177 of the Compact of Free Association between the United States and the Marshall Islands both give jurisdiction to the Nuclear Claims Tribunal. This authorizes the Tribunal to render final determination upon all past, present, and future claims of the Marshall Islands' government, citizens, and nationals that are based on, arise out of, or are in any way related to the Nuclear Testing Program.

This jurisdiction includes determining the appropriate amount of compensation payable to the people of the Rongelap, Rongerik, and Ailinginae Atolls for the periods in which they have been denied full and unrestricted use of their homelands because of the Nuclear Testing Program and subsequent radioactive contamination of these atolls.

Regarding the subject properties, the Nuclear Claims Tribunal rendered verdicts based on the values and methodologies employed in this case study. However, only a summary of a portion of the market data and calculations is set forth here.

## Marshall Island Background

The Republic of the Marshall Islands consists of 29 atolls and five islands located within 750,000 square miles just north of the equator in the central Pacific Ocean. The country is located in the easternmost portion of Micronesia, approximately 2,000 miles southwest of Hawaii. The total land area of the Marshall Islands is approximately 70 square miles (about one-third of the area of Guam), and the total lagoon area for all 29 atolls is approximately 4,300 square miles.

The 29 ring-shaped atolls are arranged in two roughly parallel chains that run in a southeast-to-northwest direction. The western chain (including the three subject atolls) is known as the Ralik Chain, and the eastern chain is known as the Ratak Chain. (*Ralik* means "sunset" in Marshallese, while *ratak* means "sunrise.") The two chains are separated by approximately 130 miles of open ocean.

The climate of the Marshall Islands is tropical maritime, due to its location near the equator and its lack of a large landmass. Temperatures range from approximately 80 to 85 degrees Fahrenheit, with nominal seasonal variations. The Marshallese are believed to have landed in the area at least 2,000 years ago. As expert navigators, they traveled freely throughout the region and had frequent contact with other Micronesian cultures.

The Marshall Islands were sighted by several Spanish explorers in the 1500s, but ships rarely visited the Marshalls in the early centuries of European contact. The islands were named after John Marshall, an English sea captain who visited the area in 1788. In the 1860s, German traders began establishing coconut plantations on the islands, and Germany subsequently annexed the Marshalls in 1885. A series of land transactions occurred around this period of German annexation. When the Japanese took control of the Marshalls in the 1914, they colonized the islands and built large fortified bases in anticipation of military action.

In 1944, American forces invaded the Marshall Islands as the first step in the United States' island-hopping push across the Pacific in World War II. After the war, the Marshalls were incorporated into the United Nations Trust Territory program and were administered by the United States.

On March 1, 1954, the Bikini Atoll's weather outlook was downgraded to "unfavorable," and several ships were directed to move 20 miles to the south to remove them from the expected nuclear fallout zone. Despite weather reports showing that winds were blowing in the direction of inhabited islands, the Castle Bravo hydrogen bomb was detonated at Bikini. At 15 megatons, it was 1,000 times the strength of the Hiroshima bomb. Within hours, a gritty, white ash enveloped islanders on Rongelap and Ailinginae Atolls. A few hours later, American weathermen were exposed to the snowstorm of radioactive fallout on Rongerik, and still later, the people of Utrik and other islands experienced the fallout "mist." Those exposed experienced nausea, vomiting, and itching of the skin and eyes. Skin burns on heavily exposed people began to develop, and their hair later fell out. The US Atomic Energy Commission issued a statement to the press calling Bravo a "routine atomic test" and stating that some Americans and Marshallese were "unexpectedly exposed to some radioactivity. There were no burns. All were reported well."

On March 7, 1954, a secret medical group was established to monitor and evaluate the Rongelap and Utrik people through Project 4.1, "Study of Response of Human Beings Exposed to Significant Beta and Gamma Radiation due to Fallout from High Yield Weapons." In April 1954, a Project 4.1 memo recommended that the exposed Rongelap people should have "no exposure for (the) rest of (their) natural lives."

In July 1976, the US Congress approved $20 million and military logistic support for a nuclear cleanup of Enewetak Atoll. A Brookhaven National Laboratory report on Rongelap showed that 69% (20 out of 29) of the Rongelap children who were under 10 years old in 1954 developed thyroid tumors. This exposure led to many thyroid problems, including thyroid cancer as well as other types of cancer. The 236 inhabitants of Rongelap and Utrik have continued to require regular medical care by American doctors following the Bravo detonation.

At the end of the 1970s, the Marshalls withdrew from the Trust Territory and became an independent republic. In 1986, the Republic of the Marshall Islands entered into a Compact of Free Association with the United States. The islands' present-day government is a combination of American and British models and has an operating parliament known as the Nitijela, which selects a president from among its ranks.

## Environmental Issues

Radioactivity from natural sources affects all properties. However, the radioactive discharge that affected Rongelap, Rongerik, and Ailinginae was an "accidental" discharge that far exceeds radiation from natural causes.

Rongelap, Rongerik, and Ailinginae lands generally do not meet the current US Federal regulatory 15-millirem standards. The Nuclear Claims Tribunal has ruled that this 15-millirem standard defines "contamination." The radioactive contamination was conveyed in an airborne plume that resulted in direct human exposure.

## Land Transaction History and Concept of Value

Land has deep cultural and psychological importance to Marshallese people. This significance is referred to in Marshallese as *Lamoren* land and stems from lineage ties to particularly named wetos, or sections of land, that may result from becoming the burial sites of older people or may be symbolized by the burial of an infant's umbilical cord on that child's matrilineal land. To the Marshallese, land is the essence of personal and social identity. It is shared with matrilineal kin. It is the most important possession possible and in many respects is regarded as sacred. It is also philosophically important. Apart from providing a birthplace, a place to live, a means of subsistence, and a place to die, land provides status in the sociological and political structure of the community. The cultural significance of land to the Marshallese and other Pacific Islanders exceeds that which is understood in the Western world, where land is viewed largely as an economic resource.

Land is of paramount importance to the Marshallese people, whose agricultural economy is based on copra production.[2] Most local foods come directly from the land. All members of society are born into land rights; the Marshallese system of land tenure provides for all eventualities and takes care of the needs of all members of its society.

The Western concept of land ownership was imported to the Marshall Islands beginning in the late 1800s. During this time, Germany was actively acquiring parcels of land to use primarily for plantations. According to a review of German land transaction records, nearly 50 land transactions took place during the late 1800s. The most notable transaction during this period involves the sale of Likiep Atoll in 1877. This atoll remains the only fee simple-owned parcel of land in the entire country.

Beginning in the 1960s, the volume of real estate transactions in the Marshall Islands began to increase. This increase in transaction activity was due to the ongoing transition from an agricultural to a money-based economy. The urbanization of Majuro Atoll and the increasing activity of the United States military also played key roles in the increase in land transaction activity during this time.

A database of Marshall Islands land transactions was compiled, beginning with the Bikini database. As part of the prior Rongelap study, the database was updated, corrected, and revised as necessary based on our physical review of documents recorded at the courthouse and attorney general's office. A summary of real estate activity in the Marshall Islands by decade (through 2000) is shown in Exhibit 1.

The majority of real estate transactions took place in the 1980s (41%), followed by the 1990s (33%). Only about 7% of the total transactions occurred between 1940 and 1969. Because of the social structure in the Marshall Islands, it was natural that government influence on real estate values and rents began early. According to an Attorney General Memorandum Synopsis dated December 4, 1968, a minimum land rent bill was passed by the Nitijela at $0.03 per square foot per year. Although it appears that the bill did not pass into law, this land rent equates to $1,307 per acre per year.

In the 1960s, the Trust Territory retained significant control over the lease of private land to noncitizens. A lengthy application process was employed to ensure that landowners were adequately compen-

---

2. *Copra* is "dried coconut meat yielding coconut oil." *Merriam-Webster's Collegiate Dictionary*, 276.

### Exhibit 1
#### Transaction Volume

| Decade | No. of Real Estate Transactions | % of Total Transactions |
|---|---|---|
| No date | 8 | 1.6% |
| 1940s | 2 | 0.4% |
| 1950s | 6 | 1.2% |
| 1960s | 28 | 5.7% |
| 1970s | 82 | 16.6% |
| 1980s | 202 | 40.9% |
| 1990s | 165 | 33.4% |
| 2000 | 1 | 0.2% |
| Totals | 494 | 100.0% |

sated. Although designed to protect the long-term interests of local landowners, the strict control may have precluded foreign investment during this time.

In or around 1979, an "Official Government Rate" of $2,500 per acre per year was established by the Cabinet of the Government of the Republic of the Marshall Islands. This government-set rate became widely accepted as a benchmark value for land regardless of frontage, size, or other characteristics. The government rate remained $2,500 per acre per year until October 1, 1989, when it was adjusted upwards to $3,000 per acre per year. In early 1996, the existing rate was reviewed and reestablished as the government rate. The government rate, as of December 2000, remained at $3,000 per acre per year.

The influence of the government rate on transaction prices cannot be overstated. Since the published government rate was implemented, many land lease transactions have been based on it. Further, many leases provide for rent reviews at five-year intervals based on changes in the established rate.

## Highest and Best Use Overview

The highest and best use of the subject properties was considered to be for military and government use. Government/military considerations for the Marshall Islands began as early as October 1945, when military planners initiated worldwide research to identify a site where the effects of nuclear bombs could be studied. The initial testing program was referred to as Operation Crossroads.

The ideal nuclear test site criteria included

- Area controlled by the United States
- Climatic conditions with predictable winds, free from storms and cold temperatures

- A large sheltered area for anchoring target vessels and measuring radiation effects
- Location within 1,000 miles of a B-29 air base
- No inhabitants or a small population that can be relocated[3]

The Marshall Islands were selected among many sites around the world as being the site most optimal for government/military uses involving the testing of nuclear weapons. The actual use of the atoll is inseparably connected to the US nuclear testing program. This is by virtue of the relocation of residents, the collection of radioactive data on the atoll, and ultimately the blanketing of the atoll with a radioactive plume that has resulted in contamination above the 15-millirem standard. Accordingly, Rongelap, Rongerik, and Ailinginae Atolls have been used for the atomic testing and residual fallout from nuclear waste, clearly a government/military use.

## Damage Analysis

In the valuation process, several approaches were used:

1. An analysis based on the Kwajalein military lease (explained in the following section of this case study)
2. A statistical model of numerous ground leases throughout the Marshall Islands (including consideration of the government rate)
3. A case study analysis whereby the aggregate figures for lost use were compared to other large-scale nuclear instances around the world

### Land Lease Rate–Kwajalein Lease Study

Portions of the nearby Kwajalein Atoll involve a lease by the US government for military-related uses. This lease represents an outstanding indicator of the government/military value of an atoll in the Marshall Islands. Whether the government uses the atoll for military purposes (as it does in Kwajalein) or for nuclear testing and radioactive waste storage (as it does in Rongelap, Rongerik, and Ailinginae), the values should reconcile.

According to independent sources, the Kwajalein lease includes 2,409.483 acres. The annual gross payment figures range from $7,210,000 in 1987 to $8,460,000 in 2000. Using the 2,409.483 acreage, the annual Kwajalein lease payments range from $2,992 per acre in 1987 to $3,511 per acre in 2000. These figures provide a relevant and independent verification of the government/military rate implemented in 1989 at $3,000 per acre per year.

---

3. Jonathan M. Weisgall, *Operation Crossroads: The Atomic Tests at Bikini Atoll* (Annapolis, MD: Naval Institute Press, 1994).

## Land Lease Rate–Statistical Analysis

Comparable land transactions in the Marshall Islands were extensively researched to estimate a loss in use value for the subject property. A review was made of historic appraisal and consulting reports, legal decisions, land use agreements, and land settlement agreements. Historic memoranda and meeting notes were reviewed, as were Nuclear Claims Tribunal, Foreign Claims Settlement, Trust Territory, and other documents. Interviews were conducted with attorneys, property owners, and other knowledgeable market participants. Further, the research included a detailed review of all documents recorded at the Majuro Courthouse and the Attorney General's Office of the Government of the Marshall Islands.

A database of all known land transactions was compiled. The first requirement was to ensure that all possible recorded transactions were examined. Visits were made to the governmental offices in the Marshall Islands, and examinations were made of hundreds of lease and sale transactions. These databases covered the primary provisions of those transactions, which included the name of the parties, the name of the land weto, the district or land location, the land area, the term of the lease, use and rental payments, or price provisions.

This analysis is based on the unit rate of US$1 per acre per year, which is the unit rate most commonly found in land lease transactions in the Marshall Islands. All documents were considered appropriate in light of the loss in use period, which extends over many decades. The most obvious difficulty in the research process involved the realities of the Marshall Islands' real estate market, particularly between 1946 and the mid-1970s, when more reliable transactions began to occur. No true market existed during the early years. The limited number of transactions that did occur involved government condemnation-style actions or payments for prior occupations. Over time, the government-related transactions became recognized by the market as legitimate indicators of land values and rents in the country. The government's influence on land value started with the 1968 land price declaration and culminated with the adoption of the official government rate in 1979.

The database initially included 585 transactions. As expected, the comparable transactions reflected a wide range of rents on a dollar-per-acre-per-year basis. Transaction documents included ground leases, bills of sale, agreements for past use, and other documents. The 585-transaction database was filtered numerous times to extract the most pertinent market data. First, the database was revised to exclude duplicate entries, partial detail transactions, and other erroneous data. The revised transaction database included 494 transactions. The next step in the filtering process was to eliminate transactions that did not reflect a land rent or price from which rent could be derived. Transactions without dates were eliminated in this stage of the filtering process. The revised database reflected 384 transactions. Although additional filtering was required, this 384-transaction database was used to extract additional details regarding rent renegotiations and escalation clauses. Market data with related parties was also excluded. Adjustments were considered for property rights conveyed, market conditions, location, size, and other property characteristics.

The conclusions for the Marshall Islands case study are complex, as they involved a variety of scenarios and a variety of atolls and islands. In general, the damages equated to approximately $16,000 per acre for the total period of lost use. In the aggregate, the damages were in excess of $1 billion.

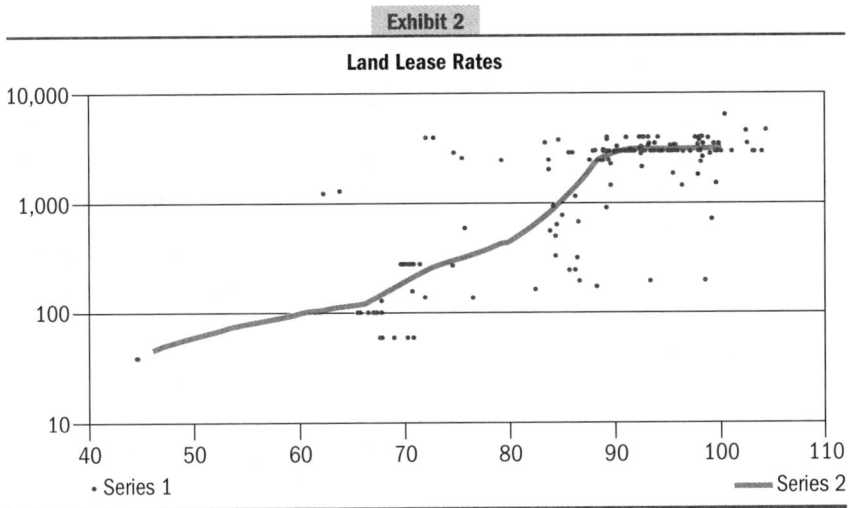

The land lease rate graph in Exhibit 2 sets forth time on the $x$-axis and the land lease rate on the $y$-axis. Series 1 represents specific land leases, while Series 2 represents the overall trend.

Statistical modeling based on the 384 transactions indicated the land rental rates shown in Exhibit 3. The Kwajalein lease payments from $2,992 per acre in 1987 to $3,511 per acre in 2000 supported and

| Exhibit 3 | |
|---|---|
| Year | Rental Rate/Acre/Year |
| 1996 | $3,130 |
| 1997 | $3,150 |
| 1998 | $3,160 |
| 1999 | $3,180 |
| 2000 | $3,190 |

reconciled with the results of this statistical analysis. Therefore, the cumulative loss of use as a result of the radioactive contamination is shown in Exhibit 4.

### Exhibit 4

| Year | Rent/Acre | Acres | Loss of Use | Cumulative Loss of Use |
|------|-----------|-------|-------------|------------------------|
| 1996 | $3,130 | 3,166.9 | $9,912,397 | $9,912,397 |
| 1997 | 3,150 | 3,166.9 | 9,975,735 | 19,888,132 |
| 1998 | 3,160 | 3,166.9 | 10,007,404 | 29,895,536 |
| 1999 | 3,180 | 3,166.9 | 10,070,742 | 39,966,278 |
| 2000 | 3,190 | 3,166.9 | 10,102,411 | $50,068,689 |

## Radioactive Case Studies

The prior analysis reflects a fractional portion of the complete computations in this case. All totaled, the damage in the Marshall Islands was in excess of $1 billion. The compensation awarded amounted to over $560 million in the Bikini Atoll case, while the compensation awarded was approximately $324 million in the Enewetak case.

In order to verify the reasonableness of a value conclusion of this magnitude, case studies of other instances involving nuclear issues around the world were reviewed. A search was made for the costs and damages associated with nuclear events such as nuclear leaks, testing, meltdowns, and so forth. The results of this search are shown in Exhibit 5.

These cases are obviously not directly comparable to the Marshall Islands case. However, they illustrate the general "price tags" associated with large-scale radiation cases. This information indi-

### Exhibit 5

#### Summary of Radioactive-Related Costs

| | | |
|---|---|---|
| 1. | Three Mile Island, Pennsylvania | $973 million |
| 2. | Chernobyl, Ukraine | $300 billion, by 2015 |
| 3. | Hanford, Washington | $35 billion, $50 billion more required |
| 4. | Paducah, Kentucky | $124 million per year |
| 5. | Yucca Mountain, Nevada | $7 billion to date |
| 6. | Nevada "downwinders" | $1.5 billion |
| 7. | Portsmouth, Ohio | $1.1 billion |
| 8. | Rocky Mountain Arsenal, Colorado | $7.7 billion |
| 9. | Oak Ridge, Tennessee | $6.49 billion |
| 10. | Pantex Plant, Texas | $227 billion |
| 11. | Fernald, Ohio | $3.15 billion |
| 12. | Savannah River, South Carolina | $50.3 billion |

cates that the loss of use for Rongelap, Rongerik, and Ailinginae could easily be in the hundreds of millions of dollars. Yucca Mountain has an annual budget of $400 to $500 million per year, yet no nuclear waste has yet to be actually stored there. The Nevada nuclear test sites resulted in the "downwinders" program, which cost $1.5 billion. Over $3 billion is expected to be spent on one nuclear facility in Ohio. As these case studies illustrate, the costs associated with repairs and compensation for nuclear issues typically range in the hundreds of millions to billions of dollars.

These case studies indicate that the damages for impacted atolls in the Marshall Islands fall within the general parameters of the costs associated with other nuclear-related events.

## Case Study 4.1

# Transmission Line Construction—Wooden Poles to Metal Pylons

*By Shawn Wilson, MAI*

In 2003 an electric utility company in Tampa, Florida, began construction of new power line links between existing power substations. These additional links were needed to improve back-up capacity on the electrical grid. The power lines connecting substation to substation are high voltage and support the transmission of 230 kilovolts of electrical current.

One of the substations involved in the project is located in the Egypt Lakes Estates neighborhood, an area of several hundred suburban homes. The neighborhood is primarily working class, with most homes constructed during the 1960s. The area is bounded by multi-lane arterial roadways, including a six-lane state road and a four-lane county road. Most of the utility infrastructure in the area parallels those busy roads.

The other streets in the neighborhood are typical two-lane residential roadways. Several of the east-west residential streets are equipped with speed control humps to deter cut-through traffic between the major roads. The neighborhood's electrical distribution lines that provide power to individual homes are aboveground and supported by wooden poles of the type commonly found in residential subdivisions.

The Egypt Lakes subdivision plat is unusual because the road rights of way may also be used for utilities. The existing power lines were located within the road right of way, beyond the edge of the pavement. Such power lines are typically located within utility easements running beside the road.

When designing the new substation connection in Egypt Lakes, engineers realized that the new transmission lines could bypass the arterial roadways if routed through the subdivision within existing road rights of way. By doing so, the power company would have no right of way acquisition cost. If the lines were instead routed along the nearby thoroughfares, the power company would have to purchase utility easements from many commercial properties at an estimated cost of $5 million. The engineers designed the more cost-effective alternative. The addition of high-voltage transmission lines on large metal poles within the existing right of way did not require a special permit, public hearings, or government approval. There was no requirement to provide any notice to property owners adjoining the project.

## Residents React

When the power company began installing the new poles, the neighborhood residents were outraged and county officials were deluged with calls.

The local newspaper published an editorial that described the project, stating, "Words cannot capture how grossly the Tampa Electric Co. has disfigured a decent, working-class neighborhood. In Egypt Lake, just northwest of Tampa's city limits, a battery of workers is sinking a long line of massive electric utility poles. They are three feet wide and up to 125 feet tall and visible from nearly three miles away. You need to see it to believe it—columns lined like towering tin soldiers on every fourth lawn, only a few feet away from people's living rooms, butting against fences, landscaping, driveways, and sidewalks."

The affected homeowners, along with county officials, requested that the poles be removed and the project rerouted to commercial streets. The utility company considered the request but ultimately denied it, stating that project deadline requirements did not allow enough time to acquire a new right of way. The utility company ordered appraisals of each impacted home. The appraiser hired by the utility stated that the new transmission lines and structures had no impact on the value of the adjoining properties.

The homeowners eventually filed suit against the utility company, claiming that the power lines constituted a continuing nuisance. For relief, they requested that the poles be removed and placed in a more suitable commercial corridor. Absent that relief, they requested a jury trial to establish compensation for the devaluation of their properties.

*Transmission Line Construction–Wooden Poles to Metal Pylons*

The utility company ordered updates of the appraisals along the corridor. This time the appraiser found slight damages, but only to those homes that had power poles on or adjacent to their front yards. Small settlement offers were extended to the homeowners and rejected.

After months of legal wrangling, a judge ruled that a jury could not order removal of the power poles because the action could interrupt the community's flow of electricity. That ruling was appealed but denied in the District Court of Appeals. The judge did rule, however, that a jury could consider financial compensation for damages to real estate value.

The coalition of homeowners raised money to cover court costs and expenses related to the lawsuit. Their attorneys agreed to work for a percentage of the final result rather than being paid along the way, but the budget was tight and the utility company had virtually unlimited financial resources.

The homeowners hired a local real estate appraiser to value their homes with and without the new power lines. The appraiser began work on the first part of the assignment but missed deadlines for the second part of the assignment. With a trial date approaching, the homeowners hired a second appraiser.

## Scope of Work

Due to time constraints and the existence of individual "before condition" appraisals that were substantially complete and already paid for, the second appraiser was to focus on damages caused by the atypical power lines and the structures supporting them. The appraiser inspected and photographed the subject properties, took measurements from the transmissions lines and the nearest power poles, and recorded the type and size of each power pole.

The degree of impact on each home varied. One of the affected streets had larger power poles, which were more evident because of a bend in the road. Some of the homes had poles clearly visible in the immediate vicinity, while others had more oblique visibility. A few of the homes had directly adjacent poles, and some poles interfered with side yard access. The second appraiser evaluated the extent of the impact and assigned an impact severity score to each home, using a scale of 1 to 100.

An impact study entitled "The Effect of High-Voltage Power Lines on the Market Value of Single-Family Homes Located on Two-Lane Streets Where the Power Lines Adjoin the Front Yards of the Residences" was prepared. A paired sales analysis was used to estimate the general impact on sale price when, all other things being fairly equal, high-voltage power lines impacted one of the homes.

The first step in preparing the paired sales analysis was to locate sales of single-unit residences that were impacted by high-voltage power lines or structures at the time of sale. Electrical transmission corridors are not typically found in residential neighborhoods, so a search for similar power line corridors within proximity of residential properties was undertaken.

The general scope of work for the paired data study was set forth as follows:

- Identify similar transmission lines proximate to single-unit homes as areas of study.
- Study those neighborhoods to identify recent sales of homes that were impacted by the power lines or power line structures.
- Analyze and confirm the sales of homes that are impacted by power lines, making note of the nature of the impact (orientation to the power line, distance to pylons, type and size of power line structure).
- Identify comparable sales of homes that have no power line impact to pair with the impacted sales.
- Analyze and confirm the nonimpacted sales.
- Pair the sales to determine the difference in value (if any) between homes without high-voltage power lines nearby and those that are impacted by power lines or power line structures, based on the nature of the impact.

## Valuing the Effect of High-Voltage Transmission Lines

Comparable neighborhoods with transmission line impacts were identified using the following elements of comparison:

- Similar power line voltage and supporting structures
- Similar roads or sections of roads (two-lane, residential)
- Single-unit residential neighborhoods along the corridor
- Power lines with front yard impact

Twenty power line corridor segments were identified as possible sources of impacted home sales. Several of the neighborhoods were determined to be less similar to the affected neighborhood because of lower levels of owner occupancy or higher levels of dissimilar improvements. Sales in these neighborhoods were given no further consideration. The subject neighborhood was considered as a source of data for the study but was not used because it had been depicted in newspaper and television coverage for three years. In addition, dozens of properties in the affected neighborhood were involved in lawsuits regarding the power line issue.

Five power line corridor segments within 50 miles of the subject neighborhood were identified as being the most comparable and subsequently researched. A three-year period was selected as the initial time frame for study, allowing sufficient time to capture an adequate amount of data but keeping the date recent enough to facilitate reliable confirmation of the transactions.

Within the corridors selected for study, the nature of the impact on the homes differed. Possible impacts on nearby homes included the following:

- Located on same side of street as high-voltage power line, no pole in yard
- Located on same side of street as power line, power pole structure located in yard
- Located on same street as power line but opposite side of street, no pole nearby
- Located on opposite side of street as power line, power pole structure clearly visible nearby

From the five corridors studied, 16 home sales impacted by proximity to high-voltage power lines were available for analysis. These properties were analyzed, mapped, tabulated, inspected, photographed, and confirmed. The nature of the impact was identified, such as "metal pylon in front yard" or "metal pole across the street in full view of the home."

A search for sales of comparable nonimpacted homes to pair with the 16 impacted home sales was then undertaken. Sales in the five comparable neighborhoods were abstracted using standard appraisal search techniques for comparable sales. From the corridors used in the initial study, approximately 851 nonimpacted sales were selected for consideration.

After researching these transactions, 59 nonimpacted sales were selected for inspection and more detailed research. The appraiser attempted to locate nonimpacted sales that were similar in terms of location (other than power line impact), bedroom and bathroom count, sale date, and condition in order to minimize the need for adjustments. These remaining properties were then mapped, field inspected, and photographed. After inspection, some nonimpacted sales were found to be insufficiently comparable for matched pair analysis and removed from consideration.

The remaining sales were sorted again, based on similar characteristics, to indicate possible matched pairs. Each of the sales was then researched in greater detail and confirmed. Final candidate sales pairings were identified. Twelve matched pairs resulted. Each pair included an impacted sale with a corresponding nonimpacted sale located in the same neighborhood.

The impact study confirmed that high-voltage power line transmission corridors are an unusual feature on two-lane residential roads in central Florida. They are even more unusual when they are oriented to the front yards of nearby homes rather than back property lines. In most cases, high-voltage lines are located along heavily traveled arterial roadways or alongside other public uses such as railroads or recreational areas.

When high-voltage power lines on two-lane streets were observed, the streets were usually high-traffic roadways that included nonresidential uses. For instance, a two-lane roadway could have several single-unit residential neighborhoods along its length as well as signalized intersections and nonresidential uses.

In some corridors, high-voltage power lines ran along the side yards of homes that were located on residential streets situated perpendicular to the power lines. Some homes backed up to high-voltage power line corridors (i.e., lines adjoined the back property line of adjoining residences).

High-voltage transmission lines require supporting power poles that are taller and wider at the base than the wooden poles commonly used for power distribution (see photo). Wooden poles are typical features in residential neighborhoods and tend to blend into the background.

Atypical power lines and supporting structures, such as large metal pylons or unusually long spans, tend to be quite noticeable in a neighborhood setting. The impact of their visibility varies from location to location and is affected by other factors such as the number and height of trees in the area, the width of the impacted road and of the right of way and the presence of other atypical structures in the neighborhood (e.g., a water tower, a cell phone tower).

The impacted sales in the matched pair analysis varied in terms of the level of power line impact. The intensity of the power line's impact on each home was based on the type and size of the power line and related structures located nearby as well as the locational characteristics of the adjoining roadway.

Among the paired sales analyzed, the indicated difference in value was not entirely consistent given the nature of the impact (i.e., power line on same side of street versus opposite side of street) across all neighborhoods studied. For instance, some neighborhoods indicated a higher impact on value for poles on the opposite side of the street, while in other neighborhoods that impact was minor. In general, the range of value diminution illustrated by the data was fairly narrow and found to be similar to the range of value diminution attributable to other external factors, such as a location on a very busy road.

In each of the paired sales analyzed, the home impacted by the power line sold for less than the home without a power line impact. The difference in value attributable to external characteristics ranged from 6.4% to 26.4%.

## Using Impact Severity Scores

Among the properties analyzed, the possible combinations of power line impact were virtually limitless. For the subject properties, this difficulty was managed by using an impact severity score. For the sales of impacted homes presented in the paired sales analysis, the analyst provided additional explanation and analysis regarding the relative scarcity of available transactions and the resulting diminished reliability of some individual pairings from differing neighborhoods. Among the paired sales analyzed, the range of impact was generally consistent and considered to be sufficiently reliable to correlate the appropriate damage calculations with the impact severity scores. The results of this study were used to estimate the loss in market value to homes impacted by the power lines installed in the affected neighborhood. Homes that suffered less impact and were assigned lower impact severity scores were compared with the data at the lower end of the range. Homes with higher impact severity scores, such as those with the largest power poles in close proximity to their front yards, were compared with the data at the upper end of the range.

Only a small number of homes with immediately adjacent power poles were available for analysis in the initial study set because the phenomenon occurs infrequently. Homes with the highest degree of impact were therefore underrepresented in the analysis. Studies of additional neighborhoods, time permitting, could be expected to yield additional impacted sales for further analysis.

The loss in value to each home was calculated by assigning a damage percentage that correlated to the property's assigned impact severity score. For instance, one home located on the street with the largest power poles had a pole in the yard that was only 27 feet from the house. The impact severity for this house was estimated to be 99 on a scale of 1 to 100, with the damage percentage therefore estimated at the top of the range indicated by the paired sales analysis (26%).

Another home was located on the opposite side of the street from the new high-voltage lines. That home was 69 feet from the power line corridor and 132 feet away from the nearest high-voltage power pole. The impact severity for this home was estimated to be 50 on a scale of 1 to 100, with the damage estimated at 13%. This information was assembled in tabular form and provided to the homeowners and their attorney.

An illustrative sample of the damage analysis is presented in the following table:

| Property | Power Line Location on Street | Pylons | Distance: Home to Power Line | Distance: Home to Pylon | Impact Severity (1 to 100) | Damage as % of Market Value |
|---|---|---|---|---|---|---|
| 2801 K | Across street | Tallest | 69 | 108 | 30 | 8% |
| 3015 S | Across street | Medium height | 69 | 132 | 50 | 13% |
| 3102 RC | Same side | Medium height | 27 | 84 | 70 | 18% |
| 2809 S | Across street | Medium height | 72 | 75 | 75 | 20% |
| 3215 S | Across street | Largest metal pylon | 75 | 90 | 85 | 22% |
| 3320 S | Same side | Largest metal pylon | 31 | 32 | 99 | 26% |
| 3218 S | Same side | Largest metal pylon | 11 | 22 | 100 | 26% |

## Conclusions

The appraisals prepared by the first appraiser provided market value estimates for the homes as if unimpacted by the new transmission corridor. Those appraised values were reduced by the damage percentage provided by the second appraiser. For instance, a home valued at $150,000 with a 20% damage estimate would have a $30,000 negative impact attributable to the new project.

A trial date was set, and depositions were taken. On the Saturday before the beginning of the trial, the case was settled. As the local newspaper reported, "Tampa Electric Co. will pay a cash settlement to Egypt Lake homeowners, whose neighborhood was invaded by giant power poles. 'We are very happy to have the matter resolved,' said attorney Paul Antinori, who represented 52 homeowners after the poles began popping up in the northwestern Hillsborough County neighborhood in July 2003….The settlement agreement prevents attorneys on either side from revealing how much money will be paid. 'Not everyone will get the same amount,' Antinori said, 'because some property owners were affected more than others. The amount will depend on property size and appraisal and damage studies that were done.'"

During the course of the project and because of the negative public opinion that it generated, the county passed an ordinance that would prevent a similar situation from happening in the future. The ordinance requires that utility companies apply for a special permit before installing any utility poles greater than 75 feet high and two feet wide in a residential neighborhood. In addition, the utility company is required to notify nearby residents and prove that alternate routes were considered. Before approving the permit, the county commission must make a finding that the poles are "visually and aesthetically compatible" with the neighborhood. The ordinance passed unanimously.

## Case Study 5.1
# Tax Assessment–Gas Wells
*By S. Warren Klutz, MAI, SRA, CCIM*

## The Assignment

At the time of the appraisal engagement in 2010, a county in southwest Virginia and a major natural gas producer were involved in litigation over the correct value of between 462 and 543 natural gas wells for the tax years 2002 through 2005 and some 440 miles of gas pipeline with compressor stations for the tax years 2003 through 2005. The county had not taxed the gas wells prior to 2003 but had taxed the compressors and pipelines. Gathering assets consist of pipes leading from wells to a main distribution point. The assessment for the gas pipelines and other gathering assets, which the current gas company believed to excessive, was based on information filed several years earlier by a predecessor gas production company.

The Virginia statute provided relatively little guidance, and there were no court cases or attorney general's opinions available to offer guidance on the correct approach to valuing the gas wells and pipeline assets. The Virginia statute provides that gas-extracting properties could be assessed in three categories:

1. Lands under development, including the gas reserves beneath the surface
2. Improvements on and in the land, including the gas wells and pipeline assets
3. Lands not under development and consisting of the reserves, which have not been proven (not relevant to this case)

The gas company took the position that the word "improvements" in the Virginia statute was limited to property that was subject, under applicable federal taxation principles, to an allowance for depreciation. Moreover, the gas company believed that the cost of actually drilling the well and the cost of fracking did not result in depreciable improvements and therefore should not be counted in any valuation methodology. (Fracking involves introducing water, chemicals, and other materials into the well bore and shooting them into the strata to fracture it and to accelerate the release of gas into the well.)

A typical well site

An example of a compressor station with three compressors

The county had originally contracted a certified general real estate appraiser specializing in tax appraisals to value the gas wells, and a uniform value of $200,000 per well had been estimated. Based on the per-well value estimate, the county estimated that the total assessment on the gas wells was about $100,000,000 for each of the four years: $96,500,000 in 2002, $99,500,000 in 2003, $106,900,000 in 2004, and $106,900,000 in 2005 and levied taxes based on those assessments. The gas company asserted that the correct assessments should have been less than $33,000,000 in each of the four years. In addition, the gas company declared that the value of the gathering assets should not have been assessed at more than $19,500,000 in the years 2003 through 2005.[1] The difference in values translated to

---

1. The assessment of the gathering assets for the tax year 2002 was not brought into issue in this case.

about $1,325,000 in taxes plus five to eight years of interest at approximately 8% could be was due the gas company.

Trust between the county and gas company had eroded completely, and the parties had tried administrative appeals and mediation. At this point they were entangled in a significant court struggle, the outcome of which affected control of the assessments in subsequent years and would weigh heavily on whichever party lost the case. At risk for the tax years 2002 through 2005 was $3,600,000 in taxes and interest, and that amount would double in later years.[2]

I was asked by H. M. "Sam" Darby, lawyer for the county, to perform a new appraisal and serve as its expert valuation witness.

## Reaction to the Engagement Invitation

The gas company had hired an equipment appraiser early on. This appraiser's report, which recognized only improvements subject to the allowance for depreciation under applicable principles of federal taxation of natural gas wells, was rendered in February of 2010. The gas company's expert was a knowledgeable and experienced personal property tax appraiser from Texas. However, he lacked a valid Virginia certified general real estate appraiser license and was not licensed as a certified general real estate appraiser in his home state. During the discovery phase of the trial and at the trial itself it became apparent that this appraiser had accumulated extensive experience working as an equipment appraiser and property tax consultant for the oil and gas industry and was the most knowledgeable person regarding the specific assets involved in the case.

It was not until May of 2010 that the gas company engaged two certified general real estate appraisers licensed in Virginia with adequate qualifications to testify. Both of these licensed appraisers readily admitted that they did not have expertise in valuing gas wells and pipeline assets. Their opinions of value essentially adopted the values concluded by the Texas equipment appraiser and also asserted that the cost of drilling and fracking a well should be excluded in estimating the cost to produce a well. Consequently, all three of the values arrived at by the gas company's appraisers relied solely on costs supplied by the gas company.

The exclusion of drilling and fracking costs resulted in cost estimates equal to approximately 37% of the company's reported actual costs. Stated differently, the three gas company appraisers excluded 63% of the gas company's reported costs to produce the wells by

---

2. The county's interest ordinance provided for 8% simple interest per year on late taxes but failed to provide explicitly for the interest rate on overpayment of taxes. The court ultimately determined that the interest rate was set by Virginia state statute at 10%. The county ultimately ended up owing approximately $1 million in interest in addition to the approximately $800,000 in overpayments that were assessed by the court for the years 2002 through 2005.

eliminating drilling and fracking costs. All three of the gas company's appraisers claimed that the costs of drilling a well vary and the fracking costs should not be included in the total cost to install a well.

## The Approach Used by the County's Expert Witness

The only wells I had previously appraised were water wells on properties involved in condemnation cases and it was common practice to include the cost of digging the well and any other costs associated involved with getting water to the surface. Costs for digging water wells and excavating for building sites, foundations, and basements were considered appropriate to include in the total construction costs of other real estate assets. Consequently, it would follow that the significant costs associated with drilling a gas well and fracking should be included.

The gas company's expert witnesses referred to fracking and drilling as intangible costs or expense items that add no value to the gas well improvements. Despite the decision of the gas company's experts not to include these costs in their valuation, a regional production manager for the gas company admitted on cross examination that a well would be worthless without fracking.

Although the county, through its attorney, asked for analyses using both an income capitalization approach and the cost approach, I was confident at the outset that, since the reserves were not being taxed by the county, the capitalization of income would not be an appropriate valuation methodology because the potential volume of gas could not be quantified if the underlying leases were not part of the appraisal.

Data analysis was difficult in this case because gas wells and gathering assets are not typically sold or purchased as separate elements in the geographic region in which the subject was located. Any sales of assets similar to the subject would certainly be included as part of a going concern and therefore would include a nontaxable business component.

If sales data on out-of-state transactions could be obtained, it would be objectionable and probably would be ruled inadmissible as evidence by the judge. I was involved in another trial two decades earlier with the same judge, and during this trial he did not permit sales evidence from outside the state of Virginia. In this earlier trial, the judge excluded the use of sales from an adjacent Tennessee county in a condemnation trial involving a Virginia property. The sales in that trial were to be used as evidence in support of an adjustment relating to an appraisal I was testifying on for a condemning authority. Ironically, the opposing attorney for the gas company in this case was the same attorney who commissioned my study in the trial two decades earlier. The opposing attorney would certainly win any objection to using out-of-state sales, if such sales were presented.

Too many variables would be encountered in any endeavor to make adjustments for bulk sales of wells and gathering assets if they had been available. Consequently, the sales comparison approach was not practical for use in this trial. In addition, no leases of assets similar to the subject were available.

A financial analysis was performed for the county by an outside gas consultant in an attempt to process an income capitalization approach, but it ultimately required too many assumptions and was based on gross sales receipts for gas flowing through the system rather than leases of the assets. This methodology would result in a value that included a business component, which is inappropriate for real estate tax assessment purposes in Virginia.

In the financial analysis prepared by the county's gas consultant, the projected gross sales receipts from gas were reduced by the estimated expenses, and the net income for several years was converted to a present value using discounted cash flow analysis. The analysis was fraught with many unsupportable assumptions and was equivalent to the unacceptable practice of valuing the gas pumps, tanks, and other real estate for a convenience store based on the total amount of sales the property generates rather than rental income. The analysis by the outside consultant included business value and would have required the deduction of all the other assets required by a corporation to generate the sales, including but not limited to executive and employee salaries, other equipment, vehicles, office equipment, business value, and the value of all the underlying land leases. Due to the nature of the asset, it was clear that use of comparable sales of gas wells and income based on anything less than leases of similar assets would not be possible.

## Competency Issues

When Sam Darby, attorney for the county, contacted me about the assignment, I informed him that I had no experience with gas well appraisals. Darby's response was, "No one else we have contacted does either, and the gas company suing the county had to go all the way to Texas to find their appraiser." The first requirement of the Competency Rule of the Uniform Standards of Professional Appraisal Practice (USPAP) had been met by my notifying the client of my lack of experience. Still, competency needed to be acquired. Comments within the Competency Rule of USPAP suggest that "Competency can be acquired in various ways, including, but not limited to, personal study by the appraiser, association with an appraiser reasonably believed to have the necessary knowledge and/or experience, or retention of others who possess the necessary knowledge and/or experience."[3]

---

3. Uniform Standards of Professional Appraisal Practice, 2010-2011 ed. (Washington, D.C.: The Appraisal Foundation, 2010), U-11.

I chose the option of self-education and learned from reviewing the available materials that the standard approach used to calculate the replacement cost of gas wells is to multiply the cost per linear foot by the well depth. In this case, well depths varied from approximately 900 feet to 7,100 feet. Data on the wells that existed each year and their depths was furnished by the gas company through prior owners of record and discovery, the Virginia Gas and Oil Board, and the Virginia Department of Mines, Minerals, and Energy.

Data on the cost per linear foot of well depth for the different tax years was extracted from the *Joint Association Survey on Drilling Costs* (JAS) published by the American Petroleum Institute. Data for several regions was used because the state of Virginia was not surveyed as a stand-alone geographic area (see Exhibit 1). While many states have published cost data, Virginia was only included within the categories of "All States" and "Other States" as presented in Columns 2, 3, and 5 of Exhibit 1. The only data category considered not to include the state of Virginia was Column 4, the Appalachian category, which did include the bordering state of West Virginia.

Due to a confidentiality order by the court, some data provided by the gas company could not be used for any purpose other than the trial. Consequently, original cost data provided by the gas company has been excluded from Exhibit 1, and other data presented regarding the gas company's records has been changed for the purposes of this case study and to comply with the court-ordered confidentiality agreement. My preliminary examination of the historical cost records maintained by the gas company, including the installation of wells going back to the early 1950s, indicated that the typical historical cost of gas wells claimed by the gas company was at a certain level before depreciation. When the cost of drilling the well and the cost of fracking were excluded, the historical cost dropped to less than half the original figure.

The "actual" per-foot costs provided by the company were analyzed and considered in the original appraisal and compared with the various cost categories in Exhibit 1. However, the gas company's

### Exhibit 1

#### Costs per Linear Foot of Well Depth

| Col. 1 | Col. 2 | Col. 3 | Col. 4 | Col. 5 | Col. 6 |
|---|---|---|---|---|---|
| Year | Onshore/Ft. Cost All States | Onshore/Ft. Cost Other States | Appalachian Avg. for Intervals 3,750-4,999 & 5,000-7,499 ft. | Onshore/Ft. Cost Other States Avg. of 3,750-4,999 & 5,000-7,499 ft. | Average Cost from Cols. 2-5 |
| 2001 | $129.65 | $69.77 | $49.17 | *$69.77 | $79.59 |
| 2002 | $136.43 | $89.05 | [1]$48.76 | [2]$118.54 | $98.20 |

* All intervals used due to lack of any well cost data in the 3,750 to 4,999 depth bracket.
[1] Data also used from Table 2.73 in the JAS report for the specified year.
[2] Data also used from Table 2.74 in the JAS report for the specified year.

reported costs were ultimately not used in the calculation of average costs in Exhibit 1, Column 6. The average of the costs from Columns 2, 3, 4, and 5, which excludes the gas company's reported actual costs, is reported in Column 6. In arriving at the cost to use for valuing the wells, I studied Exhibit 1 and decided that the appropriate costs to use were those found in Column 6, the average cost excluding the reported gas company's cost. Costs per linear foot for the year 2001 in Column 6 were used to calculate the cost for the 2002 tax year based on the practice of valuing the property in the year before the tax year in which it is assessed. While several years were considered in the appraisal report, only costs for 2001 and 2002 are shown in Exhibit 1 to demonstrate the process.

During my research, I found an article in an industry publication in which the chairman and former CEO of the gas company was quoted as stating that the average well drilling costs for the company were $1,500,000 per well. Even though the appraisals related to the years 2002 through 2005 and these comments were published in 2010, I considered the CEO's statement when making the decision to use costs other than those purported to be the company's actual costs.

## Entrepreneurial Incentive

The previously presented costs typically include an allowance for contractor's overhead and profit but do not include an allowance for entrepreneurial incentive. *Entrepreneurial incentive* is defined as "The amount an entrepreneur expects to receive for his or her contribution to a project. Entrepreneurial incentive may be distinguished from entrepreneurial profit (often called *developer's profit*) in that it is the expectation of future profit as opposed to the profit actually earned on a development or improvement."[4]

The distinction between *entrepreneurial incentive* and *entrepreneurial profit* is that entrepreneurial incentive is the projected percentage profit a developer aspires to achieve in the future, while entrepreneurial profit measures the percentage profit a developer actually realizes. Gas companies exist to make a profit just as any developer would expect to realize a profit on a real estate development.

Research on rates of return expectations and rates of return earned by gas companies yielded results similar to the 15% used in this analysis. According to Ben Dell, senior energy analyst at Bernstein Research in New York, many gas companies often imply 100% internal rates of return (*IRRs*) in initial public offerings, but when estimated costs for land, drilling, and taxes are considered, the *IRR* comes down to 14%.[5]

---

4. *The Dictionary of Real Estate Appraisal*, 5th ed. (Chicago: Appraisal Institute, 2010), 67.
5. Keith Schaefer, "Shale Gas Companies: All Talk, No Walk?" *Seeking Alpha* (April 8, 2009), http://seekingalpha.com/article/130012-shale-gas-companies-all-talk-no-walk.

My survey of developers of other property types in the region indicated that 15% was the average preferred rate of return and 15% was used as the entrepreneurial incentive for the cost approach. Indirect costs were not added as a separate item because these costs were already included in the JAS survey costs.

My use of an entrepreneurial incentive became problematic during the trial due to the failure of the county's original contract appraiser to consider it in his costs. The inclusion of an entrepreneurial incentive in costs was further discredited when a witness for the gas company read a deposition given by the chief appraiser of the Commissioner of Revenue's office for the State of Virginia. This appraiser indicated that he had "never used entrepreneurial incentive in calculating cost." The three witnesses for the gas company testified that they did not use entrepreneurial incentive.

The county's attorney attempted to impeach the claims of the three gas company witnesses and two of his own witnesses that they had never used an entrepreneurial incentive or did not think it appropriate to use it in the costs calculated for the appraisal of gas wells. Anticipating the experts' testimony, the county's attorney expected that these issues would be raised at trial. To this end, Darby submitted the Appraisal Institute textbook *The Appraisal of Real Estate* as evidence that entrepreneurial incentive was an appropriate cost component. In addition, Darby stressed the correctness of its use during my direct testimony. Despite these efforts, the court ultimately ruled that entrepreneurial incentive should be excluded from the costs.

## Depreciation

Without a proper analysis of depreciation, the cost approach is nothing more than a mathematical exercise. Market-supported depreciation estimates subtracted from accurate cost data produce a reliable indication of value through the cost approach. The derivation of depreciation percentages becomes particularly difficult when there is no sales data on which to rely.

In this appraisal the economic lives of the wells and gathering assets were estimated separately. Economic lives for the wells were estimated by analyzing market-derived information on their production data over time. The economic lives of the gathering assets were estimated based on an interview with a contractor who built and maintained these assets. This information was supported by life expectancy guidelines published in *Marshall Valuation Service*.

Gas production figures for each well were obtained from the State of Virginia Department of Mines, Minerals, and Energy (DMME) and provided in a spreadsheet that may have inadvertently displayed the production data provided by the gas company during discovery. Two groups of wells with operating histories long enough to estimate economic life were uncovered by sorting the data by date of installation. Thirty-three wells were installed in 1992 and 45 were installed in 1993. The average production for each group in thousands of cubic feet was plotted on scatter graphs to produce a trend line of best fit and provide an indication of economic life.

The data for 33 wells shown on the graph in Exhibit 2 has been changed to ensure nondisclosure of the exact production figures. The point at which the trend line intersects the horizontal axis, if extended, indicates the total economic life. Similar results were found when production data for 45 wells installed in 1993 were plotted. A 20-year economic life was concluded for the gas wells using data from the wells considered. Further study of the production data indicated that the wells continuing in operation usually maintain a production level at about 20% of their initial levels after 16 years of operation. Consequently, the wells that remained in production after 16 years were depreciated a maximum of 80% (for example, 16 years actual age ÷ 20 years total life = 80%). Wells still in production were not depreciated below 20% of cost.

The appraisal assignment required valuing compressors and approximately 440 miles of pipes with varying diameters found within the gathering systems. Research was undertaken to obtain actual contractor cost estimates. The original contractor who laid the pipe for the gathering assets owned by the gas company in the county was located. The contractor's experience with installing the pipe systems now owned by the gas company covered a period of approximately 20 years, and he was the sole contractor for 10 years in the early 1990s. Present costs for each pipe size were obtained from the contractor and trended back to the dates for each year of the valuation using historical cost multipliers from *Marshall Valuation Service.*

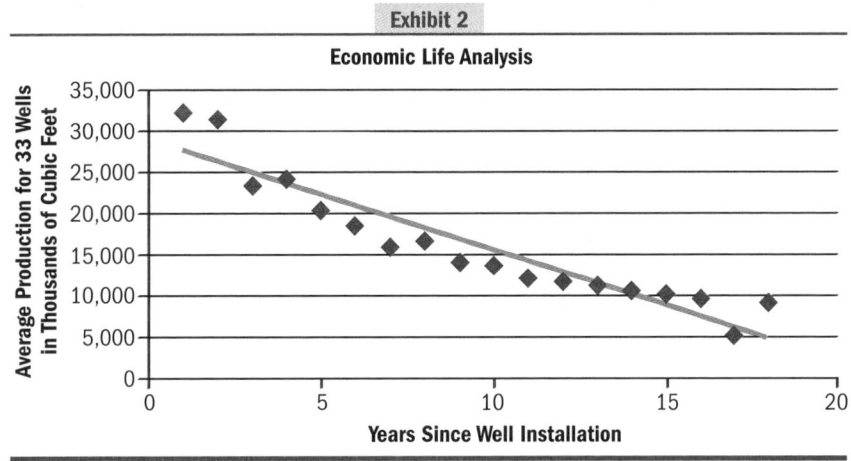

**Exhibit 2**

**Economic Life Analysis**

The contractor informed me that approximately 70% of the pipes in the county were laid above ground and 30% were laid below ground. Different costs are involved for aboveground and belowground installations for each pipe size. The cost of the pipe materials is the same, but installation costs are different due to the greater amount of work required to install the pipes below ground. The installation costs in Columns 2 and 3 of Exhibit 3 are converted to weighted costs in Column 6 using the 70% percentages for aboveground and 30% for buried piping installations. The weighted costs in Column 6 were used for calculating the piping costs within one of the several gathering systems within the county.

### Exhibit 3
#### 2010 Weighted Costs of Installing Piping Above and Below Ground (Excludes Cost of Pipe)

| Col. 1 | Col. 2 | Col. 3 | Col. 4 | Col. 5 | Col. 6 |
|---|---|---|---|---|---|
| Pipe Diameter Size | LF Costs for Surface* | LF Costs for Buried* | 70% of Surface Costs | 30% of Buried Costs | Weighted Costs Col. 4 & 5 |
| 1" | $1.00 | $3.00 | $0.70 | $0.90 | $1.60 |
| 2", 3" & 4" | $7.00 | $14.00 | $4.90 | $4.20 | $9.10 |
| 6" | $14.50 | $22.50 | $10.15 | $6.75 | $16.90 |
| 8" | $20.00 | $30.00 | $14.00 | $9.00 | $23.00 |
| 10" | $27.50 | $37.50 | $19.25 | $11.25 | $30.50 |
| 12" | $35.00 | $45.00 | $24.50 | $13.50 | $38.00 |

\* Costs in linear feet.

Use of the weighted installation costs reduces the number of columns in Exhibit 4 and produces the same total cost that would be calculated if 70% of the linear feet (LF) of a specific pipe size (in terms of diameter) was estimated at the surface cost of installation and 30% of the linear feet of a specific pipe size was estimated at the buried cost of installation. A "present day" weighted cost for installation of each pipe size was based on these percentages. Costs were then trended back to the various tax years involved in this valuation.

The following historical cost multipliers were derived from the *Marshall Valuation Service* (Section 98, page 8) for July 2010.

Historical Cost Multiplier: Historical Index/Present Index × Present Index
Present Index = 1.00
2002 Multiplier = 1,169/1,727.5 × 1 = 0.6767
2003 Multiplier = 1,192/1,727.5 × 1 = 0.6900
2004 Multiplier = 1,234.2/1,727.5 × 1 = 0.7144
2005 Multiplier = 1,340.9/1,727.5 × 1 = 0.7762

The 2010 index of 1,727.5 (rounded) is found by using linear regression for the years 2002 through 2009. (The 2010 index was not published at the time the report was written.) Pipe lengths and identification of the system have been changed to comply with the court order regarding confidentiality of data furnished by the gas company. Exhibit 4 shows an example of the methodology used to calculate the cost to install a pipe in one of the several gathering systems owned by the gas company as of the date of the report. Similar calculations were performed for several gathering systems, covering hundreds of miles for each of the tax years. Exhibit 5 converts the 2010 costs to the applicable 2002 tax year.

The depreciation for the gathering systems was established on a total economic life of 22 years using the economic age-life method (age ÷ total economic life). The depreciation estimate is supported by the discussion of piping lives with the original contractor who maintained the systems and by life expectancy guidelines published in *Marshall Valuation Service* (Section 97, page 14).

The values for the gathering assets that I concluded did not differ significantly from those determined by the gas company's appraisers. Those appraisers relied completely on the purported actual costs provided some years ago in records already in the county's possession and supplied by the previous owners of the assets.

The consistency between my value conclusion and the value conclusion of the gas company's appraisers ultimately required a refund by the county due to overassessments on the gathering assets for the years 2003-2005. The court did not rule on the value of the gathering assets or compressors, as the parties essentially agreed to their value. There was some significant history here. The gas company essentially failed to file correct information, i.e., filing information that conflicted with previous reports by a preceding owner or filing information that was internally inconsistent.

Gas wells were valued using the cost data from Exhibit 1 with an adjustment for entrepreneurial incentive included at 15%. Processing the data to produce well values for each of the four tax years included in the original appraisal report required Excel spreadsheets with 8,695 cells and approximately 6,000 calculations. The cost per foot of well depth used in the assessment year is based on those established in the previous year. For example, the $79.59 per foot cost from Exhibit 1, Column 6 was used in calculating the total well cost for 2002 (see Exhibit 6, Column 5). The process for valuing one conventional gas well with a hypothetical well depth of 3,154 feet is shown in Exhibit 6.

## The Trial

The county filed a motion about a week before the trial date attacking the qualifications of the out-of-state, nonlicensed, non-real estate

## Exhibit 4

### 2002 Costs for XYZ Gathering System as of 8/2/2010

| | Year Installed | Size (inches) | Length (feet) | Miles | 8/10 Pipe Cost/LF | Total Pipe Cost 8/10 | Weighted Inst. Cost | Tot. Install. Cost 8/2/10 | Total Cost 8/2/2010 |
|---|---|---|---|---|---|---|---|---|---|
| **Gas Co. Gathering System** | | | | | | | | | |
| XYZ Gathering System Pipe | 1995 | 2 | 110,567 | 20.94 | $2.77 | $306,271 | $9.10 | $1,006,160 | $1,312,430 |
| XYZ Gathering System Pipe | 1995 | 3 | 139,785 | 26.47 | $5.05 | $705,914 | $9.10 | $1,272,044 | $1,977,958 |
| XYZ Gathering System Pipe | 1995 | 4 | 175,400 | 33.22 | $6.57 | $1,152,378 | $9.10 | $1,596,140 | $2,748,518 |
| XYZ Gathering System Pipe | 1995 | 6 | 53,698 | 10.17 | $9.72 | $521,945 | $16.90 | $907,496 | $1,429,441 |
| XYZ Gathering System Pipe | 1995 | 8 | 56,333 | 10.67 | $17.01 | $958,224 | $23.00 | $1,295,659 | $2,253,883 |
| XYZ Gathering System Pipe | 1995 | 10 | 1,257 | 0.24 | $21.33 | $26,812 | $30.50 | $38,339 | $65,150 |
| Totals | | | 537,040 | 101.71 | | | | | |

## Exhibit 5

### XYZ Gathering System Present Costs Converted to 2002 Costs

| Pipe Size in Inches | Total Cost 8/2/2010 | Hist. Mult. | Hard Cost on 1/1/2003 | Cost Incl. 15% Entrepreneurial Incentive | Age | % Deprec. | Indicated Value |
|---|---|---|---|---|---|---|---|
| 2 | $1,312,430 | 0.6767 | $888,122 | $1,021,340 | 6 | 0.273 | $742,793 |
| 3 | $1,977,958 | 0.6767 | $1,338,484 | $1,539,257 | 6 | 0.273 | $1,119,459 |
| 4 | $2,748,518 | 0.6767 | $1,859,922 | $2,138,910 | 6 | 0.273 | $1,555,571 |
| 6 | $1,429,441 | 0.6767 | $967,303 | $1,112,398 | 6 | 0.273 | $809,017 |
| 8 | $2,253,883 | 0.6767 | $1,525,203 | $1,753,983 | 6 | 0.273 | $1,275,624 |
| 10 | $65,150 | 0.6767 | $44,087 | $50,700 | 6 | 0.273 | $36,873 |
| Total | | | | | | | $5,539,337 |

| | | | Exhibit 6 | | |
|---|---|---|---|---|---|
| Col. 1 | Col. 2 | Col. 4 | Col. 5 | Col. 6 | Col. 7 |
| Well I.D. # | Year Placed in Service | Well Depth | Cost Incl. Entrepreneurial Incentive ($79.59 × Well Depth × 1.15) | Depreciation (2001 less Yr. in Serv.)/ 20 yrs. × Col. 5 | 2002 Indicated Value (Col. 5 – 6) |
| 37145 | 1998 | 3,154 | $288,681 | $43,302 | $245,379 |

expert to testify in the case. The court overruled the motion and permitted the gas company's expert to testify. The case was tried over a two-day period in the county seat, and a retired judge with no experience in gas well or pipeline taxation presided over the trial. The judge maintained firm control of the proceedings and viewed all five experts with suspicion. Ultimately, he rejected the final conclusions of all five experts but accepted my methodology as being the most accurate, except for the inclusion of entrepreneurial incentive.

Cross examination of all the witnesses was rigorous, but my evidence was accepted by the court and evaluated. The court processed the two days of evidence and rendered its final decision in August 2011. Ultimately, the gas company's attempt to eliminate the well drilling and fracking cost were rejected by the court. My methodology, using well depth per foot to provide installation costs and depreciating the wells over 20 years using the age-life method with a 20% floor, was accepted by the court. However, the court directed the parties to reevaluate the costs shown here in Exhibit 1. In his ruling, the judge stated:

> The assets being valued here are not being sold on the open market. No comps, if you will. Therefore, what better way to establish a fair valuation of such assets than by selecting appropriate relevant categories from the tables, putting the gas company's cost data (including those associated with drilling and fracking) in the mix, and then following Klutz's valuation technique? The court is of the opinion to use the JAS categories of "Kentucky," "Appalachian," and "Other States," along with the gas company's cost data. Using average costs for depth intervals of 3,750 to 4,999 and 5,000 to 7,499. The parties are directed to engage their experts once again, or CFO, commissioner, accountant, etc., as you choose, to develop these calculations for the court's instruction. They may use linear regression as did Klutz. There shall be no addition for entrepreneurial incentive. The court is of the opinion that, if calculated accordingly, it should produce a stipulation.

## The End Result

Essentially, the court's ruling required:

1. Removing Columns 2 and 3 from Exhibit 1 and replacing them with Kentucky well costs for depth intervals of 3,750 to 4,999 feet and 5,000 to 7,499 feet and the average actual costs, including drilling and fracking

2. Averaging the cost data to arrive at the cost to be used

Depreciation would be calculated using the 20-year life with 80% as the maximum depreciation. The county was later able to obtain the JAS data for 2008 and 2009. With the dramatic increase in drilling costs, the county was able to reassess for the years 2008 through 2011 and file supplemental assessments, stopping the interest accrual on the refund. The county was also required, under uniformity principles, to reassess the other six gas companies operating in the county.

## Lessons Learned

An after-action review of the assignment following the conclusion of a trial can assist appraisers in discovering what happened, why it happened, and how to improve strengths and mitigate weaknesses. Discussions with attorneys after a trial can shed light on the impact of the appraiser's testimony on the outcome and provide suggestions for improving appraisals and testimony in the future. In this trial, the judge excluded entrepreneurial incentive. This was disturbing because the county's attorney covered the subject in sufficient detail in my direct testimony and the opposing attorney failed to bring the matter up during cross examination. The gas company's attorney had one witness read the deposition of an appraiser in the State of Virginia's Commissioner of Revenue Office and several other witnesses testify to convince the judge that entrepreneurial incentive should not be included in the cost approach. As a result, five appraisers testified that they did not use entrepreneurial incentive. I was left appearing as an appraisal heretic for including it in my cost approach, despite the introduction into evidence of a section covering entrepreneurial incentive from *The Appraisal of Real Estate*.

This case probably could have used an additional independent appraiser for the county to refute the analysis performed by the gas company's appraisers and their failure to include entrepreneurial incentive in estimating costs. Another appraiser testifying about the proper use of entrepreneurial incentive would have given some additional weight to my testimony. In addition, another appraiser could have discredited the other side's appraisers for simply adopting the costs supplied by the gas company, which did not include drilling, fracking, contractor's profit, entrepreneurial incentive, or other administrative expenses. An attorney I worked with on many court cases once told me that attorneys do not win cases with the other side's expert witnesses; they win by using their own witnesses.

The use of Excel spreadsheets was invaluable in this assignment because it allowed me to use the gas company information on the wells obtained through discovery and sort it by date of installation. The sorted data helped me recognize wells with an adequate history of gas production so that age and production figures could be plotted on an *x-y* graph. Plotting the production of wells installed in 1992 and 1993 provided ample information to compare gas production to the age of wells and derive the 20-year economic life for this group of wells.

Sorting the data also allowed me to identify wells and calculate installation costs per linear foot of depth for certain years using the gas company's supplied data. Actual costs could then be compared with published data from the *Joint Association Survey on Drilling Costs*. Extensive records from the gas company were provided in spreadsheets. If I hadn't already known how to work with data in Excel, the appraisal for this trial would not have been as thorough. Just as there is insufficient time to learn military tactics after a battle starts, an appraiser does not usually have the time to learn new skills when a trial date is on the horizon.

The scope of work for this assignment required the investment of additional time to research information about gas wells. To ensure compliance with competency requirements, I also performed an extensive literature review, which allows an appraiser to learn from others and avoid mistakes when addressing appraisal problems not encountered in the past. Ultimately, appraisers cannot broaden their skills and knowledge without accepting appraisal assignments that they have not encountered previously. This unique appraisal solidified my confidence in the knowledge I have gained through appraisal practice and the Appraisal Institute's publications and courses. The experience confirmed my opinion that basic appraisal principles can be applied to many unusual property types.

CASE STUDY 6.1

# Matrimonial Dissolution

*By Anthony S. Graziano, MAI, CRE, FRICS*

Most county courts throughout the United States are filled with real estate valuation-related litigation matters. This chapter will focus on a common appraisal practice associated with divorce cases. *Equitable distribution* is the term typically used when a married couple is in the process of a divorce and must distribute marital assets or community property between the husband and wife. Although parties to the litigation are husband and wife, an appraisers is typically engaged by an attorney who represents one of these individuals. In some cases, particularly in matters involving minimal assets, both parties agree to the court's appointing of a single appraiser to assist in the determination of real property values. Regardless of who engages the real estate appraiser, he or she is considered to be an expert witness and a friend of the court. As a result, the appraiser is responsible for assisting the "trier of fact" (the judge) in determining the appropriate value of real property assets subject to equitable distribution.

Although the National Conference of Commissioners on Uniform State Laws and the American Bar Association have adopted recommendations known as the Uniform Marriage and Divorce Act, these standardized divorce procedures have not been adopted by every state. These recommendations have been adopted by the legislature in some jurisdictions. In other states, like New Jersey, the recommendations and procedures have basically been implemented through Supreme Court decisions. In nine states, the terminology used may be different, although some of the policies have been adopted. As is the case with any litigation, appraisers must work closely with the attorneys involved to identify the appropriate local laws, case law, regulations, governing policy, and rules for equitable distribution.

As of this writing, several states consider the "division of marital assets" (also known as *marital property*) under a "community property" concept, rather than an equitable distribution. The determination of marital property and nonmarital property (immune assets) varies from state to state. The most common terminology will be used in this case study. However, for the purposes of completing appraisal assignments and communicating with other professionals and the court, appraisers are advised to clarify the appropriate word usage within the relevant jurisdiction.

Chapter 3 of this book explains in great detail the responsibilities of an expert witness in litigation matters. In the case of complex matrimonial matters, other valuation experts and professionals are often needed to appropriately process the net worth of marital assets subject to equitable distribution.

## Other Professionals Involved

In matrimonial matters involving multiple and varied assets, the plaintiff and defendant typically compile a group of required professionals, including but not limited to the following:

- Attorneys
- Accountants
- Business valuation professionals (BV appraisers)
- Personal property/machinery and equipment (M&E) appraisers
- A mediator or court master

Understanding the positions of these various professionals is critical for the real estate appraiser as the real estate value is often only a starting point in the calculation of net monetary assets.

### Attorneys

Attorneys are always advocates for their client's interests. They are, by virtue of their role, expected to interpret the law and case precedent(s) to their client's advantage and to conduct themselves in a manner that promotes the best possible outcome for their client at all times. Because valuation experts work directly with the respective attorneys during the development of the case, the advocacy role of the attorney is often unintentionally asserted on the experts. The experts must be mindful that their role requires independence, not advocacy, and that the expert's role is to assist the trier of fact.

However, remaining independent of advocacy does not mean disputing the advocate's legal interpretations and opinions. In almost all cases, legal issues may bear on the highest and best use, legal rights of ownership, and other matters that, if interpreted differently, may affect the value opinions. To remain independent, any interpretations or legal opinions that provide specific direction to the expert's conclusions should be documented in writing by the attorney and provided as "scope of assignment" legal instructions that could alter the value opinion(s) if determined or interpreted differently by the court.

There are innumerable examples of how legal issues and direction can affect the value opinion. The clearest way for an expert to avoid the appearance of advocacy is to accept the advocate's written position given their legal expertise and, relying on the legal instructions as valid, to express the value opinion and clearly identify that the value opinions considered the legal instruction(s) provided. Such legal instructions should be included in the report for examination and consideration by the trier of fact.

## Accountants

The husband and wife often employ independent accountants or auditors in matrimonial matters, particularly in complex cases. These individuals compile information provided by the valuation experts and incorporate these estimates into the financial books and records of the parties' owned entities to determine the net value subject to equitable distribution. Accountants are governed by their standards of professional practice and ethics and also come to court as expert witnesses.

## Business Valuation (BV) Appraisers

Business valuation (BV) appraisers are essentially in the same position as real estate appraisers. BV appraisers are considered friends of the court and are often required in complex cases, particularly those that involve partial interest valuations, business valuations, holding companies, limited liability partnerships, and corporations. In many cases, real estate appraisers, personal property appraisers, and machinery and equipment (M&E) appraisers all provide market value estimates to the business appraiser. These estimates are then incorporated into the enterprise appraisals for the development of the appropriate balance sheet or as a component of the enterprise valuation process.

## Personal Property and Machinery and Equipment Appraisers

Specialty valuation professionals such as personal property and M&E appraisers are often engaged by high net worth individuals. These experts are subject to their industry standards for professional practice as well as traditional court requirements for unbiased and independent value opinions.

## Court-Appointed Mediators

A court-appointed mediator or master is typically an independent individual, often a retired judge or attorney, who serves as an intermediary in an attempt to resolve valuation matters without the necessity of a trial. The mediator often serves with the authority of the trial judge and has the power to subpoena documents, examine witnesses, and review reports, stipulations, and settlement agreements. The court-appointed mediator often assists valuation professionals by focusing the scope of the assignment on the most important and critical valuation issues. The mediator is an independent court-appointed expert and trier of fact. This individual deserves the same respect as the trial judge.

# Engagement (Scope of Work and Definition of Problem)

When a real estate appraiser is contacted for an equitable distribution matter, it is most important to communicate clearly to the client and the attorney that any valuation opinions expressed must be developed in accordance with industry standards and ethics, as follows:

- Independent value opinions and the fee cannot be based on any contingency or performance measure.
- The assignment cannot be based on any predetermined conclusion or results.
- The report and analysis must be based on court rules and industry-accepted standards (USPAP), theories, principles, and learned treatises.

In discussions with the engaging party, the appraiser must define and identify the nature of the assignment, which is often very complex and may include

- a marital home
- a vacation home (or homes)
- business property
- real estate investments

Equitable distribution matters are often complicated with multiple dates of valuation. In most states, equitable distribution of premarital assets requires two valuation dates: value as of the date of the marriage and value as of the date of the divorce.

Matrimonial cases also call on the expertise of real estate appraisers for the valuation of property interests that may include

- fee simple
- leased fee
- leasehold
- sandwich leases

Although some appraisal professionals may have the necessary experience and qualifications, minority interests and discounts are typically handled by financial professionals and business valuation experts. Real estate appraisers must be cognizant of their own professional competency at all times.

In a very basic case in which a residential home is the only asset for distribution, the appraiser may provide only a summary report or a self-contained residential report in which primary parties to the comparable transactions confirm the data and conditions. In complex cases in which marital assets are extensive, however, the judge, attorneys, or court mediator might recommend short-form restricted or summary reports as an interim step to facilitate settlement or to assist the accountant and business valuation appraiser.

Regardless of the reporting format approved for settlement purposes, the appraiser should prepare the most appropriate reporting form needed to communicate a supportable value conclusion effectively when testimony is required. For more complex assignments, conclusions are often best reported using a self-contained format.

The caution to all appraisers is that the value conclusions expressed must be credible and supportable, regardless of the reporting format. The standard of practice for most experienced practitioners is that no value opinion is expressed with anything short of complete file documentation, including the exhibits, data, property description, operating information, and well-notated confirmation memorandum, all of which would be necessary to produce a complete self-contained report.

Regardless of the product delivered, the confirmation process for any comparative data considered in the development of the value opinion should include, at a minimum, discussions with one of the primary parties to each transaction. A best-case scenario is direct communication with two or three parties. These communications should be noted with a file memo, including the contact name, address, and phone number. When possible, sending a "thank you" e-mail or memo with confirming notation is the best practice.

Engagement as an expert witness in any litigation should (and must) be completed in a written formal agreement. It is sometimes effective for the engagement letter to provide for a two-phase assignment. Phase 1 identifies the scope of work and definition of the problem for each of the assets. Phase 2 defines deliverables and fees exclusive of meetings, conferences, or testimony.

No assignment relating to a litigation matter should be accepted without a defined hourly or per diem rate for other professional services such as testimony, conferences, supplemental data, exhibits, or similar services that lie outside the scope of the appraisal reports. It is also a good idea to include assumptions and limiting conditions as part of the proposal letter. Be mindful and review the standard assumptions and limiting conditions to ensure that they are consistent with the specific scope of the proposed assignment.

## Case Study

This case study highlights the process and procedures for a real estate appraiser employs to provide expert and competent valuation services for the equitable distribution of a fictional, relatively high net worth family known as Mr. and Mrs. W. R. Robinson.

The first communication on this matter was initiated by Bob Schwartz, Esq., who is representing Mrs. Robinson in a divorce matter. Schwartz explains that approximately 10 real property assets are owned by the Robinsons. He has sent an e-mail listing the assets that require appraisals and requests appraiser Ann Suarez, MAI, to quote a fee. This listing is shown in Exhibit 1.

**Exhibit 1**

**Attachment A**
**Real Property Assets of Mr. & Mrs. W. R. Robinson**

| | |
|---|---|
| 1 | 13 Bluebird Ct., Washington (family home) |
| 2 | Unit 27, Bellamia Condos, Orlando (vacation condominium) |
| 3 | 300 Campus Way, Madison (office building) |
| 4 | Captain Harry's, Washington (hardscape manufacturing plant) |
| 5 | Captain Harry's Stores (3): Jefferson, Lincoln, & Madison (hardscape retail stores) |
| 6 | 25 Broad St., Washington (apartment building) |
| 7 | Keyhole Fishing Club, Key West, FL (fishing camp) |
| 8 | 11 Logistics Ct., Franklin (industrial building) |
| 9 | Unit 15, Holiday Manor, Washington (residential condo—rented) |
| 10 | Tucson Marriot, Tucson, AZ (resort hotel) |

Ann reviews the list and recognizes immediately that although seven of the properties are located within her primary market area and relate to her area of expertise, three of the properties are located in distinctly different markets and two of the properties (the fishing camp and resort hotel) are of a property type that requires special competency to comply with USPAP.[1]

Ann recognizes that the list of assets barely identifies the properties, does not distinguish or identify ownership, and is insufficient to appropriately develop a scope of work. The list also does not identify the interest to be appraised or establish the valuation dates.

The definition of the problem, scope of work, intended use, intended users, interest appraised, and deliverables must be identified before any fee can be quoted. At this point, Ann develops a two-phase proposal that includes the following:

1. Phase 1 services identify the scope of work for each property and define relevant elements for the preparation of each required market value estimate (a real property consulting service).

2. The Phase 2 component includes preparation and delivery of the required appraisal opinions. A fixed fee structure cannot be

---

1. See the Competency Rule (U-11-12) and Advisory Opinion 22 (A-73-79) of the Uniform Standards of Professional Appraisal Practice, 2010-2011 ed. (Washington, D.C.: The Appraisal Foundation, 2010).

established until Phase 1 is completed. (Phase 2 is considered an appraisal assignment.)

As an alternative, Ann would have the option to submit an hourly rate proposal and require a fairly substantial retainer. In either case, the proposal should include the defined services for Phase 1, which are limited to a statement of the definition of the problem, scope of work, intended use, interest appraised, and intended users who will be identified on a parcel-by-parcel basis upon review and consultation with Schwartz.

Phase 2 should include a fee schedule for the appraisal reporting services plus the hourly rate for post-appraisal services. It should also include standard assumptions, limiting conditions, and special assumptions as may be appropriate. The Phase 2 proposal often provides an "opt out" provision if the fee schedule or timing are not acceptable. Shortly after Ann's proposal is delivered, she receives the requested retainer and a signed authorization for Phase 1.

## Phase 1

Upon authorization, Ann coordinates a meeting with Schwartz and Mrs. Robinson to discuss the various assets, their ownership, and the relevant dates of value associated with the assignment. The Robinsons were married on March 1, 1995, and the divorce was filed on July 30, 2011.

After accumulating the basic information, Ann proceeds with her standard due diligence regarding new appraisal assignments. In this particular instance, due diligence includes communication with appraisers in jurisdictions outside of her normal practice area, research of public and municipal records regarding the individual assets, and a drive-by inspection to take some neighborhood and property photographs. After several days of research and analysis, Ann prepares the memo shown in Exhibit 2 to file as a basis for developing a scope of work.

Ann contacts Schwartz and advises him that a BV appraiser and M&E appraiser may be required as part of the Captain Harry's valuation. Schwartz advises Ann that he has already made the arrangements and e-mails a list of the other experts involved. After the call with Schwartz, Ann drafts the narrative notes to her file shown in Exhibit 3.

### Scope of Work

As one can see upon review of Ann's file memo and notes, the nature of this assignment is varied. Clearly, one of the most critical elements to identify early on is the competency requirements of the assignment. Working outside an area in which Ann has jurisdictional competency is a factor relating to the properties in Orlando and the Florida Keys. Ann immediately communicates with competent appraisers in these jurisdictions. She will obtain the necessary temporary licenses to

## Exhibit 2

**Memo to File:** Robinson v. Robinson
**From:** Ann Suarez, MAI
**Re:** Asset Distribution
Real Property Assets, Mr. & Mrs. W. R. Robinson

**Mr. & Mrs. Robinson—Joint Ownership**

1. **13 Bluebird Ct., Washington** (family home, fee simple, market value)
2. **Unit 27, Bellamia Condos, Orlando** (family vacation condo, fee simple, market value)
3. **300 Campus Way, Madison** (office building, 15,000 sq. ft., jointly held asset, 2 tenants, 10- & 12-year leases, market value leased fee interest)
4. **Captain Harry's, Washington** (hardscape manufacturing plant, family-owned business property, fee simple, market value and market rental value to be incorporated into business valuation, BV appraisal by others)
5. **Captain Harry's Stores (3) Jefferson. Lincoln, Madison** (hardscape retail stores, market value leasehold and market rental value to be incorporated into business valuation, BV appraisal by others)

**Mr. Robinson—Personal Assets**

6. **25 Broad St., Washington** (50-unit apartment building, ownership is a family partnership, market value of fee simple, value as of marriage and divorce date)
7. **Keyhole Fishing Club, Key West** (fishing camp, ownership: Four Men, LLP, market value fee simple, value as of marriage and divorce date)
8. **11 Logistics Ct., Franklin** (50,000-sq.-ft. industrial building, long-term lease, ownership: Logic, LLC, 3 partners, market value leased fee, value as of marriage and divorce date )

**Mrs. Robinson—Personal Assets**

9. **Unit 15, Holiday Manor, Washington** (residential condominium, rented year to year, premarital asset, market value fee simple, value as of marriage and divorce date)
10. **Tucson Marriot, Tucson** (325-room resort hotel, ownership: Happy Days Family Trust, may be immune asset, to be determined)

## Exhibit 3

**Memo to File:** Robinson v. Robinson
**From:** Ann Suarez, MAI
**Re:** Asset Distribution Narrative Notes
Confirming Consultation with Bob Schwartz, Esq.

**Jointly Held Properties**

- The home at 13 Bluebird Court and Unit 27 at the Bellamia Condos are jointly held assets in fee, estimate market value for equitable distribution.
- 300 Campus Way is a jointly held investment property that is a leased office building. Valuation will be as of the date of the divorce. Given the long duration of the existing leases, the valuation will be a leased fee interest.
- The family-owned business known as "Captain Harry's" manufactures hardscape (paving) products and sells these products from three regional store outlets owned by Captain Harry's, LLC.
- "Captain Harry's" hardscape manufacturing plant is a fee-owned industrial property that is the family business and joint asset. A fee simple market value of the plant will be required, along with a market rental value. Machinery and equipment to be valued by the M&E appraiser (Alan Lee). These estimates will be incorporated within the enterprise appraisal by the BV appraiser (Ed Carey, MBA).

> **Exhibit 3**
>
> *(continued)*
>
> - Captain Harry's stores are three leased retail stores used in conjunction with Captain Harry's hardscape business. These storefronts are all owned by unrelated third parties. A market value of the leasehold (if any) and market rental estimate for each of the stores will be developed. The leasehold and market rent estimates will be incorporated by Carey in the valuation process for the Captain Harry's enterprise.
>
> **Premarital Assets of Mr. Robinson**
>
> - The 50-unit apartment building (25 Broad Street, Washington) is a Robinson family partnership between a total of 10 relatives, which existed prior to the date of marriage. Two value dates will be necessary in the jurisdiction of this equitable distribution case. This asset must be valued as of the date of marriage and as of the date of the divorce. The appraiser will provide a market value estimate that may or may not be subject to partial interest discounting by others. (A stipulation or case management order regarding minority interest discounts is often issued.)
> - The Keyhole Gang Fishing Camp is held in the ownership of an LLP in which Mr. Robinson held a one-quarter interest prior to the marriage. I will estimate the market value of the fee simple interest in the real property with the help of a local Florida appraiser. The market value may be incorporated into a net equity analysis by the accountants and/or subject to a minority discount analysis by others. As ownership of this asset predates the marriage, there will be a retrospective market value estimate as of the date of marriage and a market value estimate as of the date of divorce.
> - The 50,000-sq.-ft. industrial building on Logistics Court is a limited liability corporation of three partners and was owned by Mr. Robinson prior to the marriage. The valuation must recognize that the property is subject to a long-term lease commitment, and a leased fee interest will be required as of the date of divorce. Further research as of the date of marriage is necessary to identify whether the retrospective value estimate is a fee simple or leased fee assignment.
>
> **Premarital Assets of Mrs. Robinson**
>
> - The residential condo, Unit 15 at Holiday Manor, was the premarital home and asset of Mrs. Robinson. This property would require a fee simple valuation as the current lease term is only one year. Two valuation dates will be required: the retrospective date of marriage and the date of divorce.
> - The Tucson Marriott was owned by a family trust of Mrs. Robinson prior to the marriage. Her attorney will review trust documents and confirm through the court whether this property is an immune asset. No appraisal work will be completed on this property until further authorization is received.

inspect the properties and participate in report preparation to ensure that settlement negotiations, report content, and testimony are consistent with the local jurisdictional requirements.

Several of the properties, particularly the Captain Harry's business property, require a close working relationship between Ann, Alan Lee (the M&E appraiser), and Ed Carey, MBA (the BV appraiser).

The possible immunity of the Tucson Marriott could be an issue. This must be resolved by attorneys and the court. It may be useful for Schwartz to have some proportional estimate of this asset's value to determine the extent of litigation costs warranted for exclusion of this property from the marital assets. Ann may be requested to do some limited valuation consulting. If requested, these additional services will likely require jurisdictional competency and a hospitality specialist. This phase may be a limited-scope analysis solely for the purposes of estimating a "no greater than" proportion of value. The work may be assigned out at this point to a more qualified appraiser.

Due to the diversity of properties and varied property interests, significant documentation is necessary to prepare reports. In cases of this nature a discovery order may be established, particularly because the party (Mrs. Robinson) does not have a working relationship with the business enterprise and certain premarital assets. Discovery normally requires the appraisers to sign confidentiality agreements and provide access to all documentation, financial reports, and leases.

In a court-ordered exchange of documents associated with any litigation matter, keep in mind the old expression, "Be careful what you ask for–you just might get it." In cases in which discovery orders are established, the documentation becomes voluminous. The difficulty for appraisers who lack litigation experience is that they tend to filter documentation and provide only what they believe is relevant. This is a very dangerous situation. It is most important that all documents exchanged be reviewed in detail. Once documents become part of a discovery order, they are considered facts of the case. If issues relate to the real estate valuation, the appraiser must give consideration to all known facts, absent any legal instructions.

In cases in which a court master or mediator is appointed, the appraiser should be part of the mediation meetings to confirm the scope of work, intended use of their valuation opinions, limitations on the use, and the nature of the reporting required. Once the appraiser is involved in a matter–be it before the court or the mediator–all research, file documentation, and analysis must be completed before any value opinion is expressed, regardless of the reporting process.

Although the skills necessary for the valuation of the various Robinson assets are within basic competency levels of a state-certified general real estate appraiser, Ann should participate in each assignment and report as the principal appraiser.

Now that Ann has completed her due diligence, she prepares a matrix of services required for the requisite reporting of market value opinions. What originally arrived by e-mail and looked like a simple case of 10 individual appraisals has now–after completion of the Phase 1 due diligence–turned into an assignment that (after deferral of one of the reports) requires 19 different value estimates (see Exhibit 4).

In quoting fees, Ann must pay particular attention to the fact that at least two of the properties require out-of-area appraisers to satisfy the requirement for jurisdictional competency and four of the properties require retrospective value estimates as of the date of marriage. Preparing the Phase 1 portion of the engagement agreement has

**Exhibit 4**

**Required Value Estimates**
**Robinson v. Robinson**

|   |   | Current Values as of 7/30/2011 | | | | Retrospective as of 3/1/1995 | |
|---|---|---|---|---|---|---|---|
|   |   | Market Value Fee Simple | Market Value Leased Fee | Market Rent | Market Value Leasehold | Market Value Fee Simple | Market Value Leased Fee |
| 1 | 13 Bluebird Ct., Washington | 1 | | | | | |
| 2 | Unit 27, Bellamia Condos, Orlando, FL | 1 | | | | | |
| 3 | 300 Campus Way, Madison | | 1 | | | | |
| 4 | Captain Harry's, Washington | 1 | | 1 | | | |
| 5 | Captain Harry's Stores (3) | | | 3 | 3 | | |
| 6 | 25 Broad St., Washington | 1 | | | | 1 | |
| 7 | Keyhole Fishing Club, Key West, FL | 1 | | | | 1 | |
| 8 | 11 Logistics Ct., Franklin | | 1 | | | | 1 |
| 9 | Unit 15, Holiday Manor, Washington | 1 | | | | 1 | |
| 10 | Tucson Marriot, Tucson, AZ | To be determined upon further authorization | | | | | |
|   | Value Opinions | 6 | 2 | 4 | 3 | 3 | 1 |

given Ann the opportunity to appropriately quote the fees and define the appraisal problem and scope of work.

Based on the diversity of the assignments, Ann should expect that the market value estimates will require certain adjustments by Laura Williams, CPA, Mrs. Robinson's accountant. Williams will be responsible for estimating net equity subject to equitable distribution and premarital immune equity that is not subject to equitable distribution. At minimum, the Captain Harry's enterprise requires a business valuation. Lee will assist Ann in determining the owned real estate and machinery and equipment assets. Both Ann and Lee will provide current market value estimates to Carey for inclusion within the enterprise appraisal. Ann will also provide market rental estimates of all real estate used by this entity and leasehold values, if any, for the rented stores. Since the entity of Captain Harry's, LLC, was started six months after the marriage, all assets and value are considered marital property subject to equitable distribution. Thomas Hawkins, JSC, is the appointed mediator and will have access to all appraisal reporting.

Recognizing these factors, Ann has drafted the following statements of intended use and intended users:

- **Intended Use:** The intended use of the reports is to establish the market value of the various real estate assets of Mr. and Mrs. W. E. Robinson as of the appropriate effective dates for the purposes of equitable distribution.

- **Intended Users:** The intended users of the value opinions as developed by the appraiser would include the Superior Court of the state of jurisdiction and its agents, Bob Schwartz, Esq., Mrs. Robinson, Laura Williams, CPA, Ed Carey, MBA (the BV appraiser), and Alan Lee (the M&E appraiser).

At this point, Ann prepares the proposal for Phase 2 services. She includes Attachment A, a summary of the costs associated specifically with each valuation report (see Exhibit 5).

### Exhibit 5
### Attachment A
### Phase 2 Real Estate Appraisal Cost Proposal
### Prepared for Bob Schwartz, Esq.
### Robinson v. Robinson

| | | Market Value Fee Simple 7/30/2011 | Market Value Leased Fee 7/30/2011 | Market Rent 7/30/2011 | Market Value Leasehold 7/30/2011 | Market Value Fee Simple 3/1/1995 | Market Value Leased Fee 3/1/1995 |
|---|---|---|---|---|---|---|---|
| 1 | 13 Bluebird Ct., Washington | $1,000 | | | | | |
| 2 | Unit 27, Bellamia Condos, Orland | $1,750 | | | | | |
| 3 | 300 Campus Way, Madison | | $5,250 | | | | |
| 4 | Captain Harry's, Washington | $5,500 | | N/C | | | |
| 5 | Captain Harry's, Jefferson | | | $2,250 | $1,250 | | |
| 5b | Captain Harry's, Lincoln | | | $2,250 | $1,250 | | |
| 5c | Captain Harry's, Madison | | | $2,250 | $1,250 | | |
| 6 | 25 Broad St., Washington | $5,500 | | | | $6,500 | |
| 7 | Keyhole Fishing Club, Key West | $5,000 | | | | $6,000 | |
| 8 | 11 Logistics Ct., Franklin | | $5,500 | | | | $6,000 |
| 9 | Unit 15, Holiday Manor, Washington | $1,000 | | | | $1,000 | |
| 10 | Tucson Marriot, Tucson | | | To be determined | | | |

**Note 1:** Fees as quoted are for market value appraisals of the interest identified. They include subcontractor fees as may be needed, out of town travel, and jurisdictional certifications for the principal appraiser.

**Note 2:** Fees do not include (1) authorized coordination with Mr. Robinson's professionals, (2) review of third-party appraisal reports, (3) settlement meetings, (4) conferences or calls, or (5) additional valuation or consulting services outside the scope of the schedule.

In addition to the notes within the schedule, Ann reinforces that the fees as quoted relate to market value appraisals as defined and include additional costs for subcontractor's fees, travel, and out-of-pocket expenses associated with the Orlando and Key West properties as well as coordination of the valuation process with the intended users. She is very careful to indicate that the quoted fees do not include

- authorized coordination with Mr. Robinson's professionals
- the review of third-party appraisals
- settlement meetings
- conferences or conference calls, or

- valuation and consulting services outside the scope of those indicated within Attachment A

This process is recommended as it will prevent "scope creep" and allow the appraiser to concentrate on providing meaningful valuation services to the intended users and the court of jurisdiction.

## Phase 2

Upon delivery of a formal Phase 2 proposal, Ann is authorized to proceed as the real estate expert in the matter of Robinson v. Robinson. Early in the process of preparing the files, Ann has been advised that Mr. Robinson has engaged a local real estate appraiser, David Steele, MAI, who is well known to Ann and belongs to the same Appraisal Institute chapter. In an effort to ensure the consistency of critical elements of valuation, it has been suggested by the mediator, Hawkins, that the real estate appraisers coordinate the document discovery and exchange of required property information. Additionally, they were asked to coordinate property inspections to ensure that all property information is consistent and minimize inconvenience to tenants. This process is very effective, particularly with operating business and leased properties; it is time-efficient for the occupants and minimizes business interruptions.

Shortly after engagement, Ann receives a call from the BV appraiser, Carey. He explains that the valuation of Captain Harry's will require a current market value and market rent for the manufacturing facility. He will also need a current leasehold and market rental value for the three stores. Carey reveals that the partnership documents relating to the Key Hole Fishing Club in Key West provide a "right of first refusal" option to purchase by surviving partners if any of the partnership interests become available. Although the overall market value of the property is important, he will also need to address a provision that indicates that a purchase by one or all of the partners can be at market value or a legitimate offer, minus traditional real estate commissions typical in the area. Ann explains to Carey that this additional research was not within the scope of the assignment and communicates with Schwartz that additional market research will be necessary to verify "typical and customary real estate brokerage commissions" in the Key West area.

The court mediator assembles a meeting of all expert witnesses and attorneys. At this meeting, it is stated that the primary responsibility of Hawkins is to resolve this matter without the need for a protracted litigation and in a cost-effective fashion. Accordingly, Hawkins has requested that the appraisers prepare summary appraisal reports in an abbreviated fashion to facilitate a settlement that will be negotiated at a series of settlement conferences.

Ann and Steele jointly prepare a valuation and data reporting format that is acceptable to all intended users, specifically for the settlement process. A stipulation is prepared confirming the report format, and it includes limitations on the use of the report in the event that court testimony is required. The stipulation should also state that the appraisers will provide a comprehensive report if they are requested to testify at trial.

At the suggestion of Hawkins, Ann and Steele jointly prepare property information and document request schedules for each of the individual properties. After a review by the appropriate council, Hawkins issues a court order for the exchange of date-stamped documents as set forth in each individual schedule. The documents are to be distributed to all attorneys and experts in the matter of Robinson v. Robinson.

As approved by the attorneys and the court mediator, the real estate appraisers proceed with the joint inspection of each individual property. This process proves to be most efficient. Because each party's appraiser is present as questions are asked of the tenants, property management, and owners, the information accumulated is clear. This minimizes confusion and contradictory assumptions, which often occur in litigation practice.

Ann then proceeds to complete each of the appraisals as requested and provides the summary shown in Exhibit 6 to her client, Attorney Schwartz:

### Exhibit 6

**Client Privileged and Confidential—For Informational Purposes Only—Results of Several Complete Appraisal Reports***

**Summary of Value Conclusions**

**Robinson v. Robinson**

| | Market Value Fee Simple 7/30/2011 | Market Value Leased Fee 7/30/2011 | Market Rent 7/30/2011 | Market Value Leasehold 7/30/2011 | Market Value Fee Simple 3/1/1995 | Market Value Leased Fee 3/1/1995 |
|---|---|---|---|---|---|---|
| 1 13 Bluebird Ct., Washington | $725,000 | | | | | |
| 2 Unit 27, Bellamia Condos, Orland | $485,000 | | | | | |
| 3 300 Campus Way, Madison | | $325,000 | | | | |
| 4 Captain Harry's, Washington, | $4,250,000 | | $318,750 | | | |
| 5 Captain Harry's, Jefferson | | | $150,000 | $448,000 | | |
| 5b Captain Harry's, Lincoln | | | $150,000 | $627,000 | | |
| 5c Captain Harry's, Madison | | | $180,000 | $420,000 | | |
| 6 25 Broad St., Washington | $3,750,000 | | | | $1,950,000 | |
| 7 Keyhole Fishing Club, Key West | $1,575,000 | | | | $900,000 | |
| 8 11 Logistics Ct., Franklin | | $3,925,000 | | | $1,175,000 | |
| 9 Unit 15, Holiday Manor, Washington | $225,000 | | | | $75,900 | |
| 10 Tucson Marriot, Tucson | | | To be Determined | | | |

* This summary is a court-requested, client-privileged compilation of various value conclusions from individual complete appraisal reports and is not intended for distribution of any kind.

*Applications in Litigation Valuation: A Pragmatist's Guide*

Shortly after delivering the appraisal reports, Ann is contacted by Williams, who has completed some calculations to develop the equitable distribution net values. Williams has questions regarding a couple of the assets.

For the family home at Bluebird Court, the condominium in Orlando, and the 300 Campus Way property in Madison, the equitable distribution was prepared by simply deducting the outstanding debt from the market value estimate. Williams, however, is somewhat confused over Unit 15 in Holiday Manor and provides Ann with her worksheet (see Exhibit 7), which indicates that the outstanding mortgage debt substantially increased between the valuation dates.

### Exhibit 7
**Unit 15, Holiday Manor**
**Premarital Asset, Mrs. Robinson**
**Two-Bedroom Townhouse Condominium**

| | | |
|---|---|---|
| Market value as of 7/30/2011 | $225,000 | |
| Outstanding debt | -$150,000 | |
| Net equity | | $75,000 |
| Market value as of 3/1/1995 | $75,900 | |
| Outstanding debt | -$15,000 | |
| Net equity premarital (immune) | | $60,900 |
| Value subject to equitable distribution | | $14,100 |

Ann explains that her assignment was merely to value the fee simple interest in the property as of two specific dates. She does confirm, however, that the outstanding debt on both the date of marriage and the debt on the date of divorce were provided in the document exchange process. Ann also questioned the large increase in debt and confirmed through Mrs. Robinson that the property was refinanced in early 2000 to provide cash to purchase the family's 40-ft. fishing boat. As demonstrated in Exhibit 7, Mrs. Robinson will receive the full immunity benefit of her premarital equity of $60,900, plus her equitable share of the $14,100.

Williams also had some concern regarding 11 Logistics Court. The current market value of the property was more than three times the 1995 value, yet the mortgage debt was substantially less (see Exhibit 8).

Ann confirmed that the 1995 appraisal was completed based on discovered information that indicated the property was subject to a short-term lease entered into by a local tenant. Three years ago, a new 25-year lease was negotiated with a public, triple A-rated tenant. The remaining term is 22 years as of July 2011. Market rents in the area had escalated significantly. Mr. Robinson did not refinance the build-

### Exhibit 8
### 11 Logistics Court, Franklin
### Premarital Asset, Mr. Robinson
### 50,000-sq.-ft. Industrial Property

| | | |
|---|---|---|
| Market rent as of 7/30/2011 | $5.85/sq. ft. | |
| Lease date | 6/1/2010 | |
| Lease term | 25 years | |
| Tenant | Public, triple A-rated | |
| Leased fee market value on 7/30/2011 | $3,925,000 | |
| Outstanding debt | -$975,000 | |
| Net equity | | $2,950,000 |
| Market rent as of 3/1/1995 | $2.25 | |
| Lease date | 6/1/1992 | |
| Lease term | 5 years | |
| Tenant | Local sheet metal | |
| Fee simple market value on 3/1/1995 | $1,175,000 | |
| Outstanding debt | -$1,048,000 | |
| Net equity premarital | | $127,000 |
| Net equity of Logic, LLC | | $2,823,000 |
| Mr. Robinson's interest in Logic, LLC | 33.33% | |
| Value subject to equitable distribution | | $940,906 |

ing, and the outstanding debt was the initial debt that had amortized over the 16 years of ownership during the marriage. Given the short term of the 1995 lease, the value is considered a fee simple interest. The long-term lease remaining in 2011 would indicate that a leased fee interest is appropriate.

As agreed upon with the client, Ann delivers an appraisal report to Carey with the value conclusions for the real estate associated with the Captain Harry's operation shown in Exhibit 9. The values include a fee simple interest in the manufacturing plant, the leasehold values associated with the retail stores, and market rental values of all the real estate. Because the business enterprise was started after the marriage, retrospective values are not required.

Shortly after receiving this information, Carey calls Ann and tells her that the information was most helpful. The business valuation was very difficult because the Captain Harry's manufacturing operation essentially produces products for retail sale through its own outlets. The operation requires large capital investments in fixed assets. Carey has prepared preliminary worksheets of an asset-based analysis using an excess earnings approach. Exhibit 10 summarizes the asset-based comparison prepared by Carey for review by Ann.

This asset-based comparison demonstrates the financial scale of the fixed assets. As indicated in Note 1, the book value of owned real

### Exhibit 9
### Value Conclusions: Captain Harry's Hardscape

| Property | Location | Interest | Market Value | Market Rent |
|---|---|---|---|---|
| Hardscape manufacturing plant | Washington | Fee simple | $4,250,000 | $318,750 |
| Capt Harry's Store 1 | Jefferson | Leasehold | $448,000 | $150,000 |
| Capt Harry's Store 2 | Lincoln | Leasehold | $627,000 | $150,000 |
| Capt Harry's Store 3 | Madison | Leasehold | $420,000 | $180,000 |
| Sum of values | | | $5,745,000 | $798,750 |

### Exhibit 10
### Asset-Based Comparison

| Assets | At Book Value | At Market Value | |
|---|---|---|---|
| **Current Assets** | | | |
| Cash and cash equivalents | $1,255,800 | $1,255,800 | |
| Accounts receivable | $547,895 | $547,895 | |
| Prepaid expenses | $75,285 | $75,285 | |
| Inventory | $750,000 | $750,000 | |
| Total current assets | $2,628,980 | $2,628,980 | |
| **Property, Plant, and Equipment** | | | |
| Fixed assets (RE) | $1,240,000 | $4,250,000 | Note 1 |
| Leasehold improvements | $1,212,400 | $2,707,400 | Note 2 |
| Machinery and equipment | $925,000 | $725,000 | Note 3 |
| Total | $3,377,400 | $7,682,400 | |
| Less accumulated depreciation | -$1,750,000 | -$225,555 | Note 4 |
| Net property and equipment | $1,627,400 | $7,456,845 | |
| Total Assets | $4,256,380 | $10,085,825 | |
| **Liabilities and Equity** | | | |
| Current portion of long-term debt | -$65,255 | -$65,255 | |
| Accounts payable | -$124,788 | -$124,788 | |
| Income taxes payable | -$257,500 | -$257,500 | |
| Long-term debt (net of current) | -$1,255,000 | -$1,255,000 | |
| Total liabilities | -$1,702,543 | -$1,702,543 | |
| Stockholder equity | $2,553,837 | $8,383,282 | |

Note 1: Capt. Harry's plant added at market value
Note 2: Sum of leasehold MV ($1,495M) + leasehold improvements
Note 3: Value as estimated by Alan Lee
Note 4: Depreciation only from leasehold improvements

estate (Captain Harry's plant) is replaced with Ann's fee simple market value of $4.25 million. The accrued depreciation of this property is not deducted in the asset-based market analysis; it is implicit in Ann's market value estimate that all accrued depreciation has been deducted.

*Matrimonial Dissolution*

As indicated in Note 2, the market value of the leaseholds, which totals almost $1.5 million, has been added to the book cost of the leasehold improvements. As the leasehold improvements are recaptured during the remaining lease term, they are carried at book value less accrued depreciation (Note 4). The machinery and equipment has been added at market value based on the estimates by Lee. Again, the M&E appraisal reports the assets at the "as is" market value, so accrued depreciation is not deducted.

Recognizing that the real estate owned in fee, leaseholds, and equipment has been booked at market value, the accumulated depreciation only relates to the leasehold improvements, which are a wasting asset. Williams and Carey will carefully audit and review depreciation schedules to eliminate any redundant deduction against the value of fixed assets, which are marked to market. As indicated by the comparison, there is a significant difference between the book value of the assets and the market value of the fixed assets (property and equipment), exclusive of cash and cash equivalent.

The "earnings multiple method" is a second method used to estimate the value of the business. An analysis was prepared based on the most recent historic earnings, considered by Carey as the best estimate of normalized earnings. This analysis required an adjustment of occupancy costs to the sum of the market rents as estimated by Ann. This demonstrates why the real estate appraiser must ensure consistency and balance between the market rents and market value estimates of both fee simple and leasehold values.

The enterprise has limited market decline. Captain Harry's stores are the best customers for the Captain Harry's plant. As a result, a relatively low earnings multiple of two times the net earnings has been used in valuing the business. The net earnings were also adjusted for the excess owner's compensation. Because Captain Harry's is a family-owned enterprise, Mr. Robinson has consistently received a salary and bonuses that exceed the market norm. See Exhibit 11.

As demonstrated by the earnings multiple analysis, the majority of Captain Harry's enterprise value is found in the fixed assets of real estate, leaseholds, machinery, and equipment, even though the enterprise is relatively successful. It is not the function of this case study to teach appraisers how to value a business enterprise. However, it is important to understand that real estate value conclusions serve multiple disciplines in developing the net value of assets that are subject to equitable distribution.

This case study attempts to present relevant examples of the use and intended users of real estate appraisers' value estimates that are part of an equitable distribution matter. As demonstrated by the examples, the appraisers' estimates are a critical component in the process.

| Exhibit 11 | | | |
|---|---|---|---|
| **Analysis by Earnings Multiple** | | | |
| Gross revenue | $7,525,000 | $7,525,000 | |
| Cost of sales | -$2,633,750 | -$2,633,750 | |
| Net revenue | $4,891,250 | $4,891,250 | |
| **Operating Expenses** | | | |
| Operating | -$1,256,500 | -$1,256,500 | |
| Salaries | -$1,425,000 | -$1,425,000 | |
| Occupancy | -$240,000 | -$798,750 | Note 1 |
| Other | -$750,125 | -$750,125 | |
| Total operating expenses | -$3,671,625 | -$4,230,375 | |
| Net earnings | $1,219,625 | $660,875 | |
| Excess owner's compensation | $150,000 | $150,000 | |
| Net earnings | $1,369,625 | $810,875 | |
| Earnings multiple | 2 | 2 | |
| Indicated value of business | $2,739,250 | $1,621,750 | |
| Net asset value | $2,553,837 | $8,383,282 | |
| Enterprise value | $5,293,087 | $10,005,032 | |

**Note 1:** Sum of all facility rents at market rent

# Conclusions

It is not necessary to discuss or teach the methods and techniques for estimating the requisite market values within this case study. These techniques are covered in the comprehensive texts of the Appraisal Institute. All work associated with matrimonial litigation should be completed in compliance with the code of ethics and professional standards as set forth in USPAP. In litigation matters, the need for appraisers to confirm all data used in reports through primary sources and maintain a well-documented file with memos, e-mails, and cataloged documents cannot be overemphasized.

In addition to maintaining complete files, an appraiser involved in litigation should be prepared to be engaged for an extended period of time. It is not unusual for appraisers to be asked to modify all value opinions as of a court-ordered revised date of divorce. Appraisers should work honestly, candidly, and fairly with other professionals, and constantly maintain their objectivity and independence throughout the process. The integrity of an expert witness is his or her most valuable asset.

Appraisers should also be prepared for a request to review real estate appraisals prepared for the opposing side in litigation. These services often help to establish a factual and technical basis. It is, however, a good practice for the principal appraisers (Ann and Steele in this case) to avoid the position of "rebuttal appraiser." It would be better for another qualified appraiser to take on this role to avoid the appearance of advocacy, particularly if court testimony is required.

Although the appraiser's contribution to an equitable distribution process in a matrimonial matter has significant financial implications, the appraiser must always be aware that the job of the attorneys and judiciary is complicated by many additional issues that outweigh monetary considerations. The typical divorce is the dissolution of a family, which often involves the custody of children, the disposition of the family home and personal property, and numerous other personal factors that impact the lives of the husband, wife, and children.

Matrimonial cases often develop into very personal causes for the husband and wife. Regardless of the engaging party or the information obtained in the process, appraisers are encouraged to maintain an arm's-length professional relationship with all litigants at all times.

# Case Study 7.1

# Bankruptcy—
# Fractional Interest in a
# Leased Fee Estate

*By Michael Y. Cannon, MAI, SRA, ASA, CRE, FRICS*

## The Assignment

This unique assignment involved determining the appropriate appraisal methodology to value a 1/15 interest in a leased fee estate based on the remaining 47-plus years of a 99-year ground lease in accordance with Federal Rules of Procedures and Federal Rules of Evidence. The leased fee estate interest in the land was owned by a 14/15 fee owner and two individuals who each owned a 1/30 interest in the fee owner's estate. Together, these two individuals owned the 1/15 interest being appraised in this assignment.

The fee owners' interests were created on May 15, 1956, when two related families agreed to sell a 93.33%, or 14/15, interest in the land to a developer. The developer created a ground lease in which the developer owned the 14/15 fee owner's interest, and the two families equally divided the remainder 6.67%, or a 1/15 ownership interest, and held it as cotenants in common. The desire of the original owners was that their heirs, each owning a 1/30 fee owner's interest, would benefit from the future value of the reversion at the termination of the 99-year ground lease. The developer created a separate entity and developed the subject office building as the intermediate leaseholder, i.e., the sandwich lease position. That separate entity was then the lessee of the fee co-owners and the sublessor to the sublessee tenants renting space in the office building.

## The Property

The property, known as the "200 Building," is a 12-story, 141,679-sq.-ft. commercial office building located at 200 SE First Street in the central business district of downtown Miami. The building was built in 1958-1959 and was renovated in 1997 and again in 2005. As of the effective date of appraisal, February 29, 2008, 25 tenants leased office and retail space under various sublease agreements with the intermediate leaseholder-landlord.

The land area is 135 feet × 102.5 feet, totaling 13,838± square feet, or 0.32± acres. Parking for 250 cars is provided to the subtenants in the

200 Southeast First Building

Adjacent Parking Garage

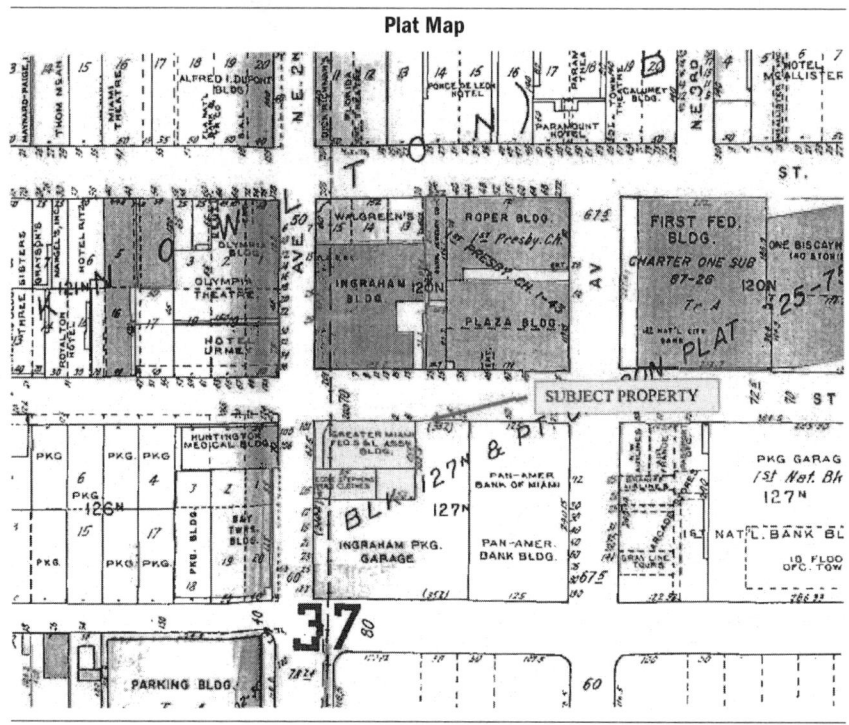

Plat Map

adjacent public parking garage, which is owned by others. A covenant running with the land in perpetuity ensures off-street parking for the subtenants and guests of the subject building on a pay-as-used basis.

## Background

On September 20, 2006, the 14/15 fee owner and its affiliate leaseholder, the leaseholder-landlord, acquired title through a special warranty deed for a reported price of $23.5 million. They financed this sale with a reported $20 million mortgage loan and a $3.5 million mezzanine loan. This enabled them to acquire a 93.33% (14/15) interest in the fee estate and a 100% interest in the leasehold estate.

On December 6, 2006, the 14/15 fee owner and its affiliate entered into a contract for the sale of the leasehold estate interest and 100% of the leased fee estate interests to be sold in their entirety, whereupon the remaining term of the 99-year ground lease (as shown in the abstract below) would be terminated effective as of the closing of the sale. The 1/15 fee co-owners objected to the pending sale and filed a petition in the Circuit Court to set aside the sale.

---

**Abstract of the Lease taken from the Public Records**

Case 07-17999-AJC        Document 205        Filed 12/21/2007        page 28 of 31

Description of Lease

Ninety-Nine Year Lease dated May 15, 1956 by and between T.J. Galatis joined by Marjorie L. Galatis, his wife, Dorothea Galatis Roach, also known as Dorothea Galatis Roach and Marguerite Galatis Plasman, joined by Howard Plasman, her husband as Lessors and Edward N. Claughton, sometimes known as Edward N. Claughton, Jr., as Lessee, recorded in Deed Book 4275, Page 298, modified by that certain Supplement and Amendment to Leases, dated January 24, 1962, recorded February 5, 1962 in Official Records Book 3009, Page 218; assigned by Assignment of Lease dated August 13, 1957, recorded in Official Record Book 391, Page 481; further assigned by Assignment of Lease dated July 10, 1958, recorded in Official Records Book 922, Page 178; further assigned by Assignment of Lease dated May 6, 1982, recorded in Official Records Book 11434, Page 637; further assigned by Assumption of Lease recorded May 30, 1997 in Official Records Book 17658, Page 4545, as assigned April 2, 2001 in Official Records Book 19576, Page 3624, being further assigned (Lessee's Interest) by Assignment and Assumption of Lessee's Interest in Ground Lease and Related Interest and Assignment and Assumption of Covenant Running with the Land recorded on September 20, 2006 and recorded in Official Records Book 24928 at Page 0947, being further assigned (Lessor's Interest) by Assignment and Assumption of Lessor's Interest in Ground Lease and Related Interest and Assignment and Assumption of Covenant Running with the Land recorded on September 20, 2006 and recorded in Official Records Book 24928 at page 941 of the Public Records of Miami-Dade County, Florida.

---

On September 26, 2007, the owner of the 14/15 fee interest, joined by its affiliate leaseholder, filed debtors-in-possession Chapter 11 bankruptcy protection in the US Bankruptcy Court for the Southern District of Florida, Miami Division. The debtors listed $35 million in assets and $23.5 million in debt.

On October 31, 2007, the debtors, as plaintiff, filed a complaint seeking relief and final judgment to authorize the sale of the interests of all owners under the Federal Rules, 11 U.S.C. §363(h)(3). On December 13, 2007, the co-owners of the 1/15 fee interest filed their answer and affirmative defenses not to force them to sell the combination of their 1/30 interests in the pending sale of all interests to a third-party purchaser. The bankruptcy court, having jurisdiction, was to determine the value of the 1/15 combined ownership interest that would be payable from the net proceeds of sale under Section 11 U.S.C. §363 (Use, Sale, or Lease of Property).

On January 9, 2008, the adversary proceeding came before the bankruptcy court for trial, and the court, as fact-finder, considered testimony of witnesses and the arguments of counsel representing all parties. The court reviewed all exhibits introduced as evidence, made findings of fact and conclusions of law in accordance with Federal Rule of Bankruptcy Procedure 7052, and approved the sale of the leasehold and leased fee estate interests (in the entirety) to the unrelated third party.

Section 363(h) of the Bankruptcy Code authorizes a sale free and clear of the interests of the co-owners if certain conditions are met. Section 363(h) provides that a debtor or trustee may sell off both (a) the fee estate's interest in the property and (b) all co-owners' interests based on the following:

1. Partition in kind of such property among the estate and such co-owners is impractical.
2. Sale of the estate's undivided interest in such property would realize significantly less for the estate than sale of such property free of the interests of such co-owners.
3. The benefit to the estate of a sale of such property free of the interests of co-owners outweighs the detriment, if any, to such co-owners.
4. Such property is not used in the production, transmission, or distribution for sale of electric energy or of natural or synthetic gas for heat, light, or power.[1]

In this case, a partition in kind was impractical because the property was improved with an office building and could not be subdivided in kind among the owners.

Subsections 2 and 3 above carry the burden of proof on the debtor with respect to all of Section 363(h) requirements, and the parties stipulated that the property did not meet the test of Subsection 4 above.

In support of the debtor's position that a sale of 100% of the fee simple and leasehold interests would result in a substantially greater return for the ownership interest in the estate, testimony was offered

---

1. Title II, Chapter 3, Subchapter IV, U.S.C. §363–Use, Sale, or Lease of Property.

that the buyer would not be willing to purchase the property unless it acquired 100% of the fee interests with the ground lease terminated upon the closing of the sale of the property.

The 1/15 fee owners objected to the sale but did not contend that the amount of the purchase price was less than the fair market value. The 1/15 fee owners argued to the court that if they had to sell their interest, they were entitled to a distribution from the actual net cash proceeds (approximated $30 million of the $31,620,000 pending sale price) based on their allocated ownership interests. This would result in a distribution of $1 million to each of the 1/30 fee owners, totaling $2 million for their combined 1/15 interest ($30,000,000 × 0.06667 = $2,000,000).

The court was not persuaded by this argument and read the statute to require that the interests of a co-owner be valued based upon the nature of the interest as it existed prior to the sale. At this point, the court requested expert appraisal opinions from all parties.

The buyer testified that several potential lenders said they would not be able to finance the transaction unless 100% of the fee owner's interests were acquired in the leasehold interest. The court concurred and stated that the only remaining issue under Section 363(h) was whether the benefit to the debtor's leasehold estate of a sale free and clear of the ownership interests of the co-owners' fee interests outweighs the detriment, if any, to the co-owners according to Section 11 U.S.C. §363 (h)(3). Cases in which bankruptcy courts have found that the detriment to a co-owner outweighs the benefit to the estate generally involve situations in which a sale will displace a co-owner or otherwise result in serious hardship.

In this matter, the owners of the 1/15 interest in the leased fee estate testified that the unknown potential future value of their ownership interest in the property may substantially appreciate, thereby benefitting them and their heirs in the future. The court sympathized with this position, noting that the owners acquired their ownership interest from their mother when the lease was executed on May 15, 1956, and they agreed to a supplement and amendment to the lease on January 24, 1962.

The court concluded that the 1/15 fee interest appreciating in value over time was not realistic, nor was it a factor for analysis in the case because, at the conclusion of the lease in just over 47 years, the co-owners would own a minority fee interest as "tenants in common" with the 14/15 fee owner. The minority interest would be subject to a partition lawsuit at that future time, which would result in a future sale of the entire property. The court then stated:

> [W]hen sold now, the fee interest of the co-owners would receive the present value of their interest in the property, and if they prudently reinvested their appropriate share of the sale proceeds, the amount would be substantially greater than what it would be in a 47 plus year ride in the future.
>
> The fee owners have the right to receive their respective rental income plus the reversionary interest in their fee interest upon the termination or expiration of the leasehold.

# Method for Valuing the Interests in the Fee Owner's Estate

The court was required to determine the correct method for valuing the interests in the fee owner's estate under Section 11 U.S.C. §363(h). Then the court would advise the trustee to distribute the proceeds of sale accordingly, based on the presumption that this sale would occur and that the proceeds would be distributed. The court was mindful that the sale to this unrelated third party was unlikely to ever close for the stated amount and that the property may sell to another purchaser for a different amount. If so, the method for valuing the fee owner's estate interest would then apply.

In this instance, for the purpose of the court's determination, the $31,620,000 sale price was determined to be the fair market value of the property. However, the court still needed to determine how much should be paid to the owners of the 1/15 and the 14/15 fee interests from the proceeds of sale under Section 363(j) of the Bankruptcy Code. This section directs the court to distribute the proceeds of sale, less costs and expenses of sale, to the fee co-owners' estate based on the value of their respective interests. Section 363(j) states the following:

> After a sale of property to which subsection (g) or (h) of this section applies, the trustee shall distribute to the debtor's spouse or the co-owners of such property, as the case may be, and to the estate, the proceeds of such sale, less the costs and expenses, not including any compensation of the trustee, of such sale, according to the interests of such spouse or co-owners, and of the estate.

## Contract Rent

The amount of the rent collectively paid and to be paid to the owners of the 1/15 fee interest was the fixed rent from February 29, 2008, (the effective date) through to the termination of the lease on May 14, 2055. In the proceedings, it was noted that the contract rent paid and to be paid to the fee co-owners was most favorable to the leaseholder-landlord, resulting in a very positive and favorable leasehold position.

The annual rent paid and to be paid monthly by the intermediate leaseholder-landlord to the fee owners totaled $49,000 annually and was apportioned at $45,733.33 to the 14/15 fee owner and $3,266.67 to the 1/15 fee owners paid in monthly installments for the remaining term of the lease.

## Differing Appraisal Methodologies

The court received and reviewed two appraisal reports. The first appraiser was engaged by the 1/15 fee owner defendant's counsel. The second appraiser (the author of this case study) was engaged by the 14/15 fee owner's counsel on behalf of the debtor as the plaintiff.

*First Appraiser*
The first appraiser's valuation was based on the following premise:

> The present value of the contractual ground rent payments and the present value of the estimated residual market value of the subject land "as if" vacant (meaning that the existing building did not exist) and inflated to the current appraised value of the land only until the end of the lease term, discounted to present value.

The first appraiser testified:

> Should the residual value be based on the estimated market value of the land and improvements using the current contract price inflated until the end of the lease, the value of the leased fee position would be significantly greater, that if the assumption is made that the pending sale contract will close, then the second appraiser's analysis is an acceptable methodology and one with which the first appraiser agrees.

And that appraiser further stated:

> There are no known covenants, conditions and restrictions impacting the site that are considered to affect the marketability or Highest and Best Use "as if" vacant[.][2]

The first appraiser concluded that the most likely buyer of the land only as if vacant would be an investor (for land speculation) or a developer. For the purpose of his analysis, the first appraiser used the sales comparison approach to analyze recent land sale transactions and current listings of land offered in and around the central business district.

Using this methodology, the appraiser concluded a value from the three land sales and two land listings, which ranged from $277.31 to $340.67 per square foot. The appraiser compared these sales and listings to the $31,620,000 sale price of the subject property (an occupied office building), which equated to $232 per rentable square foot. The appraiser stated that this sale represented an increase in value of approximately 35% over the acquisition price of $23.5 million ($172 per square foot) in early March 2006, indicating a continuing strong interest in Miami CBD office buildings.

The land value opinion ranged from $275 to $345 per square foot, with an indicated land value of $4.2 million, or $303 per square foot of land area. This method was deemed to be hypothetical and not relevant for the intended use.

The first appraiser valued all the co-owners' leased fee interests at $2,450,200, based on the total annual ground lease rent obligations of $49,000, and apportioned the value of the 1/15 interest at $163,000.

The leased fee analysis cash flow schedule is presented on the following page.

---

2. One material fact was not considered. The subject property's ownership receives the benefit from a perpetual covenant running with the land at a public garage adjacent to the subject property that is owned by others.

## First Appraiser's Value of the Leased Fee Interest

**200 SE First Street** — Leased Fee Analysis

| Y/E 5/30 | Contract Rent | Reversion Proceeds | Net Cash Flow | PV Factor @ 6.00% | PV of Cash Flow |
|---|---|---|---|---|---|
| 2008 | $49,000 | | $49,000 | 0.9433962 | $46,226 |
| 2009 | 49,000 | | 49,000 | 0.8899964 | $43,610 |
| 2010 | 49,000 | | 49,000 | 0.8396193 | $41,141 |
| 2011 | 49,000 | | 49,000 | 0.7920937 | $38,813 |
| 2012 | 49,000 | | 49,000 | 0.7472582 | $36,616 |
| 2013 | 49,000 | | 49,000 | 0.7049605 | $34,543 |
| 2014 | 49,000 | | 49,000 | 0.6650571 | $32,588 |
| 2015 | 49,000 | | 49,000 | 0.6274124 | $30,743 |
| 2016 | 49,000 | | 49,000 | 0.5918985 | $29,003 |
| 2017 | 49,000 | | 49,000 | 0.5583948 | $27,361 |
| 2018 | 49,000 | | 49,000 | 0.5267875 | $25,813 |
| 2019 | 49,000 | | 49,000 | 0.4969694 | $24,351 |
| 2020 | 49,000 | | 49,000 | 0.4688390 | $22,973 |
| 2021 | 49,000 | | 49,000 | 0.4423010 | $21,673 |
| 2022 | 49,000 | | 49,000 | 0.4172651 | $20,446 |
| 2023 | 49,000 | | 49,000 | 0.3936463 | $19,289 |
| 2024 | 49,000 | | 49,000 | 0.3713644 | $18,197 |
| 2025 | 49,000 | | 49,000 | 0.3503438 | $17,167 |
| 2026 | 49,000 | | 49,000 | 0.3305130 | $16,195 |
| 2027 | 49,000 | | 49,000 | 0.3118047 | $15,278 |
| 2028 | 49,000 | | 49,000 | 0.2941554 | $14,414 |
| 2029 | 49,000 | | 49,000 | 0.2775051 | $13,598 |
| 2030 | 49,000 | | 49,000 | 0.2617973 | $12,828 |
| 2031 | 49,000 | | 49,000 | 0.2469785 | $12,102 |
| 2032 | 49,000 | | 49,000 | 0.2329986 | $11,417 |
| 2033 | 49,000 | | 49,000 | 0.2198100 | $10,771 |
| 2034 | 49,000 | | 49,000 | 0.2073680 | $10,161 |
| 2035 | 49,000 | | 49,000 | 0.1956301 | $9,586 |
| 2036 | 49,000 | | 49,000 | 0.1845567 | $9,043 |
| 2037 | 49,000 | | 49,000 | 0.1741101 | $8,531 |
| 2038 | 49,000 | | 49,000 | 0.1642548 | $8,048 |
| 2039 | 49,000 | | 49,000 | 0.1549574 | $7,593 |
| 2040 | 49,000 | | 49,000 | 0.1461862 | $7,163 |
| 2041 | 49,000 | | 49,000 | 0.1379115 | $6,758 |
| 2042 | 49,000 | | 49,000 | 0.1301052 | $6,375 |
| 2043 | 49,000 | | 49,000 | 0.1227408 | $6,014 |
| 2044 | 49,000 | | 49,000 | 0.1157932 | $5,674 |
| 2045 | 49,000 | | 49,000 | 0.1092389 | $5,353 |
| 2046 | 49,000 | | 49,000 | 0.1030555 | $5,050 |
| 2047 | 49,000 | | 49,000 | 0.0972222 | $4,764 |
| 2048 | 49,000 | | 49,000 | 0.0917190 | $4,494 |
| 2049 | 49,000 | | 49,000 | 0.0865274 | $4,240 |
| 2050 | 49,000 | | 49,000 | 0.0816296 | $4,000 |
| 2051 | 49,000 | | 49,000 | 0.0770091 | $3,773 |
| 2052 | 49,000 | | 49,000 | 0.0726501 | $3,560 |
| 2053 | 49,000 | | 49,000 | 0.0685378 | $3,358 |
| 2054 | 49,000 | | 49,000 | 0.0646583 | $3,168 |
| 2055 | 49,000 | 27,596,358 | 27,645,358 | 0.0609984 | $1,686,323 |
| Indicated leased fee value (rounded) | | | | | $2,450,200 |
| Value of 1/15 interest (rounded) | | | | | $163,000 |

## *Second Appraiser*

The second appraiser's methodology took into consideration Section 11 U.S.C. §363 by using the net sales proceeds to the sellers of the pending sales agreement, and the appraiser requested the settlement statement (on the following page) that was approved by all parties and by the court for use as the current value basis for the reversion.

## Settlement Statement

| J. Summary of borrower's transaction | | K. Summary of seller's transaction | |
|---|---|---|---|
| 100. Gross amount due from borrower: | | 400. Gross amount due to seller: | |
| 101. Contract sales price | 31,620,000.00 | 401. Contract sales price | 31,620,000.00 |
| 102. Personal property | | 402. Personal property | |
| 103. Settlement charges to borrower (Line 1400) | | 403. | |
| 104. | | 404. | |
| 105. | | 405. | |
| **Adjustments for items paid by seller in advance:** | | **Adjustments for items paid by seller in advance:** | |
| 106. | | 406. | |
| 107. County taxes | | 407. County taxes | |
| 108. Assessments | | 408. Assessments | |
| 109. | | 409. | |
| 110. | | 410. | |
| 111. | | 411. | |
| 112. | | 412. | |
| 120. Gross amount due from borrower: | 31,620,000.00 | 420. Gross amount due to seller: | 31,620,000.00 |
| 200. Amounts paid or in behalf of borrower: | | 500. Reductions in amount due to seller: | |
| 201. Deposit or earnest money | 1,000,000.00 | 501. Excess deposit (see instructions) | |
| 202. Principal amount of new loan(s) | | 502. Settlement charges to seller (line 1400) | 1,182,808.34 |
| 203. Existing loan(s) taken subject to | | 503. Existing loan(s) taken subject to | |
| 204. Principal amount of second mortgage | | 504. Payoff of first mortgage loan | |
| 205. | | 505. Payoff of second mortgage loan | |
| 206. | | 506. Deposits held by seller | |
| 207. Principal amt of mortgage held by seller | | 507. Principal amt of mortgage held by seller | |
| 208. | | 508. | |
| 209. | | 509. | |
| **Adjustments for items unpaid by seller:** | | **Adjustments for items unpaid by seller:** | |
| 210. County taxes 2040 from 01/01/08 to 02/29/08 | 43,824.62 | 510. County taxes 2040 from 01/01/08 to 02/29/08 | 43,824.62 |
| 211. County taxes 2050 from 01/01/08 to 02/29/08 | 8,764.92 | 511. County taxes 2050 from 01/01/08 to 02/29/08 | 8,764.92 |
| 212. Rent Roll with lease charges from 01/01/08 to 02/29/08 | 7,883.79 | 512. Rent Roll with lease charges from 01/01/08 to 02/29/08 | 7,883.79 |
| 213. Security deposits | 169,520.60 | 513. Security deposits | 169,520.60 |
| 214. License fee proration from 01/01/08 to 02/29/08 | 890.25 | 514. License fee proration from 01/01/08 to 02/29/08 | 890.25 |
| 215. | | 515. | |
| 216. | | 516. | |
| 217. | | 517. | |
| 218. | | 518. | |
| 219. | | 519. | |
| 220. Total paid by/for borrower: | 1,230,884.18 | 520. Total reductions in amount due seller: | 1,413,692.52 |
| 300. Cash at settlement from/to borrower: | | 600. Cash at settlement to/from seller: | |
| 301. Gross amount due from borrower (line 120) | 31,620,000.00 | 601. Gross amount due to seller (line 420) | 31,620,000.00 |
| 302. Less amount paid by/for the borrower (line 220) | (1,230,884.18) | 602. Less total reductions in amount due seller (line 520) | (1,413,692.52) |
| 303. Cash (☑ From ☐ To) Borrower: | 30,389,115.82 | 603. Cash (☑ To ☐ From) Seller: | 30,206,307.48 |

*Bankruptcy–Fractional Interest in a Leased Fee Estate*

The appraiser's market analysis supported the assumption that, if the subject building improvements were adequately maintained and prudently managed, the existing use of the office building would be extended and would most likely be the future use of the property upon termination of the leasehold 47-plus years in the future. The appraiser identified competitive office buildings built more than 70 years ago that have continued to be functional and concluded that the 50-year-old subject office building could have a similar physical longevity and an extended economic life beyond the remaining lease term of 47-plus years.

The second appraiser also addressed the benefit of the existing covenant running with the land for the subtenants' perpetual use of off-street parking in the adjacent parking garage facility owned by others.

The following section of the case study reproduces edited and redacted portions of the report the second appraiser submitted to the court.

## Edited and Redacted Abstract of the Second Appraiser's Report

### Summary of Salient Facts and Opinions

| | |
|---|---|
| Property Address: | 200 SE First Street, Miami, Florida |
| Property Description: | An existing 12-story, 141,679-square-foot office building built in 1958-1959 and renovated in 1997-2005, on a land parcel containing 13,838± square feet (0.32± acres). The building is leased to 25 subleasehold tenants with a reported occupancy of 85%. Common area factor is 14%. Available parking of 250 spaces is provided in the adjacent parking garage per a covenant running with the land. |
| Current Fee Holders (Lessor/Landlord): | ▓▓▓▓▓, LLC is the fee owner of a 14/15 interest, and ▓▓▓▓▓ and ▓▓▓▓▓ each own a 1/30 interest, combined, they are the fee owner of a 1/15 interest in the fee title of ownership. |
| Current Leaseholder (Lessor and Sub-Landlord): | ▓▓▓▓▓, LLC |
| Lease Agreement Date(s): | Lease execution date: 5/15/1956<br>Supplement and amendment to lease: 1/24/1962<br>Lease expiration date: 5/14/2055 |
| Remaining Term of Lease: | 47 Years, 2 Months and 14 Days |
| Annual Rent for the Remaining Term of the Leasehold: | Assumes that the total rent paid and to be paid per the supplement and amendment to the lease of $49,000 per year and that the apportioned rent to the 1/15 fee interest owner is and will be $3,266.67 per year for the remaining term of the ground lease. |
| Date of Contract for Purchase and Sale: | December 6, 2006 |
| Buyer: | ▓▓▓▓▓, Inc. |
| Date of Closing: | Estimated to be on February 29, 2008 |
| Purchase Price: | $31,620,000 |
| Net Sales Proceeds to Seller(s) (Per Settlement Statement): | $30,206,307.48 |
| Property Rights Appraised: | A 1/15 fee interest in the ground lease |
| Use of this Appraisal: | For the exclusive and restricted use in the bankruptcy proceedings by the court as fact finder to determine the equitable apportionment of the pending sale price net proceeds for distribution to the 1/15 fee interest owners collectively. |
| **APPRAISED VALUE of the 1/15 Fee Interest Effective as of February 29, 2008** | **$375,000** |

[Based upon the pending sale. If this sale does not close, the appraised value is void per 363(h).]

## Purpose

The purpose of this appraisal is to develop an opinion of the appraised value of a 1/15 ownership interest in the leased fee estate as of an effective date of February 29, 2008, which is the estimated date of the property sale closing of the leaseholder's interest, the co-owner's 14/15 interest, and the subject's 1/15 interest of two co-owners (two 1/30 interests combined) in the captioned property.

## Intended Use

The intended use of this appraisal is to assist the fact-finder in making a determination for the equitable apportionment of the sales proceeds from the property to be paid by ▇▇▇▇▇▇▇▇ for the ownership interests in the subject property.

## Lessor's Interest

The lessor's, seller's, and co-owner's interest is a 14/15 interest owned by ▇▇▇▇▇▇▇▇▇▇▇▇ LLC. The 1/15 interest being appraised is owned by ▇▇▇▇▇▇▇▇ (a 1/30 interest) and ▇▇▇▇▇▇▇▇ (a 1/30 interest) as co-fee holders, which are combined to equal the 1/15 interest.

The interest of the lessor (also known as the *fee holder* or *landlord*) is defined as the *leased fee estate interest*, which has only the right to receive rent from the lessee for the remaining term of the lease and the right of repossession of the property at the expiration of the lease if in good standing. This future repossession of the property is commonly known as the *reversion of fee title* to the fee holder.

## Lessee's Interest

The interest of the lessee (also known as the *leaseholder* or *tenant*) is defined as the leasehold estate interest, which has the right to the exclusive use and occupancy rights of the property during the remaining term of the lease, subject to the lease terms, conditions, and the payment of rent to the lessors over the remaining term of the lease.

## Condition of this Appraisal

Since the price of the ownership interest in the existing real property (in its entirety) has been established, in accordance with the contract for purchase and sale of real property to ▇▇▇▇▇▇▇▇▇▇▇, Inc., and the cash proceeds to be paid have been established at the estimated closing date, the definition of *market value* may apply. However, this appraisal does not render an opinion as to whether the purchase price is above or below market value (as defined).

*Market price* (as defined) may apply. The differences between these two concepts are defined as follows:

### Market Value, As Defined
The most probable price which a property should bring in a competitive and open market under all conditions requisite to a fair sale, the buyer and seller each acting prudently, knowledgeably, and assuming the price is not affected by undue stimulus. Implicit in this definition is the consummation of a sale as of a specified date and the passing of title from seller to buyer under conditions whereby:

(1) buyer and seller are typically motivated;
(2) both parties are well informed or well advised, and each acting in what they consider their best interests;
(3) a reasonable time is allowed for exposure in the open market;
(4) payment is made in terms of cash in U.S. dollars or in terms of financial arrangements comparable thereto; and
(5) the price represents the normal consideration for the property sold unaffected by special or creative financing or sales concessions granted by anyone associated with the sale.

Source: *The Dictionary of Real Estate*; 12 CFR Part 34.42[g]

### Market Price, As Defined
The amount actually paid in a sale transaction that may or may not have been sold under all conditions requisite to a fair sale. *Market price* is an accomplished fact and involves no assumptions of prudent conduct by the parties to a transaction or any conditions set forth in the concept of *market value*.

## Applicable Definitions

In the appraisal report, the second appraiser provided the court with appraisal assumptions and conditions, along with definitions applicable to the appraisal problem:

- Market value
- Market price
- Fee simple estate interest
- Lease interests such as leased fee (estate) interests, leasehold interests, the intermediate sandwich leasehold position, and the sublease tenant's interest
- Leased fee estate value
- Leasehold estate value

These definitions were abstracted from *The Appraisal of Real Estate, The Dictionary of Real Estate Appraisal,* and *The Encyclo-*

*pedia of Real Estate Terms* with further clarifications specific to the scope of work performed by the second appraiser.

## Leased Fee Discount Rate

The leased fee discount rate may be thought of as the interest rate that reflects the competitive rate of return on an investment. The discounted present value factor of this rate converts future rent payments into a present worth opinion.

The risk component of the leased fee discount rate is compared to the rate of return on capital that is commensurate with the risk-reward benefit of the investment. Therefore, the leased fee discount rate can be based on a safe rate, which is the yield rate of return on a long-term riskless investment. The difference between the total rate of return of a leased fee discount rate and the safe rate is the premium required to compensate for the security of the capital invested, the illiquidity of the capital invested, and the burden of management relating to the ownership interest of the investment.

The remaining term of this lease (from the effective date of appraisal) is 47 years, 2 months, and 14 days. This long-term leasehold period binds the fee holders to the financial terms set forth by contract terms in the lease.

For the purpose of this appraisal, it is concluded that the leaseholder's rent paid to the fee owners is deemed to represent a riskless return for a real estate investment because the rental amount is far below current market rent norms and is most favorable to the leasehold (tenant's) interest. Therefore, a marketable yield rate of return would be similar to an annuity investment (e.g., a long-term US government bond or similar security investments) plus a premium for lack of liquidity, risk, and burden of management.

A review of national investment surveys of triple net leases reveals that rates of return and yield rates range from 6.0% to 7.5% for long-term, quality leaseholds that have increasing revenues over the lease terms. Interest rates on 30-year mortgages average 5.42% and reflect a more secure position. The coupon rate on a AAA–rated tax-exempt insured revenue bond yields 4.49%, and 30-year Treasury Notes, the most riskless investment, currently are set at 3.375%.

## Leased Fee Discount Rate Conclusion

In analyzing the structure of this leasehold, the appraiser compared the characteristics and quality of this lease income stream with alternative, competitive income streams that reflect various yield rates. The appraiser reached the following conclusions:

- The contract rent paid and to be paid is deemed most favorable to the lessee intermediate landlord, resulting in a very positive and favorable leasehold. This warrants a discount rate commensurate with a long-term and basically riskless annuity plus premiums for illiquidity and burden of management. Long-term annuities (e.g., US Government Treasury Notes and other competitive securities) fall within a range that would be 250 to 350 basis points below what long-term triple net leases would be sold for in the secondary marketplace and 50 to 150 basis points above a fixed-rate mortgage loan rate.

- The subject leaseholder's fixed rent is flat with no rent increases over the remaining lease term. This warrants a discount rate of return at 6.0%, and the reversion discount rate warrants an additional 100 basis points due to the risk of uncertainty as to the future forecast of the resale price 47-plus years in the future.[3]

It is therefore concluded for the purpose of the appraisal that the leased fee discount rate for the apportioned 1/15 annual rent, as of the effective date, is 6.0%. And the reversionary discount rate for the apportioned 1/15 interest of the reversion, as of the effective date, is 7.0%.

## Value of the Leased Fee Interest

The present value of the 1/15 co-owners' interest in this leased fee estate is best analyzed and apportioned value using the income capitalization approach. Using this approach, the appraiser calculates the expected annual apportioned rent of $49,000 per year paid and to be paid to the 1/15 fee owners at $272.22 per month ($3,266.67 annually) for the remaining term of the leasehold (47 years, 2 months, and 14 days), which terminates on May 14, 2055.

This monthly rent, converted to an annual amount for the purpose of appraisal, must be discounted to a present worth because the value of the total rent to be received over the remaining term of this lease has a greater present worth in a lump-sum payment than its worth if received over a period of 47-plus years.

The co-owners of the leased fee interest also have their apportioned reversionary value, which is the present worth of the

---

3. Various rates were illustrated in the addenda of the appraisal report to support this opinion.

property in the entirety 47-plus years in the future, discounted to present worth.

Therefore, the prospective property's value, forecasted 47-plus years hence, must also be discounted at a market yield rate, discounted to a present worth.

The sum of the present worth of the future rent to be received from the effective date plus the present worth of the reversion is the current value of the 1/15 leased fee interest in the real property being appraised, as of the effective date, February 29, 2008:

| Concluded Opinions | |
|---|---|
| Present worth of future rent payments | $51,755 |
| Present worth of the reversion | $323,424 |
| Value of the 1/15 co-owners' interest in the leased fee estate as of February 29, 2008 | $375,000 (rounded) |

Based upon an independent exercise of my professional appraisal judgment and experience, the calculations for this valuation are as follows:

| Assumptions and Conditions | | | |
|---|---|---|---|
| Ownership interest | | | A 1/15 interest |
| Ownership interest factor | | | 0.066666667 |
| Effective date of analysis (date of value) | | | February 29, 2008 |
| Growth rate | | | 3.0% |
| Discount rate for the rent payments | | | 6.0% |
| Discount rate for the reversion | | | 7.0% |
| Remaining lease term | | | 47 years, 2 months, 14 days |
| Total fixed rent | | $49,000 | |
| Annual proration of a 1/15 interest | | $3,266.67 | $3,266.67 |
| ($49,000 × 0.066666667 = $2,366.66 ÷ 12 = $272.22/mo.) | | | |
| Prorations of fixed rent | | | |
| March and April 2008 | | $272.22 × 2 = | $544.44 |
| May 1 thru May 14, 2008 | $272.22 ÷ 14 days | × $8.95/day = | $125.30 |
| Total first-year income | | $3,936.41 | |
| Analysis of the Present Worth of the Reversion | | | |
| | Contract sale price | $31,620,000 | |
| | Less: Seller's reductions | −($1,413,693) | (4.47%) |
| | Net cash to seller | $30,206,307 | |
| **Net Cash Proceeds** | Growth Rate @ 3% Factor (47-plus Years Hence) | | Future Price at Lease Expiration |
| $30,206,307.00 | × 4.132251879 | = | $124,820,069 |
| **Allocation of a 1/15 Interest for the Reversion (Factor)** | Present Worth @ 7.0% Discount Rate (47-plus Years Hence) | | Present Worth of the Reversion |
| 0.066666667 | × $125,520,573 | = | $8,368,038 |
| $8,321,337.92 | × 0.03886679 | = | $323,423.69 |
| Present Worth of the Reversion | | | $323,424 (rounded) |
| (See the DCF analysis on the following page.) | | | |

## Value of a 1/15 Interest in the Leased Fee Estate as of February 29, 2008, via a DCF Analysis

| Period | Year | Apportioned Monthly Rent | Apportioned Annual Rent[1] | Times | PV Factor @ 6.00% | Equals | Present Value |
|---|---|---|---|---|---|---|---|
| 1 | 2008 | $328.03 | $3,936.41 | × | 0.9433962 | = | $3,714 |
| 2 | 2009 | $272.22 | $3,266.67 | × | 0.8899964 | = | $2,907 |
| 3 | 2010 | $272.22 | $3,266.67 | × | 0.8396193 | = | $2,743 |
| 4 | 2011 | $272.22 | $3,266.67 | × | 0.7920937 | = | $2,588 |
| 5 | 2012 | $272.22 | $3,266.67 | × | 0.7472582 | = | $2,441 |
| 6 | 2013 | $272.22 | $3,266.67 | × | 0.7049605 | = | $2,303 |
| 7 | 2014 | $272.22 | $3,266.67 | × | 0.6650571 | = | $2,173 |
| 8 | 2015 | $272.22 | $3,266.67 | × | 0.6274124 | = | $2,050 |
| 9 | 2016 | $272.22 | $3,266.67 | × | 0.5918985 | = | $1,934 |
| 10 | 2017 | $272.22 | $3,266.67 | × | 0.5583948 | = | $1,824 |
| 11 | 2018 | $272.22 | $3,266.67 | × | 0.5267875 | = | $1,721 |
| 12 | 2019 | $272.22 | $3,266.67 | × | 0.4969694 | = | $1,623 |
| 13 | 2020 | $272.22 | $3,266.67 | × | 0.4688390 | = | $1,532 |
| 14 | 2021 | $272.22 | $3,266.67 | × | 0.4423010 | = | $1,445 |
| 15 | 2022 | $272.22 | $3,266.67 | × | 0.4172651 | = | $1,363 |
| 16 | 2023 | $272.22 | $3,266.67 | × | 0.3936463 | = | $1,286 |
| 17 | 2024 | $272.22 | $3,266.67 | × | 0.3713644 | = | $1,213 |
| 18 | 2025 | $272.22 | $3,266.67 | × | 0.3503438 | = | $1,144 |
| 19 | 2026 | $272.22 | $3,266.67 | × | 0.3305130 | = | $1,080 |
| 20 | 2027 | $272.22 | $3,266.67 | × | 0.3118047 | = | $1,019 |
| 21 | 2028 | $272.22 | $3,266.67 | × | 0.2941554 | = | $961 |
| 22 | 2029 | $272.22 | $3,266.67 | × | 0.2775051 | = | $907 |
| 23 | 2030 | $272.22 | $3,266.67 | × | 0.2617973 | = | $855 |
| 24 | 2031 | $272.22 | $3,266.67 | × | 0.2469785 | = | $807 |
| 25 | 2032 | $272.22 | $3,266.67 | × | 0.2329986 | = | $761 |
| 26 | 2033 | $272.22 | $3,266.67 | × | 0.2198100 | = | $718 |
| 27 | 2034 | $272.22 | $3,266.67 | × | 0.2073680 | = | $677 |
| 28 | 2035 | $272.22 | $3,266.67 | × | 0.1956301 | = | $639 |
| 29 | 2036 | $272.22 | $3,266.67 | × | 0.1845567 | = | $603 |
| 30 | 2037 | $272.22 | $3,266.67 | × | 0.1741101 | = | $569 |
| 31 | 2038 | $272.22 | $3,266.67 | × | 0.1642548 | = | $537 |
| 32 | 2039 | $272.22 | $3,266.67 | × | 0.1549574 | = | $506 |
| 33 | 2040 | $272.22 | $3,266.67 | × | 0.1461862 | = | $478 |
| 34 | 2041 | $272.22 | $3,266.67 | × | 0.1379115 | = | $451 |
| 35 | 2042 | $272.22 | $3,266.67 | × | 0.1301052 | = | $425 |
| 36 | 2043 | $272.22 | $3,266.67 | × | 0.1227408 | = | $401 |
| 37 | 2044 | $272.22 | $3,266.67 | × | 0.1157932 | = | $378 |
| 38 | 2045 | $272.22 | $3,266.67 | × | 0.1092389 | = | $357 |
| 39 | 2046 | $272.22 | $3,266.67 | × | 0.1030555 | = | $337 |
| 40 | 2047 | $272.22 | $3,266.67 | × | 0.0972222 | = | $318 |
| 41 | 2048 | $272.22 | $3,266.67 | × | 0.0917190 | = | $300 |
| 42 | 2049 | $272.22 | $3,266.67 | × | 0.0865274 | = | $283 |
| 43 | 2050 | $272.22 | $3,266.67 | × | 0.0816296 | = | $267 |
| 44 | 2051 | $272.22 | $3,266.67 | × | 0.0770091 | = | $252 |
| 45 | 2052 | $272.22 | $3,266.67 | × | 0.0726501 | = | $237 |
| 46 | 2053 | $272.22 | $3,266.67 | × | 0.0685378 | = | $224 |
| 47 | 2054 | $272.22 | $3,266.67 | × | 0.0646583 | = | $211 |
| Total(s) | | | $154,203 | | | | $51,556 |

Present Worth of Future Rent Payments $51,556
Present Worth of the Reversion* $323,424
$374,980
Value of a 1/15 Interest in the Leased Fee as of February 29, 2008 $375,000 (RD)

\* does not include debit for tenant security deposits

1. Assumes that rent was paid and would be paid, per the remaining lease term under the amendment to lease

*Prepared and analyzed by Michael Y. Cannon MAI,SRA, Integra Realty Resources-Miami (January 2008)*

> In summary, the second appraiser's valuation methodology was consistent with the rules of the court, and the appraised value of the 1/15 fee interest was based on a growth rate for the reversion of the agreed-upon pending sale price, which was deemed to be the market value of the property per the court's determination.
>
> The appraiser stated, however, that if the pending sale did not close, this appraisal method would be applicable to another agreed-upon property sale price as the basis for calculations plus the present value of the allocated rental income to be paid over the remaining term of the ground lease discounted to present value. The sum would be the appraised value of the co-owners' 1/15 interest in the leased fee estate.

## Appraisal Comparison Analysis

The court stated that the basic appraisal methodology of the two appraisals had certain similarities, but noted the differences in the appraisers' assumptions.

### First Appraiser's Valuation Assumptions

- That the existing building and improvements do not exist as of the effective date and the building will be demolished at the expiration of the ground lease and the site will be assembled with adjacent properties for redevelopment as a high-rise office with street-level retail storefronts.
- That the discount rate for the future apportioned rent to be received by the owners of the 1/15 fee interest is 6% as of the effective date.
- That the inflation rate will average 4% over the remaining term of the ground lease.
- That the discount rate for the reversion of the property back to the co-owners of the leased fee interests is 6% as of the effective date.

### Second Appraiser's Valuation Assumptions

- That the existing property will continue to be prudently managed, maintained, and leased to office and retail tenants for the remaining term and beyond the remaining term of the 99-year ground lease.
- That the discount rate for the present worth of the future apportioned rent to be received by the co-owners of the 1/15 interest is 6% as of the effective date.

- That the growth rate of the agreed-upon property value should average 3% over the remaining term of the ground lease.
- That the discount rate for the present worth of the reversion of the property back to the fee owners is 7% as of the effective date.

The chart below further identifies the appraisal differences.

| | Appraisal Comparison Differences | |
|---|---|---|
| **Relevant items** | **Stated by the First Appraiser** | **Stated by the Second Appraiser** |
| Effective date of appraised value | January 10, 2008 | February 29, 2008 |
| Remaining term of lease | 568 Months | 47 years, 2 months, 14 days or 566 months, 14 days |
| Annual contract rent of the 1/15 fee owners' interest | Stated to be $3,267. Analysis based on $49,000 and applied as an apportionment to the 1/15 co-owners | $3,266.67 |
| Contract sales price of 100% interests | Not considered | $31,620,000 |
| Net cash to seller (per closing statement) | Not considered | $30,206,307 |
| Concluded a land value "as if vacant" | $4,200,000 | Not addressed nor considered |
| Term/period of DCF model | 48 Years | 47 years, 2 months, 14 days |
| Growth rate | 4% | 3% |
| Future worth factor @ 3% | - | 4.13225189 |
| Future worth factor @ 4% | 6.570528 | - |
| Discount rate for rent income | 6% | 6% |
| Reversion rate | 6% | 7% |
| Future resale price of the property upon lease expiration (47 plus years hence) | Not addressed | $124,820,071 |
| Future value of land (only) at lease expiration (47 plus years hence) | $27,596,358 | Not addressed nor considered |
| Present value of future rent payments to the 1/15 co-owners' fee interest | $50,925 | $51,556 |
| Indicated leased fee of all co-owners' interest | $2,450,000 | Not considered a part of scope of work |
| Value of a 1/15 interest | $163,000 (RD) | $375,000 (RD) |

## Court's Determination

The court respectfully rejected the argument of the co-owners of the 1/15 fee interest that they were entitled to a 1/15 distribution of the net sales proceeds of the pending sale price totaling approximately $2 million. The court stated that the statute requires that the interest of a co-owner of the fee interest be valued based upon the nature of such interest as it existed prior to the sale. In other words, prior to the sale closing, the co-owners of fee interests have only the right to receive contract rent for the remaining term of the lease plus the present value of its reversionary interest in the fee upon the expiration of the lease.

The court reserved its position that if the current property sale did not close, the method to determine the proper distribution of the co-owners' 1/15 interest would be adjusted to another purchase price if it differed in amount.

The court found that the second appraiser used a methodology that was consistent with the requirements of the statute and that correctly took into account the fact that the property was being sold at the present time, i.e., the intended use of the appraisal.

The court went on to say the following:

> In contrast, the first appraiser valued the property based upon the assumption that the property will not be sold, will remain subject to the lease, and will be returned to the present owners in the year 2055, at the expiration of the lease.
>
> This approach may be a valid appraisal methodology, but it ignores the fact that the purpose of the instant proceeding is to authorize a sale of the property to a third party for the present Fair Market Value.
>
> In other words, the property is not going to be returned to the current owners at the end of the lease. It is being sold now for cash, and the cash must be divided among the co-owners, as provided by the statute.

The basic difference in methodology, other than two differing discount rates, was the basis for the reversion. The first appraiser based the reversion on the land value "as if" vacant. The second appraiser based the reversion on the court's determinate price of the pending sale.

The court found that the second appraiser's methodology and approach was correct for valuing the co-owners' leased fee estate interest in accordance with 11 U.S.C. §33(j), stating the following:

> **Conclusion**
> The court values the 1/15 co-owner's fee interest in the property at the second appraiser's opinion at $375,000 ($187,500 for each of the 1/30 fee owner's interest based upon the proceeds of the pending sale price of $31,620,000.)

The court also restated that

> If the sale of the property is to another purchaser for a different amount . . . then the 1/15th fee interest will necessarily be adjusted accordingly relative to their pro-rata share.

## Appraisal Issues That Must Be Considered

Under the Scope of Work Rule of the Uniform Standards of Professional Appraisal Practice, the appraiser, as an expert witness, must set forth the appropriate appraisal methodology and theory to be employed in a judicial proceeding, which is more than just citing the basic three approaches to value.

The appraiser, if declared to be an expert witness in a court proceeding, must acquire and use the court's rules under the Jurisdictional Exception Rule of USPAP. The appraiser must incorporate rules of the court and state them as being applicable for a credible opinion of value to be reported.

The appraiser needs to "step out of the box" and learn why the appraiser's professional appraisal services are being sought by the court, in this case to resolve a dispute resolution matter.

## Lessons Learned

The most important lesson to be learned in this type of assignment is to understand and use the rules of the court. In this case, the first appraiser did not consider that the property would be sold at the present time, but rather assumed that it would be returned to the fee owners at the end of the lease. This method produced an inappropriate appraised value opinion of $163,000. This was deemed to be an extreme hypothetical condition since the intended use of the appraisal by the court as fact-finder was to determine the amount that the two 1/30 fee co-owners should receive if all ownership interests were sold as of the effective date.

The second appraiser considered the amount of the then-pending sale price stated in the contract and used a methodology that was consistent with the requirements of the statute and took into account that the property was being sold at the present time. The method used resulted in a appraised value of $375,000 and was consistent with the purposes of the court's determination.

In contrast, the two 1/30 fee co-owners argued that they were entitled to a direct allocation of their combined interests of 6.67% (1/15) of the pending sale. This argument would have resulted in an allocation of $2 million. This position was also deemed inappropriate under the Federal Rule Statute 11 U.S.C. §33(j).

In bankruptcy court, the judge, as fact-finder, relies on Federal Rules of Procedures and Federal Rules of Evidence. The expert appraiser must be cognizant of those rules to avoid impeachment of opinions presented to the court.

CASE STUDY 8.1

# Lease Renewal–The Periodic Setting of Market Rent in a Long-Term Lease

*By John G. Ellis, MAI, CRE, FRICS*

Long-term leases often have valuation clauses that call for an appraisal of market rent at a specific point in time. Sometimes this appraisal occurs 10 years or 25 years after the start of the lease. It may recur at periodic intervals, or it may coincide with the exercise of an option to extend the lease term. For such assignments, the appraiser must carefully read and consider the entire lease, particularly those sections dealing with the allowable uses of the property and the valuation (or rent resetting) provisions of the document. These sections of the same lease may provide a consistent set of instructions, or they may appear to suggest different interpretations of the property's potential uses to be considered in the appraisal. In the case study that follows, the allowable uses for the subject premises as defined in the lease also formed the basis for the appraisal of market rent. However, the appraiser is cautioned to consider this issue carefully and be aware of situations in which such consistency is lacking. This case study also illustrates how an appraisal assignment can transition into subsequent phases of service, including litigation support and expert testimony.

## The Assignment

At the time I was engaged to perform this appraisal of market rent, the situation had already escalated to the point of litigation. The issue centered on a disagreement between the landlord, whose multitenant property included a large theater space, and a tenant, a church that was the current lessee of the theater space. The parties had agreed to retain a retired judge who would hear the case as a full trial. The primary issue in the litigation was the amount of rent to be paid for the subject theater space over the 10-year extension option period. The lease required the rent to be set at "fair market value" as of November 1, 2008, which was the first day of the extended term.

Two other leases between the same parties were also being extended. These covered basement space and second-floor office space. While the basement and the office spaces were appraised as part of the same assignment, the focus of this case study is the theater lease.

The issue of how the subject theater premises could be used was of critical importance to the appraisal and the trial that followed.

My client in the assignment was the legal counsel for the church (i.e., the tenant). I was interviewed for the assignment and retained several months before the trial was scheduled to begin. There was ample time to conduct the necessary market research and analysis.

This case study will discuss the history of the subject property and its local market, the lease and its key provisions, the highest and best use analysis, the appraisal process, the value opinion, and the work done by the landlord's appraiser as well as the deposition testimony, pretrial litigation support, the trial, and its outcome.[1]

## A Brief History of the Subject Property

In 1993, a growing religious organization (the church) entered into a lease with the North End Theater, which is near the north end of the historic theater district in the older urban core of the city.[2] The North End Theater had been built as a 1920s movie palace, but with the advent of multiscreen cinemas the demand for large-screen, single-auditorium theaters had diminished so much that traditional movie theater use was no longer a viable option for this historic facility or for several others like it.

When the five-year lease term expired in 1998, the owner of the North End Theater demanded a substantial increase in the church's rent. Rather than pay the higher rent, the church terminated its occupancy and relocated to the subject theater, another former movie palace from the 1920s located about four blocks south. The subject theater was located in a building with a basement that was originally built out as a restaurant and more recently used as a large discount shoe store. Above the ground floor were 12 floors of office and other commercial space. The interior of the theater included an orchestra seating level with 1,305 seats, a balcony with 1,020 seats, and a formal lobby and foyer.

## The Lease

The original term of the new lease began on November 1, 1998, and ran for 10 years with an option to extend the lease for an additional 10-year

---

1. The circumstances of this case are accurate. The identities of some of the parties and properties have been omitted or slightly modified to protect information that may not be publicly available.
2. The North End Theater is not the subject property. The lease for the subject theater was originally signed in 1998. However, some history about the church and the neighborhood is helpful for a thorough understanding of the case. There were 14 theaters in the immediate area developed between the 1890s and 1930s. Some of the theaters have historic designations. However, the use of the term *historic* in this chapter refers to the age and character of the neighborhood, not the property status of a historic landmark.

The subject property, a former theater being used as a church

period. The lease was written with a rental rate that increased in fixed steps over the primary term according to the following rent schedule:

| | |
|---|---|
| Months 1 through 6: | $7,000 per month |
| Months 7 through 24: | $10,000 per month |
| Years 3 and 4: | $10,500 per month |
| Years 5 and 6: | $11,000 per month |
| Years 7 through 10: | $12,000 per month |

The church (as the tenant) was responsible for its share of liability and property insurance, all utilities and maintenance for the theater space, and a proportionate share of the real estate taxes levied against the property. The lease was, in effect, a triple net lease. The lease also contained a provision specifying that "The allowable uses of the premises shall be as a church and for religious assembly purposes only. The lessee may also use the space for movie theater uses provided, however, that if the lessee intends to use the space for movie theater purposes, it must first provide an opportunity for Urban Theaters to serve as the operator of the movie theater operations."

The city enacted an adaptive reuse ordinance shortly after the year 2000 that allowed for the conversion of some of the older buildings in the vicinity into housing, even though prior code requirements (especially as they related to parking) could not be satisfied. The economic boom from 2002 through 2006 resulted in a substantial increase in the residential population in the subject theater's vicinity and led to the conversion of some of the other historic theaters into nightclubs, restaurants, and multitenant retail developments, which were supported by the growing resident population. These newcomers to the neighborhood were significantly more affluent than those living in this central city neighborhood prior to 2000.

The congregation of the church grew during the first 10 years of the lease (1998 to 2008), and the church intended to exercise its option to continue as a tenant in the building for the 10-year option period. The church gave notice to the property owner of its intention to exercise the option and included a rent offer that was about 5% higher than the $12,000 per month rent in effect at the end of the initial term.

The landlord submitted a demand for $97,800 per month in rent at the start of the extended term and cited information on rents being charged for spaces used as concert venues and nightclubs as the primary support for this increased amount.

The parties sought and obtained a pretrial hearing for the purpose of determining whether the use provision in the lease was valid and restrictive. The court ruled that the use provision was indeed legal and cited the case of *Wu v. Interstate Consolidated Industries* in support of this ruling.[3] However, the court did not rule on the appropriate rent amount at that time. As a result, the lease and the court's ruling became the foundation on which the appraisers could build their analyses once they were brought into the assignment.

At this point I was retained by the church's counsel to perform an appraisal of market rent. As a first step, I carefully read the lease and the court's ruling.

## Highest and Best Use

The appropriate investigations for the appraisal were similar to what would be required in many other assignments. Although the highest and best use investigation was not unique to this appraisal, it

---

3. *Wu v. Interstate Consolidated Industries* (1991) 226 Cal. App.3d 1511, 1514 [277 Cal. Rptr. 546]. In the *Wu* case, the lessees of a motion picture theater building had exercised their renewal option. The lessors attempted to raise the rent to fair market rental value based on the highest and best use of the premises without considering the use provisions of the lease. The lessees brought an action for declaratory relief and breach of contract, contending that the lease provision allowing for an increase to fair market rental value must be interpreted as requiring a determination of the rent based on the particular purpose for which the premises were leased. The trial court granted summary judgment for the lessees. The Court of Appeal affirmed. It held that the only reasonable interpretation of the term *fair market rental value* as used in the lease was that rent was to be established with reference to the nature of the premises and the purpose for which they had been leased.

warranted special emphasis. Since the property rights conveyed by the lease did not allow the lessee to modify the underlying land, the highest and best use of the land was not relevant to the appraisal. The highest and best use of the property as improved focused only on the premises described in the lease.

## Legally Permissible Uses

The zoning of the property allowed for general commercial uses, which included retail, restaurant, office, and a variety of entertainment uses, some of which required a variance or conditional use permit. Churches and movie theaters were within this larger group of legally permissible uses under zoning. The lease itself, however, imposed significant restrictions on the uses that could be legally conducted within the subject premises. Specifically, the lease limited the allowed uses to church, religious assembly, and (under certain circumstances) movie theater uses.

## Physically Possible Uses

The subject premises are configured as a large theater auditorium with a ground-floor entry, a lobby area, and two staircases leading to a second-level foyer that provides access to the mezzanine level of the theater. The premises also include a backstage area, service rooms, and other facilities related to the support of the original theater operations. To the extent that a movie theater use was to be considered, it would be physically possible to conduct such a use as a single-screen operation. However, there was no practical way to convert the theater to a multiscreen format. Continuation of the church and religious assembly uses was also physically possible.

## Financially Feasible Uses

The limitations on converting the theater to a multiscreen format were partially physical and partially financial. Accordingly, only a single-screen format could be evaluated for financial feasibility. A careful analysis of the history of the city's historic theater district revealed that at its peak there had been 14 movie palaces within a one-mile radius of the subject property. Between 1920 and 1980, 12 of those had ceased operation. The final two were shuttered between 1980 and 1995. Two of the theaters continued to occasionally show art films or function as venues for small film festivals. However, these limited movie screening uses were insufficient to cover all of the ownership and operating costs of the facilities. As a result, use as a movie theater was not deemed to be financially feasible. The remaining uses for consideration were church and religious assembly. An analysis of the regional market revealed two other historic theaters in the subject's vicinity that had been leased to other churches. A regional search revealed that eight other lease transactions involved theaters that had been leased to religious organizations for use as churches. The rental income from these church-oriented leases generated a positive cash flow (income exceeding operating expenses) for the respective theater spaces. Accordingly, use of the subject facility as a church or for religious assembly purposes was deemed to be the only financially feasible use of the subject premises.

## Maximally Productive Use

The facility's use for church and religious assembly purposes was the only use that satisfied the other three tests and was concluded to be the maximally productive use.

# The Appraisal Process

After the completion of the highest and best use analysis, the next step was to attempt to gather a sufficient body of comparable data that would allow for meaningful comparison to the subject premises, ultimately leading to an opinion of market rent.

Church leases were relatively scarce, and the leasing of churches within theaters was even more limited. However, with an objectively defined set of research parameters, I identified eight transactions that, in my opinion, were relevant and appropriate comparables. My research included a countywide search for lease transactions in which the tenant was a church. Considering the specialized nature of the subject premises, I considered leases starting as long ago as 10 years prior to the November 1, 2008, date of value.

I reviewed published sources of transaction data but focused my efforts on extensive interviews with brokers, leasing agents, and church representatives. Through those efforts, I identified two brokers who were actively involved in the leasing of church properties. Information from these brokers included both long-term, exclusive-use leases between a single church and property owner as well as transactions in which multiple churches used the same physical premises on a shared basis at different times during the week. Because the subject property was leased on an exclusive-use basis to a single church, I limited my final set of comparables to those properties that were also leased on an exclusive-use basis.

The subject premises contain 2,325 seats; this was the largest facility of all of the leased premises I found. Some of the smaller facilities had fewer than 200 seats. In making my final data selection, I used 400 seats as a cut-off point. Ministers and other participants in this market described the smaller facilities as being insufficient to support a congregation for an extended period of time. I reviewed transactions in which the lessee of the subject church was also the lessee in other theater properties and included some of these leases in my final data set if they satisfied the selection parameters. Those that were smaller than 400 seats or were leased prior to 1998 were excluded from my final data set.

The November 1998 lease of the subject premises was used as a comparable, recognizing that a market conditions adjustment would be an important element in my analysis of this property. However, I also recognized that even this dated lease of the subject premises still enjoyed the benefits of an identical location, the same physical premises that were under consideration, and the exact use specified for the purpose of my appraisal assignment. I also identified leases from the North End Theater (the former premises of the church), which included two separate lease transactions in 2000 and 2006.

My final data set included eight transactions, six of which were churches leasing a theater and one that represented a purpose-built church that had been leased to a different church organization. One of the North End Theater leases involved a lessee that was not a church. A summary of the lease comparables is shown in Exhibit 1.

The 2006 lease of the North End Theater allowed the screening of motion pictures and limited live entertainment. This facility was located in a former office building in which the upper floors had been converted to residential use. Accordingly, the entertainment uses had strict limitations on their hours of operation. This comparable had significant similarities to the subject property in terms of location and physical characteristics. However, the differences in use between the subject property and the 2006 transaction of the North End Theater warranted a careful analysis of use differences as part of the appraisal process.[4] The North End Theater was also leased in May 2000 as a facility with 2,093 seats. For the 2006 transaction, 136 seats had been added back to the facility, and the transaction involved a facility with 2,229 seats. In terms of seating capacity and location, the North End Theater property was the most similar to the subject (other than the subject facility itself).

The data fell into three distinct groups in terms of similarity to the subject and overall relevance to the analysis:

- **The lease of the subject theater**
  As noted, this property is the same physical entity as the property being appraised and has the same location. The fact that the transaction precedes the date of value by 10 years warrants extra attention in the analysis due to the significant passage of time.

---

4. As noted in the case of *Wu v. Interstate Consolidated Industries*, the appropriate basis for the appraisal is to focus on the allowable use within the subject premises. The case does not mandate consideration of only comparables with identical uses but rather requires that the appraisal process recognize the use limitations found in the subject lease.

## Exhibit 1

| Item | Property Name/Location | No. of Seats | Leased Area (±sq. ft.) | Start Date | Term Basis | Rent Per Month | Rent Per Seat per Month | Rent Per Sq. Ft. per Month | Comments |
|---|---|---|---|---|---|---|---|---|---|
| 1 | - North End Theater<br>- Same street as subject<br>- Four blocks N of subject<br>- Within the downtown core | 2,229 | 20,866 | 11/15/06 | 126 mos., triple net | $11,000 | $4.93 | $0.53 | - Rent adjusted on the 25th mo. and every 12-mo. period thereafter<br>- Rent adjustment is based on CPI factor<br>- 2 option periods of 5 yrs. each<br>- Space includes backstage area, offices, and the portion of the basement immediately below the stage |
| 2 | - North End Theater<br>- Same street as subject<br>- Four blocks N of subject<br>- Within the downtown core | 2,093 | 20,866 | 05/01/00 | 36 mos., triple net | $11,000 | $5.26 | $0.53 | - The lease had set annual rent escalations<br>- The tenant was Iglesia del Cuerpo de Christo, which used the theater for religious assembly<br>- The tenant terminated the lease after 10 mos. |
| 3 | - Purpose-built church<br>- Adams Blvd.<br>- Four miles SW of subject<br>- Outside the downtown core | 1,800 | 24,625 | 03/05/08 | 6 mos., gross modified | $28,000 | $15.56 | $1.14 | - The church/tenant occupied the premises for 9 mos. while attempting to raise funds to purchase the property<br>- The tenant paid utilities<br>- Additional amenity of 2,000± sq. ft. of basement area |
| 4 | - Miracle Theater<br>- Inglewood, CA<br>- 12 miles SW of subject<br>- Outside of downtown core | 400 | 8,120 | 12/01/02 | Mo.-to-mo., triple net | $4,500 | $11.25 | $0.55 | - The theater was leased to a church tenant on a mo.-to-mo. basis for 5 yrs.<br>- In Dec. 2007 the space went vacant<br>- In Apr. 2008 there was an offer (from a church) for $6,500/mo. ($16.25 per seat) that was declined as the property was listed for sale |

## Exhibit 1
*(continued)*

| Item | Property Name/ Location | No. of Seats | Leased Area (±sq. ft.) | Start Date | Term Basis | Rent Per Month | Per Seat per Month | Per Sq. Ft. per Month | Comments |
|---|---|---|---|---|---|---|---|---|---|
| 5 | - Suburban Theater<br>- Panorama City, CA<br>- 20 miles NW of subject<br>- Outside of downtown core | 700 | 11,000 | 09/01/08 | 36 mos., triple net | $10,800 | $15.43 | $0.98 | - The theater was leased to The Church<br>- Premises include 2 theater spaces of approximately 300 and 400 seats, respectively<br>- Original lease date commenced 09/01/02 |
| 6 | - Avenue Theater<br>- 7 miles E of subject<br>- Outside of downtown core | 690 | 9,700 | 06/01/06 | 72 mos., triple net | $5,000 | $7.25 | $0.52 | - The space is leased to The Church, which has leased the space since 1996<br>- The current lease represents an option exercised at market rent<br>- Annual rent adjustments are based on CPI factor |
| 7 | - Harbor Theater<br>- 20 miles S of subject<br>- Outside of downtown core | 937 | 10,300 | 10/01/07 | Mo.-to-mo., modified gross | $4,675 | $4.99 | $0.45 | - Adjustment in mo.-to-mo. rental agreement, representing holdover period of lease<br>- Original lease began 06/15/00 at $4,000/mo. |
| 8 | - Subject theater | 2,325 | 31,683 | 11/01/98 | 120 mos., triple net | $10,000 | $4.30 | $0.32 | - Discounted rent at $7,000/mo. for mos. 1 to 6<br>- Lease includes set increases every other year<br>- Lessee has one option to extend for a 10-yr. term<br>- Space is to be used exclusively as church (religious assembly) or movie theater |

- **The North End Theater**
  This property has a documented history of housing large church operations in a facility that is almost as large as the subject premises. This property is the closest to the subject premises in size and is the only other lease comparable that was also in the historic theater district of the downtown core.
- **The entire body of comparable lease transactions**
  All of these lease transactions were located within the same county as the subject property and contained at least 400 seats.

Before proceeding with the analysis, it was necessary to determine the primary unit of comparison. I considered the guidance of published texts and market participants' evaluations of similar properties as well as the unit of comparison that had the closest correlation (or the tightest range). The primary candidates were monthly rent per seat and monthly rent per square foot.

In terms of correlation, the highest monthly rent on a per-square-foot basis was 3.56 times the lowest monthly rent. The highest rent on a per-seat basis was 3.62 times the lowest monthly rent. This test showed no material difference favoring one unit of measurement over the other.

Regarding published reference material, I reviewed two Appraisal Institute texts: *Real Estate Valuation in Litigation*, second edition, and *The Appraisal of Real Estate*, 13th edition. *Real Estate Valuation in Litigation* provides guidance on applying a per-seat analysis for theaters/churches.[5] In *The Appraisal of Real Estate*, the price per seat is identified as the typical unit of comparison for theaters and auditoriums.[6]

Interviews to confirm the comparable rental data were also helpful in evaluating the use of these units of comparison by market participants. For every comparable, each person interviewed knew the number of seats (to the nearest 100) within the facility. The brokers who handled the transactions also knew the approximate square footage, but the church representatives (the lessees in these transactions) were not aware of (or did not recall) the square footage of their churches. As a result of these investigations, I determined that the primary unit of comparison applicable for this assignment in the local market was the monthly rent per seat.

I completed the valuation analysis using four variations of a direct comparison study. The first study involved a time-trend analysis applied to the 1998 lease of the subject premises. Given the scarcity of data concerning church leases, I looked to the next most meaning-

---

5. J. D. Eaton, *Real Estate Valuation in Litigation*, 2nd ed. (Chicago: Appraisal Institute, 1995), 230.
6. *The Appraisal of Real Estate*, 13th ed. (Chicago: Appraisal Institute, 2008), 306. No specific guidance with regard to churches is provided in this text.

ful data set with readily available market information: retail property leases in the immediate vicinity. I completed a trending analysis of retail lease rates over the 10-year period and supplemented it with an analysis of the economic changes that transpired over the relevant time span. The data analyzed was also controlled for consistency of use, recognizing that the subject's use in 1998 would be the same for the 2008 lease extension. This study showed an increase of approximately 25% to 30% between 1998 and 2006, a period of relative stability during 2007, and a roughly 10% decline from the end of 2007 to November 2008. The net effect of the time-trend analysis was that relevant commercial lease tenancies in the subject's neighborhood were leasing at rates in 2008 that were about 15% higher than rates for the same property with the same use as of 1998. This 15% rate was applied to the subject's 1998 lease rate to develop one of the value indications in my comparison study.[7] This analysis is summarized as follows:

November 1998 lease rate × market conditions factor = November 2008 indicated market rent
$$\$10{,}000 \times 1.15 = \$11{,}500$$

The subject's time-adjusted rent is equal to $4.95 per seat per month.

A similar analysis was conducted using the two lease transactions of the North End Theater. In this study I also used a market conditions adjustment estimated as follows:

- 2006 to 2007: rents rose 5%
- 2007 to 2008: rents declined 10%
- Net adjustment: downward 5%

For this important comparable, I also adjusted for the difference in location, noting that the North End Theater's location was slightly inferior to the subject's. The North End Theater is at the northerly edge of the historic theater district, while the subject premises are closer to the center in an area where commercial retail lease rates were approximately 20% higher. A portion of this difference is explained by the population density study (described later), so the location adjustment is shown in two parts. For the 2006 lease of the North End Theater, I considered the more flexible use provisions of the North End Theater lease but also recognized the strict limitation on operating hours. After interviewing the operator of the North End Theater lease, I reached the opinion that these two factors were

---

7. The rent for the first six months at $7,000 included a rent concession that allowed the lessee an opportunity to complete its own build-out and installation of fixtures. At the time of the 1998 lease, the subject space had not previously been used as a church. In 2008, the continuation of the church use would not require a period for modification of the premises. As a result, the starting rent for this study was the stabilized rate of $10,000 per month.

offsetting and no quantified adjustment was warranted even though the uses were different.

A final difference between the subject premises and the North End Theater was the availability of parking. The North End Theater was in a building that had a five-level, on-site parking garage, while the nearest parking for the subject premises was in public lots located across the street. I applied a 3% downward adjustment for the superior parking at the North End.[8] Applying the adjustments to the North End Theater lease transaction, I derived the value indication shown in Exhibit 2.

| Exhibit 2 | | |
|---|---|---|
| | Adjustment Factor | After Adjustment |
| Unadjusted monthly rent per seat | | $4.93 |
| Change in market conditions | 0.95 | $4.68 |
| Location (population density) | 1.10 | $5.15 |
| Location (commercial rent levels not already captured by population density) | 1.10 | $5.67 |
| Parking | 0.97 | $5.50 |

The population density study was applied to the entire data set. All of the brokers and church representatives interviewed as part of my research agreed that a higher density population in close proximity to a particular church is deemed to be a positive attribute for that facility, although none could specifically translate the dollar equivalence in monthly rent. In an effort to quantify this general observation, I calculated the population density within a two-mile radius of each comparable property and divided that population by the number of seats within the facility to derive a population per seat within two miles.[9] I then reviewed the results of my analysis by comparing the rent per seat per month to the population per seat. The results of this analysis are shown in Exhibit 3.

The population density study shows a divided market, with half of the comparables (including the subject) reflecting a population density of fewer than 100 people per seat within the surrounding two-mile area and the other half having a density greater than 150. The data reflecting the lower density is given more weight in the analysis.

---

8. The parking adjustment of 3% was based on a broker opinion survey. The two parking configurations were described to local brokers, who were asked their opinions of the difference in achievable rent. Most responses were qualitative (such as "there would be a small adjustment"). The 3% conclusion ultimately represented my best interpretation of these qualitative survey responses.
9. The two-mile radius is a distance commonly used by the local school district to analyze potential demand for new charter schools.

### Exhibit 3

| Item | Theater | Rent per Month | No. of Seats | Population within 2 Miles | 2-mile Population per Seat | Rent per per Month |
|---|---|---|---|---|---|---|
| 7 | Harbor Theatre | $4,675 | 937 | 61,421 | 66 | $4.99 |
| 2 | North End Theater | $11,000 | 2,229 | 193,734 | 87 | $4.93 |
| 2 | North End Theater | $11,000 | 2,229 | 193,734 | 87 | $4.93 |
| 8 | Subject theater | $10,000 | 2,325 | 224,090 | 96 | $4.30 |
| 3 | Purpose-built church | $28,000 | 1,800 | 280,519 | 156 | $15.56 |
| 6 | Avenue Theater | $5,000 | 670 | 151,465 | 226 | $7.46 |
| 5 | Suburban Theatre | $10,800 | 700 | 173,789 | 248 | $15.43 |
| 4 | Miracle Theater | $4,500 | 400 | 165,620 | 414 | $11.25 |

However, since the data in this study has not been adjusted for market conditions or other factors, an upward adjustment is warranted. In my opinion, the population density study indicated a market rent for the subject at a rate of $5.50 per seat per month.

Finally, I completed a typical direct comparison study using all eight of the lease comparables. Adjustments were made for market conditions, size (number of seats), location (including prevailing neighborhood rates and population density), expense provisions of the leases, availability of parking, and physical condition of the premises. The ratio of leased square feet per seat was also examined and considered in a qualitative manner. The result of this study was a monthly rent within the range of $5 to $6 per seat. As a result of the four studies completed, I generated the indications of monthly rent shown in Exhibit 4.

### Exhibit 4

| | Rent per Seat | | Number of Seats | | Monthly Rent Indication |
|---|---|---|---|---|---|
| Subject theater lease study | $4.95 | × | 2,325 | = | $11,509 |
| North End Theater lease study | $5.50 | × | 2,325 | = | $12,788 |
| Population density study | $5.50 | × | 2,325 | = | $12,788 |
| Comparison study | $5.00 to $6.00 | × | 2,325 | = | $11,625 to $13,950 |

In reconciling the indications of the direct comparison analyses, I observed a point of central tendency slightly lower than $13,000 per month. I also noted that five of the eight comparables had monthly rent set at an increment of $1,000, and four out of the five comparables with monthly rents of $10,000 or more had monthly rent set at an increment of $1,000. As a result of the analysis, I rounded my conclusion to the nearest $1,000 and reached a conclusion of a total monthly rent of $13,000 per month on a triple net basis, which is equal to $5.59 per seat per month.

# The Appraisal for the Landlord

The landlord's appraiser was very experienced in valuing properties in the downtown commercial core. He had appraised at least six major mixed-use historic buildings in this area over the prior decade, some on more than one occasion. His experience included an appraisal of the mixed-use building that contained the subject church. He was very well informed about the changes that had occurred in the local market over the last 10 years and had been provided with additional lease data from his client concerning recent leases of commercial spaces in and near the area, including properties that had been constructed as theaters and were now serving different uses.

The landlord's appraiser also researched the market for the leasing of theater spaces by churches. His research was expanded to include shared-use rental agreements in which more than one church organization would use the same physical premises on different days of the week or even during different time periods in the same day. The landlord's appraiser had data that generally fell into three categories:

- Leases of theater and church facilities subject to an exclusive-use arrangement by a single religious organization
- Theater premises used for non-church purposes
- Rental arrangements providing for the shared use of the same church or theater facility by multiple religious organizations

The analysis developed by the landlord's appraiser placed significant reliance on the lease transaction of a historic theater located west of the downtown commercial core, the Mid-Wil Theater. His appraisal reported that it had been leased in 2003 at a monthly rate of $60,000 on a triple net basis. Under the terms of the lease, the facility was used for a variety of musical concerts, theatrical productions, and major corporate events. The property had been extensively refurbished immediately prior to the commencement of the lease.

The landlord's appraiser also considered other leases of theaters used for entertainment-oriented purposes and shared-use rental arrangements that (according to his data analysis) provided some level of support for a lease rate around $60,000 per month. While the landlord's appraiser also identified leases of theaters and church facilities leased exclusively for religious purposes, these transactions were interpreted as not being representative of the highest and best use of the subject premises and were given little weight in the final rent conclusion expressed by the landlord's appraiser, which was $60,000 per month on a triple net basis.

## Deposition Testimony

During his deposition, the landlord's appraiser testified about his prior experience in the local market, including the fact that he had performed a prior appraisal of the building that housed the subject church. He further testified that he no longer had copies of that report or any part of his work file related to the prior engagement due to relocating his office several years ago.[10] He also testified extensively about the comparable lease transactions that were used as the factual basis for his appraisal opinion as well as his interpretation of the use clause within the subject lease and its relevance to the appraisal assignment.

His reasoning on the use issue followed the premise that religious assemblies often include gatherings featuring music, meals, refreshments, and so on. In addition, the use provisions at some of the entertainment-oriented venues used as lease comparables would have allowed for religious assembly. Therefore, he believed it was reasonable to assert that comparables of that type represented valid data for consideration because there was sufficient overlap in the terms of the allowable uses specified in the subject lease and the actual uses to which the lease comparable premises were put.

In regard to the lease of the Mid-Wil Theater, which had a rental rate that coincided exactly with the appraiser's conclusion and was stated as being the most relevant comparable lease transaction, the appraiser testified that he had confirmed the transaction by interviewing a representative of the lessee but had not seen the actual lease document.

## Pretrial Litigation Support

In performing all aspects of service for any appraisal assignment, the appraiser must fulfill the role of "one who is expected to perform valuation services competently and in a manner that is independent, impartial, and objective."[11] This requirement continues while the appraiser performs litigation support services and expert testimony following the completion of his or her appraisal.

Two well-qualified and competent appraisers often come to different conclusions after each performs a thorough and proper appraisal. However, there are some common reasons for material differences in opinion. It may be that one, or possibly even both, of the appraisers:

- Relied on information that was factually incorrect
- Was unaware of material information that, if known, would have influenced the final opinion

---

10. The prior appraisal had been done for lending purposes more than five years prior to the time of the current engagement, so there was no violation of the record-keeping provisions of the Ethics Rule of USPAP.
11. *Uniform Standards of Professional Appraisal Practice*, 2010-2011 ed. (Washington D.C.: The Appraisal Foundation), U-1

- Made an error in calculation
- Adopted an inappropriate assumption as a basis for the appraisal, or
- Applied incorrect appraisal methodology

An appraiser has special knowledge and training in valuation issues and is uniquely qualified to help determine whether an appraiser on the other side has erred in any of these ways. The Appraisal Institute text *Real Estate Valuation in Litigation*, second edition, addresses the issue of litigation support as follows:

> Appraisers must take particular care to ensure that their analyses, opinions, and conclusions concerning real estate are arrived at without bias in favor of the client or the accommodation of their personal interests. But, after arriving at an unbiased analysis, opinion, or conclusion, the appraiser may defend or advocate the correctness of his or her value estimate. . . . Every appraiser who testifies in court has a job to do and he is assisted in this job by legal counsel. The appraiser must convince the trier of fact that his estimate of value is correct; in so doing, the incorrectness, or error, of the other appraiser's estimate becomes apparent. If the appraiser does not believe his estimate of value is correct and the other appraiser's estimate is incorrect, he should not be on the witness stand.[12]

Following the deposition of the landlord's appraiser, I performed additional research to further demonstrate the correctness of my opinion. Based on my review of the other appraiser's deposition, it seemed possible that the appraisal report he prepared for the building containing the subject church may be useful for comparing valuation data and methodologies between the older report and the one prepared for the case at hand. Also, because of the importance of the Mid-Wil Theater lease transaction in supporting the opinion of the landlord's appraiser, additional investigation into this transaction was warranted to determine whether or not the appraiser had an accurate understanding of the facts surrounding the lease.

In helping my client get a copy of the prior appraisal report, I identified a loan on the property that had been issued at about the same time that the other appraiser had appraised the property. My attorney/client was successful in obtaining an appraisal report prepared in 2001 by the landlord's appraiser.

The 2001 appraisal contained some information that was important in developing a cross examination. The 2001 report contained a reference to the leasing of the North End Theater and indicated that the leasing of this theater was supportive of the then-current rent being paid for the subject church.

At that time (in 2001), the subject church was occupied under the terms of the 1998 lease. The date of the report was three years beyond the start date of the lease and seven years prior to the end of the base

---

12. *Real Estate Valuation in Litigation*, 2nd ed., 535.

term and potential start of the 10-year option period. The analysis of the rent for the theater premises in the 2001 appraisal report contained no reference to any data outside of the downtown historic core and concluded with the following paragraph:

> The leasing of theaters in the area is limited. The appraiser obtained information on one recent lease, that of the North End Theater, formerly occupied by the subject church. This church has 2,093 seats. It was leased in April 2000 for $11,000 per month, plus $750 per month for expenses, a lease rate comparable to that at the subject. Thus the lease to the theater appears to be at market rent levels.

At the time this statement was written, the lease for the subject theater space was set at $10,500 per month. The other appraiser's reliance on an analysis of the North End Theater lease was very similar to one of the studies I had performed in completing my appraisal.

In an effort to obtain the actual lease of the Mid-Wil Theater, I located one of the parties' representatives who had it in his files. In response to a subpoena, he produced a copy of the lease for use at trial. This Mid-Wil Theater lease was important because it showed that the actual lease rate was about 20% less than the $60,000 reported by the other appraiser.

## The Trial

By the agreement of the parties, the trial was heard by a retired Superior Court judge but was convened under all rules of evidence applicable to a Superior Court trial in order to protect the rights of appeal for both parties.

The opinion of market rental value expressed by the landlord's appraiser was more than four times the amount that I set forth in my appraisal. In working his way toward a final verdict on the issue of market rental value, the judge appeared to consider the following questions:

- Did the use provision in the subject lease impose limitations that would prohibit these premises from being used for music concerts, live entertainment, and restaurant/bar operations that were found in some of the comparable properties?
- Did the use of comparable lease transactions in which the lessee could conduct entertainment-oriented uses automatically exclude those transactions from consideration as comparable data?
- Did the appraisers perform their analysis based on published and recognized procedures?

### The Use Provision

The judge indicated that the use provision of the lease, limiting the potential uses to church, religious assembly, and (under certain circumstances) movie theater uses, did in fact preclude the subject from being used for live musical concerts, other live entertainment, and restaurant and bar operations. The judge also indicated that the concept of a shared-use agreement was materially different from an exclusive-use arrangement and that the intervening step of transitioning from exclusive use to shared use created a different type of transaction that was not the same as the lease agreement that governed the subject premises.

### Use of Non-Church Comparables

The judge indicated testimony on comparables that were physically similar to the subject premises but used for purposes other than churches. The judge recognized that the subject's use was limited to church, religious assembly, and movie theater uses but indicated that comparable properties that did not have identical use provisions specified in their leases may still be relevant for analysis as long as the differences between the provisions were evaluated in the comparison process. For this reason, the North End Theater lease could be considered both for the older lease transaction limited to church uses and the more recent lease that allowed for other types of live entertainment.

### Did Appraisers Rely on Recognized Methods?

The judge's verdict was ultimately based on a price-per-seat analysis, which came directly from testimony that I provided concerning the use of appropriate units of comparison as set forth in published texts from the Appraisal Institute. The landlord's appraiser relied on a total monthly rent method of comparison, without any citation to published appraisal texts. Thus, the published literature of the Appraisal Institute had a direct bearing on the verdict in the case.

### The Final Decision

The judge's final decision in the case was based on a monthly rental amount of $5.59 per seat, which the judge entered as $12,996.75 per month. The judge's ruling also included an awarding of costs and fees to my client, meaning that (barring a reversal on appeal) the landlord would ultimately be responsible for paying all of the legal fees incurred by my client in pursuing this matter through trial.

# Conclusion

Most market value appraisals of income-producing properties include an analysis of the market rent for the subject property. The analysis of market rent in such appraisals may be somewhat abbreviated or superficial, depending on the significance that the estimate of market rent has on the overall outcome of the market value determination. However, when the *primary* focus of the appraisal is to develop an opinion of market rent, the appraiser must consider the additional scrutiny to which the appraisal may be subjected. Care in the selection of comparables (to ensure objectivity) and diligent research to ensure as thorough an understanding of the data as possible are necessary steps in producing an appraisal of market rent that can withstand the rigors of cross examination.

The subject lease itself controls the property rights available to the lessee. In the case at hand, the court determined that market rent should reflect the same restrictions as indicated in the use provisions of the lease. Under these circumstances, the highest and best use and ultimately the rental value cannot reflect property rights that the lessee does not possess under the terms of the lease. Because it is applicable here, the *Wu* case sets a legal precedent in applying this concept to highest and best use analysis.[13] The judge's decision in this case appeared to reflect a perceived inconsistency between the analysis and testimony of the landlord's appraiser and the guidelines established at the pretrial hearing based partially on the *Wu* decision.

When a judge issues rulings on pretrial motions, it is important for the appraiser to become aware of those rulings. If the rulings create a need for a new set of appraisal assumptions, the appraiser should inform his or her client and then perform the additional analysis to bring his or her work into compliance with the rulings on the pretrial motions.

Once the appraiser has the appropriate foundation for the analysis, he or she can proceed to complete the appraisal in an objective and unbiased manner and can be confident in defending his or her opinion during the pretrial and expert testimony phases of the assignment.

### Acknowledgments
The author would like to thank Steven S. Karic, Esq., of Hamburg, Karic, Edwards & Martin for the opportunity to handle this assignment and to acknowledge his comprehensive grasp of the law and thorough trial preparation that ultimately led to a favorable ruling. I would like to also acknowledge the professional work of Senior Analyst Ryan J. Dobbins at Integra Realty Resources–Los Angeles, whose exhaustive research and insightful analysis were critical to the outcome of the case.

---

13. It is possible for the use provisions of a lease to conflict with the valuation provisions (within the same lease) that apply to the resetting of rent. It is not uncommon for long-term leases (especially ground leases) to specify a predetermined use at the time of a parcel's original development but to provide for a hypothetical valuation of the land at its highest and best use as if vacant at the time rent is to be reset in the future. The appraiser must examine this issue carefully and seek legal advice if needed.

# Glossary

**advocacy**
1. The work or profession of an advocate.
2. The act of pleading for or actively supporting a cause or proposal. [2]

**bench trial.** A trial before a judge without a jury. • The judge decides questions of fact as well as questions of law. Also termed *trial to the bench*; *nonjury trial*; *court trial*; *trial before the court* (abbr. TBC); *judge trial*. [2]

**case in chief**
1. The evidence presented at trial by a party between the time the party calls the first witness and the time the party rests.
2. The part of a trial in which a party presents evidence to support the claim or defense. [2]

**cross examination.** The process of questioning a witness whose direct testimony is adverse to the position of the party undertaking the questioning. The purpose of cross examination is to dilute, neutralize, or completely destroy the effect of the witness's direct testimony. [1]

**deposition.** A legal process in which an attorney asks oral questions of a person involved in a legal action or of a witness for one of the parties involved. The person who is deposed is called the *deponent*. The deposition is conducted under oath outside of the

---

**Sources**
[1] *The Dictionary of Real Estate Appraisal*, 5th ed. (Chicago: Appraisal Institute, 2010).*
[2] Bryan A. Garner, *Black's Law Dictionary*, 9th ed. (St. Paul, Minn.: West Group, 2009).
[3] Uniform Standards of Professional Appraisal Practice, 2010-2011 ed. (Washington, D.C.: The Appraisal Foundation, 2010).
[4] ___, 2012-2013 ed. (Washington, D.C.: The Appraisal Foundation, 2012).
* Note that the fifth edition of *The Dictionary of Real Estate Appraisal* was published in 2010. Definitions from that dictionary may include parenthetical references to *Black's Law Dictionary*, eighth edition, and USPAP, 2010-2011 edition.

courtroom, usually in one of the lawyer's offices. The testimony of an appraiser in a deposition regarding his or her opinion about a parcel of real estate is considered an *oral report*. [1]

**direct examination.** In a trial or other court proceeding, the initial questioning of a witness by the party who called the witness to testify. [1]

**discovery (1).** A legal procedure in which lawyers prepare for trial by obtaining factual information from an expert or fact witness(es) through written or oral questions. In discovery, an attorney may also have court authority to examine the files of all appraisals and related information for the purpose of preparing a case. [1]

**discovery (2)**
1. The act of process of finding or learning something that was previously unknown.
2. Compulsory disclosure, at a party's request, of information that relates to the litigation.
3. The facts or documents disclosed.
4. The pretrial phase of a lawsuit during which depositions, interrogatories, and other forms of discovery are conducted. [2]

**docket.** 2. A schedule of pending cases. Also termed *court calendar*; *cause list*; *trial calendar*. [2]

**exhibit**
1. A document, record, or other tangible object formally introduced as evidence in court.
2. A document attached to and made part of a pleading, motion, contract, or other instrument. [2]

**expert.** A person who is presumed to have special knowledge of, or skill in, a particular field due to education, experience, or study. [1]

**expert testimony.** Testimony of persons who are presumed to have special knowledge of, or skill in, a particular field due to education, experience, or study. The *Daubert* and *Kumho Tire* decisions of the US Supreme Court discuss four considerations in determining the reliability of expert testimony–testing, peer review, error rates, and acceptability in the relevant scientific community. [1]

**expert witness (1).** A person qualified to give expert testimony. [1]

**expert witness (2).** A witness qualified by knowledge, skill, experience, training, or education to provide a scientific, technical, or other specialized opinion about the evidence or a fact issue. Also termed *skilled witness*. [2]

**extraordinary assumption (1).** An assumption, directly related to a specific assignment, which, if found to be false, could alter the appraiser's opinions or conclusions. Extraordinary assumptions presume as fact otherwise uncertain information about physical, legal, or economic characteristics of the subject property; or about conditions external to the property such as market conditions or trends; or about the integrity of data used in an analysis. (USPAP, 2010-2011 ed.) [1]

**extraordinary assumption (2).** An assumption, directly related to a specific assignment, as of the effective date of the assignment results, which, if found to be false, could alter the appraiser's opinions or conclusions. Extraordinary assumptions presume as fact otherwise uncertain information about physical, legal, or economic characteristics of the subject property; or about conditions external to the property, such as market conditions or trends; or about the integrity of data used in an analysis. [4]

**fact-finder.** One or more persons—such as jurors in a trial or administrative-law judges in a hearing—who hear testimony and review evidence to rule on a factual issue. Also termed *finder of fact*; *fact-trier* or *trier of fact* (in a judicial proceeding); *fact-finding board* (for a group or committee). [2]

**hearsay.** Traditionally, testimony that is given by a witness who relates not what he or she knows personally, but what others have said, and that is therefore dependent on the credibility of someone other than the witness. (*Black's*) [1]

**hypothetical condition (1).** That which is contrary to what exists but is supposed for the purpose of analysis. Hypothetical conditions assume conditions contrary to known facts about physical, legal, or economic characteristics of the subject property; or about conditions external to the property, such as market conditions or trends; or about the integrity of data used in an analysis. (USPAP, 2010-2011 ed.) [1]

**hypothetical condition (2).** A condition, directly related to a specific assignment, which is contrary to what is known by the appraiser to exist on the effective date of the assignment results, but is used for the purpose of analysis. Hypothetical conditions are contrary to known facts about physical, legal, or economic characteristics of the subject property; or about conditions external to the property, such as market conditions or trends; or about the integrity of data used in an analysis. [4]

**jurisdictional exception.** An assignment condition established by applicable law or regulation, which precludes an appraiser from complying with a part of USPAP. (USPAP, 2010-2011 ed.) [1]

**jury instruction (usu. pl.).** A direction or guideline that a judge gives a jury concerning the law of the case. Often shortened to *instruction*. Also termed *jury charge*; *charge*; *jury direction*; *direction*. [2]

**legal instruction.** *See* **jury instruction.**

**material witness.** A witness who can testify about matters having some logical connection with the consequential facts, esp. if few others, if any, know about those matters. [2]

**motion in limine.** A pretrial request that certain inadmissible evidence not be referred to or offered at trial. • Typically, a party makes this motion when it believes that mere mention of the evidence during trial would be highly prejudicial and could not be remedied by an instruction to disregard. If, after the motion is granted, the opposing party mentions or attempts to offer the evidence in the jury's presence, a mistrial may be ordered. A ruling on a motion in limine does not always preserve evidentiary error for appellate purposes. To raise such an error on appeal, a party may be required to formally object when the evidence is actually admitted or excluded during trial. [2]

**predicate fact**
1. A fact from which a presumption or inference arises.
2. A fact necessary to the operation of an evidentiary rule. • For example, there must actually be a conspiracy for the co-conspirator exception to the hearsay rule to apply. [2]

**produce**
1. To bring into existence; to create.
2. To provide (a document, witness, etc.) in response to subpoena or discovery request. [2]

**protective order**
1. A court order prohibiting or restricting a party from engaging in conduct (esp. a legal procedure such as discovery) that unduly annoys or burdens the opposing party or a third-party witness.
2. RESTRAINING ORDER (1). [2]

**reasonable.** In law, just, rational, appropriate, ordinary, or usual in the circumstances. It may refer to care, cause, compensation, doubt (in a criminal trial), and a host of other actions or activities. [1]

**rebuttal testimony.** Testimony that is produced to refute the testimony presented by the opposition in a court case. [1]

**recross examination.** A second cross-examination, after redirect examination. Often shortened to *recross.* [2]

**redirect examination.** A second direct examination, after cross-examination, the scope ordinarily being limited to matters covered during cross-examination. Often shortened to redirect. Also termed (in England) *reexamination.* [2]

**scope of work.** The type and extent of research and analyses in an assignment. (USPAP, 2010-2011 ed.) [1]

**subpoena duces tecum (1).** A subpoena ordering the witness to appear and to bring specified documents, records, or things. (*Black's*) *See also* **discovery**. [1]

**subpoena duces tecum (2).** A subpoena ordering the witness to appear in court and to bring specified documents, records, or things. [2]

**time certain.** 1. A definite, specific date and time. [2]

**trier of fact.** *See* **fact-finder.**

# Index

access
   change in, 107, 145
   easement, 57
   loss of, 48-49
adjustment of comparable sales, 179-180, 308-311
advocacy, 16-17, 260-261, 277-278
   appearance of, 27, 30
after situation, 47-50, 55-60, 84-85, 109-110, 125-127, 155-158, 168-170
allocation of value, 284
annoyance. *See* nuisance, case study
appraisal fees, 6, 8, 268-271
appraisal report, 13-16, 262-263
appraisal review, 16, 27, 277
   See also litigation support services
appraiser, as consultant, 16-17, 261
appraiser-attorney relationship, 16-17, 26, 30, 260-261
   *See also* litigation support services
appraiser's credibility, 27
   *See also* ethics
appraiser's qualifications. *See* qualifications of appraiser
appraiser's testimony. *See* testimony by appraiser
asset comparison, 274-275
assignment. *See* engagement

assumptions and limiting conditions. *See* general assumptions and limiting conditions
attorney-appraiser relationship. *See* appraiser-attorney relationship

bankruptcy, appraising for, 281-283
   case study, 279-298
before situation, 40-44, 54-55, 83-84, 105-106, 117-122, 154-155, 161-162, 168
bench trial, 20
benefits
   general, 121-122
   special, 122, 151-160
   treatment of, in appraisal process, 155-159

case in chief, 6
case management, 3-6
Chapter 11. *See* bankruptcy, appraising for
charts, as exhibits, 15, 23-24, 256-257
church leases, 300-302
class action, 205-206
   case study, 205-219
commitment, executing the, 13-17

comparative analysis of leases, 304-312

compensable damages, 53

conflict of interest, 3

consistent use theory, 11-12

consulting appraiser. *See* appraiser, as consultant

contaminated property. *See* environmental contamination

contract rent, 284

corner clip, case study, 35-52

cost approach, 61-76
  applicability and limitations, 55, 61, 106, 114

cost to cure, 36, 51, 126, 138, 143-144, 155-159, 168-170

court-appointed mediator, 261

credibility of appraisal witness. See appraiser's credibility

cross examination, 2-297, 255
  limits of, 29
  purpose of, 27
  *See also* rebuttal testimony *and* recross examination

damages, 115, 143
  from lack of easement, 168-170, 181
  from LUST, 200-202
  from radiation, 227-231
  study, 50

*Daubert*, 24

demeanor on witness stand, 25-29

deposition, 7-9, 31, 216-218, 313

depreciation, 250-253, 275-276

diminution in value. *See* damages

direct examination, 25-27

discovery, 4-9, 14
  exchange of appraisal reports, 268, 271-274

dissolution of marriage cases, appraising for, 259-263
  case study, 259-278

divorce cases, appraising for. See dissolution of marriage cases, appraising for

docket, 4-5

drainage, 125

easement
  access, 57, 61-62
  case study, 53-79, 81-102, 117-149
  parking, 61-62
  permanent, 42, 56, 94, 117, 122, 124-125
  pipeline, 81-82, 84-85
  temporary construction, 84, 96, 117, 138
  transmission line, 56
  utility, 183-188
  value impact of existing, 42, 62, 94-96, 97-102
  waterline, 161-170, 171-182

engagement, 3-12, 243-246, 262-263

engagement letter, 6-7, 13

engineering consultant, 5-6

entrepreneurial incentive, 249-250, 256

environmental contamination
  case study, 205-219
  class action, 205-219
  definitions, 190-191
  disclosure, 208-209
  leaking underground storage tank, 192-194, 206
  on-site, 206-209
  radioactive contamination, 221-231
  service station, 189-203
  weapons testing site, 224-231

equitable distribution, 259, 262
ethics, 21
exhibits
   in appraisal reports, 15-16
   in trials and depositions, 7-8, 16, 25-26, 31
expert, qualifying as, 24-25
expert witness, 8-9, 19-33
   characteristics, 20
   competency, 246-249
   cross examination, 27-29, 255
   defined, 21
   notes subject to inspection, 26
   opposing, 216-218, 246-247
   preparation for witness stand, 23-24, 26
expert witness fee. *See* appraisal fees
extraordinary assumptions, 9-10

fact-finder, 10
fact witness, 8-9
fair market value. *See* market value
field research by associates, 29
fractional interest, 279-283

gas wells, case study, 243-257
general assumptions and limiting conditions, 285-286, 295-296
general benefits. *See* benefits
grade change, 122
graphs, as exhibits, 15, 25-26, 111-113

hazardous waste, 206-209
hearsay rule, 26-27

highest and best use
   after situation, 49, 85, 110, 139, 145, 156-157
   before situation, 42-43, 106, 129-130, 154
   of environmentally impacted property, 193-194
   of residential waterfront property, 165-166, 180-181
   of theater space, 302-304
hotels, 53-54
hypothetical conditions, 10-11, 186-187

impact severity scores, 240-242
impact study, 236-242
income capitalization approach, 76, 132-136, 141-142, 146
   applicability and limitations, 55, 106-107, 114
ingress and egress. *See* access
interviewing market participants, 26-27, 186-187

jurisdictional exceptions, 11, 298

KISS, 7

land valuation, 44-45, 62-67, 83-84, 106, 114, 131, 139, 145, 224-226
leaking underground storage tank, 192-193
   case study, 189-203
lease analysis, 200-201, 299-302, 312-313
   land leases, 227-230

leased fee estate, 279, 286, 289, 291-295
leasehold estate, 279, 289
lease renewal, case study, 299-318
legal instruction, 11-12, 284, 297-298, 302, 317
lender questionnaire, 203
    See also interviewing market participants
limiting conditions. See general assumptions and limiting conditions
litigation support services, 16-17, 313-315
    appraisal review, 16, 277, 314
litigation timeline, 4-5, 277
loss of parking area. See parking area, loss of
lost income, 200-201
LUST. See leaking underground storage tank

maps, as exhibits, 15, 25
market rent analysis, 299-313, 317
market value, 284, 290
matched pairs technique. See paired data analysis
material witness, defined, 8
    See also fact witness
measure of damage. See damages
motion in limine, 10

nonconforming use, 120, 130
normal pool, 175-177
nuclear weapons testing site, 221-224
    case study, 221-231
nuisance, case study, 50, 233-242

opinion of value, 13, 21-22

paired data analysis, 97-102, 194-197, 236-242
parking area, loss of, 110-114, 120
    case study, 103-116
part taken, 46, 124-125
permanent easement, case study, 53-79, 81-102
petroleum pipeline, case study, 81-102
phased assignments, 6-7, 14, 264-265
Phase 1 and Phase 2. See phased assignments
photographs, as exhibits, 15, 25
postmortem, 32
predicate fact, 6
predicate witness, 9
preparation for trial. See trial preparation
probability of rezoning. See rezoning, reasonable probability of
production, 7
professional ethics. See ethics
property taxes. See tax assessment, case study
protective order, 8
proximity
    damage, 205-219
    hazardous materials, 205-209
    radioactive contamination, 221-231

qualifications of appraiser, 24-25
    adherence to code of ethics, 247-248
qualifying as an expert, 24-25

radioactive contamination, 221-224, 230-231
  case study, 221-231
reasonable probability, 10, 22
  of rezoning, 43, 49
rebuttal testimony, 30-32, 256
  limits of, 30-31
recross examination, 29-30
  limits of, 30
redirect examination, 29-30
  limits of, 29-30
rehearsal of testimony, 26
remainder property, 49, 125-126
  value, 46, 51, 109, 128-129, 142, 147
restoration cost. *See* cost to cure
review of appraisal. *See* appraisal review
rezoning, reasonable probability of, 43, 49
right of way, 36, 44, 46, 122
  *See also* easement
road widening, 103, 107-109
  case study, 103-116, 151-159

sales comparison approach, 76, 83-84, 97-102, 131-132, 139-140, 145-146, 166-170, 178-180, 194-197, 304-312, 316
  applicability and limitations, 13-14, 36, 55, 106, 114
sandwich lease, 279
scope of work, 4-6, 13
  of case study, 35-36, 127-129, 161, 185-186, 221-222, 236-237, 257, 262-266
scripted testimony, 26
septic tank, partial taking of, 151-160
  case study, 151-160

service station
  case study, 189-203
  leaking underground storage tank, 192-194, 197-200
setback requirements in after situation, 49, 175-177
settlement, 78-79, 218-219
  statement, 287
severance damage. *See* damages
sewage disposal system, private. *See* septic tank, partial taking of
special benefits, 154
  case study, 151-160
standards of practice. *See* Uniform Standards of Professional Appraisal Practice (USPAP)
state law, 259-260
subpoena duces tecum, 7
surveyors, 175-177
surveys, 74-75

tax assessment, case study, 243-257
temporary construction easement, 84, 96, 117, 138
testimony by appraiser, 9, 23-32
  cross examination, 2-297
  by deposition, 31
  direct examination, 25-27
  hearsay evidence, 26-27
  preparing for, 23-24, 26-27
  qualifying as an expert, 24-25
  rebuttal testimony, 30-32
  redirect examination, 29-30
  witness's notes subject to inspection, 26, 268
theaters, case study, 299-318
time certain, 4-5
time series analysis, 210-216

*Index*

title insurance claims, appraising for, 161, 171, 181
   case study, 161-170, 171-182
training, as expert witness, 20-21
transmission line easement, 56
   case study, 53-79, 233-242
tree, valuation of, 187-188
trial postmortem. *See* postmortem
trial preparation, 23-24, 26, 30
   appraiser-attorney pretrial conference, 23, 26
   discovery, 4-9, 14
trier of fact, 10, 259

Uniform Standards of Professional Appraisal Practice (USPAP), 3-4, 6-7, 9n2, 10-11, 14, 16, 247
use provision, 315-316
utility line easement, case study, 183-188

valuation witness. *See* expert witness
visual aids. *See* exhibits

waterline easement
   case study, 161-170, 171-182
   missing, 161-170
   and property boundary, 171-182
water transmission line, 184-185